A Research Agenda for Digital Transformation

Elgar Research Agendas outline the future of research in a given area. Leading scholars are given the space to explore their subject in provocative ways, and map out the potential directions of travel. They are relevant but also visionary.

Forward-looking and innovative, Elgar Research Agendas are an essential resource for PhD students, scholars and anybody who wants to be at the forefront of research.

For a full list of Edward Elgar published titles, including the titles in this series, visit our website at www.e-elgar.com.

A Research Agenda for Digital Transformation

Multidisciplinary Perspectives

Edited by

JOHN QI DONG

Associate Professor of Information Systems, Nanyang Business School, Nanyang Technological University, Singapore

PETER C. VERHOEF

Professor of Marketing, Faculty of Economics and Business, University of Groningen, the Netherlands

Elgar Research Agendas

Edward Elgar PUBLISHING

Cheltenham, UK • Northampton, MA, USA

Published by
Edward Elgar Publishing Limited
The Lypiatts
15 Lansdown Road
Cheltenham
Glos GL50 2JA
UK

Edward Elgar Publishing, Inc.
William Pratt House
9 Dewey Court
Northampton
Massachusetts 01060
USA

A catalogue record for this book
is available from the British Library

Library of Congress Control Number: 2024941200

This book is available electronically in the **Elgar**online
Business subject collection
https://dx.doi.org/10.4337/9781035306435

MIX
Paper | Supporting responsible forestry
FSC® C013056
FSC www.fsc.org

ISBN 978 1 0353 0642 8 (cased)
ISBN 978 1 0353 0643 5 (eBook)

Printed and bound in Great Britain by
TJ Books Limited, Padstow, Cornwall

Contents

Contributors

Marjolein Aerts-Veenstra, University of Groningen, the Netherlands

Ilke Bakir, University of Groningen, the Netherlands

Albert Boonstra, University of Groningen, the Netherlands

Jan vom Brocke, University of Münster, Germany

Thijs Broekhuizen, University of Groningen, the Netherlands

John Qi Dong, Nanyang Technological University, Singapore

Felix Eggers, Copenhagen Business School, Denmark

Nicolai Etienne Fabian, University of Groningen, the Netherlands

P. K. Kannan, University of Maryland, USA

Hager Khechine, Laval University, Canada

Gregor Kipping, University of Liechtenstein, Liechtenstein

Guy Alain Sylvanus Kouyo, Laval University, Canada

H. Alice Li, Ohio State University, USA

Peter Maas, University of St Gallen, Switzerland

Daniel Malan, Trinity College Dublin, Ireland

Dinh Khoi Nguyen, Open University of the Netherlands, the Netherlands

Rohit Nishant, Queen's University Belfast, United Kingdom

Werner J. Reinartz, University of Cologne, Germany

Kees Jan Roodbergen, University of Groningen, the Netherlands

Christopher Schumacher, University of St Gallen, Switzerland

Chee-Wee Tan, Hong Kong Polytechnic University, Hong Kong

A. Berfu Ünal, University of Groningen, the Netherlands

Peter C. Verhoef, University of Groningen, the Netherlands

Manuel Weber, ERCIS – European Research Center for Information Systems, Germany

Julian R. K. Wichmann, Tilburg University, the Netherlands

Jaap E. Wieringa, University of Groningen, the Netherlands

Bingqing Xiong, Deakin University, Australia

1 Introduction to *A Research Agenda for Digital Transformation*

John Qi Dong and Peter C. Verhoef

Digital transformation has been fundamentally changing the business world. By deeply altering the way of doing business by firms, disrupting the rule of the game across industries, and changing consumers' expectations and behaviors, we are living in the age of competing on digital business models (Nguyen et al., 2023; Verhoef et al., 2021). While there are different definitions and understanding of digital transformation, particularly across multiple levels, we consider it as "a change in how a firm employs digital technologies, to develop a new digital business model that helps to create and appropriate more value for the firm" (Verhoef et al., 2021: 889). Different from other digital changes aiming to digitize a specific work task or digitalize a specific business process (e.g., Fabian et al., 2023), digital transformation is different in its revolutionary nature and profound changes in business models. We believe that digital transformation is a business model innovation, aiming to develop new ways of creating and capturing value in the market. In this sense, it is not only relevant to transforming an incumbent firms' business model to a new digital one, but also speaks to digital native firms (e.g., Uber and Airbnb) that create a new digital business model that is entirely new to an industry.

Despite significant changes stemming from digital transformation and new digital business models, academic research on digital transformation is primarily conducted within specific business disciplines. Given that the essence of digital transformation resides on business model innovation—which require synergistic changes across all functional areas in an organization—discipline-specific insights can rarely have the holistic picture of how digital transformation takes place and why one firm is more successful to ascertain value-increasing outcomes than another firm. We propose that multidisciplinary perspectives need to emerge and be co-present to synthesize our understanding about distinct aspects of digital transformation, such as strategy, organization, information systems, supply chains, and marketing, as well as privacy and business ethics. As a first step, it is important to gather insights across these business disciplines and lay out a foundation for future research to take multidisciplinary perspectives. To address this notable gap in the literature and urgent the need to facilitate digital transformation research with multidisciplinary perspectives, we invite leading scholars across multiple business disciplines to share their in-depth knowledge on digital transformation in this book. The book consists of three parts each with multiple chapters (Figure 1.1), focusing on multidisciplinary perspectives on digital transformation, capabilities and resources of digital transformation, and implementation and impact of digital transformation, respectively.

Digital Transformation		
Part 1: Multidisciplinary Perspectives	**Part 2: Capabilities and Resources**	**Part 3: Implementation and Impact**
• Strategic Innovation Perspective *(Chapter 2)* • Process-Oriented Perspective *(Chapter 3)* • Market-Oriented Perspective *(Chapter 4)*	• Data Science *(Chapter 5)* • Digital Platforms *(Chapter 6)* • Open Innovation *(Chapter 7)* • Supply Chain and Logistics *(Chapter 8)*	• Change Management *(Chapter 9)* • Cybersecurity Management *(Chapter 10)* • Data Analysis *(Chapter 11)* • Business Ethics *(Chapter 12)*

Figure 1.1 Overview of book chapters

Part I: multidisciplinary perspectives on digital transformation

In Part I of the book, we first present multidisciplinary perspective on digital transformation from innovation-, process-, and market-oriented perspectives, respectively. Chapter 2 focuses on digital transformation from a strategic innovation perspective using small and median enterprises (SMEs) as an example, which have been largely understudied but widely needed in practice. While most research has been focused on large firms' digital transformation, SMEs constitute the majority of organizations in most countries and regions and are going through a transition toward digital business models. This chapter deepens our understanding of the temporal dimensions of strategic decisions for digital transformation in SMEs. The authors investigate how future orientation (i.e., a strategic focus as attention devoted to future perceptions) and future horizon (i.e., the temporal distance as time horizon for envisioning future events) impact digital transformation and, more importantly, contrast these effects with their impacts on radical innovation. By using detailed data from 268 SMEs in the Netherlands, they find that future orientation fosters both digital transformation and radical innovation in SMEs, suggesting that a long-term oriented strategic focus is crucial for digital transformation and innovation. Digital transformation benefits form a shorter future horizon, which usually allows more experimental learning with lower uncertainty. This could be particularly important for SMEs, which have limited resources and lower tolerance of risk. Differently, radical innovation benefits more from an extended time horizon. SMEs often need to cautiously allocate precious resources and only those with a long-term horizon would be willing to pursue radical innovation.

Chapter 3 discusses the role of business process management (BPM) in value creation and proposes a process-oriented perspective on digital transformation. BPM has had a long-standing attention within specifically information systems research. The general idea is that a specific task is value creating, when technology and people interact in a process. Technology is an enabler of this process. For the management of digital transformation, it is important to consider that (1) digital technologies do not automatically have a positive impact on firm value; (2) innovative process design does not necessarily result from technology use alone; and (3) the value created through process design is contingent on an appropriate task–technology–people fit in the specific application context. A process-oriented approach to digital transformation tangible both for researchers and practitioners is discussed and a conceptualization of BPM that adopts a holistic view of digital transformation is presented called the BPM billboard. A case study is described that shows how the billboard can be used to improve digital transformation success.

Chapter 4 presents a market-oriented perspective and discusses the implications of digital transformation for marketing strategy. The authors suggest that digital transformation in the context of marketing strategy refers to the incorporation and comprehensive use of digital technologies to create, communicate, deliver, and exchange offerings that have value for customers, clients, partners, and society at large. After shortly discussing the old marketing strategy paradigm, they discuss how digital transformation is reshaping it. The authors pledge that specifically new technologies are constantly changing how marketing operates. This includes older technologies, such as digital platforms and social media, but also novel technologies, such as artificial intelligence (AI) and large language models (i.e., ChatGPT). Specifically, new digital technologies impact the customer journey in general, which is the process a customer goes through when interacting with a firm. This journey includes various touchpoints across the pre-purchase, purchase, and post-purchase phases (Lemon and Verhoef, 2016). Moreover, new technologies are also revolutionizing how firms approach customer experience and marketing, providing opportunities to deliver highly personalized, convenient, and seamless experiences to customers, thereby increasing their satisfaction, loyalty, and, ultimately, profitability for the firm. Subsequently, it is discussed how digital technologies are affecting the classic four Ps in marketing: product, price, promotion, and place (distribution). These changes are very strong. In terms of promotion, for example, we observe a strong increase in online marketing, social media marketing with increasing importance of analytics to target the right customers with the right messages at the right time. The advancements in digital product lines and customized offerings to customers also create pricing challenges and new pricing opportunities for firms. For example, dynamic pricing and yield management have become much more common. Products are also becoming increasingly digital or have digital components, while distribution with the upcoming of e-commerce and digital platforms is also strongly affected.

Part II: capabilities and resources of digital transformation

In Part II of the book, we delve further into the capabilities and resources for digital transformation, including data science, digital platforms, digital ecosystems, and digital supply chains. Chapter 5 discusses how to share and analyze customer data in a privacy-concerned world. One important capability in digital transformation is data science. Data science has become very important with increasing presence of data, which is especially omnipresent in a digital environment. When firms utilize their data in a good way and derive relevant insights in their firm strategy and customer solutions, they can create value for the firm (Verhoef et al., 2022). Recently, new developments have become relevant, specifically the strong upcoming of machine learning and large language models. This creates even more opportunities for value creation. However, an important caveat is that consumers are concerned about their privacy (e.g., Beke et al., 2022), while governments are regulating the use of data. With regard to the consumer perspective on privacy, it discusses the use of the PRICAL measure to assess the privacy calculus (Beke et al., 2022). This chapter, though, mainly focus on how data science and new techniques can be used in such an environment. Firms must make a trade-off between data utility and privacy protection. Data utility generally increases when you have more and detailed data, but this generally is at the expense of privacy protection.

There are well-known privacy protection tools. However, compelling examples in the literature demonstrate that these privacy protection methods that we discuss above are inherently un-private and there is a lack of actual privacy control. Differential privacy is discussed as a privacy protection approach that explicitly takes the perspective of controlling privacy risk. It is based on a mathematical definition of privacy that provides protection by adding noise to data while maintaining data utility. New machine learning techniques, such as Generative Adversarial Networks, can be used to find a good balance between data utility and privacy risk. The chapter ends by presenting an integrated framework that balances the consumer perspective and the firm perspective with their data science toolbox. It is clear that firms should develop specific data science capabilities understanding consumers' privacy requirements to find an optimal balance that is further shaped by privacy legislation.

Chapter 6 investigates the role of digital platforms in transforming retailing. As already discussed in Chapter 4 digital platforms have a strong impact on the marketplace and distribution. Digital platforms are omnipresent and include firms such as Amazon, Zalando, and Uber. The chapter provides a nice overview of multiple platform types and their specific characteristics. Next, it discusses the consequences of platformization for the retailing industry. This industry has been strongly affected and classic offline retailers have faced or are facing major problems in multiple markets. The chapter discusses how platforms affect specific main competences of retailers, such as assortment size and curation, customer experience creation, and service. These consequences can be huge. For example, platforms have extensive assortments in multiple markets, whereas offline retailers due to their square meter limitations have limited assortment sizes both in terms of depth and breadth. Three strategies are discussed about how to deal with platformization: (1) assortment extension thereby choosing head-on competition, (2) assortment specialization thereby deflecting competition, and (3) service focus aiming to evade competition. Each of these strategies has its own advantages and disadvantages and should be considered seriously. The chapter discusses multiple examples of these strategies.

Chapter 7 discusses how to create and realize value via open innovation in digital transformation, where co-creation becomes essential as the locus of value creation is shifting nowadays from individual businesses to clusters of businesses and individuals on digital platforms and ecosystems. While open innovation platforms offer vast potential for value creation, there are threats to realizing and sustaining it over time. In order to create and realize value, the authors propose a virtuous cycle of value co-creation and value co-realization for platform sustained growth, in which digital resource provision plays a key role. This cycle underscores the interdependence of value co-creation and co-realization and articulates such interdependence from a dynamic, co-evolution viewpoint.

Chapter 8 shifts the focus to another important area—digital transformation of supply chains and logistics. The authors take food distributors as a notable example, given that food delivery platforms are growing rapidly across countries and regions, to show the expanding possibilities of digital technologies that urge companies to reinvent their networks, operations, and business models to reduce environmental impacts and labor shortages. Using empirical data from a logistics company, bundling—where goods of different suppliers are jointly delivered to customers by the same logistics arrangement—is proposed as an effective path of digital transformation for food distributors to create value as well as reduce cost and emissions. To this end, digital collaborations between companies require an increased effort in data exchange and business model transformation.

Part III: implementation and impact of digital transformation

In Part III of the book, we focus on the implementation and impact of digital transformation. Chapter 9 discusses the processes and challenges in change management for digital transformation. The author presents a duality perspective to manage digital transformation processes to recognize and embrace the inherent complexity, where duality refers to the interplay of contrasting or complementary forces that contribute to a balanced understanding. It is suggested that managers and organizational members can better understand the tensions that arise during digital transformation by acknowledging the existence of relevant dualities. Based on a systematic diagnosis, those who manage digital transformation should recognize the dualities by developing a context-dependent, firm-specific change strategy according to an organization's characteristics, challenges, and the available technologies for achieving success. An analytical framework is provided to facilitate a balanced understanding of digital transformation processes by addressing the most common dualities that may arise from changes.

Chapter 10 discusses another key challenge related to cybersecurity in the digital transformation age. The authors present a human–machine collaborative approach based on AI tools. As human users are often the weakest link in an organization's cybersecurity, it is crucial to involve humans in developing cybersecurity solutions, who can be equipped with AI-based systems to provide personalized and relevant cybersecurity policy suggestions by analyzing the digitally transformed work data to better understand each individual user's tasks and issues. By suggesting AI involvement in cybersecurity policy specifications, an application of using AI-based systems to improve cybersecurity policy compliance, as well as an AI-based security, education, training, and awareness recommendation system, this approach can help organizations save resources and time in training human resources for cybersecurity in digital transformation processes.

Chapter 11 focuses on the challenge of digital transformation related to privacy concerns on the consumer side. The authors empirically conduct a multilevel latent class analysis for more than 15,000 consumers across 24 countries to segment consumers based on willingness to share (WTS) personal information with firms in the digital transformation age, investigate how the privacy calculus and consumers' relationships with firms affect WTS, and explore how WTS varies nationally and internationally. This is a timely large-scale empirical endeavor as advancing digital transformation enables firms to access consumers globally, who will not be effectively served with low WTS providing little input to firms' big data. The results show three meaningful consumer segments—privacy-concerned consumers, privacy pragmatists, and relationship seekers—that are considerably different from each other and can predict WTS.

Chapter 12 further extends the discussion from privacy concerns to business ethics in general under the digital transformation context. Three ethical implications of digital transformation are discussed regarding the concerns on digital technologies, the perceptions of those who engage with digital technologies, and the actual outcomes of technological changes. A literature review with a particular focus on AI as the representative digital technology is conducted for publications in leading journals in the ethics, corporate social responsibility, and management field defined by the Association of Business Schools. Fifty-eight resulting articles were coded and analyzed to uncover ethical implications of digital transformation. Several management and governance recommendations are provided, with directions for future research.

Concluding remarks

We hope you will enjoy reading this book on various important topics about digital transformation across multiple business disciplines. Hopefully, the insights from this book showcase essential areas of digital transformation research within and beyond each discipline and inspire future scholarly endeavors to better understand digital transformation from multidisciplinary perspectives, contributing to a more successful digital era. Finally, we want to thank all contributing authors for providing 11 valuable chapters on digital transformation. It has been a great pleasure to work with so many excellent scholars from multiple business disciplines.

References

Beke, F. T., Eggers, F., Verhoef, P. C., & Wieringa, J. E. (2022). Consumers' privacy calculus: The PRICAL index development and validation. *International Journal of Research in Marketing*, *39*(1), 20–41.

Fabian, N. E., Dong, J. Q., Broekhuizen, T., & Verhoef, P. C. (2023). Business value of SME digitalisation: When does it pay off more? *European Journal of Information Systems*. https://doi.org/10.1080/0960085X.2023.2167671.

Lemon, K. N., & Verhoef, P. C. (2016). Understanding customer experience throughout the customer journey. *Journal of Marketing*, *80*(6). https://doi.org/10.1509/jm.15.0420.

Nguyen, D. K., Broekhuizen, T., Dong, J. Q., & Verhoef, P. C. (2023). Leveraging synergy to drive digital transformation: A systems-theoretic perspective. *Information & Management*, *60*(7), 103836.

Verhoef, P. C., Broekhuizen, T., Bart, Y., Bhattacharya, A., Dong, J. Q., Fabian, N. E., & Haenlein, M. (2021). Digital transformation: A multidisciplinary reflection and research agenda. *Journal of Business Research*, *122*, 889–901.

Verhoef, P. C., Kooge, E., Walk, N., & Wieringa, J. E. (2022). *Creating Value with Data Analytics in Marketing: Mastering Data Science*. Routledge, London.

PART I

Multidisciplinary perspectives on digital transformation

2 A strategic innovation perspective on digital transformation: the example of small and medium enterprises

Thijs Broekhuizen, Dinh Khoi Nguyen and Nicolai Etienne Fabian

Small and medium enterprises (SMEs) face mounting pressure to respond to digital technologies and new digital entrants. To remain competitive, they need to innovate by developing incrementally and radically new products as well as by introducing new business models through digital transformation (Fabian et al., 2023; Verhoef et al., 2021). While there is a strong sense of urgency to expedite digital transformation (Baiyere et al., 2020; Vial, 2019; Vom Brocke et al., 2021; Wessel et al., 2021), many SMEs struggle to manage its complexity (Eller et al., 2020; Fabian et al., 2023). The development of new digital business models is particularly challenging for SMEs, as it fundamentally alters the organization's identity, value proposition, target segments, and competencies, and/or requires substantial short-term investments that may potentially endanger firm survivability. Factors such as a lack of specialized personnel (Bouncken & Barwinski, 2021), the complexity of embracing new digital technologies (Eller et al., 2020), and the need for deep organizational changes and identity (Wessel et al., 2021) can overwhelm and paralyze SMEs (Fabian et al., 2023). Adding to the complexity is the fact that digital transformation unfolds over time, requires continued attention and commitment, and entails great uncertainty regarding the development of technologies and performance outcomes (Nguyen et al., 2023).

Prior research has explored the role of time to understand how firms balance exploration (identifying new opportunities) and exploitation (leveraging existing opportunities) (Mathias et al., 2018) regarding strategic planning (Das, 1987), corporate social responsibility (Choi et al., 2023), durability of capital investments (Souder & Bromiley, 2012), and innovation (Barreto et al., 2022).

A firm's orientation and interpretation of the future determine the timing and intensity of updating and leveraging its business model in response to dynamic events, such as the advent of digital technologies (Blank, 2019; Wenzel et al., 2020). Hence, temporal dimensions play a significant role in shaping strategic decisions for SMEs related to digital transformation and radical innovation. They determine how SMEs envision and prepare for technological advancements while ensuring agility and adaptability within shorter time frames to stay competitive in the dynamic digital landscape. In the short term, incremental technologies are often employed for continuous innovation to further exploit existing core capabilities and enhance business model performance. More radical technologies may take longer to develop but can extend the SME's existing business model and further improve existing core capabilities to better address existing and future customers with a radically improved product. The most pervasive and complex form is the adoption of new technologies to create new digital business models that take advantage of or respond to disruptive opportunities or counter competitors' disruptive business models. For these two latter, more radical forms of innovation, SMEs must consider the future to allocate attention and resources strategically.

The aim of this study is to gain a deeper understanding of how the temporal dimensions influence digital transformation. To better understand the (relative) impact of the temporal dimensions, we compare the effects of two temporal dimensions, namely future orientation and future horizon on digital transformation, and contrast them with their impact on another type of innovation that requires significant development time: radical innovation. This comparison between innovation contexts aims to provide a more comprehensive and nuanced understanding of how temporal dimensions influence each type of innovation. Comparing the two may reveal unique distinctions, evidence diverse learning strategies, and yield divergent outcomes, aiding in more informed decision-making for the pursuit of both types of innovation.

Research on digital transformation highlights that SMEs pursuing digital transformation benefit from experimentation and iterative testing (Fabian et al., 2023; Nguyen et al., 2023). Popular management books such as *The Lean Startup* by Eric Ries (2011), *Launch!* by Scott Duffy (2014), and *Testing Business Ideas* by Bland and Osterwalder (2019) also emphasize the need for agile build–measure–learn feedback loops to validate market assumptions and accelerate learning when introducing new (digital) business models. These approaches validate market assumptions and accelerate learning when introducing new (digital) business models. By building minimum viable products – barely, finished, iterative, incremental prototypes – SMEs can test the waters, learn quickly from customers, and adjust accordingly to cater to their changing needs (McGrath, 2010). This suggests that SMEs not only benefit from more strongly considering the future, but also from using shorter time frames to define the distant future.

Building on this understanding, we argue that researchers must consider two temporal dimensions to fully understand digital transformation (and how their effects differ from those of radical innovation), particularly for SMEs. First, SMEs benefit from a strong future orientation, which involves devoting significant time to envisioning and preparing for the use of digital technologies. Second, they should not look too far into the future, and benefit from a shorter time horizon to foster agility and incorporate experimentation into their strategies. Radical innovation is expected to also benefit from a stronger future orientation as it helps SMEs to consider how new technologies can improve or enhance value in the future, but here a longer time horizon may align well with the more structured engineering development path – also known as the waterfall approach – that involves clear milestones and well-defined (product) requirements. To test our hypotheses, we use a unique data set consisting of Dutch SME firms and their (digital) innovation activities. Based on the analysis of 268 firms, we find that SMEs' digital transformation is fostered by a stronger future orientation and shorter time horizon. We further demonstrate the relevance of firms' future orientation and future horizon, as they impact digital transformation and radical innovation performance differently; while firms with a stronger future orientation generate greater radical innovation performance as well as digital transformation.

In this chapter, we aim to contribute to the literature in two ways. First, in an attempt to gain a better understanding of the predictive validity of the two temporal dimensions, we explore whether the strengths of the effects of the temporal dimensions on business model innovation (i.e., digital transformation) differ from another important type of innovation (i.e., radical innovation). The results of this comparison show a differential effect of future horizon on digital transformation and radical innovation. This finding advances past research focusing on the effects of temporal dimensions on a single outcome (Nadkarni et al., 2016; Nadkarni & Chen, 2014) and emphasizes the relevance of including the time horizon as it explains the different organizational learning processes that underlie the two innovation outcomes. Shorter future horizon facilitates organizational learning for digital transformation through experimentation and iteration by focusing on market information processing and proactivity (cf., Slater & Narver, 1995). Conversely, a longer horizon is beneficial for less uncertain learning pathways that underlie the technological and engineering-focused development of radical innovations.

Second, our investigation diverges from existing studies in the field of temporal orientation by focusing on a diverse range of SMEs. Traditional research in this area has been limited to examining either large firms (Desjardine & Shi, 2021; Gamache & McNamara, 2019; Nadkarni & Chen, 2014) or family firms (Le Breton-Miller & Miller, 2011; Lumpkin & Brigham, 2011). We believe that the SME context provides unique theoretical insights that are distinct from those acquired from studying large corporations or a subset of SMEs, as it offers a research context in which a diverse group of SMEs must respond to digital technologies to navigate future challenges. Currently, little is known about how SMEs' future orientation and future horizon affect innovation outcomes. The existing literature presents a mixed view on SMEs and their approach to innovation. On the one hand, studies grounded in the behavioral theory of the firm suggest that SMEs, constrained by limited resources, are generally more risk-averse and favor shorter time horizons for their innovations (Argote & Greve, 2007; Woschke et al., 2017). On the other hand, other research emphasizes that SMEs often exhibit a high level of entrepreneurial orientation (Runyan et al., 2008), creating a culture conducive to risk-taking and disruptive innovation (Karimi & Walter, 2016; Wiklund & Shepherd, 2005). Our study seeks to explore these contrasting views by examining the temporal dimensions in SMEs. Specifically, we investigate whether shorter time horizons expedite digital transformation and limit radical innovation. Hence, our research illuminates how future orientation and future horizon differentially influence SMEs' innovation outcomes. With SMEs representing a major part of the firms in the European Union, we make an important contribution to better understand how SMEs manage digital transformation and radical innovation. These insights hold managerial significance as they demonstrate how temporal dimensions link to the attainment of specific innovation outcomes.

Theoretical background

Digital Transformation: The Introduction of a New Digital Business Model

Digital transformation describes a deep change to the fabric of the organization that combines changes to the business model as well as organizational identity (Hanelt et al., 2021; Verhoef et al., 2021; Vial, 2019; Wessel et al., 2021). It closely relates to adjacent phenomena such as information technology (IT) transformation (Wessel et al., 2021), but also differs from other innovation-related phenomena such as radical innovation (Zhou et al., 2005). Digital transformation refers to the integration of digital technology into all areas of a business, resulting in fundamental changes to the logic and functioning of the business (Verhoef et al., 2021), leading to a new way of creating and capturing value (Teece, 2010). Therefore, in contrast to radical innovation, which mainly focuses on the development of radically new products and services that are new to the market, digital transformation entails many organizational changes on different levels. It involves the incorporation of new technologies such as big data, the Internet of Things, and artificial intelligence (AI) to improve organizational processes, increase efficiency, and enhance the customer experience (Teece, 2010; Verhoef et al., 2021). We take an organizational view on digital transformation and treat it as a dynamic process that allows firms to ultimately introduce new digital business models.

A business model refers to the system of interconnected activities performed by a firm and its partners to create value for its customers (Teece, 2010). To create value, firms develop a value proposition in the form of a product or service that is valued by some customers and which is backed up by an activity system that links resources, activities, and components to help deliver this value (Zott et al., 2011). A revenue model, or monetization method, allows the firm to capture some of the value it creates (Teece, 2018). Business models are crucial for a firm's long-term survival and growth as they form the very basis of how the firm functions, yet they are subject to change by internal and external market pressures (Broekhuizen et al., 2018). Digital transformation often involves the development of a new business model that leverages digital technologies or big data to create value in a way that was not previously possible (Vial, 2019). For instance, a firm might use big data analytics to better understand and predict customer behavior, or it might use the Internet of Things to improve supply chain efficiency (Verhoef et al., 2021). The adoption of a new business model through digital transformation can bring about significant changes to the way a company operates and the value it delivers to customers. It involves a great risk of failure due to technological and market uncertainty. Prior to the start of digital transformation, firms face technological uncertainty regarding the ability to effectively make use of digital technology, as well as market uncertainty by not knowing whether the customer likes the new value proposition and whether other market partners (suppliers, retailers) are willing to accept the changes without causing channel conflicts.

Digital transformation is a risky endeavor that fails more often than it succeeds[1] because it requires fundamental shifts to the business without any guarantee of success (Fabian et al., 2023). SMEs especially, while nimble and agile, are also resource-constrained and often lack the ability to quickly implement changes of such size (Eller et al., 2020). For instance, digital transformation may imply the use of disruptive technologies that may devalue or even make existing market-based and/or technological competencies obsolete (Christensen et al., 2015; Christensen & Overdorf, 2000). Furthermore, digital transformation also has the potential to cannibalize its business model without having established a new one. In sum, digital transformation poses significant market- and technological-based challenges for SME firms. On the one hand, SMEs need to adopt new technologies and market competencies in the short term to further improve their existing business and exploit existing competencies. On the other hand, they need corporate foresight and to play the long game in order to develop new competencies to fully reinvent themselves and establish new digital business models. As such, digital transformation is strongly influenced by the future orientation and interpretation of the future by the explorative versus exploitative business model change (Osiyevskyy & Dewald, 2015).

Temporal Dimensions: Future Orientation and Future Horizon

The role of time and how it shapes strategic decisions (e.g., short-term and long-term investments) and performance (e.g., firm value, firm growth) has been a prominent topic of debate in organization theory and strategy (Das, 1991; Flammer & Bansal, 2017; Gavetti & Levinthal, 2000; Reilly et al., 2016). Much of this literature explores how employees, who are embedded in organizations, conceptualize, experience, and manage the concept of time (cf., Park et al., 2017). Time has been conceptualized in terms of perception and behaviors. While the organizational behavior literature mostly considers time as manifested in *behaviors* of individual employees such as polychromic (Conte & Gintoft, 2009), urgency, or hurriedness (Jansen & Kristof-Brown, 2005), and pacing styles (Gevers et al., 2015), strategic research often relies on their *perception* of organizations toward, for example, eras of time (past, present, and future) (Gamache & McNamara, 2019; Nadkarni & Chen, 2014), or time horizon (Bluedorn & Martin, 2008; Nadkarni et al., 2016). In their review of how time horizons affect resource allocation, Reilly et al. (2016) explain that strategic decisions are heavily affected by references to the past (where the firm has been), the present (where the firm is), or the future (where the firm would like to be).

Based on our review of the digital transformation literature of SMEs, we suggest that, with respect to the eras of time (past, present, and future), the future plays a more prominent role than the past or present in explaining digital transformation. While interpretations of the past and present may play a role in shaping the existing organizational identity, activities, customer segments, and competencies, the burdens of an organizational identity change, overcoming inertia, and legacy costs require firms to be forward-looking (Fabian et al., 2023). In terms of the temporal dimensions, we argue that two of them are important, namely (a) future orientation that displays the importance of the future, and (b) the future horizons that the firm considers regarding the future, and provide how firms treat or interpret the future horizon.

Future orientation is defined as a firm's strategic focus on the future or the extent to which it considers and plans for the long-term consequences of its actions. Unlike some research that views future orientation as a cultural attribute,[2] we align with Nadkarni and Chen (2014) in treating future orientation as a strategic focus. This is particularly relevant for SMEs undergoing digital transformation, as such a strategic directive is risky and change-inducing (Vial, 2019). Previous studies have confirmed that a strategic focus on the future significantly influences risk-taking, innovation, and entrepreneurial activities (Desjardine & Shi, 2021; Nadkarni & Chen, 2014). This line of thought suggests that managers with a strong future orientation are more adept at identifying emerging trends and consumer demands in the industry. Consequently, they are better positioned to develop new products and engage in scenario planning to make future-proof decisions (Nadkarni & Chen, 2014).

Future horizon refers to the length of time, or distance, that a firm considers when thinking about the distant future (Nadkarni et al., 2016). Future time horizon, also known as temporal depth, is another aspect of a firm's strategic orientation (Das, 1987). A firm with a long-distance orientation may be more likely to consider the impacts of its actions over a longer time horizon (e.g., 30 years) while a firm with a short-distance orientation may only consider the near-term future and treat it as distant. Past research has shown that the future horizon might be a double-edged sword in strategic planning (Bluedorn & Martin, 2008; Nadkarni et al., 2016). Firms with longer future time horizons are capable of foresight and responding to future opportunities and threats as well as overcoming myopia and short-termism, contributing to their sustained competitive advantages. However, a long-term vision may lead to situations in which firms myopically overemphasize the long term and prevent firms from effectively addressing short-term changes (Levinthal & March, 1993). Overcommitment to the long term creates a type of rigidity that shades firms from urgent upcoming events and shock. On the other hand, firms with a shorter future horizon act on a shorter time window which allows them to be timelier and more responsive (Nadkarni et al., 2016).

Notably, and as presented in Table 2.1, there is a highly related temporal construct of long-term orientation (LTO) in the strategic management literature, defined as "the tendency to prioritize the long-range implications and impact of decisions and actions that come to fruition after an extended time period" (Lin et al., 2019; see also Martin et al., 2016), and in the cross-cultural literature, defined as "the extent to which a society looks forward to the future rather than resorting to the past to solve the problems in the present or the future" (Hofstede, 2010). In both cases, LTO can be seen as a combination of future orientation (focusing on the future) and a longer future time horizon (emphasizing the long-term versus the short-term impacts) (Lin et al., 2019). Rather than convoluting the time dimensions, this study opts to use two separate constructs of future orientation and future time horizon because of two important reasons. First, we argue that both future orientation and future horizon are relevant to digital transformation, but that they may have opposite effects (Gupta & Bose, 2022; Hanelt et al., 2021; Warner & Wäger, 2019). Second, we aim to juxtapose the effects of the temporal dimensions on digital transformation with those of radical innovation to highlight the different impact that the future horizon has on the two innovation outcomes based on differences in organizational learning. Radical innovation faces high technological risk because state-of-the-art technologies are extremely expensive and require major investments (Sorescu et al., 2003; Wind & Mahajan, 1997), yet radical innovation often addresses well-understood needs of existing target customers (e.g., a new technological liquid crystal method to enhance the picture quality of televisions), the perceived market risk tends to be lower than for digital transformation (Chandy & Tellis, 2000; Srinivasan et al., 2002; Zhou et al., 2005). This has important consequences for how SMEs can effectively learn and reduce uncertainty. Radical innovation can benefit from taking a longer future horizon, as the innovation steps in the new product development (NPD) process can be more clearly defined and planned, while digital transformation can benefit from shorter distances that promote quick experimentation, trial-and-error approaches, and continued adaptation (Argote et al., 2020; Argote & Miron-Spektor, 2011). Figure 2.1 illustrates the difference between long and short future horizons.

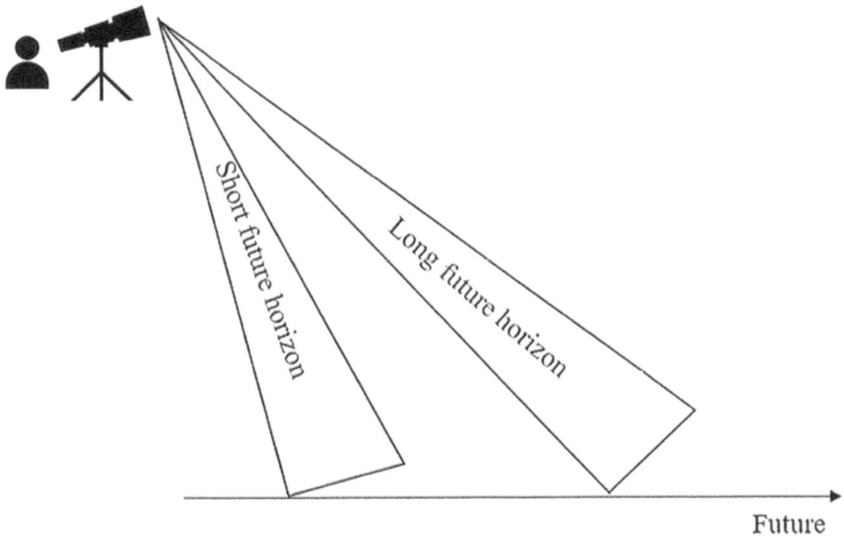

Figure 2.1 Long versus short future horizon

Table 2.1 Definitions and descriptions of future orientation, future time horizon, and long-term orientation

Concept	Definition	Description of concept	Selected reference	Inclusion in this study
Future orientation	The extent to which firms devote their attention to perceptions of the future	A relatively stable tendency in evaluating and interpreting time	Nadkarni & Chen (2014); Gamache & McNamara (2019); Desjardine & Shi (2021)	✓
Future time horizon	Distance into the future that firms consider when contemplating events that may happen	Time horizons that firms consider when thinking about future events	Nadkarni et al. (2016); Bluedorn & Martin (2008)	✓

Concept	Definition	Description of concept	Selected reference	Inclusion in this study
Long-term orientation	The tendency to prioritize the long-range implications and impact of decisions and actions that come to fruition after an extended time period	The fostering of virtues oriented towards future rewards, like perseverance and thrift	Le Breton-Miller and Miller (2011); Martin et al. (2016); Lin et al. (2019)	*x*
		The extent to which a society looks forward to the future rather than resorting to the past to solve the problems in the present or the future	Hofstede (2010)	

Hypotheses

To demonstrate the relevance of our multidimensional view, we explore the relationships between future orientation, time horizon, and digital transformation. To understand how temporal dimensions may affect digital transformation and radical innovation differently, we compare the effect sizes and direction of the temporal dimensions as predictors of both innovation outcomes. Below, we explain how future orientation and future horizon facilitate both digital transformation and radical innovation. Figure 2.2 presents our conceptual model.

The Effects of Future Orientation on Digital Transformation and Radical Innovation

Digital transformation requires a fundamental change to the logic of the business. As such, SMEs need to adopt new digital technologies into the business and also develop the necessary capabilities to handle such technologies (Vial, 2019). As such, digital transformation involves making significant changes

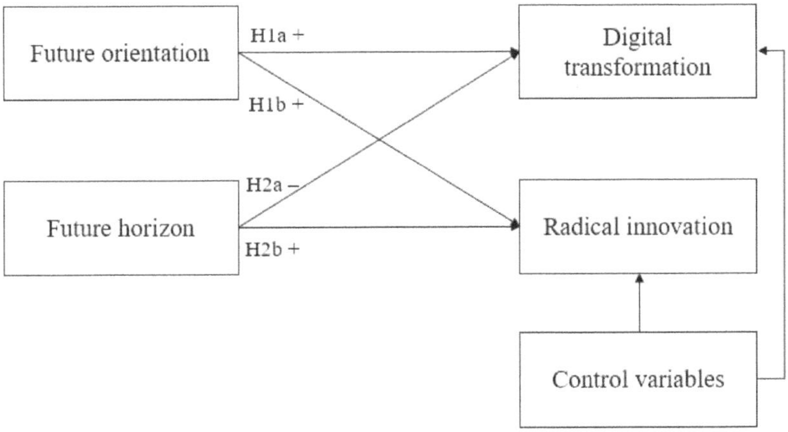

Figure 2.2 Conceptual model

to an organization's processes, systems, and operations to adapt to and take advantage of new technologies. These changes can be complex, costly, and time-consuming, and they may not provide immediate benefits. For example, changes can be rooted in changing the value proposition (e.g., from product to services), the value network (e.g., creating a platform and connecting different actors), or the use of digital channels (e.g., e-commerce) (De Reuver et al., 2018; Dremel et al., 2020; Fabian et al., 2023; Suseno et al., 2018). In the second step, SMEs must be then able to not only create value but also appropriate it and establish an effective revenue model. While successful digital business models tend to be more profitable as they require less labor and less physical infrastructure, and have greater scalability and lower distribution costs (Fabian et al., 2023; Verhoef et al., 2021), attaining sufficient revenues in fiercely competitive (platform) markets that are dominated by large data-moguls is highly complex.

Research considers digital transformation as a process that unfolds over time (Baiyere et al., 2020; Vial, 2019; Wessel et al., 2021). The constant updates necessary for successful digital transformation are at odds with a waterfall approach, which consequently diminishes the business value of digital transformation for SMEs (Fabian et al., 2023). As such, the SME's future orientation plays an integral role in facilitating success. Future orientation ensures that the SME commits to and sustains the efforts required for digital transformation. Digital transformation requires a substantial commitment from the firm's leadership in terms of resources (Nguyen et al., 2023; Vial, 2019). Such resources include human resources, IT resources, and also financial resources to build and nurture new revenue streams (Verhoef et al., 2021). Moreover, future orientation ensures that short-term financial goals are foregone in favor of future gains. It also involves a willingness to embrace change and adapt to new circumstances (Lin et al., 2019). All of these characteristics are important to successful digital transformation, as it requires an SME to think beyond the present and to be willing to make changes that may not have immediate benefits, but that are necessary for long-term success in a rapidly evolving digital landscape.

Different studies, relying on different theoretical perspectives, have theorized about this relationship in different ways (see Xiao et al., 2022 for an overview). In this chapter, we apply a learning perspective (Argote et al., 2020; Argote & Miron-Spektor, 2011) to explain this relationship. We expect that SMEs with a stronger future orientation are more likely to be aware of digital transformation and the changing environment. By considering the future, they are more likely to be confronted with these technologies, and that may provide them with an advantage over competitor firms. Recent research shows that such awareness of new digital technologies is a prerequisite to digital transformation (Day & Schoemaker, 2016; Warner & Wäger, 2019), as SMEs need to familiarize themselves firstly by carefully selecting the right technologies from a wide range of potential technologies to develop new business models (Nguyen et al., 2023). Therefore, we expect the following hypothesis:

H1a: An SME's future orientation is positively associated with digital transformation.

Many of the previously mentioned properties of digital transformation also apply to radical innovation. While the scope of radical innovation differs (mostly focused on introducing products or services that make use of radically new technologies), radical innovation also benefits from a greater awareness of future developments that allow SMEs to remain competitive and make substantial resource investments (Nadkarni & Chen, 2014). For instance, a stronger future orientation helps to monitor and anticipate changing market trends and customer demands. By staying attuned to potential shifts in customer preferences and technological advancements, these SMEs can develop groundbreaking products or services that cater to unmet market demands (Eggers & Park, 2018). Furthermore, the structured NPD processes of radical innovation also require substantial resource investments, including financial, human, and technological (Brentani, 2001). A stronger future orientation helps to allow SMEs to prioritize and commits resources to high-risk, high-potential projects. Finally, future orientation helps to establish forward-looking external collaborations that promote the exchange of novel, nonredundant knowledge that can be recombined to form novel ways to apply radical technologies (Broekhuizen et al., 2023; Leifer et al., 2001; Polier, 2019). Market visioning, an aspect of future orientation, which relates to the organization's capability to develop new market applications for an advanced technology, fosters the development and early success of radically new, high-tech products (Reid & de Brentani, 2012). As such, we expect the following hypothesis:

H1b: An SME's future orientation is positively associated with radical innovation.

The Effects of Time Horizon on Digital Transformation and Radical Innovation

SMEs may differ in their temporal depth or perceptions of time horizon; while some SMEs may use long periods to consider the distant future, others may treat the future using much shorter time frames (Flammer & Bansal, 2017; Nadkarni et al., 2016). A longer time horizon means that the SME thinks or plans further into the future, while a shorter future horizon means that it only considers the near-term future (Bluedorn & Martin, 2008; Nadkarni & Chen, 2014). An SME that considers the next ten years as the distant future uses a longer future horizon than an SME that views the next one to two years as the distant future. In general, SMEs with a longer time horizon tend to have a longer-term perspective and may be more focused on long-term planning and goal-setting. Conversely, those with a shorter time horizon may be more focused on the present and near-term future.

Research finds mixed results regarding the performance effects of time horizon (Sampson & Shi, 2023). A shorter time horizon may be detrimental because managers may become myopic and forgo profitable investments in order to make the short-term earnings expected by shareholders (Graham et al., 2005), and avoid long-term projects, such as corporate social responsibility (Wang & Bansal, 2012). Yet, other research, especially in the field of digital transformation and business model innovation, warns against using longer time horizons (Blank, 2019) because it limits organizational learning needed to come up with new and competitive business models, and being preoccupied with the long-term effects may also lead to myopic situations that prevent SMEs from effectively addressing short-term changes (Levinthal & March, 1993). According to Blank (2019), the rapid influx of technologies and digital disruptors make past time considerations outdated. Blank (2019: 3) argues that "in the 20th century [...] new disruptive ideas took years to research, engineer, and deliver. That's no longer true in the 21st century."

For digital transformation, while future orientation is essential to become aware of and acquainted with new digital technologies, we expect that longer time horizon may be detrimental to learning and reacting quickly, thereby limiting the potential to reduce technological and market risks. This notion is particularly relevant when studying SMEs, as they are constrained by resources and less responsive to risks and uncertainties (Argote & Greve, 2007). Popularized by practitioners and academic research (Blank, 2013; Fabian et al., 2023; Ries, 2011), the adage is to use shorter time horizons and install build–measure–learn feedback loops to validate market assumptions that accelerate learning and introduce flexibility in the design (agile approach). Relative to the agile approach, the waterfall approach is less equipped to deal with the dynamic and uncertain nature of digital transformation, as it depends on upfront planning, huge upfront investments, and a different focus on retrieving and catering to customer needs (Table 2.2). The dynamic nature of the digital transformation process and the deep changes to the organization require SMEs to employ experimentation and step-by-step organizational learning (Fabian et al., 2023). As such, digital transformation is dependent on constant feedback loops between the future and the present. Subsequently, a longer time horizon may distract SMEs from the more immediate concerns. In addition, digital technology itself is highly dynamic in nature. Thus, technologies have a shorter shelf life which runs in contrast to a longer future time horizon. In sum, we expect that a shorter future time horizon is more beneficial to reap benefits from digital transformation.

H2a: An SME's future horizon is negatively associated with digital transformation.

While digital transformation requires constant experimentation, agility, and organizational learning to fine-tune business model changes and build new competencies along the transition, radical innovation may share some of the same characteristics for attaining knowledge based on previous experience (Eggers & Park, 2018), but its development is less dependent on constant experimentation and market updating. Instead, radical innovation often involves the under-the-radar development of new-to-the-market products and services. A recent historical study of Chen and Habibi (2023) reveals that during recessions firms adopt shorter time horizons leading to defensive tactics (i.e., cost cutting) that reduce innovation. In contrast, during recovery and growth, firms take on a long-term outlook, leading to increased research and development (R&D) expenditures and consequently fostering greater productivity in breakthrough innovation. Supporting this idea, Nadkarni and Chen (2014) link CEOs' forward-looking focus with an increased rate of product innovation, especially in dynamic environments. This suggests that a future-oriented mindset with longer time horizons can help establish an environment that stimulates radical innovation. Based on the above, we expect that SMEs with a longer time horizon are more likely to foster radical innovation. This long-term perspective enables them to envision and embrace new technologies, dedicate resources toward structured (NPD) projects, and build innovative products and services leveraging groundbreaking technologies.

H2b: An SME's future horizon is positively associated with radical innovation.

Table 2.2 Differences between the agile and waterfall approach

Element	Agile approach	Waterfall approach
Hands-on learning	Emphasized	Not emphasized
Testing assumptions	Encouraged	Not encouraged
Long-term planning	Flexible	Inflexible
Customer-oriented	Yes, via market updates	Yes, via focus groups or market research
Pivoting	Allowed	Not allowed
Prototyping	Encouraged	Not encouraged
Gathering and documenting requirements	Iterative	Upfront
Design	Emergent	Upfront

Note: Based on Blank (2013); McGrath (2010); McDonald & Eisenhardt (2020); Ries (2011).

Methodology

Research Context and Data Collection

We empirically explore the relevance of the temporal dimensions among a broad set of SMEs. SMEs recognize and use alternative future orientations and horizon to address some inherent challenges such as overcoming the liability of smallness (Kahle et al., 2020; Radziwon & Bogers, 2019; Van de Vrande et al., 2009) and the liability of newness (Cafferata et al., 2009; Gimenez-Fernandez et al., 2020; Singh et al., 1986) that are relevant to SMEs' digital transformation. Focusing on SMEs also entails a practical advantage as it is relatively easy to capture the mindset of this kind of company because decision power tends to be rather concentrated in SMEs.

To test our hypotheses, we rely on data that were collected within the scope of the 2019 edition of the Northern Netherlands Innovation Monitor. The Innovation Monitor asks SMEs to report on the innovation activities and performance of SMEs in this particular region. The data were collected between March and April 2019. The sample consists of close to 5,935 SMEs that received an invitation (and two reminders) to participate in an online survey. In total, we initially collected 436 surveys. After list-wise deletion, we obtained a final sample of 268 SMEs.

The sampled SMEs originate from a variety of industries, including manufacturing, agriculture, forestry & fishing (22.8 percent), professional, scientific and technical services (24.6 percent), other services (10.8 percent), construction (3.7 percent), information and communication (11.6 percent), wholesale and retail (13.1 percent), accommodation and food services (1.9 percent), rental, transportation, and warehousing (5.2 percent), and miscellaneous (6.3 percent). The SMEs are on average 28 years old (M = 28.40; SD = 37.06) and have on average 23 employees (M = 23.15; SD = 38.58).

Collecting self-reported data triggers the risk of response bias. To minimize this risk, we applied two research strategies. First, to motivate respondents to focus on response accuracy instead of speed, we promised each respondent a customized benchmark report in which the scores of the company are compared with their peers.[3] Second, we emphasized that the collected data would not be used as input to awards or rankings, thereby minimizing the risk that respondents would be incentivized to inflate their responses.

Measures

Digital transformation. We measure digital transformation as a second-order, reflective construct comprising digital business model (i.e., the degree to which SMEs introduce new digital value system elements to their business model) and digital capabilities development (i.e., the degree to which SMEs develop their digital capabilities) (Fabian et al., 2023; Nguyen et al., 2023). To measure the scale, we use 12 items that are all measured on 5-point scales. We take the mean of these 12 items to calculate a composite score where a higher score indicates a higher degree of digital transformation.

Radical innovation. In line with prior research (Belderbos et al., 2006; Faems et al., 2010; Oerlemans et al., 2013), radical innovation is operationalized as the degree to which the SMEs' revenues in 2018 are generated by new-to-the-market innovations that were introduced in the time frame 2016–2018. This focus reflects the ability to introduce more radical forms of innovation that are "new to the market" and not just "new to the firm."

Future orientation. We measure future orientation following Shipp et al. (2009), representing the degree to which SMEs consider the future in their current decision-making. We use two items with 5-point Likert scale to measure this construct.

Future horizon. This variable represents the SME's interpretation of the distant future. We ask the respondents to indicate how far away the distant future is, and use the number of years (with a maximum of 50) as a proxy for the interpretation of the distance toward the future (Nadkarni et al., 2016). Table 2.3 lists all items for each construct.

Table 2.3 Measures of key constructs

Construct	Measurement items	Scale
Future orientation	When making a strategic decision, to what degree does your firm take into account ... (): 1. The (expected) situation in the near future 2. The (expected) situation at the long term	5-point scale: 1 = very little; 5 = very strongly
Future horizon	If we talk about the long term, we usually think of the following number of years ahead: 0 5 10 15 20 25 30 35 40 45 50 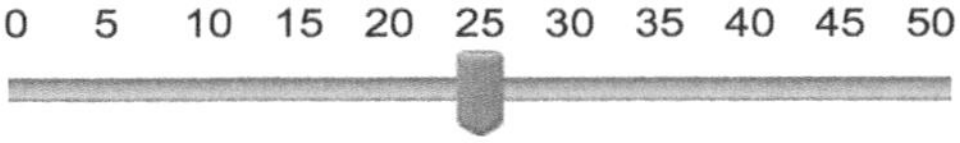	0 to 50 years
Digital transformation	1. Digital technology has changed the way how we do business 2. Digital technology has changed our internal operations 3. Digital technology has changed the collaboration with partners 4. The knowledge to use digital technology to improve the customer's journey (analyzing and collecting data) 5. We have entered new geographical markets and serve new customers with the help of digital technology	5-point scale 1 = not at all, 5 = to a great extent

Construct	Measurement items	Scale
Digital transformation	6. Our role in the value system has changed (e.g., extending markets via online channels, entering new business fields) Improvements realized in: 7. The ability and knowledge of the employees to use digital technologies 8. The ability to manage and analyze data of clients, competitors and other market data to capture value from it 9. The ability to find the best and most suitable digital technologies 10. The ability to integrate new digital technologies into our business activities 11. The ability to change business activities to create additional value for clients with new digital technology 12. The ability, knowledge, and awareness to handle digital technology ethically (privacy, security)	5-point scale 1= not at all, 5= to a great extent
Radical innovation	Indicate how your company revenues are generated by the following innovations and existing products/services (total = 100%): (a) New-to-the markets innovations (b) New-to-the-firm innovations (c) Existing products	Percentage of (a) to total revenues

Control variables. Following past research on digital transformation (Fabian et al., 2023; Nguyen et al., 2023) and radical innovation (Belderbos et al., 2006; Faems et al., 2010; Oerlemans et al., 2013), we control for a number of firm and industry characteristics. We control for *firm age* (in years) and *firm size* (number of employees) to capture differences in resource availability and life cycle differences (Laforet, 2013) and ability to manage ambidexterity (Mathias et al., 2018) that can be correlated with our dependent variables. As research suggests that family firms differ from nonfamily firms in their approach to innovation (Duran et al., 2015), we also include a *family firm* dummy variable (0 = no family firm, 1 = family firm) based on whether the family owns the firm.

To ascertain whether the direction of the time may play a role, we also control for the time orientations toward different time eras (i.e., past orientation and present orientation) as they might impact innovation and digital transformation (Nadkarni & Chen, 2014).

SMEs' launch of process innovations can influence their innovation and digital transformation (Laforet, 2013; Van Auken et al., 2008). We control for *process innovation* using a summative index of three questions indicating whether the SME has introduced in the past three years using the following activities: (i) new or improved production methods, (ii) logistic, supply, and distribution solutions, and (iii) maintenance, procurement, and administrative activities.

Finally, we control for industry effects using eight industry dummies, and geographical location (as proxied by the SME's location in one of the three provinces of the northern Netherlands).

Measurement Validation

We deploy a factor analysis to ensure the validity and reliability of our multi-item constructs. Using confirmatory factor analysis and item-to-total correlations, we confirm the unidimensionality of our latent constructs (digital transformation and future orientation). We find evidence for convergent validity, as the factor loadings are significant ($p < 0.01$, Table 2.4). Furthermore, the average variance extracted (AVE) of the constructs clearly exceeds the 0.5 threshold (Fornell & Larcker, 1981). We find evidence for discriminant validity as the square root AVE of three constructs is higher than the correlation among them. The low cross-loadings of all items also support sufficient discriminant validity. In terms of reliability, composite reliabilities and Cronbach's alphas for the constructs were above 0.7. Table 2.4 displays the descriptive statistics of our independent, dependent, and control variables.

Given the use of a single source, we tried to limit common method variance (CMV) in the survey design using mixed measurement (binary, percentage, Likert) (Podsakoff et al., 2003). We conducted a marker variable test, using the two weakest non-negative correlations (.01 and .02) as proxies for CMV (Lindell & Whitney, 2001). We calculated the partial correlations of the significant associations with the two performance measures, and they all remained statistically significant with the change from 1.33 percent to 9.29 percent. These tests provide evidence that common method bias does not seriously inflate our correlations.

Data Analysis

We use Ordinary Least Squares OLS regression to examine the associations of future orientation and future horizon on digital transformation. Because radical innovation is measured by the percentage of revenue generated by new-to-the-market innovations, we rely on double-censored Tobit regres-

Table 2.4 Descriptive statistics and correlations

	Mean	SD	(1)	(2)	(3)	(4)	(5)	(6)	(7)	(8)	(9)
(1) Digital transformation	2.744	0.933									
(2) Radical innovation	0.273	0.345	0.04								
(3) Future orientation	4.082	0.856	0.21*	0.24*							
(4) Future horizon	8.201	8.091	-0.12	0.19*	0.12*						
(5) Past orientation	3.513	0.977	0.03	0.06	0.19*	0.05					
(6) Present orientation	4.119	0.883	0.11	0.11	0.51*	**0.01**	0.48*				
(7) Firm age	28.39	37.06	0.04	-0.18*	-0.09	0.07	-0.12	-0.06			
(8) Firm size	23.15	38.58	0.18*	-0.18*	-0.08	-0.04	-0.04	-0.04	0.48*		
(9) Family firm	0.440	0.497	-0.00	-0.07	-0.12*	-0.03	**0.02**	-0.10	0.27*	0.00	
(10) Process innovation	1.085	1.000	0.43*	0.04	0.17*	-0.02	-0.08	-0.05	0.10	0.24*	0.04

Note: * $p < 0.05$, $N = 268$. Correlations in bold are used as proxies for CMV.

sion to analyze the effects of future orientation and future horizon on digital transformation (Haleblian et al., 2012; Laursen & Salter, 2006). We have 26 observations with the value of radical innovation performance equal to 1 and 100 observations with the value of radical innovation performance equal to 0. Our percentage measure is censored by 0 (the lower bound) and 1 (the upper bound) and, thus, the double-censored Tobit model is an appropriate approach.

Results

Hypothesis Testing

Table 2.5 shows the results of our analyses to predict digital transformation using OLS regression. Model 1 (in Table 2.5) is our baseline model, which only includes the control variables. The results in Model 2 (Table 2.5) indicate the existence of a positive linear relationship between future orientation and digital transformation ($b = 0.155$, $p = 0.036$), supporting H1a. We also find support for H2a as the association between future horizon and digital transformation is negative and significant ($b = -0.013$, $p = 0.037$).

Table 2.6 shows the results of the Tobit analysis.[4] In support of H1b and H2b, we find that both future orientation ($b = 0.139$, $p = 0.003$) and future horizon ($b = 0.008$, $p = 0.038$) increase radical innovation.

Table 2.5 OLS analyses with digital transformation

	Hypothesis	(1)	(2)
Firm age		-0.001 (0.002)	-0.001 (0.002)
Firm size		0.003 (0.002)	0.003 (0.002)
Family firm		-0.004 (0.109)	0.005 (0.109)
Past orientation		-0.017 (0.061)	0.008 (0.060)
Present orientation		0.136 (0.066)	0.055 (0.074)
Process innovation		0.374** (0.052)	0.344** (0.053)
Future orientation	H1a: +		0.155* (0.074)
Future horizon	H2a: -		-0.013* (0.006)
Industry dummies		Yes	Yes
Province dummies		Yes	Yes
N		260	260
R2		0.303	0.325

Note: * $p < 0.05$; ** $p < 0.01$.

Table 2.6 Tobit analyses with radical innovation

	Hypothesis	(1)	(2)
Firm age		-0.002 (0.001)	-0.002* (0.001)
Firm size		-0.001 (0.001)	-0.001 (0.001)
Family firm		-0.040 (0.068)	-0.009 (0.066)

	Hypothesis	(1)	(2)
Past orientation		0.023 (0.037)	0.024 (0.037)
Present orientation		0.035 (0.041)	-0.026 (0.046)
Process innovation		0.077* (0.033)	0.049 (0.032)
Future orientation	H1b: +		0.139** (0.046)
Future horizon	H2b: +		0.008* (0.004)
Industry dummies		Yes	Yes
Province dummies		Yes	Yes
N		268	268
Pseudo R2		0.066	0.105

Note: * $p < 0.05$; ** $p < 0.01$.

In terms of control variables, we find that process innovation (in Table 2.5, Model 2) has a strong positive influence on digital transformation ($b = 0.344$, $p = 0.001$), but not on radical innovation ($b = 0.049$, $p = 0.133$) (in Table 2.6, Model 2). This underlines our assumption of the dynamic and iterative nature of digital transformation by suggesting that process innovations further stimulate the development of new digital business models. Finally, the controls for the time orientations toward different time eras (i.e., past orientation and present orientation) show that such perceptions neither have an influence on digital transformation nor on radical innovation.

Post Hoc Analysis

As an additional test, we also investigate the possible interaction effect between future orientation and future horizon on digital transformation and radical innovation. The existence of such an interaction effect may provide valuable insights into how these two temporal dimensions synergistically influence an SME's capacity for digital transformation and radical innovation. The insignificance of these interaction terms ($p > 0.10$) suggests that there is no (dis) synergy between the two temporal dimensions.

Discussion and conclusion

This study investigates the role that time plays in the development of new digital business models and radical innovation. It examines the impact of two distinct temporal dimensions, future orientation and future horizon, on digital transformation, and juxtaposes their impacts with those observed for radical innovation. The study findings suggest that a stronger future orientation can foster SMEs' digital transformation and radical innovation. Yet, future horizon has distinctive and opposite effects: while digital transformation benefits from shorter horizons, radical innovation thrives under longer horizons.

First, we contribute to the temporal orientation literature by disentangling the role of future orientation and future horizon and their impact on two important yet distinct types of innovation, digital transformation versus radical innovation, whereas earlier research often focused on the impacts of temporal dimensions on a single outcome (Desjardine & Shi, 2021; Nadkarni et al., 2016; Nadkarni & Chen, 2014). We broaden this discussion by considering both digital transformation and radical innovation, thereby shedding light on the differential impacts of future horizon. In line with organizational learning literature, we find that future horizon affects how SMEs learn to improve different innovation processes. Digital transformation benefits strongly from shorter time horizon and thereby from continuous adaption, testing the waters as well as trial-and-error approaches to benefit from new technologies (Fabian et al., 2023; Warner & Wäger, 2019). Moreover, SMEs may avoid myopia by adopting a longer future horizon, which is beneficial to identifying emerging needs and developing products that are new to the market (Nadkarni et al., 2016). In contrast, a longer horizon is beneficial for less uncertain learning pathways that underlie the technological and engineering-focused development of radical innovations. Looking far into the future helps SMEs to steer away from incremental improvements by realizing the limitations of current technologies and predict the products and services of the future (Tellis et al., 2009; Yadav et al., 2007). Thus, a longer future horizon allows SMEs to imagine future scenarios, thereby more accurately predicting emerging needs or anticipating coming (disruption) risks to the NPD process (Chandy & Tellis, 1998; Nadkarni & Chen, 2014; Tellis et al., 2009). SMEs are generally multi-outcome oriented, and this raises the important question of how they may handle the paradox and achieve the ability to foster both innovation outcomes simultaneously (Le Breton-Miller & Miller, 2011) (see managerial implications, below).

Second, while temporal orientation research has mostly focused on large corporations and generic outcomes (Desjardine & Shi, 2021; Gamache &

McNamara, 2019; Nadkarni & Chen, 2014) as well as on family firms (Le Breton-Miller & Miller, 2006, 2011; Lumpkin & Brigham, 2011), we shift the scope toward SMEs future orientation and interpretation affects their strategic responses regarding specific innovation outcomes. The investigation of the SME context offers theoretical insights that are distinct from those gained from studying large corporations, as it offers a rich research context in which a diverse group of SMEs must respond to digital technologies to navigate future challenges. This study aims to measure the temporal dimensions of SMEs to shed light on whether shorter time horizons expedite digital transformation and limit radical innovation. The absence of a main effect of family firms (and lack of significant correlations) on both innovation outcomes in our results may suggest that the stronger future orientation toward generational continuity and stronger commitment to employees is cancelled out by a greater reluctance to take risks and resistance to change in a rapidly changing business environment (Ano & Bent, 2022; Sharma et al., 1997). Alternatively, family firms may represent a diverse set of SMEs in themselves, such that other characteristics drive innovation outcomes. Our research illuminates how future orientation and future horizon differentially influence SMEs' innovation outcomes. With SMEs representing a major part of the firms in the European Union, we make an important contribution to better understand how SMEs manage digital transformation and/or radical innovation.

Implications for Management

Managers are faced with the difficulty of balancing different future distances. Similar to ambidexterity that requires the balancing of exploration and exploitation, strategists need to balance the near and distant future. Research shows that such a "multitemporal orientation" can be useful when managing for the long run while staying healthy and occupied with gaining immediate results in the short run. Our results suggest that SMEs may want to develop a multitemporal orientation toward the near future by engaging in digital transformation to gather market insights and updates to innovate the business model, while simultaneously devoting significant attention to the distant future to prepare for and make progress on radical innovation. To adapt to and harmonize with the contradictory requirements for the future of both digital transformation and radical innovation, it is essential to integrate both short-term and long-term orientations. The short-term focus is crucial for digital transformation, while a long-term perspective is vital for radical innovation. This paradoxical challenge mirrors the requirements for ambidexterity. Insights from this area of study can be adapted to cultivate a multi-temporal orientation. For instance, SMEs can make organizational structural adjustments to deal with the different requirements and set up different business units that independently prioritize a short (long) future horizon depending on the desired innovation outcome. Furthermore, contextually, SMEs can link longer- and shorter-term future horizons via time-layered product and project portfolios (Le Breton-Miller & Miller, 2011).

To guide managers of SMEs on how to balance the near and distant future, we provide the example of ChatGPT as an important digital technology for a service marketing company that can be used for digital transformation (e.g., developing a new digital business model), as well as for radical innovation (e.g., using ChatGPT to create radically different products). The AI technology has short-term and long-term effects, and SMEs can effectively steer results by taking on different future horizon. To achieve digital transformation, SMEs can experiment with the technology in the short term to ultimately realize the automation of customer service employees in the more distant future.[5] To achieve radical innovation, SMEs may establish dedicated teams that aim to build radically new products based on ChatGPT technology through corporate foresight (Bouschery et al., 2023). Such teams are likely to be comprised of individuals with diverse backgrounds and skill sets, including data analysts, trend forecasters, and strategic planners, who regularly scan the environment for emerging trends and disruptive events, such as new disruptive technologies, regulatory changes, or demographic shifts. To manage both outcomes simultaneously, SME firms can apply time layering by focusing on the nearer future first to gain quick market feedback and develop AI capabilities. Subsequently, with this attained knowledge and developed AI capabilities, SMEs can introduce new business models that completely replace all customer service personnel by an online virtual agent, as well as build radically new products in the longer run that leverage the AI technology; for instance, by introducing a novel software package that helps advertisers to evaluate their own social media campaigns.

Limitations and Future Research

Our research faces several limitations, which also constitute interesting avenues for future research. The first limitation of our research is related to the issue of generalizability. We analyzed data on SMEs that are situated in a particular region (i.e., the northern part of the Netherlands). Although the focus on SMEs made sense for an initial exploration of the temporal orientations of a broad set of SMEs, we do not know the extent to which our findings are generalizable to other types of firms, cultures, and innovation outcomes. Therefore, we encourage national culture research to go beyond the traditional use of LTO of Hofstede (2010) or future orientation as part of GLOBE temporal orientation, and encourage others to investigate the temporal dimensions (future orientation and horizon) for alternative firm types (corporations) and innovation outcomes (e.g., disruptive innovation, platform innovation).

In this chapter, we relied on a cross-sectional survey design to analyze the impact of SMEs' temporal dimensions on their digital transformation and radical innovation. Our survey approach allowed the collection of primary data on SMEs' perceptions of the future, which would be difficult to collect from secondary data. At the same time, an inherent limitation of cross-sectional surveys is that they increase the risk of endogeneity issues that are difficult to address within the scope of this methodological design. We refrain from making strong causal claims in this chapter and instead frame our results as a first empirical exploration to demonstrate the relevance of using temporal dimensions to link to different innovation outcomes like digital transformation and radical innovation.

Finally, it needs to be stressed that we conducted a firm-level examination of temporality based on the perceptions of key representatives of the firm. Future research can expand the scope and assess the multiple viewpoints of all employees to get a richer understanding of how future is interpreted by a larger pool of employees. Thus, team- and individual-level research may also lead to fruitful insights. In addition, similar to digital transformation which has been investigated at different levels such as ecosystems (Tan et al., 2020), future orientation may also play a big role in determining innovation outcomes of collaboration consortia. Therefore, we point future efforts toward investigating the importance of time dimensions in interorganizational settings such as alliances and ecosystems.[6]

Notes

1. Estimates typically range that from two-thirds (https://www.consultancy.uk/news/2656/two-thirds-of-digital-transformation-projects-fail) to up to 84 perc-ent (https://www.forbes.com/sites/brucerogers/2016/01/07/why-84-of-companies-fail-at-digital-transformation/) of digital transformation initiatives fail to deliver to their promise.
2. The term "future orientation" has also been linked with corporate culture (Tellis et al., 2009) or national culture (Hofstede, 2010). From a cultural perspective, future orientation includes the collective attitudes, beliefs, and behaviors within the organization (Tellis et al., 2009) or the nation (Hofstede, 2010). A culture of future orientation implies that all individuals at all levels habitually think and act with the long term in mind, even in the absence of explicit strategic directions. Our focus lies on explaining the effect of future

orientation as a strategic focus by highlighting the importance of SMEs incorporating the future to direct their (innovation) activities.
3. In these benchmark reports, we provided respondents their individual score as well as the average scores of their size, age, industry, and innovation pyramid group.
4. We also used OLS regressions for our analyses with radical innovation performance as a dependent variable. Our results remain robust using this alternative regression approach.
5. See https://www.theatlantic.com/ideas/archive/2023/01/chatgpt-ai-economy-automation-jobs/672767/.
6. The authors thank Dries Faems and Frank Bos for their willingness to share data on the temporal orientation, and the discussions that ensued.

References

Ano, B., & Bent, R. (2022). Human determinants influencing the digital transformation strategy of multigenerational family businesses: A multiple-case study of five French growth-oriented family firms. *Journal of Family Business Management, 12*(4), 876–891.

Argote, L., & Greve, H. R. (2007). A behavioral theory of the firm—40 years and counting: Introduction and impact. *Organization Science, 18*(3), 337–349.

Argote, L., Lee, S., & Park, J. (2020). Organizational learning processes and outcomes: Major findings and future research directions. *Management Science, 67*(9), 5399–5429.

Argote, L., & Miron-Spektor, E. (2011). Organizational learning: From experience to knowledge. *Organization Science, 22*(5), 1123–1137.

Baiyere, A., Salmela, H., Tapanainen, T., Mendling, J., Pentland, B. T., & Recker, J. (2020). Digital transformation and the new logics of business process management. *European Journal of Information Systems, 29*(3), 238–259.

Barreto, T. S., Lanivich, S. E., & Cox, K. C. (2022). Temporal orientation as a robust predictor of innovation. *Journal of Business Research, 138*(2), 287–300.

Belderbos, R., Carree, M., & Lokshin, B. (2006). Complementarity in R&D cooperation strategies. *Review of Industrial Organization, 28*(4), 401–426.

Bland, D. J., & Osterwalder, A. (2019). *Testing Business Ideas: A Field Guide for Rapid Experimentation*. Wiley.

Blank, S. (2013). Why the lean start-up changes everything. *Havard Business Review, 91*(5), 63–72.

Blank, S. (2019). McKinsey's three horizons model defined innovation for years: Here's why it no longer applies. *Harvard Business Review*, 1–5. https://hbr.org/2019/02/mckinseys-three-horizons-model-defined-innovation-for-years-heres-why-it-no-longer-applies.

Bluedorn, A. C., & Martin, G. (2008). The time frames of entrepreneurs. *Journal of Business Venturing, 23*(1), 1–20.

Bouncken, R., & Barwinski, R. (2021). Shared digital identity and rich knowledge ties in global 3D printing—A drizzle in the clouds? *Global Strategy Journal, 11*(1), 81–108.

Bouschery, S. G., Blazevic, V., & Piller, F. T. (2023). Augmenting human innovation teams with artificial intelligence: Exploring transformer-based language models. *Journal of Product Innovation Management, 40*(2), 139–153.

Brentani, U. de. (2001). Innovative versus incremental new business services: Different keys for achieving success. *Journal of Product Innovation Management, 18*(3), 169–187.

Broekhuizen, T., Bakker, T., & Postma, T. J. B. M. (2018). Implementing new business models: What challenges lie ahead? *Business Horizons, 61*(4), 555–566.

Broekhuizen, T., Dekker, H., de Faria, P., Firk, S., Nguyen, D. K., & Sofka, W. (2023). AI for managing open innovation: Opportunities, challenges, and a research agenda. *Journal of Business Research, 167*(2), 114196.

Cafferata, R., Abatecola, G., & Poggesi, S. (2009). Revisiting Stinchcombe's "liability of newness": A systematic literature review. *International Journal of Globalisation and Small Business, 3*(4), 374–392.

Chandy, R. K., & Tellis, G. J. (1998). Organizing for radical product innovation: The overlooked role of willingness to cannibalize. *Journal of Marketing Research, 35*(4), 474–487.

Chandy, R. K., & Tellis, G. J. (2000). The incumbent's curse? Incumbency, size, and radical product innovation. *Journal of Marketing, 64*(3), 1–17.

Chen, S., & Habibi, M. (2023). A temporal approach to innovation management in recessionary times. *Industrial Marketing Management, 113*, 215–231.

Choi, J. J., Kim, J., & Shenkar, O. (2023). Temporal orientation and corporate social responsibility: Global evidence. *Journal of Management Studies, 60*(1), 82–119.

Christensen, C. M., & Overdorf, M. (2000). Meeting the challenge of disruptive change. *Harvard Business Review*, 66–76. https://hbr.org/2000/03/meeting-the-challenge-of-disruptive-change.

Christensen, C. M., Raynor, M., & McDonald, R. M. (2015). What is disruptive innovation? *Harvard Business Review*. https://hbr.org/2015/12/what-is-disruptive-innovation.

Conte, J. M., & Gintoft, J. N. (2009). Polychronicity, big five personality dimensions, and sales performance. *Human Performance, 18*(4), 427–444.

Das, T. K. (1987). Strategic planning and individual temporal orientation. *Strategic Management Journal, 8*(2), 203–209.

Das, T. K. (1991). Time: The hidden dimension in strategic planning. *Long Range Planning, 24*(3), 49–57.

Day, G. S., & Schoemaker, P. J. H. (2016). Adapting to fast-changing markets and technologies. *California Management Review, 58*(4), 59–77.

De Reuver, M., Sørensen, C., & Basole, R. C. (2018). The digital platform: A research agenda. *Journal of Information Technology, 33*(2), 124–135.

Desjardine, M. R., & Shi, W. (2021). How temporal focus shapes the influence of executive compensation on risk taking. *Academy of Management Journal, 64*(1), 265–292.

Dremel, C., Herterich, M. M., Wulf, J., & vom Brocke, J. (2020). Actualizing big data analytics affordances: A revelatory case study. *Information & Management, 57*(1), 103121.

Duffy, S. (2014). *Launch!: The Critical 90 Days from Idea to Market*. Piatkus.

Duran, P., Kammerlander, N., Van Essen, M., & Zellweger, T. (2015). Doing more with less: Innovation input and output in family firms. *Academy of Management Journal, 59*(4), 1224–1264.

Eggers, J. P., & Park, K. F. (2018). Incumbent adaptation to technological change: The past, present, and future of research on heterogeneous incumbent response. *Academy of Management Annals, 12*(1), 357–389.

Eller, R., Alford, P., Kallmünzer, A., & Peters, M. (2020). Antecedents, consequences, and challenges of small and medium-sized enterprise digitalization. *Journal of Business Research, 112*, 119–127.

Fabian, N., Dong, J. Q., Broekhuizen, T., & Verhoef, P. C. (2023). Business value of SME digitalisation: When does it pay off more? *European Journal of Information Systems*. https://doi.org/10.1080/0960085X.2023.2167671.

Faems, D., De Visser, M., Andries, P., & Van Looy, B. (2010). Technology alliance portfolios and financial performance: Value-enhancing and cost-increasing effects of open innovation. *Journal of Product Innovation Management, 27*(6), 785–796.

Flammer, C., & Bansal, P. (2017). Does a long-term orientation create value? Evidence from a regression discontinuity. *Strategic Management Journal, 38*(9), 1827–1847.

Fornell, C., & Larcker, D. F. (1981). Evaluating structural equation models with unobservable variables and measurement error. *Journal of Marketing Research, 18*(1), 39–50.

Gamache, D. L., & McNamara, G. (2019). Responding to bad press: How CEO temporal focus influences the sensitivity to negative media coverage of acquisitions. *Academy of Management Journal, 62*(3), 918–943.

Gavetti, G., & Levinthal, D. A. (2000). Looking forward and looking backward: Cognitive and experiential search. *Administrative Science Quarterly, 45*(1), 113–137.

Gevers, J., Mohammed, S., & Baytalskaya, N. (2015). The conceptualisation and measurement of pacing styles. *Applied Psychology, 64*(3), 499–540.

Gimenez-Fernandez, E. M., Sandulli, F. D., & Bogers, M. (2020). Unpacking liabilities of newness and smallness in innovative start-ups: Investigating the differences in innovation performance between new and older small firms. *Research Policy, 49*(10), 104049.

Graham, J. R., Harvey, C. R., & Rajgopal, S. (2005). The economic implications of corporate financial reporting. *Journal of Accounting and Economics, 40*(1–3), 3–73.

Gupta, G., & Bose, I. (2022). Digital transformation in entrepreneurial firms through information exchange with operating environment. *Information & Management, 59*(3). https://doi.org/10.1016/j.im.2019.103243.

Haleblian, J., McNamara, G., Kolev, K., & Dykes, B. J. (2012). Exploring firm characteristics that differentiate leaders from followers in industry merger waves: A competitive dynamics perspective. *Strategic Management Journal, 33*(9), 1037–1052.

Hanelt, A., Bohnsack, R., Marz, D., & Antunes Marante, C. (2021). A systematic review of the literature on digital transformation: Insights and implications for strategy and organizational change. *Journal of Management Studies, 58*(5), 1159–1197.

Hofstede, G. (2010). The GLOBE debate: Back to relevance. *Journal of International Business Studies, 41*(8), 1339–1346.

Jansen, K. J., & Kristof-Brown, A. L. (2005). Marching to the beat of a different drummer: Examining the impact of pacing congruence. *Organizational Behavior and Human Decision Processes, 97*(2), 93–105.

Kahle, J. H., Marcon, É., Ghezzi, A., & Frank, A. G. (2020). Smart products value creation in SMEs innovation ecosystems. *Technological Forecasting and Social Change, 156*, 120024.

Karimi, J., & Walter, Z. (2016). Corporate entrepreneurship, disruptive business model innovation adoption, and its performance: The case of the newspaper industry. *Long Range Planning, 49*(3), 342–360.

Laforet, S. (2013). Innovation characteristics of young and old family-owned businesses. *Journal of Small Business and Enterprise Development, 20*(1), 204–224.
Laursen, K., & Salter, A. (2006). Open for innovation: The role of openness in explaining innovation performance among U.K. manufacturing firms. *Strategic Management Journal, 27*(2), 131–150.
Le Breton-Miller, I., & Miller, D. (2006). Why do some family businesses out-compete? Governance, long-term orientations, and sustainable capability. *Entrepreneurship Theory and Practice, 30*(6), 731–746.
Le Breton-Miller, I., & Miller, D. (2011). Commentary: Family firms and the advantage of multitemporality. *Entrepreneurship Theory and Practice, 35*(6), 1171–1177.
Leifer, R., O'Connor, G. C., & Rice, M. (2001). Implementing radical innovation in mature firms: The role of hubs. *Academy of Management Perspectives, 15*(3), 102–113.
Levinthal, D. A., & March, J. G. (1993). The myopia of learning. *Strategic Management Journal, 14*(S2), 95–112.
Lin, Y., Shi, W., Prescott, J. E., & Yang, H. (2019). In the eye of the beholder: Top managers' long-term orientation, industry context, and decision-making processes. *Journal of Management, 45*(8), 3114–3145.
Lindell, M. K., & Whitney, D. J. (2001). Accounting for common method variance in cross-sectional research designs. *Journal of Applied Psychology, 86*(1), 114–121.
Lumpkin, G. T., & Brigham, K. H. (2011). Long-term orientation and intertemporal choice in family firms. *Entrepreneurship Theory and Practice, 35*(6), 1149–1169.
Martin, G. P., Wiseman, R. M., & Gomez-Mejia, L. R. (2016). Going short-term or long-term? CEO stock options and temporal orientation in the presence of slack. *Strategic Management Journal, 37*(12), 2463–2480.
Mathias, B. D., McKenny, A. F., & Russell Crook, T. (2018). Managing the tensions between exploration and exploitation: The role of time. *Strategic Entrepreneurship Journal, 12*(3), 316–334.
McDonald, R. M., & Eisenhardt, K. M. (2020). Parallel play: Startups, nascent markets, and effective business-model design. *Administrative Science Quarterly, 65*(2), 483–523.
McGrath, R. G. (2010). Business models: A discovery driven approach. *Long Range Planning, 43*(2–3), 247–261.
Nadkarni, S., & Chen, J. (2014). Bridging yesterday, today, and tomorrow: CEO temporal focus, environmental dynamism, and rate of new product introduction. *Academy of Management Journal, 57*(6), 1810–1833.
Nadkarni, S., Chen, T., & Chen, J. (2016). The clock is ticking! Executive temporal depth, industry velocity, and competitive aggressiveness. *Strategic Management Journal, 37*(6), 1132–1153.
Nguyen, D. K., Broekhuizen, T., Dong, J. Q., & Verhoef, P. C. (2023). Leveraging synergy to drive digital transformation: A systems-theoretic perspective. *Information & Management, 60*(7), 103836.
Oerlemans, L. A. G., Knoben, J., & Pretorius, M. W. (2013). Alliance portfolio diversity, radical and incremental innovation: The moderating role of technology management. *Technovation, 33*(6–7), 234–246.
Osiyevskyy, O., & Dewald, J. (2015). Explorative versus exploitative business model change: The cognitive antecedents of firm-level responses to disruptive innovation. *Strategic Entrepreneurship Journal, 9*(1), 58–78.
Park, G., Schwartz, H. A., Sap, M., Kern, M. L., Weingarten, E., Eichstaedt, J. C., Berger, J., Stillwell, D. J., Kosinski, M., Ungar, L. H., & Seligman, M. E. P. (2017). Living in

the past, present, and future: Measuring temporal orientation with language. *Journal of Personality*, *85*(2), 270–280.
Podsakoff, P. M., MacKenzie, S. B., Lee, J.-Yeon, & Podsakoff, N. P. (2003). Common method biases in behavioral research: A critical review of the literature and recommended remedies. *Journal of Applied Psychology*, *88*(5), 879–903.
Polier, S. (2019). Empirical study on forward-looking external search. In *Forward-looking External Search as a Driver for Innovation* (pp. 61–179). Springer Gabler.
Radziwon, A., & Bogers, M. (2019). Open innovation in SMEs: Exploring inter-organizational relationships in an ecosystem. *Technological Forecasting and Social Change*, *146*, 573–587.
Reid, S. E., & de Brentani, U. (2012). Market vision and the front end of NPD for radical innovation: The impact of moderating effects. *Journal of Product Innovation Management*, *29*(S1), 124–139.
Reilly, G., Souder, D., & Ranucci, R. (2016). Time horizon of investments in the resource allocation process: Review and framework for next steps. *Journal of Management*, *42*(5), 1169–1194.
Ries, E. (2011). *The Lean Startup*. Crown Business.
Runyan, R., Droge, C., & Swinney, J. (2008). Entrepreneurial orientation versus small business orientation: What are their relationships to firm performance? *Journal of Small Business Management*, *46*(4), 567–588.
Sampson, R. C., & Shi, Y. (2023). Are U.S. firms becoming more short-term oriented? Evidence of shifting firm time horizons from implied discount rates, 1980–2013. *Strategic Management Journal*, *44*(1), 231–263.
Sharma, P., Chrisman, J. J., & Chua, J. H. (1997). Strategic management of the family business: Past research and future challenges. *Family Business Review*, *10*(1), 1–35.
Shipp, A. J., Edwards, J. R., & Lambert, L. S. (2009). Conceptualization and measurement of temporal focus: The subjective experience of the past, present, and future. *Organizational Behavior and Human Decision Processes*, *110*(1), 1–22.
Singh, J. V., Tucker, D. J., & House, R. J. (1986). Organizational legitimacy and the liability of newness. *Administrative Science Quarterly*, *31*(2), 171.
Slater, S. F., & Narver, J. C. (1995). Market orientation and the learning organization. *Journal of Marketing*, *59*(3), 63–74.
Sorescu, A. B., Chandy, R. K., & Prabhu, J. C. (2003). Sources and financial consequences of radical innovation: Insights from pharmaceuticals. *Journal of Marketing*, *67*(4), 82–102.
Souder, D., & Bromiley, P. (2012). Explaining temporal orientation: Evidence from the durability of firms' capital investments. *Strategic Management Journal*, *33*(5), 550–569.
Srinivasan, R., Lilien, G. L., & Rangaswamy, A. (2002). Technological opportunism and radical technology adoption: An application to e-business. *Journal of Marketing*, *66*(3), 47–60.
Suseno, Y., Laurell, C., & Sick, N. (2018). Assessing value creation in digital innovation ecosystems: A social media analytics approach. *Journal of Strategic Information Systems*, *27*(4), 335–349.
Tan, F. T. C., Ondrus, J., Tan, B., & Oh, J. (2020). Digital transformation of business ecosystems: Evidence from the Korean pop industry. *Information Systems Journal*, *30*(5), 866–898.
Teece, D. J. (2010). Business models, business strategy and innovation. *Long Range Planning*, *43*(2–3), 172–194.

Teece, D. J. (2018). Business models and dynamic capabilities. *Long Range Planning*, *51*(1), 40–49.
Tellis, G. J., Prabhu, J. C., & Chandy, R. K. (2009). Radical innovation across nations: The preeminence of corporate culture. *Journal of Marketing*, *73*(1), 3–23.
Van Auken, H., Madrid-Guijarro, A., & García-Pérez-de-Lema, D. (2008). Innovation and performance in Spanish manufacturing SMEs. *International Journal of Entrepreneurship and Innovation Management*, *8*(1), 36–56.
Van de Vrande, V., De Jong, J. P. J., Vanhaverbeke, W., & De Rochemont, M. (2009). Open innovation in SMEs: Trends, motives and management challenges. *Technovation*, *29*(6–7), 423–437.
Verhoef, P. C., Broekhuizen, T., Bart, Y., Bhattacharya, A., Dong, J. Q., Fabian, N., & Haenlein, M. (2021). Digital transformation: A multidisciplinary reflection and research agenda. *Journal of Business Research*, *122*(4), 889–901.
Vial, G. (2019). Understanding digital transformation: A review and a research agenda. *Journal of Strategic Information Systems*, *28*(2), 118–144.
Vom Brocke, J., Schmid, A. M., Simons, A., & Safrudin, N. (2021). IT-enabled organizational transformation: A structured literature review. *Business Process Management Journal*, *27*(1), 204–229.
Wang, T., & Bansal, P. (2012). Social responsibility in new ventures: Profiting from a long-term orientation. *Strategic Management Journal*, *33*(10), 1135–1153.
Warner, K. S. R., & Wäger, M. (2019). Building dynamic capabilities for digital transformation: An ongoing process of strategic renewal. *Long Range Planning*, *52*(3), 326–349.
Wenzel, M., Stanske, S., & Lieberman, M. B. (2020). Strategic responses to crisis. *Strategic Management Journal*, *41*(7/18), V7–V18.
Wessel, L., Baiyere, A., Ologeanu-Taddei, R., Cha, J., & Jensen, T. B. (2021). Unpacking the difference between digital transformation and IT-enabled organizational transformation. *Journal of the Association for Information Systems*, *22*(1), 102–129.
Wiklund, J., & Shepherd, D. (2005). Entrepreneurial orientation and small business performance: A configurational approach. *Journal of Business Venturing*, *20*(1), 71–91.
Wind, J., & Mahajan, V. (1997). Issues and opportunities in new product development: An introduction to the special issue. *Journal of Marketing Research*, *34*(1), 1–12.
Woschke, T., Haase, H., & Kratzer, J. (2017). Resource scarcity in SMEs: Effects on incremental and radical innovations. *Management Research Review*, *40*(2), 195–217.
Xiao, T., Makhija, M., & Karim, S. (2022). A knowledge recombination perspective of innovation: Review and new research directions. *Journal of Management*, *48*(6), 1724–1777.
Yadav, M. S., Prabhu, J. C., & Chandy, R. K. (2007). Managing the future: CEO attention and innovation outcomes. *Journal of Marketing*, *71*(4), 84–101.
Zhou, K. Z., Kin, C., Yim, B., & Tse, D. K. (2005). The effects of strategic orientations on technology- and market-based breakthrough innovations. *Journal of Marketing*, *69*(4), 42–60. https://doi.org/10.1509/jmkg.69.2.42.60756
Zott, C., Amit, R., & Massa, L. (2011). The business model: Recent developments and future research. *Journal of Management*, *37*(4), 1019–1042.

3 A process-oriented perspective on digital transformation

Jan vom Brocke, Manuel Weber and Gregor Kipping

Digitalization is omnipresent and companies of all kinds are striving to leverage digital technologies to create added business value (Badakhshan et al., 2022; Verhoef et al., 2021). However, companies are also struggling to realize this potential for two reasons. First, technology and its adoption are evolving at an ever-faster pace. The artificial intelligence (AI) platform ChatGPT, for example, jumped to a million users just five days after its launch in November 2022. In comparison, Instagram, founded in 2010, took 2.5 months to reach similar user levels, Airbnb, launched in 2008, took 2.5 years, and Netflix, launched in 1999, took 3.5 years. During the adoption process, organizations need to consider various aspects related to how the technology will fit into the organizational context in order to identify and realize the technology's benefits. This process is shaped by expectations, attitudes, beliefs, and personal opinions about how to become more efficient and successful (Fink, 1998; Karahanna et al., 1999). However, it is unclear how to implement such technology in a way that reliably creates value-adding business innovations and master digital transformation. Actors often get carried away by the "wonders of digital technology" being inspired, not least, by the vendors' promises and it takes a long time to generate successful value-adding use cases.

Secondly, companies are under increasing competitive pressure and seeking to generate competitive advantages through digital technologies (Yoo et al., 2012). Methods, such as design thinking and their application in practice, facilitate the creation of ideas. Nevertheless, organizations struggle to get those ideas off the ground accurately evaluating the resources needed to implement new ideas effectively and efficiently. Many organizations perform an "innovation theater" rather than creating profound digital innovation and transformation (Blank, 2019). Thus, value realization often fails to live up to its potential, instead hindering many organizations' attempts to keep up with change and lead digital transformation.

This chapter demonstrates how looking at an organization's processes can help bridge the gap between "technological excitement" and "innovation theater." The term "processes" is used to refer broadly to what an organization does or, more specifically, what happens within that organization. We intentionally set aside the methods traditionally used to model business processes in order to capture the rich dynamics of various levels (Cagnin & Nakagawa, 2021; Pentland et al., 2021) related to digital transformation both in organizations and interorganizational settings and ecosystems (vom Brocke, Mendling, & Rosemann, 2021). We build on extensive knowledge from the field of business process management (BPM) (e.g., Beverungen et al., 2021; Dumas et al., 2018; Hammer, 2015; Mendling et al., 2020; vom Brocke & Rosemann, 2015; Weske et al., 2018) and show how organizations can successfully link technology and innovation (Schmiedel & vom Brocke, 2015; Van Looy, 2021).

To this end, we first provide conceptual foundations for value-creating information technology (IT) mechanisms in organizations based on information systems (IS) and process research. Second, we adopt a normative perspective and present a management framework for developing digital transformation capabilities from a process management point of view. Third, we present the results of applying this framework at a case study company, Hilti, identifying four specific archetypes of contexts and their corresponding logics for digital transformation. We then conclude with a summary that highlights how this strategy can be applied in practice and its implications for future research.

Theoretical background

A Socio-technical Systems View

IS have been described as essentially socio-technical systems in which humans perform tasks using technology (Bostrom & Heinen, 1977). The question of how people apply technology in their specific social context is at the core of this perspective. Seminal research has found that socio-technical systems consist of two subsystems – a social system and a technical system. Both are independent but do interact with each other. While the technical system consists of tasks, technologies, and processes, the social system is associated with people, their relationships, and the structure and hierarchies in which they are embedded. Both systems have their purposes and neither should be favored over the other. On the contrary, IS research specifically sets out to investigate the many relationships between the technical and social subsystems (Bostrom & Heinen, 1977) with a focus on the design, use, and impact of these IS in context (Dov et al., 2017). This is necessary because the results produced by the IS system are the product of the interactions between the two subsystems. IS design is, thus, an integrated view of both the technical and social aspects of a holistic system that produces a common outcome (Appelbaum, 1997). Applying a socio-technical perspective has been found to increase systems acceptance among stakeholders, especially end users, who have to handle certain tasks and use specific technologies within the processes of the given socio-technical system (Baxter & Sommerville, 2011; Sarker et al., 2019).

A Socio-technical Process View

Processes have been shown to be important in various research domains (Recker, 2014) including psychology, linguistics, anthropology, politics, and economics (Cornwell, 2015). In the broadest sense, a process brings about change through a sequence of temporally and causally related activities or events. To this end, the term has been appropriated by various disciplines in different ways (Pettigrew, 1997; van de Ven & Poole, 1995; Wurm et al., 2021). For example, in sociology, processes reveal the temporal aspects of a given phenomenon (e.g., life trajectories) (Abbott, 1995). In contrast, computer science uses the term to depict the computational sequences designed to accomplish specific outcomes. In the natural sciences, researchers focus on processes to unravel mechanisms that explain how certain phenomena evolve and produce distinct outcomes (Cornwell, 2015; Leenders et al., 2016), while in management and business, research emphasizes the importance of designing processes to facilitate the operation of the business (Champy & Hammer, 1993; Dumas et al., 2018).

In general, processes are only one way to organize and coordinate work or resources in the organizational context. However, using a process view has been found to support organizational design for two reasons (vom Brocke, van der Aalst et al., 2021). First, a process view is a means to integrate both technical and social aspects of design as processes reveal how people perform tasks using technology. Second, a process view is a means to conceptualize the various dynamics within an organization, as they reveal how an organization's states change. These aspects embody, respectively, the potential to integrate and the potential to capture change, which makes the process view particularly relevant to understanding and shaping digital transformation.

Process research has developed further, from a focus on well-structured processes to the exploration and analysis of diverse, and specifically emerging, processes. Indeed, according to Zairi (1997: 64): "A process is an approach for converting inputs into outputs. It is the way in which all the resources of an organization are used in a reliable, repeatable, and consistent way to achieve its goals." In an attempt to conceptualize processes even further, Zairi (1997: 64) identified the following process characteristics: "(1) predictable and definable inputs; (2) a linear, logical sequence or flow; (3) a set of clearly definable tasks or activities; (4) a predictable and desired outcome or result" (cited in Bulletpoint, 1996). However, contemporary process research embraces a much wider range of processes in seeking to account for non-predictable inputs and outputs as well as nonlinear workflows (vom Brocke et al., 2016). More recently, methods and tools have been developed for analyzing processes based on digital trace data or process mining (van der Aalst, 2016). This new field, referred to as process science, has been established with a focus on analyzing data to (1) identify processes, (2) understand processes, and (3) intervene in processes (vom Brocke, van der Aalst et al., 2021).

Thus, over time, research has developed a more detailed understanding of the factors that differentiate processes. For example, vom Brocke et al. (2016) identified the following dimensions, each of which has a varying degree of expression: value contribution, competitiveness, knowledge intensity, creativity, interdependence, and variability. Processes can be further categorized into one of three subcategories: (i) core processes, which add value to external customers and, thus, realize the business objectives, (ii) management (governance) goals, or (iii) support (enabling) processes, which support process in subcategory (i) or (ii) and add value to internal customers, such as employees (Hammer, 2015).

An IT Value-based View

Within digital transformation, process design focused on utilizing IT is of particular importance. As demonstrated above, adopting and using IT in an isolated manner does not automatically add value for an organization. Rather, it is important that organizations account for the transformational character of IT or, more specifically, develop and perform new processes through it. In this regard, digital transformation is, essentially, about generating value through IT. Indeed, this area has been well studied in recent decades in IS through the research into the development, use, and impact of IT in organizations (Benbasat & Zmud, 1999; vom Brocke et al., 2013).

On the one hand, IT has fundamentally changed the way we work and live and has been shown to be a key driver of innovation. On the other hand, IT alone does not generate the desired transformation and innovation; this is only achieved in combination with careful and creative process design. Second Life, a virtual world in which humans interacted, communicating and trading using avatars, provides a useful example. Many companies started online stores and universities built campuses on Second Life – endeavors that amounted to a multimillion dollar investment. Yet, despite this enthusiasm, Second Life never took off as people and organizations never truly adopted it. Nevertheless, many of us are currently getting excited about the metaverse, a somewhat similar digital world that extends physical space into a virtual space in which people can communicate and trade. The future will show whether history will repeat itself. How can the metaverse deliver what Second Life could not? What has changed regarding the technology and the context, the time and space in which this new technology will be applied? The COVID-19 pandemic highlighted how much of an impact the context has on technology adoption. For example, web conferencing systems have existed for a long time, at least 20 years. Yet, it was only when the global pandemic hit that people fully leveraged the ability to easily meet online and that meeting online became socially and culturally accepted (Hacker et al., 2020).

To better evaluate the value-creation potential of digital technology, we can apply theories from IS and process research. The IT business value model, for instance, can be used to conceptualize key mechanisms for creating value through IT (vom Brocke et al., 2012; Figure 3.1).

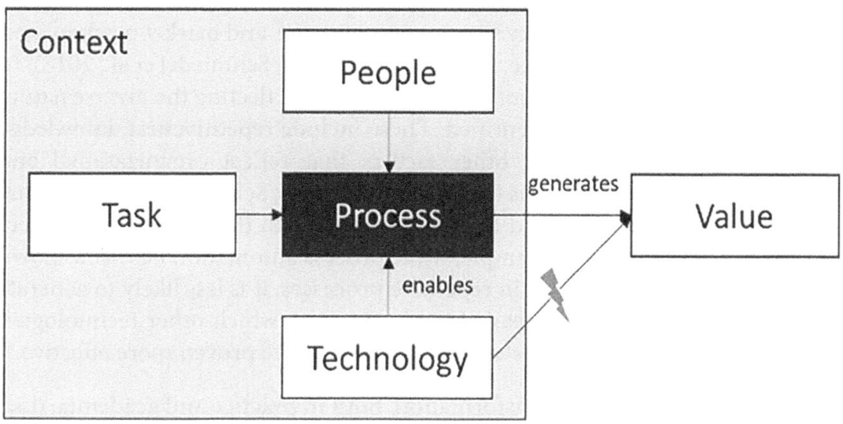

Source: vom Brocke et al. (2012).

Figure 3.1 IT business value model

The IT business value model identifies three key aspects in the management of digital transformation:

- First, digital transformation must take into account that IT does not necessarily have a positive impact on corporate value but offers opportunities to design processes, the execution of which then can add value. The added value created by digital technologies through process design must warrant the effort of using the technology. Added value can take various forms, for example, increased transparency about delivery status, faster delivery times from online stores, and more resilient and sustainable operations.
- Second, digital transformation must take into account that innovative process design does not necessarily result from technology use alone. Rather, innovative use scenarios in which people use technology to perform tasks need to be designed. Hence, digital transformation is about socio-technical design, in which aspects of tasks, technology, and people are all considered. Furthermore, different digital technologies serve very different purposes: robots enable automation, while video conferencing tools support collaboration.
- Third, digital transformation must take into account that the value created through process design is contingent on an appropriate task–technology–people fit in the specific application context. Relevant context-related factors include the industry sector, company size, and market mechanisms, among others (vom Brocke, Zelt et al., 2016; Zelt, Schmiedel et al., 2018). In addition, more detailed context-related factors reflecting the diverse nature of processes have been identified. These include repetitiveness, knowledge intensity, creativity, and other factors that reflect organizational and environmental dimensions (vom Brocke, Zelt, & Schmiedel, 2015). Digital innovation initiatives need to closely engage with this context to be effective because, by way of example, while process automation has been shown to generate positive value in repetitive processes, it is less likely to generate value in more creative areas of the business in which other technologies, such as collaboration tools and social media, have proven more effective.

Most discourse on digital transformation, both in practice and academia, does not sufficiently account for these mechanisms of IT value creation. Often, innovative technologies are brought to the fore, such as large language models, and research asks, more generally, how these technologies can be used and what impact they can have in business. The process-oriented approach presented in this chapter enables a more detailed and differentiated discourse that identifies specific application contexts and describes them through factors and design elements.

To this end, the IT business value model (Figure 3.1) can be applied to identify the value potential of different emergent digital technologies. Recently, for example, research has identified the value-creation mechanisms of process mining. This technology supports managerial decisions by visualizing and analyzing digital trace data to make behaviors within organizations visible (Badakhshan et al., 2022) and facilitates the design of new processes based on the analysis of event logs created during process execution (Grisold et al., 2021; vom Brocke & Grisold, 2020). Other studies have investigated the value creation potential of big data analytics (BDA) (Müller et al., 2018). In service innovation, for instance, it has been found that BDA can support the implementation of service automation and human-material service practices. Such BDA technologies are generative and, therefore, constitute key resources for organizations seeking to enable service innovation (Lehrer et al., 2018). Similarly, research has evaluated the value-creation mechanisms of in-memory technology (vom Brocke et al., 2014), service-oriented architectures (vom Brocke et al., 2009), and enterprise architecture technology (Boh & Yellin, 2006) by identifying the specific opportunities these technologies present for process design and execution in specific use contexts. Process research has also started to investigate application scenarios for the use of large language models specific to task characteristics (Grisold et al., 2023).

A common strategy for identifying the value-creating mechanisms of emergent digital technology is to use an affordance theory perspective to distinguish between (i) features and (ii) action potentials of IT, such as process mining, to achieve (iii) predefined goals. The features, action potentials, and goals must then be reconciled by the respective stakeholders within their social context (Seidel et al., 2013). Yet, in practice, organizations may still face many challenges when using and implementing process mining (Grisold et al., 2021). In the meantime, scholars have identified a set of interrelated affordances that lead to added value for businesses, such as increased process efficiency, monetary value, and nonmonetary value (Badakhshan et al., 2022). More specifically, using process mining, they identified four beneficial outcomes: "(1) perceiving end-to-end process visualizations and performance indicators; (2) sense-making of process-related information; (3) data-driven decision making; and (4) implementing interventions based on the obtained insights" (Badakhshan et al., 2022: 2). Process mining enables firms to visualize the socio-technical components of their individual processes (Leonardi & Treem, 2020).

To successfully master digital transformation, companies must identify and understand the drivers and developments within their organization, their management structures and processes, and their environment (Nguyen, 2022).

In addition to coordinating internal socio-technical resources and elements (including people and their tasks), external developments must be accounted for. The rapid progress of digital technologies and their increased adoption in modern organizations requires continuous reflection on and adaption of internal processes as competitive advantage can only be achieved if organizations link tangible and intangible assets with the introduction of complementary new IT (Powell & Dent-Micallef, 1997). Such an example is the smart service ecosystem, in which physical products (such as cars) are increasingly augmented with digital services (such as mobility and entertainment services) (Herterich et al., 2023). To date, the traditional (and general) BPM research community has taken a predominantly internal view of processes and considered environmental conditions and changes in less detail. In contrast, modern process science accounts for more of the many interweaving relationships between organizations and their environments in addition to the emerging and evolving nature of processes (vom Brocke, van der Aalst et al., 2021).

According to contingency theory, organizations succeed when they create the best possible fit between themselves and their environment. Thus, process design is increasingly considering contextual factors in order to adapt to the complexity and dynamics of the business environment (Rosemann & Recker, 2006; vom Brocke, Zelt et al., 2016; Weber et al., 2021). Specifically, digital technologies have been studied to facilitate the development of context-sensitive processes, that is, processes that capture real-time data during run-time (e.g., digital trace data from enterprise resource planning (ERP) systems, sensors, or even body devices), analyze the data, and adjust the process execution accordingly (Weber et al., 2021). For instance, waste collection processes have been developed that sense actual refuse levels in bins (Kamm et al., 2020) and neuro-adaptive processes have been developed that collect body data (e.g., via smartwatches) and then adapt to the emotional and cognitive state of the wearer (vom Brocke et al., 2020). Indeed, adaptability itself is also a process of constantly modifying processes according to changing situations. A process-oriented view can, therefore, help us better understand and manage change throughout the duration of digital transformation projects and programs.

Based on this current state of research, we can identify two specific reasons why a process lens is particularly useful for managing digital transformation:

- First, a process lens facilitates the integration of various aspects of tasks, technologies, and peoples, one of the key drivers for value generation (referred to as our "Integration Argument").

- Second, a process lens facilitates sensitivity to the dynamic reality of (Langley et al., 2013; Reinecke & Ansari, 2017) organizations (referred to as our "Dynamics Argument").

We now turn to the question of how a process-oriented approach to digital transformation can take shape in practice.

Towards process-oriented digital transformation management

In this section, we intend to make the process-oriented approach to digital transformation tangible both for practitioners and researchers. We present a conceptualization of BPM that adopts a holistic view of the management of processes. Specifically, we present a visual inquiry tool (Avdiji et al., 2020) called the "BPM Billboard" (vom Brocke, Mendling, & Rosemann, 2021). Built upon existing literature and empirical research, the BPM Billboard identifies the core action areas of BPM and describes how they relate to value generation (Figure 3.2).

The BPM Billboard conceptualizes process management along two axes. Horizontally it identifies a holistic set of BPM capabilities that account for the socio-technical nature of managing processes. Vertically, the Billboard illustrates how the link between the strategy and concrete value-creating projects can be established. The vertical elements are as follows (vom Brocke, Mendling, Rosemann et al., 2021):

(1) *Strategy*: Strategic alignment of the organization with the BPM project
(2) *Context*: The relationship between the BPM project and the organizational context
(3) *Capability*: Capabilities required for the implementation of the BPM project
(4) *Projects*: Related (other) projects that have a strategic impact relevant to the BPM project
(5) *Results*: Measurable tangible and intangible outcomes (goals).

Both practitioners and researchers can use the BPM Billboard as a reference model for managing digital transformation initiatives in a way that considers the organizational requirements and needs. The framework is already widely used in industry (e.g., by companies such as SAP SE and Hilti, and in public administration) (Weber & vom Brocke, 2023). It is used to plan and scale ini-

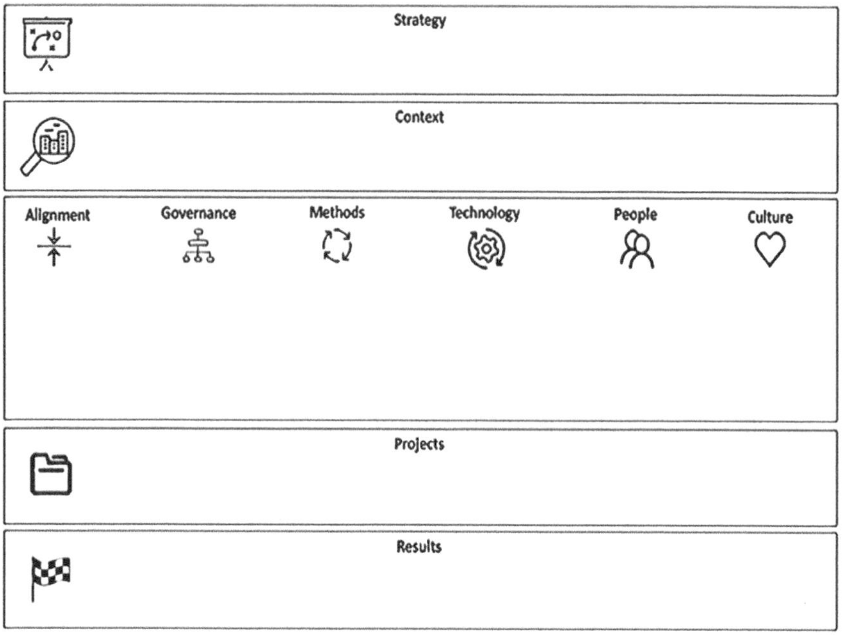

Source: vom Brocke, Mendling et al. (2021).

Figure 3.2 BPM Billboard

tiatives, as well as to communicate the strategic value of digital transformation programs to the various stakeholders. The Billboard has also been used to assess and further develop existing initiatives and to assess the value-adding potential of emerging technologies.

The Hilti case study: a process-oriented digital transformation

Hilti is a global company headquartered in Liechtenstein that develops construction tools and services. Hilti employs approximately 30,000 employees worldwide. Several years ago, Hilti standardized its global processes across several areas including finance, logistics, and research and development (R&D) (vom Brocke et al., 2015, 2017; vom Brocke, Schmiedel et al., 2016). Supported by a document management system based in Microsoft Sharepoint, they create and manage several thousand process documents. They also use the system to design (build) and disseminate process knowledge throughout the company and to all the relevant stakeholders (vom Brocke, Weber, & Grisold, 2021a; Weber et al., 2021). Over several decades, Hilti has mastered several challenges in its digitalization endeavors and their day-to-day work has changed radically in the process. Providing several success stories along its journey, Hilti has become a "digital enterprise" and a master of innovation and transformation that is currently at its peak.

The digital journey has its roots in the company's early days when, in 1951, the founder, Martin Hilti, laid the foundations for its success. His vision was to build a global IS to conduct business worldwide. Initially, the idea was to improve operations by working toward excellence and striving to satisfy their customers' needs. This prompted Hilti to design stable company-wide processes and implement common data structures. To this end, they launched the Global Processes and Data (GPD) project. Its objective was to break down functional silos by overcoming local data storage and use through a global system supporting the knowledge use and sharing processes within Hilti. Initially, approximately 20,000 users were working with SAP, their ERP software. In addition, 6,000 employees used the SAP mobile solutions and applications on their working devices (vom Brocke et al., 2011, 2017).

Over the years, Hilti has developed several digital capabilities that have been key to its success. A decisive factor in that success was its strong ability to successfully implement transformations from the conception of an idea to its realization. This was not only achieved through the adoption and use of IT but also through the ability to adapt organizational structures to new situations. Thus, since 1951, Hilti has transformed itself from a small production manufacturer of machines for the construction industry into a global player and one of the world's leading technology companies. Today, Hilti offers products and develops its own system solutions, services, and software for expanding its existing product range – ultimately offering customers added value in the process (vom Brocke et al., 2017).

A Cockpit for Establishing a Context-sensitive Approach to Digital Transformation

When applying the Billboard, Hilti considered different contextual requirements when planning and scaling their digital transformation journey (vom Brocke, Weber, & Grisold, 2021b; Weber et al., 2021). Research has shown that process management is dependent on contextual factors (vom Brocke, Zelt et al., 2016) that can also be described through the theory of contingent BPM (Zelt et al., 2019). According to this theory, various contextual factors need to be taken into account including (i) the degree of value contribution, (ii) repetitiveness, (iii) knowledge intensity, (iv) creativity, (v) interdependence, and (vi) variability (vom Brocke, Zelt, Recker et al., 2016). With Hilti, we were able to evaluate all processes according to these factors using the measurement instrument provided by Zelt et al. (2018). Details of that study and our methodological approach are described in vom Brocke, Weber, and Grisold (2021b). Based on the data collected and spider diagrams plotted for each dimension of each process, we engaged in a card-sorting exercise with the global process experts and discussed the results with a view to identifying the key dimensions that were most relevant to the company's processes. This led us to group the concepts "knowledge intensity," "creativity," and "process variability" into one dimension called "process variability" and the concepts "standardization" and "process interdependence-process steps" under the heading "process frequency." We defined the dimension "process variability" as the degree to which strong processes respond to external developments and dynamic situations. We then used "frequency" to make statements about how often a process or process instance is executed in a certain period. The BPM Context Matrix we produced through this exercise is presented in Figure 3.3.

This 2x2 matrix contains four types of processes that we refer to as process clusters:

Reliability Cluster: Processes in this cluster are run infrequently with little variability in each iteration. In this situation, process users run the risk of forgetting procedures or necessary tasks. In general, it would be useful to assist users in obtaining simple, easy-to-understand, and relevant process information and documentation. The best possible support can be achieved through checklists or knowledge management systems.

Performance Cluster: Processes in this cluster are high frequency (i.e., they are performed often). In addition, these processes have a low variability and require minimal adaption in each iteration. The aim here is process automation, which can be achieved through workflow management systems and tools. Process mining can help by allowing process logs of these high-frequency processes to be captured efficiently (Grisold et al., 2021). Robotic process automation technology can also be particularly useful in this setting (Plattfaut et al., 2022).

Innovation Cluster: The processes in this cluster are low frequency and executed rarely. Simultaneously, they require a high degree of deviation and variability in each iteration. These are often creative processes that can be best supported by messaging or project management systems. Furthermore, as the

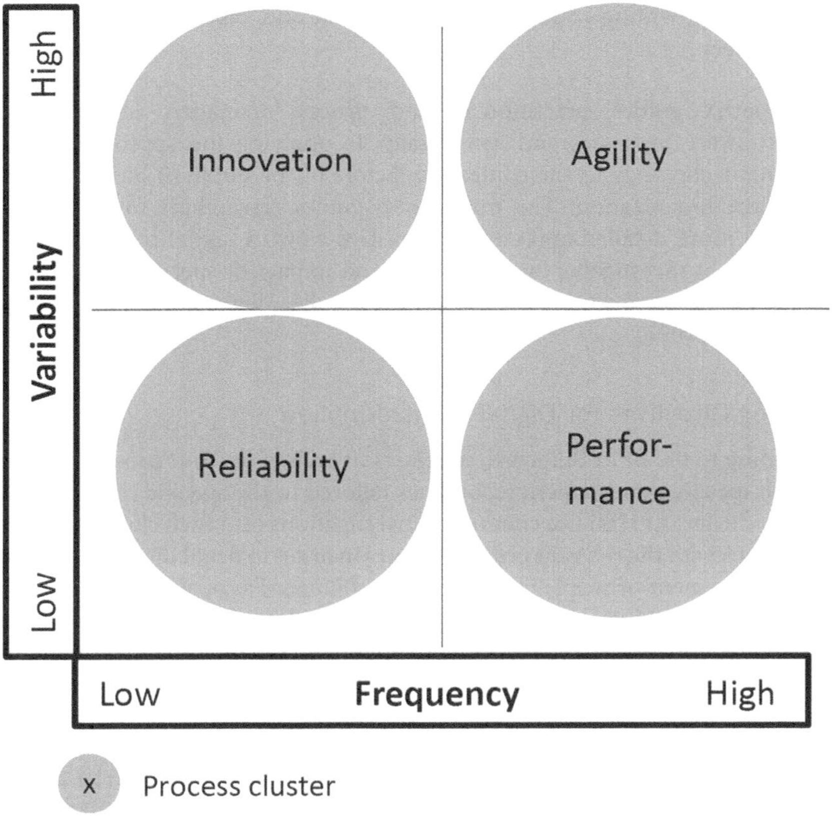

Source: vom Brocke, Weber, and Grisold (2021a); Weber et al. (2021).

Figure 3.3 BPM context matrix

results of creative processes are usually not known in advance, it is desirable to enable collaborative interaction between the process participants in a manner that also considers process transparency (Richter et al., 2009; Simons et al., 2019). So that process stakeholders are not restricted in their creativity, detailed process descriptions and models should be avoided as they would have a restrictive effect.

Agility Cluster: Processes in this cluster are high frequency and are executed very often with a high degree of variability. In most cases, these processes are complex and require continuous monitoring, including the measurement of variability. It should also be noted that the management of these processes is particularly difficult. Process analysis methodologies and tools can be the solution to providing continuous measurement and support for the process stakeholders.

The matrix guides practitioners and process managers in designing context-aware processes and, specifically, in applying the appropriate type of digital technology to the contextual factors of the different business areas across the organization. The matrix also guides researchers toward establishing a more detailed and context-sensitive view in digital transformation research that investigates the design use and impact of specific digital technology in various business contexts (vom Brocke, Weber, & Grisold, 2021a; Weber et al., 2021).

Deriving Directives for Digital Transformation

According to the BPM Billboard, processes in each of the four process clusters require specific management techniques tailored to the specific requirements of each cluster. At Hilti, we conducted investigations into each cluster through workshops with the relevant process owners in order to detail the requirements and management principles for each of the Billboard's capability areas. Table 3.1 summarizes the results and shows how the Billboard is used to account for different contextual requirements in an organization's digital transformation.

To briefly illustrate the approach, we start with the performance cluster. Here, the key challenge is to ensure efficient and compliant processes. Steps are taken to describe, analyze, and automate processes. Digital technology can be used to automate specific processes using, for example, workflow management systems or robotic process automation. In contrast, in the innovation cluster, creative problem-solving is key and, while the flow of the process may vary, the process benefits from an inspirational and supportive environment (e.g., regarding access to resources). Digital technology can be used to support project management and collaboration through a governance structure that provides, for example, access to expert networks. In the reliability cluster, where processes are low frequency with low variability, digitalization can support employees by facilitating access to the enterprise content needed to conduct the process in the prescribed way. In the agility cluster, processes are high frequency with high variability. Therefore, the management of complexity is key and digitalization can help, in particular, create behavioral visibility (Leonardi & Treem, 2020). This helps identify deviance, understand it, and discuss measures for reducing and managing the complexity of the task effectively (vom Brocke, van der Aalst et al., 2021).

Table 3.1 Management of the process clusters across the six capability areas in BPM

	Agility	Performance	Innovation	Reliability
Key Challenge	Sensitive & adaptive for change	Efficient and compliant	Find innovative solutions	Accessibility
Information Technology	Process mining	Process automation	Project management	Content management
Strategic Alignment	# variants	Efficiency KPIs	Impact of the solution	Effectiveness
Governance	Shop floor meetings	Constant oversight	Expert networks	Expert groups
Methods	Reference models	Process models	Stage-gate processes	Checklists
People	Quantitative skills	Routinized	Problem-solving skills	Conscientious
Culture	Continuous improvement	Discipline	Spirit of research	Liability

Sources: vom Brocke, Weber, and Grisold (2021a); Weber et al. (2021).

A Deep Dive into Digital Transformation through Process Science

Digital technology can be used to analyze how processes are executed. Based on digital trace data, algorithms can capture the various activities conducted within an organization, in its supply chain, and in its broader environment. Indeed, the use of process mining to analyze digital trace data is increasingly attracting interest in digital transformation research and practice. However, most of the work being done remains descriptive and does not help us understand the reason for the phenomena observed or support decisions on the path to digital transformation. Although digital trace data allows researchers to infer what happened during a process, datasets rarely provide information on the reasons for certain actions or deviations. More recently, the field of process science was established with the aim of generating holistic research on processes on three distinct levels: descriptive process science, explanatory process science, and prescriptive process science (vom Brocke, van der Aalst et al., 2021). Some examples will allow us to illustrate the principles of process science and how it contributes to digital transformation research.

Grisold et al. (2020) have proposed using process mining techniques to support theorizing about opportunities in organizations and conducting both computational and empirical investigations. In that vein, Hartl et al. (2023) utilized "temporal bracketing" to bring more contextual knowledge to the analysis of digital traces. Other studies have used process mining to examine digital trace data, the so-called digital footprints of organizational routines. They examined the data for four routines of a global manufacturing company over several months and then made statements about the complexity and changes that occurred over time, including statements about spatiotemporal aspects. Wurm et al. (2021) used process analytics to study the complexity of selected processes at Hilti, our case study company. Figure 3.4 highlights the variability of one of these routines – an order-to-cash routine, executed in Austria and Switzerland. The process is initiated by the receipt of a customer order and ends with the receipt of the customer's payment (with the receipt of the cash). The results show that the complexity changes continuously over time for all four routines. It can also be seen that the absolute complexity of all four routines starts low, increases constantly, and then changes again toward the end of the routine. New variants and factors that are added during the process need to be taken into account, for example, the change in payment targets for the customers. It is also evident that the complexity remains the same or decreases with the number of repeat executions over time. As this data was collected during the COVID-19 crisis, it also reflects the increase in the relative complexity of this order-to-cash routine that occurred during the pandemic (Wurm et al., 2021). Pilot projects have been conducted, using Hilti as a case study, to better understand digital technology's transformative power in each of the four clusters.

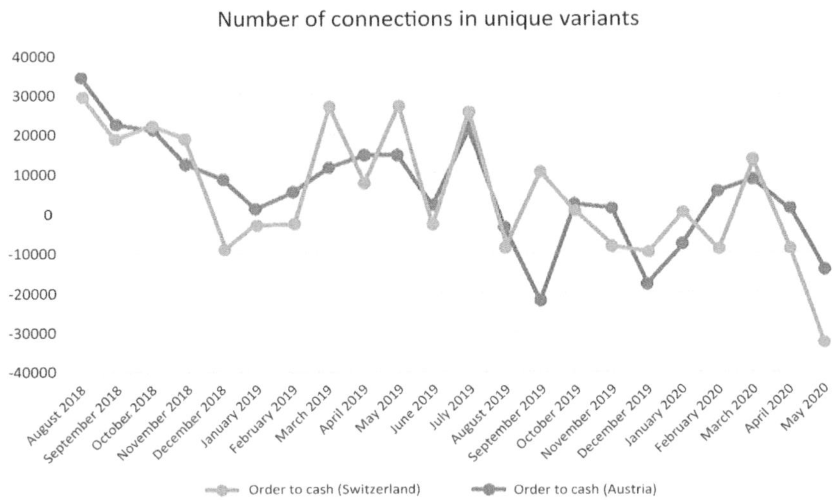

Source: Wurm et al. (2021).

Figure 3.4 Illustration of the variability of an order-to-cash process

Recognizing the Various Logics of Digital Transformation

The process-oriented approach to managing digital transformation presented in this chapter reveals that there is no one-size-fits-all solution to digital transformation and that strategies need to be tailored to each process and its specific requirements as additional value is only created for organizations when digital technology helps processes perform better. Through the Hilti case study, we have identified four different logics of digital transformation that will be useful for many companies. Nevertheless, additional context types and logics of digital transformation can, and most likely will, be identified based on each organization's individual data. Figure 3.5 outlines the four logics identified in the Hilti case to provide further specific illustration and guidance for practice and research.

The context clusters help process designers identify the relevant process logic and visualize context-sensitive processes. A specific matching between digital technologies and processes can then be derived using the context clusters. Referring to Figure 3.5, we show how to match an IS with the appropriate

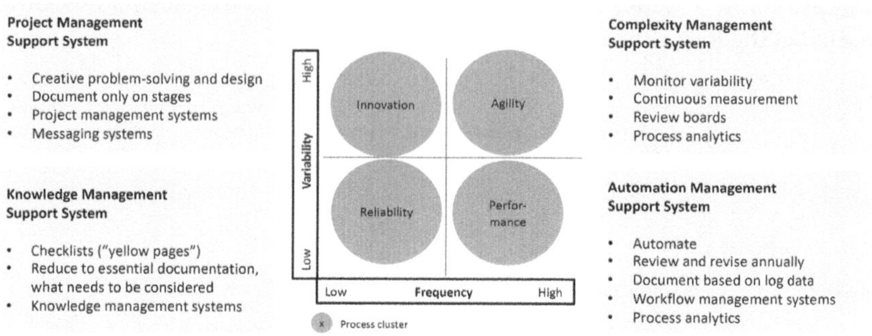

Source: vom Brocke, Weber, and Grisold (2021a); Weber et al. (2021).

Figure 3.5 Four digital transformation logics

process cluster. We have detailed examples of digital technologies and the requirements needed to fulfill their different functions. Next, the figure demonstrates the different possible affordances based on the contextual requirements of a process and where it is situated within the four clusters. We argue that companies often select digital technology that is perceived as modern or popular but then fail to respond to the relevant requirements of the organization and the people and process involved (vom Brocke, Weber, & Grisold, 2021a; vom Brocke, Zelt et al., 2016; Weber et al., 2021). The four digital transformation logics (DTLs) help practitioners avoid this shortfall by helping them successfully match emergent digital technology with different types of processes. The DTLs identified in our research serve as examples of how different digital technology adds value in different business contexts. However, the concept for the DTL is not limited to these four DTLs. Therefore, we invite future research to identify additional DTLs by analyzing other case studies and applying a wider set of measurement instruments. However, that there are different DTLs and that the value of any given digital transformation depends on how well the implementation strategy for the technology takes into account the logic inherent in the specific application context is an important finding that has emerged from our research.

Conclusion

In this chapter, we have presented a process-oriented view of digital transformation that rests on the understanding that digital technologies do not generate value per se but do so through the opportunities they represent for the design and execution of processes. Processes must be designed carefully and consider the specific application context. Therefore, we have introduced a management framework – the BPM Billboard – that can be used to develop the capabilities necessary to systematically and successfully implement digital transformations in organizations. We applied this framework to a case study company, Hilti, and, in this process, have derived four archetypes of organizational contexts – performance, innovation, reliability, and agility – and discussed their different relevant logics of digital transformation – automation management, project management, knowledge management, and complexity management.

Based on this analysis, we have formulated four key takeaways. These briefly summarize our chapter and will help practitioners successfully and efficiently implement their digital transformation endeavors.

(1) Successful value generation through the integration of information and digital technologies is not achieved through adoption alone but through the successful transformation of socio-technical resources and alignment with corporate goals.
(2) The adoption of digital technologies must, therefore, consider socio-technical, temporal, and spatial aspects. The successful balancing and coordination of space and time is essential to how digital technologies effectively implement corporate strategies.
(3) The numerous possible combinations of IT processes, purpose, context, and expectations can quickly lead to complex situations. Especially in dynamic and uncertain times, it is important to have a detailed understanding of these factors. We argue that a one-size-fits-all approach is not sufficient, but that a context-aware approach can help companies apply the right technologies in the right processes.
(4) For a long time, the management of organizations was characterized by silo thinking. We have outlined a process-oriented view that helps break down functional silos and support digital transformation from an end-to-end perspective.

Based on these findings, future digital transformation research should continue to investigate the capturing, explaining, and influencing dynamics related to digital technology use in context. Although there has already been extensive research on how the implementation of digital technologies is changing existing business processes, more research is needed to further understand both the complexity and dynamics of specific use cases. Future research needs to be more specific rather than speaking about digital transformation in general terms. It is essential to examine more specific case study application contexts in which the relevant technologies offer certain possibilities for action and, thereby, deliver targeted strategic value.

Such research will produce results that can also be used to shape digital transformation in practice. These theories will be less grand but return results for more confined areas of application in shorter timeframes. Increasingly, research has called for more design-oriented digital transformation research to generate knowledge that supports innovative problem-solving and design (Seckler et al., 2021). Such contributions will include models and methods, like the BPM Billboard presented here, that will support decision-makers in the many choices they must make during their digital transformation journey. It has also been suggested that theories may not be sufficient given the current speed of change in business contexts, and a plea for more situated and temporal forms of knowledge representation has been made, particularly in the form of patterns. To this end, researchers are encouraged to share data and develop methodologies like our BPM Billboard to provide further insight into the many dynamics of value generation with digital technologies.

References

Abbott, A. (1995). Sequence analysis: New methods for old ideas. *Annual Review of Sociology*, *21*(1), 93–113.

Appelbaum, S. H. (1997). Socio-technical systems theory: An intervention strategy for organizational development. *Management Decision*, *35*(6), 452–463.

Avdiji, H., Elikan, D., Missonier, S., & Pigneur, Y. (2020). A design theory for visual inquiry tools. *Journal of the Association for Information Systems*, *21*(3), 3.

Badakhshan, P., Wurm, B., Grisold, T., Geyer-Klingeberg, J., Mendling, J., & vom Brocke, J. (2022). Creating business value with process mining. *The Journal of Strategic Information Systems*, *31*(4), 101745.

Baxter, G., & Sommerville, I. (2011). Socio-technical systems: From design methods to systems engineering. *Interacting with Computers*, *23*(1), 4–17.

Benbasat, I., & Zmud, R. W. (1999). Empirical research in information systems: The practice of relevance. *MIS Quarterly*, *23*(1), 3.

Beverungen, D., Buijs, J. C., Becker, J., Di Ciccio, C., van der Aalst, W. M., Bartelheimer, C., vom Brocke, J., Comuzzi, M., Kraume, K., & Leopold, H. (2021). Seven paradoxes of business process management in a hyper-connected world. *Business & Information Systems Engineering*, *63*(2), 145–156.

Blank, S. (2019). Why companies do "innovation theater" instead of actual innovation. *Harvard Business Review*, *5*(93), 6.

Boh, W. F., & Yellin, D. (2006). Using enterprise architecture standards in managing information technology. *Journal of Management Information Systems*, *23*(3), 163–207.

Bostrom, R. P., & Heinen, J. S. (1977). MIS problems and failures: A socio-technical perspective. Part I: The causes. *MIS Quarterly*, *1*(3), 17–32.
Bulletpoint (1996). Creating a change culture – not about structures, but winning hearts and minds. *Sample Issue*, 12–13.
Cagnin, M. I., & Nakagawa, E. Y. (2021). Towards dynamic processes-of-business processes: A new understanding. *Business Process Management Journal*, *27*(5), 1545–1568.
Champy, J., & Hammer, M. (1993). *Reengineering the Cooperation: A Manifesto for Business Revolution*. Revolution.
Cornwell, B. (2015). *Social Sequence Analysis: Methods and Applications*. Cambridge University Press.
Dov, T., Seidel, S., & vom Brocke, J. (2017). Stimulating dialog between information systems research and practice. *European Journal of Information Systems*, *26*(6), 541–545.
Dumas, M., La Rosa, M., Mendling, J., & Reijers, H. A. (2018). *Fundamentals of Business Process Management*. Springer.
Fink, D. (1998). Guidelines for the successful adoption of information technology in small and medium enterprises. *International Journal of Information Management*, *18*(4), 243–253.
Grisold, T., Mendling, J., Otto, M., & vom Brocke, J. (2021). Adoption, use and management of process mining in practice. *Business Process Management Journal*, *27*(2), 369–387.
Grisold, T., vom Brocke, J., Kratsch, W., Mendling, J., & Vidgof, M. (2023). *Using Large Language Models in Business Processes*. 21st International Conference on Business Process Management, Utrecht, Netherlands.
Grisold, T., Wurm, B., Mendling, J., & vom Brocke, J. (2020). Using process mining to support theorizing about change in organizations. Proceedings of the 53rd Hawaii International Conference on System Sciences.
Hacker, J., vom Brocke, J., Handali, J., Otto, M., & Schneider, J. (2020). Virtually in this together - how web-conferencing systems enabled a new virtual togetherness during the COVID-19 crisis. *European Journal of Information Systems*, *29*(5), 563–584.
Hammer, M. (2015). What is business process management? In J. vom Brocke & M. Rosemann (Eds.), *Handbook on Business Process Management 1* (pp. 3–16). Springer.
Hartl, S., Franzoi, S., Grisold, T., & vom Brocke, J. (2023). Explaining change with digital trace data: A framework for temporal bracketing. 56th Hawaii International Conference on System Sciences, Maui, Hawaii.
Herterich, M. M., Dremel, C., Wulf, J., & vom Brocke, J. (2023). The emergence of smart service ecosystems: The role of socio of smart service ecosystems–theosystems. *Information Systems Journal*, *33*(3), 524–566.
Kamm, M., Gau, M., Schneider, J., & vom Brocke, J. (2020). Smart waste collection processes: A case study about smart device implementation. Proceedings of the 53rd Hawaii International Conference on System Sciences. https://hdl.handle.net/10125/64552.
Karahanna, E., Straub, D. W., & Chervany, N. L. (1999). Information technology adoption across time: A cross-sectional comparison of pre-adoption and post-adoption beliefs. *MIS Quarterly*, *23*(2), 183–213.
Langley, A., Smallman, C., Tsoukas, H., & van de Ven, A. H. (2013). Process studies of change in organization and management: Unveiling temporality, activity, and flow. *Academy of Management Journal*, *56*(1), 1–13.

Leenders, R. T. A., Contractor, N. S., & DeChurch, L. A. (2016). Once upon a time: Understanding team processes as relational event networks. *Organizational Psychology Review*, *6*(1), 92–115.
Lehrer, C., Wieneke, A., vom Brocke, J., Jung, R., & Seidel, S. (2018). How big data analytics enables service innovation: Materiality, affordance, and the individualization of service. *Journal of Management Information Systems*, *35*(2), 424–460.
Leonardi, P. M., & Treem, J. W. (2020). Behavioral visibility: A new paradigm for organization studies in the age of digitization, digitalization, and datafication. *Organization Studies*, *41*(12), 1601–1625.
Mendling, J., Pentland, B., & Recker, J. (2020). Building a complementary agenda for business process management and digital innovation. *European Journal of Information Systems*, *29*(3), 208–219.
Müller, O., Fay, M., & vom Brocke, J. (2018). The effect of big data and analytics on firm performance: An econometric analysis considering industry characteristics. *Journal of Management Information Systems*, *35*(2), 488–509.
Nguyen, K. (2022). Driving digital transformation: Integrative insights on organizational, environmental and managerial drivers. Thesis, University of Groningen.
Pentland, B., Vaast, E., & Wolf, J. R. (2021). Theorizing process dynamics with directed graphs: A diachronic analysis of digital trace data. *MIS Quarterly*, *45*(2), 967–984.
Pettigrew, A. M. (1997). What is a processual analysis? *Scandinavian Management Journal*, *13*(4), 337–348.
Plattfaut, R., Borghoff, V., Godefroid, M., Koch, J., Trampler, M., & Coners, A. (2022). The critical success factors for robotic process automation. *Computers in Industry*, *138*, 103646.
Powell, T. C., & Dent-Micallef, A. (1997). Information technology as competitive advantage: The role of human, business, and technology resources. *Strategic Management Journal*, *18*(5), 375–405.
Recker, J. (2014). Suggestions for the next wave of BPM research: Strengthening the theoretical core and exploring the protective belt. *Journal of Information Technology Theory and Application*, *15*(2), 5–20.
Reinecke, J., & Ansari, S. (2017). Time, temporality and process studies. In A. Langley & H. Tsoukas (Eds.), *The Sage Handbook of Process Organization Studies* (pp. 402–416). Sage.
Richter, D., Riemer, K., vom Brocke, J., & Große Böckmann, S. (2009). Internet social networking: Distinguishing phenomenon and practical manifestation. Proceedings of the 17th European Conference on Information Systems, Verona, Italy.
Rosemann, M., & Recker, J. (2006). Context-aware process design: Exploring the extrinsic drivers for process flexibility. In T. Latour & M. Petit (Eds.), *Proceedings 18th International Conference on Advanced Information Systems Engineering. Proceedings of Workshops and Doctoral Consortium* (pp. 149–158). Namur University Press.
Sarker, S., Chatterjee, S., Xiao, X., & Elbanna, A. (2019). The sociotechnical axis of cohesion for the IS discipline: Its historical legacy and its continued relevance. *MIS Quarterly*, *43*(3), 695–720.
Schmiedel, T., & vom Brocke, J. (2015). Business process management: Potentials and challenges of driving innovation. In J. vom Brocke & T. Schmiedel (Eds.), *BPM: Driving Innovation in a Digital World* (pp. 3–16). Springer.
Seckler, C., Mauer, R., & vom Brocke, J. (2021). Design science in entrepreneurship: Conceptual foundations and guiding principles. *Journal of Business Venturing Design*, *1*(1–2), 100004.

Seidel, S., Recker, J., & vom Brocke, J. (2013). Sensemaking and sustainable practicing: Functional affordances of information systems in green transformations. *MIS Quarterly*, *37*(4), 1275–1299.
Simons, A., Kaiser, L. F., & vom Brocke, J. (2019). Enterprise crowdfunding: Foundations, applications, and research findings. *Business & Information Systems Engineering*, *61*(1), 113–121.
van de Ven, A. H., & Poole, M. S. (1995). Explaining development and change in organizations. *Academy of Management Review*, *20*(3), 510–540.
van der Aalst, W. M. (2016). *Process Mining*. Springer.
Van Looy, A. (2021). A quantitative and qualitative study of the link between business process management and digital innovation. *Information & Management*, *58*(2), 103413.
Verhoef, P. C., Broekhuizen, T., Bart, Y., Bhattacharya, A., Dong, J. Q., Fabian, N., & Haenlein, M. (2021). Digital transformation: A multidisciplinary reflection and research agenda. *Journal of Business Research*, *122*, 889–901.
vom Brocke, J., Debortoli, S., Müller, O., & Reuter, N. (2014). How in-memory technology can create business value: Insights from the Hilti case. *Communications of the Association for Information Systems*, *34*(1), 151–167.
vom Brocke, J., Fay, M., Schmiedel, T., Petry, M., Krause, F., & Teinzer, T. (2017). A journey of digital innovation and transformation: The case of Hilti. In G. Oswald & M. Kleinemeier (Eds.), *Shaping the Digital Enterprise* (pp. 237–251). Springer International.
vom Brocke, J., & Grisold, T. (2020). Erfolgreich Digitalisieren – Ansätze für ein modernes Prozessmanagement. *Controlling*, *32*(S), 102–107.
vom Brocke, J., Hevner, A., Léger, P. M., Walla, P., & Riedl, R. (2020). Advancing a NeuroIS research agenda with four areas of societal contributions. *European Journal of Information Systems*, *29*(1), 9–24.
vom Brocke, J., Mendling, J., & Rosemann, M. (Eds.) (2021). *Business Process Management Cases: Digital Innovation and Business Transformation in Practice* (Vol. 2). Springer.
vom Brocke, J., Mendling, J., Rosemann, M., & Weber, M. (2021). The BPM billboard – a tool for planning and scoping BPM initiatives. BPTrends Class Notes: BPM Research and Education. https://www.bptrends.com/class-notes-the-bpm-billboard-a-tool-for-planning-and-scoping-bpm-initiatives/.
vom Brocke, J., Petry, M., & Gonser, T. (2012). Business process management. In A. Uhl & L. A. Gollenia (Eds.), *A Handbook of Business Transformation Management Methodology* (pp. 137–172). Routledge.
vom Brocke, J., Petry, M., & Schmiedel, T. (2011). How Hilti masters transformation. *360°: The Business Transformation Journal*, *1*, 38–47.
vom Brocke, J., Petry, M., Schmiedel, T., & Sonnenberg, C. (2015). How organizational culture facilitates a global BPM project: The case of Hilti. In J. vom Brocke & M. Rosemann (Eds.), *Handbook on Business Process Management 2: Strategic Alignment, Governance, People and Culture* (pp. 693–713). Springer.
vom Brocke, J., Riedl, R., & Léger, P. M. (2013). Application strategies for neuroscience in information systems design science research. *Journal of Computer Information Systems*, *53*(3), 1–13.
vom Brocke, J., & Rosemann, M. (2015). Business process management. In C. L. Cooper (Ed.), *Wiley Encyclopedia of Management* (Vol. 7, pp. 1–9). John Wiley & Sons.

vom Brocke, J., Schmiedel, T., Simons, A., Schmid, A., Petry, M., & Baeck, C. (2016). From local IT needs to global process transformation: Hilti's customer service program. *Business Process Management Journal, 22*(3), 594–613.

vom Brocke, J., Sonnenberg, C., & Simons, A. (2009). Value-oriented information systems design: The concept of potentials modeling and its application to service-oriented architectures. *Business & Information Systems Engineering, 1*, 223–233.

vom Brocke, J., van der Aalst, W. M., Grisold, T., Kremser, W., Mendling, J., Pentland, B., Recker, J., Roeglinger, M., Rosemann, M., & Weber, B. (2021). Process science: The interdisciplinary study of continuous change (working paper). https://ssrn.com/abstract=3916817.

vom Brocke, J., Weber, M., & Grisold, T. (2021a). A matrix for context-aware business process management: Empirical evidence from Hilti. In M. De Leoni, M. Song, & M. Röglinger (Eds.), *Proceedings of the Industry Forum at BPM 2021* (Vol. 3112, pp. 39–50). CEUR Workshop Proceedings.

vom Brocke, J., Weber, M., & Grisold, T. (2021b). Design Science Research for High Practical Relevance: Dancing through space and time. In P. Rohner, J. Schelp, & S. Aier (Eds.), *Engineering the Transformation of the Enterprise: A Design Science Research Perspective* (pp. 115–136). Springer Nature.

vom Brocke, J., Zelt, S., & Schmiedel, T. (2016). On the role of context in business process management. *International Journal of Information Management, 36*(3), 486–495.

Weber, M., Grisold, T., vom Brocke, J., & Kamm, M. (2021). Context-aware business process modelling: Empirical insights from a project with a globally operating company. Proceedings of the 29th European Conference in Information Systems.

Weber, M., & vom Brocke, J. (2023). Managing BPM projects and their implications on organizations: Experiences from research and teaching. In J. Köpke, O. López-Pintado, R. Plattfaut, J.-R. Rehse, K. Gdowska, F. Gonzalez-Lopez, J. Munoz-Gama, K. Smit, & J. M. E. M. Van Der Werf (Eds.), *Business Process Management: Blockchain, Robotic Process Automation and Educators Forum* (Vol. 491, pp. 240–249). Springer Nature.

Weske, M., Montali, M., Weber, I., & vom Brocke, J. (Eds.) (2018). *Business Process Management: 16th International Conference, BPM 2018, Sydney, NSW, Australia, September 9–14, 2018, Proceedings* (Vol. 11080). Springer International.

Wurm, B., Grisold, T., Mendling, J., & vom Brocke, J. (2021). Measuring fluctuations of complexity in organizational routines. *Academy of Management Proceedings, 1*, 13388.

Yoo, Y., Boland Jr, R. J., Lyytinen, K., & Majchrzak, A. (2012). Organizing for innovation in the digitized world. *Organization Science, 23*(5), 1398–1408.

Zairi, M. (1997). Business process management: A boundaryless approach to modern competitiveness. *Business Process Management Journal, 3*(1), 64–80.

Zelt, S., Recker, J., Schmiedel, T., & vom Brocke, J. (2018). Development and validation of an instrument to measure and manage organizational process variety. *PLoS One, 13*(10).

Zelt, S., Recker, J., Schmiedel, T., & vom Brocke, J. (2019). A theory of contingent business process management. *Business Process Management Journal, 25*(6), 1291–1316.

Zelt, S., Schmiedel, T., & vom Brocke, J. (2018). Understanding the nature of processes: An information-processing perspective. *Business Process Management Journal, 24*(1), 67–88.

4 A market-oriented perspective on digital transformation

P. K. Kannan and H. Alice Li

In the digital age, digital transformation and marketing strategy are two interdependent elements essential for business success. Given the shift toward digital platforms for communication and commerce, companies must integrate digital technologies into their marketing strategies to reach and engage their audience effectively. This necessitates a profound understanding of the digital landscape and a willingness to innovate marketing strategies and tactics continually. Therefore, businesses that embrace digital transformation and use it to enhance their marketing strategies stand to reap significant benefits and gain a competitive edge.

Digital transformation is defined as a change in how a firm employs digital technologies to develop a new digital business model that helps to create and appropriate more value for the firm (Verhoef et al. 2021). It refers to the integration of digital technology into all areas of a business, resulting in fundamental changes to how the business operates and delivers value to customers. As a process, it implies the profound and accelerated transformation of business activities, competencies, and models to fully leverage the changes and opportunities that digital technologies afford. It is marked by a shift from legacy systems to new, agile technologies aimed at improving and optimizing organizational performance, yielding superior customer value, and creating innovative, digitally driven business processes. In this process, firms transition from traditional, often manual, processes to automated, digital ones, integrating technologies like cloud computing, the Internet of Things (IoT), artificial intelligence (AI), and blockchain into their operations. This transformational process also involves a cultural shift. Organizations must foster a culture of continuous learning, innovation, and adaptability to keep pace with rapidly evolving technologies and consumer demands.

The impact of digital transformation on a firm is multidimensional. First, it leads to enhanced customer experiences. Firms can utilize data analytics, AI, and other technologies to gain deeper insights into customer behaviors and preferences (Dong and Yang 2019), enabling more personalized and effective interactions. This customer centricity often can translate to increased customer loyalty and revenue growth. Second, digital transformation fosters operational efficiency. Automating routine tasks and leveraging technologies for real-time data analysis and decision-making can significantly reduce operational costs and enhance productivity. Third, it enables business model innovation. By leveraging digital technologies, companies can create new, often disruptive, business models that can provide a competitive advantage. For example, leveraging platform-based models and social media can facilitate the creation of digital ecosystems, allowing firms to collaborate and co-create value with a network of partners, suppliers, and customers (Dong and Wu 2015). Finally, digital transformation can enhance the firm's agility and resilience, allowing it to adapt more effectively to changing market conditions, consumer preferences, and emerging risks. This adaptability is crucial in navigating the uncertainties and volatilities in today's digital age (Kalaignanam et al. 2021). Thus, digital transformation is a comprehensive and ongoing process involving technological adoption, cultural change, and business model innovation. It has a transformational impact on firms, driving enhanced customer experiences, operational efficiency, business model innovation, and organizational agility, which are pivotal for sustaining competitiveness in the contemporary business landscape.

Digital transformation in the context of marketing strategy refers to the incorporation and comprehensive use of digital technologies to create, communicate, deliver, and exchange offerings that have value for customers, clients, partners, and society at large (Verhoef and Bijmolt 2019). It typically involves leveraging data analytics, digital communications, and digital platforms to enhance customer experiences, streamline operations, and create new business models. Digital transformation in marketing can significantly impact customer engagement, enabling brands to interact with their customers in a more personalized and immediate manner. It also allows organizations to leverage data-driven insights to optimize marketing strategies, target the right audience segments, enhance customer relationships, and achieve a competitive advantage. This process requires a holistic approach, rethinking traditional marketing paradigms and embracing technological innovations to meet evolving customer needs and expectations.

The process of digital transformation enables marketing managers to take advantage of new opportunities created by technology and data to drive growth, improve efficiency and customer experiences, and stay ahead of the competition. In a digital transformation context, a company's marketing strategy must adapt to new technologies and customer behavior. This may involve a shift to digital channels for customer acquisition, engagement and retention, data-driven decision-making, design of new marketing systems and processes, and a focus on creating personalized customer experiences. An effective digital marketing strategy will likely involve a mix of social media marketing, search engine optimization (SEO), content marketing, email marketing, and influencer marketing, among other tactics, all enabled by advances in AI and machine learning (ML).

The conventional marketing strategy paradigm

We first summarize the conventional marketing strategy paradigm based on the framework commonly proposed in extant literature (Dolan 2014). Figure 4.1 illustrates the important elements in the marketing strategy process. The process begins with an environmental analysis that evaluates the five Cs – customers, collaborators, competition, context, and the company. A firm analyzes the environment within which it operates and makes the aspiration decisions of how to segment the market and target the right segments with an appropriate positioning strategy. The action plan, consisting of product, price, promotion, and distribution strategies, is developed in such a way that it aligns clearly with the targeting and positioning strategies. These strategies and tactics impact the business outcome in terms of impacting customer acquisition, retention, and margins and firm-level metrics of sales, profits, growth rate, brand equity, and market position.

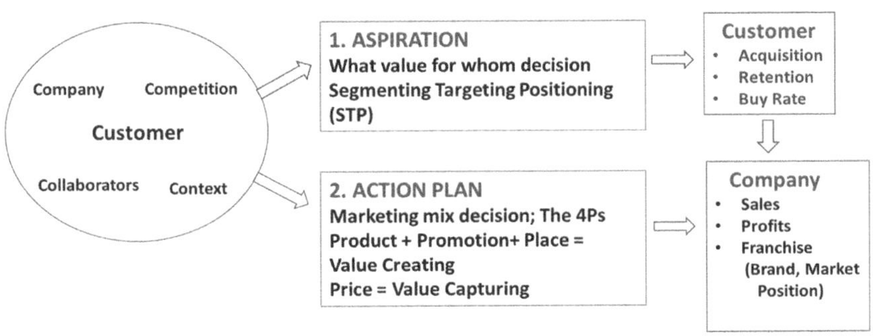

Source: Dolan (2014).

Figure 4.1 The marketing strategy paradigm

One may be tempted to ask where digital technology appears within this marketing strategy framework shown in Figure 4.1. Technology appears in Context within the environment, clubbed with culture politics, geography law, regulation, and so on. We argue that this paradigm does not sufficiently capture the critical role that digital technology and transformation plays in the marketing strategy process. Why? It is because the key touchpoints in the marketing process and strategies evolve as digital technology develops. The framework encompasses not only the elements identified in Figure 4.1 but also the interfaces between them, as shown by the arrows in the figure. It emphasizes the focus on uncovering issues in digital transformation that will have a direct or indirect impact on the firm. In order to understand the impact of digital transformation on marketing strategy, it is necessary to understand how it has created new institutions, innovations, and business processes that have drastically changed the environment within which a firm operates, how the aspiration decision and actions are impacted, and how this leads to focus on conventional and emerging outcome metrics.

We will now provide an overview of how this framework has changed with digital transformation and what it implies for the various elements of this framework as they are impacted by digital technologies.

The new marketing strategy paradigm

If we examine how digital technology has changed the environment in the last two decades, we will see institutions that did not exist two decades ago but which play a critical role in the marketing strategy planning, and implementation processes. In Figure 4.2, we have the e-commerce and retail platforms, social media platforms, and search engines that play a critical role in marketing products and services. All these new institutions are a direct result of the evolution of digital technologies like the Internet, mobile, cloud computing, voice tech, AI and ML, chatbots, and robots. Metaverse environments may emerge in the future. This shows why it is necessary to explicitly include technology as an important element of the marketing strategy paradigm – it makes the marketing strategy paradigm dynamic and forward-looking which is essential for developing strategies.

E-commerce platforms, search engines, social media platforms, and omnichannel and cross-device options, all critically impact and change the customer journey. One can argue that technology is the main driver of customer preferences, habits and cultural changes, work from home, social media

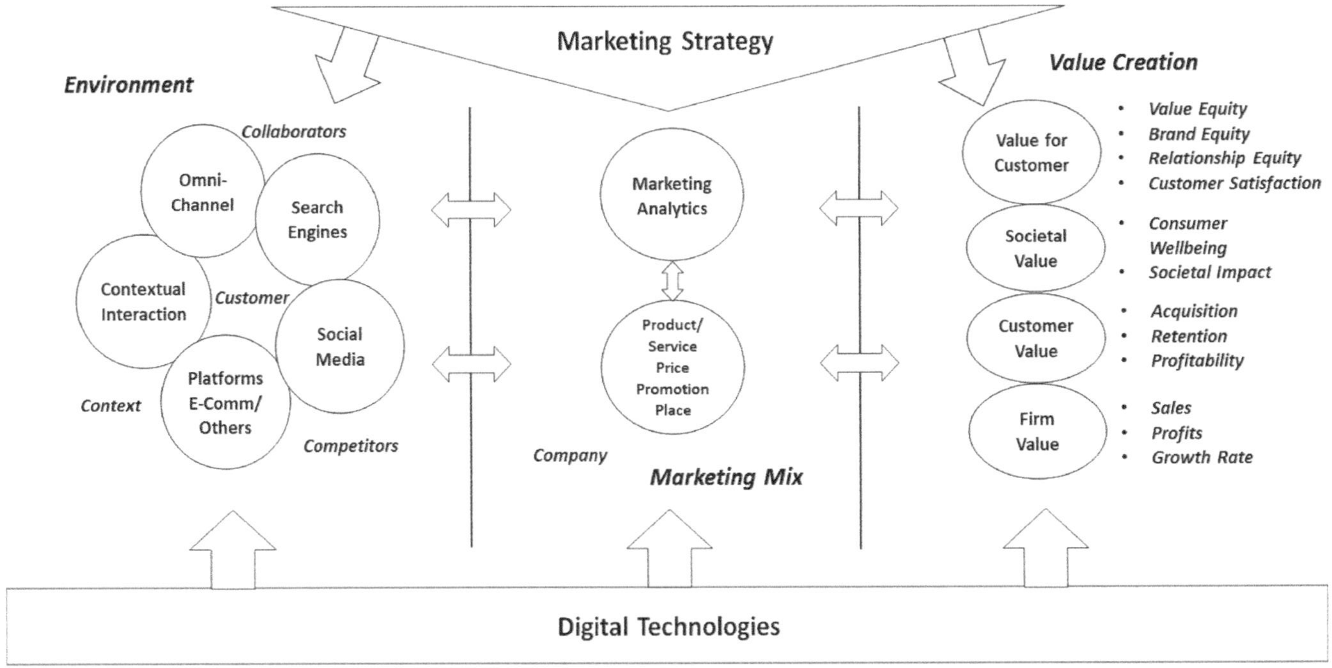

Source: Authors.

Figure 4.2 The pervasive technology paradigm

influencers, and so on. So, understanding the trends in technology, the role it plays in shaping the environment and customer preferences is important. With the rapid advancement of digital technologies, all five Cs in the environment within which firms operate are experiencing significant change. In particular, digital technologies are reducing information asymmetries between customers and sellers in various ways. Consumer behavior is changing due to access to various search technologies, both online and in mobile contexts. This changing consumer behavior affects information acquisition related to quality and price, the search process, quality and price expectations, and the resulting implications for firms.

Digital technologies play a key role in facilitating customer–customer interactions through various online media, such as word-of-mouth, online reviews and ratings, social media interactions, and user-generated content. The emergence of platforms, created through digital innovations, facilitates customer-to-customer interactions for ideation in new product/service development. Additionally, the different types of platforms connect customers and sellers in platform-based markets and those that leverage two-sided markets for revenue generation. In addition, brands are building their own platforms (Wichmann et al. 2022). These platforms are collaborators that connect a firm to its market using digital technologies.

Similarly, firms also have to deal with search engines, which function both as collaborators and platforms in acquiring customers and competing with other firms. Digital technologies interact with different contexts, including geography, privacy and security risks, regulation, and piracy. We refer to these as contextual interactions and analyze their implications for digital marketing. Technology also impacts marketing decisions of four Ps, new product designs, fueled by technology and upending markets, which we will examine in greater detail later in the chapter.

Finally, value creation (the right-hand part of Figure 4.2) encompasses value creation not only for firms and customers, but also for societies – social value creation. Rapid developments in technology can lead to unequal sharing of value creation between firms and customers while ignoring social impact. Our framework recognizes societal value creation as an integral part of value creation activities of the firm impacting all stakeholders. Therefore, firms need to consider how digital technologies can impact – both positively and negatively – the stakeholders and be cautious in how technology is implemented in marketing processes. A good example is the protection of consumer privacy and avoiding the negative impact of social media on different demographics, specifically teens.

Digital technologies ushering transformation

The emergence of new digital technology has been the driver of the changes in the environment and customer journey. The pace of change is only going to accelerate further – AI, metaverse, and blockchain technologies will further change the marketing process. Since November 2022, AI technologies, specifically generative AI technologies like ChatGPT, are ushering in new tools and opportunities for marketing.

The top left section of Figure 4.3 illustrates the impact of technology on the customer journey. The passage describes how technology impacts the customer journey, which is the process a customer goes through when interacting with a firm. This journey includes various touchpoints across the pre-purchase, purchase, and post-purchase phases. The customer journey is an iterative and dynamic process that involves different customer behaviors, such as awareness, consideration, evaluation, purchase, loyalty, and advocacy (Lemon and Verhoef 2016).

The customer journey has been influenced by technological advancements that have impacted on each stage of the process. The evolution of platforms such as search engines, social media, and e-commerce (both online and offline) has played a significant role in this evolution. Additionally, the development of digital channels, including online and mobile, has increased the accessibility of customers to firms, while ubiquitous connectivity technologies have ensured that customers can be reached anytime and anywhere they choose (Kannan and Li 2017; Verhoef et al. 2017).

Sophisticated technology has enabled firms to collect customer behavioral and demographic data, allowing for precise targeting in digital channels through display ads, paid search, and emails. Additionally, search engines enable firms to reach the right customers at the right time during their search process, helping to acquire them at the lowest cost possible. On the customer side, firms that provide omni-channel options increase the flexibility of channels, allowing customers to be in contact with the firm at all times. This approach also allows firms to reach customers more frequently at the right times, ultimately leading to a better customer experience.

Technological advances have greatly reduced search costs for customers, making it easier to find the products or services that meet their needs through the simplicity, convenience, and ease of use of these technologies. Firms that have taken advantage of these technologies have been able to provide person-

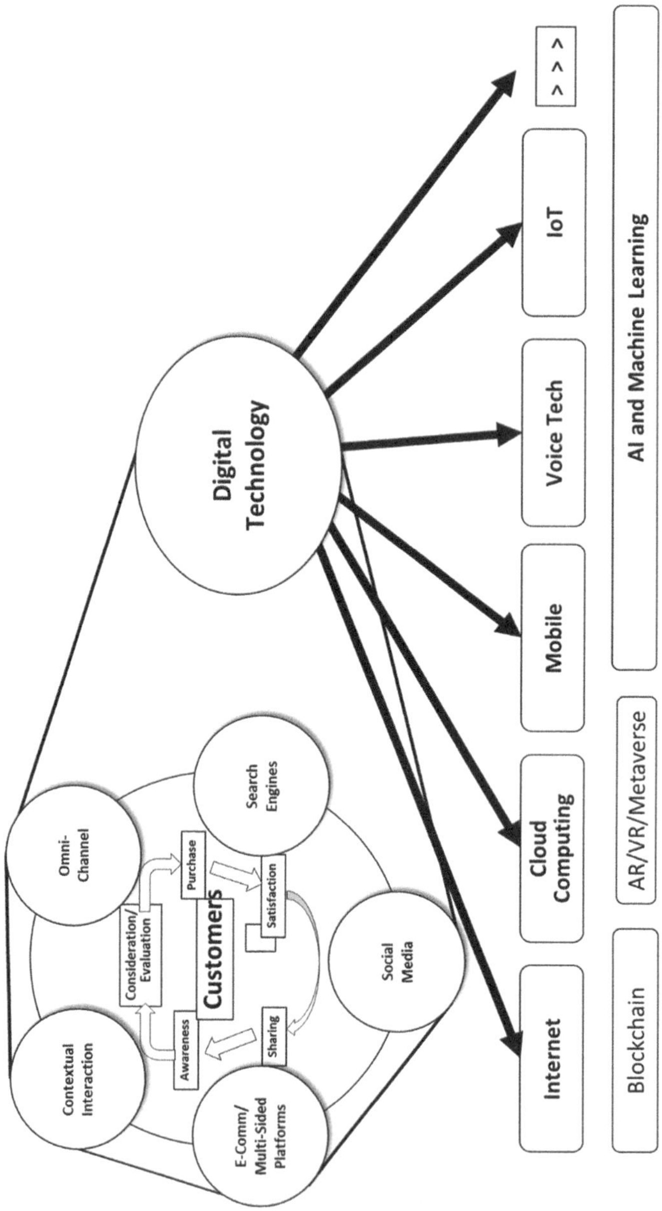

Source: Author.

Figure 4.3 Digital technology and the environment

alized recommendations and services to their customers, making the purchase process more convenient. This use of technology allows firms to offer superior value to their customers, leading to increased spending and customer loyalty.

Emerging technologies have the potential to greatly enhance the customer experience at every touchpoint in the customer journey. For instance, augmented reality (AR) and virtual reality (VR) technologies can be utilized to create immersive advertising experiences for customers. This is a marked departure from traditional marketing media, where customers are mere observers. With AR and VR, firms can create a heightened level of awareness that was previously impossible with current technologies. These new technologies hold significant promise for firms looking to improve customer experience and engagement (Hall and Takahashi 2017; Wedel et al. 2020). In addition to creating immersive advertising experiences, AR and VR technologies also offer a new way for customers to experience products. One notable example is Tiffany and Co., which adopted AR technology in its app to enhance the shopping process for engagement rings. With the app, customers can see how different diamond ring styles look on their fingers under different lighting conditions, providing a better understanding of the products and helping with evaluation and consideration. This application of AR technology provides a more personalized and interactive shopping experience, ultimately leading to greater customer engagement and satisfaction.

AI and ML methods offer powerful tools for marketers to improve the effectiveness of targeting potential consumers at the early stages of the customer journey and personalizing content and offerings. These technologies can analyze vast amounts of data to identify patterns and preferences, allowing firms to tailor their marketing efforts to individual customers. At the transaction level, technologies, fingerprint recognition, face recognition, and voice verification are now facilitating the transaction process by freeing customers from remembering transaction codes, leading to faster and more convenient transactions. Technologies such as AI robots and chatbots are ushering in new innovations in service, improving efficiencies while at the same time improving effectiveness of the service encounters (Mende et al. 2019). These developments demonstrate how technology continues to shape and improve the customer experience at every stage of the customer journey.

The advent of generative artificial intelligence (Gen AI) is revolutionizing marketing, paving the way for hyper-personalization and predictive strategies that dynamically reshape the customer journey. Gen AI, with its ability to generate data, simulate user behaviors, and automate creative processes, offers marketers the capability to craft highly personalized and contextually relevant content, significantly enhancing customer engagement and conversion rates. By analyzing vast datasets, it identifies nuanced consumer patterns, anticipates needs, and predicts future behaviors, enabling marketers to proactively address customer desires and pain points. Furthermore, Gen AI disrupts traditional advertising creation by automating and optimizing content generation, producing creative solutions that are tailored to individual consumer profiles and purchasing histories. This transformation enables a shift toward a more customer-centric marketing paradigm, where messages are not only targeted but also autonomously evolved based on continuous learning from user interactions. This synergy of AI and marketing heralds an era where customer experiences are not just understood and responded to, but also anticipated and proactively shaped by technology (Huang and Rust 2021a; Deveau et al. 2023).

Firms are increasingly using monitoring technologies that incorporate sensors and customer-level data on search, transactions, and usage to track customers' consumption experiences and anticipate future demand. By doing so, firms can induce customers to make repeat purchases at the appropriate time, either at the touch of a button or automatically. These technologies enable firms to provide a more seamless and personalized customer experience, which in turn can lead to increased customer loyalty and repeat business. As the technology continues to improve, we can expect to see even more sophisticated monitoring systems that provide even greater insight into customer behavior and preferences.

The IoT is opening up a new category of connected products, such as smart home appliances, thermostats, and self-driving cars, that offer highly personalized services and experiences to customers based on the data collected about them. By incorporating sensors and connectivity into everyday products, firms can offer customers more convenient, efficient, and personalized experiences. For example, a smart thermostat can learn a customer's preferences and automatically adjust the temperature to their liking, while a self-driving car can offer a customized entertainment experience based on the individual's preferences and behavior. As more products become connected to the IoT, we can expect to see even greater opportunities for firms to provide highly tailored and personalized experiences to their customers.

The ability to collect and analyze such vast amounts of data has also led to the emergence of predictive analytics, which can help firms anticipate customers' needs and preferences, and offer them relevant products and services before they even express a need for them. Furthermore, the combination of Gen AI, ML, and big data has enabled the development of robots, chatbots, and virtual assistants that can provide customers with 24/7 support and assistance without the need for human intervention (Huang and Rust 2021b). This not only saves time and resources for the firm but also provides convenience and instant gratification to customers.

Overall, technological advancements are revolutionizing how firms approach customer experience and marketing, providing opportunities to deliver highly personalized, convenient, and seamless experiences to customers, thereby increasing their satisfaction, loyalty, and, ultimately, profitability for the firm.

Digital effects on marketing mix

Product/Service

Within the boundaries of the firm, digital technologies are changing the concept of products in three ways to provide customers with new value propositions. First, digital technologies augment the core product with digital services and information stream. Second, digital technologies and networks with information stream help release the dormant value inherent in the products. Third, digital technologies morph products into digital services – servitization. We examine these trends and the opportunities they create for customizing and personalizing customer offerings. By varying the core product or service and the augmented digital services, firms can create unique value propositions for different customer segments.

The rise of digital technologies and the digital environment are rapidly transforming the traditional concept of a product. In a digital world, customers can access more information about products and make more informed purchasing decisions. This has led to an increased emphasis on product quality, customization, and innovation. Companies must also consider how their products fit into the larger customer experience and ecosystem.

In fact, the conventional view of a product is no longer valid (Vargo and Lusch 2017) as service has become integral to the product. In addition, information and data stream along with AI technologies are revolutionizing the concept of servitization (Huang and Rust 2021a). For example, self-driving cars with AI-enabled navigation capabilities and data stream are changing the nature of a product. This means that the previous approach of viewing the core product with additional services is now being replaced by a new perspective, in which the value of the core product is derived from its digital enhancements.

The networking of products through the IoT enables communication among products, providing enhanced value through digital services. This technology also enables a sharing economy model for a fleet of automobiles or a collection of homes (e.g., Airbnb, Uber). In this model, digital technology allows for the efficient sharing and use of resources, enabling more sustainable and cost-effective business practices. This represents a significant shift in the traditional concept of a product, as the value of a product is no longer solely derived from its physical attributes but also from its digital connectivity and the services it can provide.

In addition, the digital transformation has led to the blending of products and services, as customers increasingly expect to receive a complete solution rather than just a product. This has given rise to the concept of product-service systems (PSS), which offer a combination of physical products, software, and digital services to meet the needs of customers. PSS can be designed to increase the value customers derive from the overall offering (so that they will be willing to pay more for them). For instance, a fitness equipment company may offer a subscription-based service that provides customers with personalized workout plans and nutrition advice based on their biometric data collected from smart devices. Such digital services enhance the value of the core product and create a more compelling value proposition for customers. The implications of this trend for pricing and marketing are significant, as companies need to take into account the value of digital services when setting prices and communicating the benefits of their offerings to customers.

Li, Jain, and Kannan (2019) found that offering a free sample of a product can increase sales of the premium version, but the design of the free sample is crucial. Specifically, rather than being substitutes, free samples of the entire content can be very effective in increasing revenues. Furthermore, they find that higher-quality samples have a greater impact on the sales of popular content. In the context of software-as-a-service (SaaS), Li (2022) finds that the traditional notion of "the more, the merrier" when it comes to free-trial usage may not always hold true. Li's research found that when usage is broken down into frequency and variety, more frequent usage during the free-trial period tends to lead to higher conversion rates. However, exploring a greater variety of software during the free-trial period can actually have a negative impact on conversion rates. This suggests that SaaS providers should focus on encouraging more frequent usage of their software during free trials rather than trying to promote exploration of different features or offerings.

Pricing

The advancements in digital product lines and customized offerings to customers create pricing challenges for firms. Digital technologies also reduce menu costs and provide opportunities for dynamic pricing and yield management in product and service categories that were traditionally sold with list prices. These developments, along with online auctions, search keywords, display ads, and name-your-own-price strategies, have raised interesting research questions that we review. Moreover, as more firms adopt online and mobile channels to target and transact business with customers, the relationship between pricing and channels (both offline and online) is becoming an important issue.

Digital technologies have enhanced price transparency and intensified price competition. As a result, companies must consider how their pricing strategy aligns with the broader market and how they can utilize pricing to distinguish their products and services. Dynamic pricing and personalized pricing are becoming more widespread. Additionally, the freemium pricing model has gained significant popularity in the digital landscape, particularly for digital products associated with low marginal costs like content, SaaS, cloud services, and more.

The digital landscape presents various pricing model opportunities for firms, particularly regarding digital products and services. These products and services are often associated with minimal or zero marginal costs for production and distribution. When a firm offers various product formats in both conventional and digital versions, these different formats can be utilized as a price discrimination mechanism, ultimately resulting in increased profits. In the meantime, consumers exhibit heterogeneity in their perception of substitutability and complementarity, particularly in terms of the degree of complementarity between product formats. By bundling multiple formats under these conditions, firms can increase their profits.

Pricing in the digital environment is more dynamic compared to the offline situation due to several reasons. Consumers' search cost is low, and they search for products and services more frequently. Competitive pressures prompt firms to implement rapid changes in pricing strategies, and retailers can respond quickly due to low menu costs. The increasing use of auctions in customer acquisition, such as in search engines and retargeting, attracts more selective customers to retailers' websites. Online retailers can measure demand, track competitors' prices, and make price adjustments faster due to lower menu costs.

As IoT, ubiquitous connectivity, and networked products continue to advance, pricing of products augmented with digital services will become a crucial area of research. Therefore, the pricing of information access and connectivity is anticipated to emerge as an essential research domain.

Promotion

Regarding promotion, in addition to traditional means of communication like print, radio, and television, the digital environment offers new ways for firms to reach customers and promote their products and services through emails, display advertisements, and social media. There are new ways in which social media is being harnessed by firms to reach customer segments using influencers (Haenlein et al. 2020). The effectiveness of these new media and their contribution over traditional media in building brands and affecting outcome variables of interest has been researched. More recent forms of promotional tools include location-based mobile promotions and personalized promotions.

Managers and academics are grappling with questions about the effectiveness of new media and their incremental contributions over traditional media in brand building and affecting outcome variables of interest (Li and Kannan 2014). Newer forms of promotional tools, such as influencer marketing, location-based mobile promotions, and personalized promotions, are being increasingly employed and have significant implications for firms in providing value to customers. These novel channels for customer communications and promotions are not only online and mobile but also sub-channels within each of these environments, including social channels, search engines, and email, which assist firms in providing substantial value to customers. The newer online environments of video game ecosystems and metaverse provide interesting possibilities for firms to promote their brand and engage with customers (Yoo et al. 2023; Haenlein et al. 2023). AR, virtual assistants, chatbots, geofencing, and proximity marketing all provide exciting and engaging ways to promote brands, products, and services.

Place

The advent of the Internet dramatically changed the distribution of products and services. Companies are now optimizing their online presence, including their website, mobile presence, and various digital platforms, to reach their target audience. Traditional channels such as television, radio, and print have been redefined and complemented by a surge of digital platforms, notably social media, email marketing, SEO, and content marketing, each encapsulating a unique conduit through which brands communicate their value propositions. Personalization and data-driven insights are becoming increasingly important in creating effective channel strategies.

Digital technologies empower businesses with the tools to craft highly targeted and personalized marketing campaigns. Big data and analytics facilitate marketers in deciphering intricate patterns of consumer behavior, thereby sculpting marketing messages that resonate with specific audience segments. Consequently, businesses are capacitated to optimize their marketing spend, directing resources toward channels and messages that guarantee the highest return on investment. Moreover, programmatic advertising, enabled by sophisticated algorithms, automates the buying of ads and being able to target audiences more precisely, which increases the chances of success of the marketing campaigns and reduces the cost for the company. The advent of social media has not only expanded the horizons of marketing channels but has also transformed them into a two-way communication stream. Customers are no longer passive recipients of marketing messages; they actively engage, respond, and communicate with brands, thereby influencing marketing strategies and narratives. The reciprocal communication fostered by digital channels like social media platforms, forums, and blogs has also heightened the significance of online reputation management within the digital marketing framework.

With the growing importance of customer experience and engagement, and the increasing control customers have over their information search, firms must actively design and coordinate their omni-channel interactions to create a seamless customer journey (Verhoef et al. 2015). The growth of brand platforms is one way to provide such a capability (Wichmann et al. 2022). The availability of real-time data on customer touchpoints can aid in developing a personalized omni-channel strategy at the individual customer level. Customer relationship management (CRM) systems and other AI-driven tools facilitate the delivery of individualized messages and offers to customers in real time, enhancing customer experience and loyalty across channels at every touchpoint.

Digital impact on marketing outcomes

The impact of digital technologies on outcomes (the four ellipses on the right in Figure 4.2 under Value Creation) can be measured across different dimensions – in creating value for customers, value for the society, and in extracting value for the firm (customer value), and the overall impact reflecting in firm value. These outcomes reflect how effectively the firm has been able to leverage the opportunities provided by digital technologies to create value for customers and for itself. As depicted in Figure 4.2, the firm leverages the interactions between digital technologies and its environment, as well as its own strategic and tactical actions, to achieve these outcomes. One of the main outcomes of these interactions and decisions by the firm is creating value for customers – there are three main dimensions on which they are created (value equity, brand equity, and relationship equity; see Rust et al. 2005) and these equities (along with societal value) collectively determine how satisfied the customer is with the firm and its offering. The societal value has emerged as an important component of the overall value creation – the focus on "doing good," creating societal value, protecting the environment, and the activities that make up ESG (environmental, social, and governance) orientation make up this important component. All these value creation activities by the firm impact the value it can extract from the customers – in terms of lowering their acquisition costs, retaining them for a longer time, and increasing their spending and profitability with the firm – all leading to increased customer lifetime value. At the aggregate level, this value extraction impacts the firm value as a function of its sales, profits, and growth rate. Different channels and media contribute to these outcome measures in different ways, and the understanding of these measures is necessary for appropriate and effective marketing actions.

Finally, marketing research focuses on acquiring and processing information generated by digital technologies to better understand the environment, actions, and outcomes and to inform the firm's marketing strategies. This includes understanding customer browsing and search behavior on websites, mobile sites, on platforms of various types, analyzing online reviews, social interactions, and tags to gauge customer perceptions of the brand, and developing specific methodologies and metrics (see Wedel and Kannan 2016).

Implications for practice

As businesses continue to adapt to digital transformation, it has raised new questions and challenges for both practitioners and academics in the field of marketing. Below is a non-exhaustive list of the questions and implications that call for consideration from a practitioner perspective.

First, marketing capabilities have shifted from conventional approaches toward more tech-intensive strategies. Data analytics capability is essential in deciphering the troves of consumer data available, enabling firms to derive insights into consumer behaviors, preferences, and pain points (Wedel and

Kannan 2016; Dong and Yang 2019). The aptitude to leverage AI and ML for predictive analytics and customer segmentation allows marketers to formulate targeted and personalized marketing interventions. Furthermore, digital content creation capability, encompassing video production, graphics design, and copywriting tailored for digital platforms, becomes crucial in capturing the dwindling attention span of online audiences. This calls for a proactive and continuous upgrade of marketing capabilities infusing them with state-of-the-art technologies. This is a learning mindset that the top management team needs to inculcate within the firm.

Second, along with capabilities, marketing assets have also evolved, accentuating the significance of digital assets in constructing a robust online presence. The website, often regarded as the digital face of a business, must not only be aesthetically appealing but also user-friendly, mobile-optimized, and SEO-integrated, ensuring visibility and accessibility. Social media profiles, another pivotal digital asset, serve as platforms for brands to engage, interact, and build relationships with consumers, demanding consistent, relevant, and authentic content that resonates with the audience (Dong and Wu 2015). Additionally, customer databases, enriched with relevant and actionable consumer data, become invaluable assets for enabling personalized marketing, enhancing customer relationship management, and fostering loyalty.

The synergy between marketing capabilities and assets becomes an essential ingredient for success and chief marketing officers (CMOs) need to ensure that these are aligned. The ability to strategically utilize digital assets through adept capabilities can yield a competitive advantage, enabling firms to navigate through the digital marketing opportunities. For instance, a well-curated website can serve as a potent lead generation tool only when marketers possess the capability to leverage SEO effectively, ensuring visibility among the target audience. It is also important to ensure that data privacy and security are interwoven into digital marketing capabilities and assets to engender consumer trust.

Third, the ability of networked products to transmit usage data and enable personalized experiences raises questions about how firms can effectively utilize this data and create value for customers. Understanding the role of customers in the design process is also important as well as ethical use of the data, as it can lead to the creation of more user-friendly products. Finally, the impact of ubiquitous connectivity on product delivery and the potential for virtual and AR integration also present interesting marketing opportunities.

Fourth, regarding pricing, the digital environment has led to increasingly dynamic pricing, with firms changing prices based on contextual factors such as time of day and day of the week. This raises important questions about pricing, price matching, and the implications for price competition and customer expectations. As digital transformation continues to penetrate different verticals and markets, it is crucial to examine the impact of dynamic pricing on these areas.

Fifth, while the emergence of social media has opened up new opportunities to engage customers, increased polarization of political views, fragmented markets, and filter bubbles provide challenges which the marketing leaders of a firm have to carefully navigate. Some of the problems involve promotions meant for a specific segment going against the beliefs of another segment. In 2023, Bud Light faced a backlash from its traditional consumer segments when the company reached out to a LGBTQ+ influencer to pitch the product to that community during Pride month. Adidas got into a similar situation in 2022 when its celebrity spokesperson Kanye West behaved in a manner unbecoming of a spokesperson for a brand. Brands in social media are open to instant mass feedback and backlash from consumers which means marketing managers need to make their decisions carefully. Brand buzz can change in real time as a function of such events and impact brand reputation (Rust et al. 2021).

Sixth, with digital transformation and new technologies, established brand loyalties are under threat. An article in the *Wall Street Journal* shows how technology developments affect customer preferences. With new electric vehicles (EVs) arriving, early customers are very eager to try out new brands, and brand loyalty no longer exists for these newer versions of automobiles (McLain 2022).

Finally, CMOs need to embrace and own technology developments within their own organizations, rather than relegate them to chief technology officers and chief information officers. They need to disrupt the markets with technology leading from the front. With increasing number of channels and options to reach customers, media mix allocation decisions are becoming difficult. It is important that CMOs collect data from campaigns and use data-driven decision-making to make optimal choices and proactively seek out new channels enabled by technology advances.

Implications for research

Future research about promotion in the digital environment may prioritize exploring how targeting can be effectively coordinated across various channels and devices, as this can significantly impact customer acquisition costs and media mix decisions. Research is needed to improve the estimation accuracy of customer acquisition costs and the efficiency and effectiveness of marketing spending. It is imperative to gauge the spillovers between online and offline channels and between online and mobile channels, through a better understanding of customers' purchase journeys. Another area that requires further research is reconciling the marketing mix decisions made at the aggregate level with attribution estimates based on individual-level customer data. This research can aid in developing more effective customer acquisition strategies.

The important implications for research (as well as practice) are that we have to embrace technology as a fundamental element of marketing. As researchers, we need to view marketing from a technology perspective as much as we do from other stakeholder perspectives. In the past, many of the developments in marketing have come from practitioners, with researchers examining the phenomenon after they have been implemented in practice. With rapid technological changes and digital transformation, researchers need to focus on digital technology as a key element of marketing and how it will define marketing processes in the future.

Studying technology as a key element of marketing is a critical necessity. For example, we can anticipate the impact of technology in leveling the playing field for brands just as we saw in the case of EVs, the EV technology makes it easy for an entrant to compete against an established brand. Similarly, mobile app introduction in the hospitality industry by travel intermediaries like Expedia and Booking.com has cut into the market share of hotel chains significantly and changed the competitive landscape (Gu and Kannan 2021).

A technology perspective helps in better understanding marketing impact. Here's an example: Technology should be viewed as a double-edged sword rather than assuming technology always has a positive impact. There can be a dark side to technology adoption as recent examples of personalization implementation have exposed customers to privacy violations.

A technology perspective helps to view the benefits of technology adoption from a holistic perspective, rather than from a narrow application specific perspective. A recent study on adopting AI technology for business process automation in the banking context shows spillover to customer facing interactions, even though the process automated was an upstream operation (Ordanini et al. 2023). Also, the customer centricity impact of technology adoption need not be uniform across users. Another recent study shows the benefits of adopting and personalizing online content for education – using AI technology benefits smarter students more than the others (Kim et al. 2023).

Conclusion

The growing significance of technology in marketing highlights the essential need for both academics and practitioners to acknowledge and embrace it as a critical aspect of their work. With technology becoming a necessity for businesses to stay competitive in the market and provide customers with the best possible experiences, ignoring or resisting it can lead to missed opportunities and reduced customer satisfaction. Therefore, marketers must keep up with the latest technological advancements and find innovative ways to integrate them into their marketing strategies to ensure success in the market.

Adopting technology transformation to enhance customer experiences throughout the path to purchase may not always be a winning strategy for firms. The success of implementing such technology depends on various factors such as the product/service category and the degree of competition in the industry. It is essential for firms to closely monitor the usage of technological innovations by customers and their impact on the outcome variable of interest. Market research using observational techniques and surveys can help understand the real impact of technology. Managers cannot assume positive outcomes simply because other firms have had positive experiences with technology. They need to account for market and customer differences that can impact the outcome.

References

Deveau, R., S. J. Griffin, and S. Reis (2023), "AI-powered marketing and sales reach new heights with generative AI," McKinsey Insights Article, May. https://www.mckinsey.com/capabilities/growth-marketing-and-sales/our-insights/ai-powered-marketing-and-sales-reach-new-heights-with-generative-ai.

Dolan, R. J. (2014), *Marketing Reading: Framework for Marketing Strategy Formation*. Boston, MA: Harvard Business Publishing.

Dong, J. Q. and W. Wu (2015), "Business value of social media technologies: Evidence from online user innovation communities," *Journal of Strategic Information Systems*, 24(2), 113–127.

Dong, J. Q. and C.-H. Yang (2019), "Business value of big data analytics: A system-theoretic approach and empirical test," *Information and Management*. https://doi.org/10.1016/j.im.2018.11.001.

Gu, X. and P. K. Kannan (2021), "The dark side of mobile app adoption: Examining the impact on customers' multichannel purchase," *Journal of Marketing Research*, 58(2), 246–264.

Haenlein, M., E. Anadol, T. Farnsworth, H. Hugo, J. Hunichen, and D. Welte (2020), "Navigating the new era of influencer marketing: How to be successful on Instagram, TikTok, & Co.," *California Management Review*, 63(1), 5–25.

Haenlein, M., B. Libai, and E. Muller (2023), "Satiation and cross promotion: Selling and swapping users in mobile games," *International Journal of Research in Marketing* 40(2), 342–361.

Hall, S. and R. Takahashi (2017), "Augmented and virtual reality: The promise and peril of immersive technologies." https://www.weforum.org/agenda/2017/09/augmented-and-virtual-reality-will-change-how-we-create-and-consume-and-bring-new-risks/.

Huang, M.-H. and R. T. Rust (2021a), "A strategic framework for artificial intelligence in marketing," *Journal of the Academy of Marketing Science*, 49(1), 30–50.

Huang, M.-H. and R. T. Rust (2021b), "Engaged to a robot: The role of AI in service," *Journal of Service Research*, 24(1), 30–41.

Kalaignanam, K., Tuli, K. R., Kushwaha, T., Lee, L., and Gal, D. (2021). Marketing Agility: The Concept, Antecedents, and a Research Agenda. *Journal of Marketing*, 85(1), 35–58. https://doi.org/10.1177/0022242920952760

Kannan, P. K. and H. Li (2017), "Digital marketing: A framework, review and research agenda," *International Journal of Research in Marketing*, 34(1), 22–45.

Kartik, K., T. Kapil, K. Tarun, L. Leonard, and G. David (2021), "Marketing agility: The concept, antecedents, and a research agenda," *Journal of Marketing*, 85(1), 35–58.

Kim, C., P. K. Kannan, R. Agarwal, and W. Rand (2023), "Improving the efficacy of online learning using artificial intelligence" (working paper).

Lemon, K. N. and P. C. Verhoef (2016), "Understanding customer experience throughout the customer journey," *Journal of Marketing*, 80(6), 69–96.

Li, H. (2022), "Converting free users to paid subscribers in the SaaS context: The impact of marketing touchpoints, message content, and usage," *Production and Operations Management*, 31(5), 2185–2203. https://doi.org/10.1111/poms.13672.

Li, H., S. Jain, and P. K. Kannan (2019), "Optimal design of free samples for digital products and services," *Journal of Marketing Research*, 56(3), 419–438.

Li, H. and P. K. Kannan (2014), "Attributing conversions in a multichannel online marketing environment: An empirical model and a field experiment," *Journal of Marketing Research*, 51(1), 40–56.

McLain, S. (2022), "With new EVs arriving, brand loyalty goes out the window," *The Wall Street Journal*, December 22.

Mende, M., M. L. Scott, J. van Doorn, D. Grewal, and I. Shanks (2019), "Service robots rising: How humanoid robots influence service experiences and elicit compensatory consumer responses," *Journal of Marketing Research*, 56(4), 535–556.

Ordanini, A., A. Nanni, and P. K. Kannan (2023), "Spillover effects from AI automation: Evidence from the banking mortgage process" (working paper).

Rust, R. T., K. N. Lemon, and D. Narayandas (2005), *Customer Equity Management*. Upper Saddle River, NJ: Prentice Hall.

Rust, R. T., W. Rand, M.-H. Huang, A. T. Stephen, G. Brooks, and T. Chabuk (2021), "Real-time brand reputation tracking using social media," *Journal of Marketing*, 85(4), 21–43. https://doi.org/10.1177/0022242921995173.

Vargo, S. L., and R. F. Lusch (2017), "Service-dominant logic 2025," *International Journal of Research in Marketing*, 34(1), 46–67.

Verhoef, P. C. and T. H. A. Bijmolt (2019), "Marketing perspectives on digital business models: A framework and overview of the special issue," *International Journal of Research in Marketing*, 36(2). https://doi.org/10.1016/j.ijresmar.2019.08.001.

Verhoef, P. C., T. Broekhuizen, Y. Bart, A. Bhattacharya, J. Q. Dong, N. Fabian, and M. Haenlein (2021), "Digital transformation: A multidisciplinary reflection and research agenda," *Journal of Business Research*, 122, 889–901.

Verhoef, P. C., P. K. Kannan, and J. J. Inman (2015), "From multi-channel retailing to omni-channel retailing: Introduction to the special issue on multi-channel retailing," *Journal of Retailing*, 91(2), 174–181.

Verhoef, P. C., A. T. Stephen, P. K. Kannan, X. Luo, V. Abhishek, M. Andrews, Y. Bart, H. Datta, N. Fong, D. L. Hoffman, M. M. Hu, T. Novak, W. Rand, and Y. Zhang (2017), "Consumer connectivity in a complex, technology-enabled, and mobile-oriented world with smart products," *Journal of Interactive Marketing*, 40(1), 1–8.

Wedel, M., E. Bigne, and J. Zhang (2020), "Virtual and augmented reality: Advancing research in consumer marketing," *International Journal of Research in Marketing*, 37(3), 443–465.

Wedel, M. and P. K. Kannan (2016), "Marketing analytics for data-rich environments," *Journal of Marketing*, 80(6), 97–121.

Wichmann, J. R. K., N. Wiegand, and W. J. Reinartz (2022), "The platformization of brands," *Journal of Marketing*, 86(1), 109–131.

Yoo, K., R. Welden, K. Hewett, and M. Haenlein (2023), "The merchants of meta: A research agenda to understand the future of retailing in the metaverse," *Journal of Retailing*, 99(2), 173–192.

PART II

Capabilities and resources of digital transformation

5 Data science and privacy concerns in digital transformation

Jaap E. Wieringa

Over the past decades, there has been a remarkable surge in the amount of data generated across various sectors of society. With the ease and affordability of collecting personal data in today's digital world, customer data are now available in abundance and in great detail (Sheth & Kellstadt 2021). These data come from a wide range of sources, including social media platforms, sensors, and electronic devices (Petrescu, Krishen, & Bui 2020). For businesses and organizations, this wealth of data has become indispensable, enabling them to gain a better understanding of their customers and provide products and services that are better suited to their needs and preferences. However, these data are often unstructured, complex, and voluminous, making them challenging to manage and analyze.

Also, the methodologies for analyzing customer data have evolved considerably over time. Wedel and Kannan (2016) present an overview of these methodological advancements since the beginning of the twentieth century, ranging from basic statistical analyses to machine learning. At the time, they noted that machine learning methods were already applied in practice but had not received much attention from marketing scholars. However, more recently, this trend has shifted (see Brei 2020; France & Ghose 2019; Sheth 2021 for comprehensive overviews). The combination of the increased availability of data and the emergence of powerful tools to analyze them is closely tied to digital transformation and has revolutionized how organizations operate, deliver value to customers, and compete in the modern business landscape. Currently, the big data market generates over 55 billion dollars in revenue, and it is expected to grow to 103 billion dollars by 2027 (Statista 2022).

The growing availability of detailed personal data and the unbridled opportunities that this provides have led to an increased awareness of the importance of protecting them from unauthorized access and use. A recent study conducted across Europe by DDMA (2023) reveals that about two-thirds of the Dutch population is concerned about their online privacy, a figure that has remained stable over the past few years. In response to concerns about privacy, legislation has been put in place around the globe. According to Verhoef et al. (2021b), privacy laws in Europe and Canada are the strictest, followed by the United States and Australia. The development of privacy legislation in emerging countries is still in its early stages, but progress is being made.

Addressing privacy concerns and putting privacy legislation into business practice can be challenging and frequently sparks extensive debates within organizations (Martin & Palmatier 2020). These discussions revolve around striking an appropriate balance between a sufficient level of privacy protection and harnessing the valuable insights that detailed data on individual customer attitudes and behaviors can provide. Such trade-offs are typically difficult to make due to a lack of objective ways to navigate the balance between data utility and privacy protection. Moreover, ethical aspects of the use of data of individuals further complicate this process. Industry federations may facilitate organizations in making these trade-offs. For example, the Data & Insights Network in the Netherlands is developing privacy guidelines for affiliated marketing research agencies to address these challenges.

Organizations are not the only entities that must navigate a privacy balance. Also at the more micro level of customers, an important privacy balance can be identified. A customer who is asked to share his or her personal data with an organization will also consider the benefits that this will bring and weigh this against any potential negative outcomes. Consequently, also on the customer side, a trade-off is made between positive and negative privacy consequences; those that are experienced by individual customers. In some of the studies that investigate this privacy balance, the balance is viewed as an implicit process where, for example, trust in a company might alleviate the perceived privacy risks that consumers associate with sharing their data (Wang, Beatty, & Foxx 2004). In other work, the privacy balance is studied more explicitly, and the so-called privacy calculus is put forward as an important mechanism that drives consumers' decisions on whether to share their personal data or not.

In this chapter, we review the literature on both types of privacy balances and summarize how earlier scholarly work has increased our understanding of the privacy decisions of consumers and organizations. Furthermore, we draw attention to the fact that these two perspectives are connected. On the one hand, the data-sharing decisions of consumers affect the quality, the level of detail, and the volume of data assets that organizations can analyze. Furthermore, customers are increasingly recognizing the potential value their data holds for organizations, particularly those pursuing digital transformation. On the other hand, firms realize that their privacy measures can also be used as a unique selling point to attract new customers and retain existing ones. The interplay between customer and organizational privacy balances leads to the so-called "market for privacy," where privacy and/or data can be viewed as a type of currency that has value in a market where there is demand and supply for personally identifiable data. While the existence of this "market for privacy" is discussed in a number of papers, there is not much scholarly work that jointly considers the customer and the firm privacy balancing acts in one coherent setting. In this chapter, we bring these two perspectives together and propose a conceptual framework that connects the two.

The setup of this chapter is as follows. In the next section, we outline the importance of data and data science for digital transformation. Then we turn to the customers' perspective and discuss their privacy balance. In the subsequent section, we review the literature on the firm's privacy balance, followed by a section where we connect the two perspectives and present our proposed conceptual framework that links the elements of both privacy balances. In the final section, we discuss our conclusions and present managerial recommendations as well as a research agenda that follows from our proposed conceptual two-sided privacy model.

The role of data and data science in digital transformation

In their discussion of strategic imperatives of digital transformation, Verhoef et al. (2021a) consider having "big data capabilities" as one of the key resources that are required for a successful transformation to a new digital business model. Digital transformation involves many strategic choices to optimize processes, improve customer experiences, and stay competitive in the digital age. Sound digital data and strong digital data science skills enable organizations to make informed decisions based on data analyses, enabling firms to create and appropriate more value from their digital transformation efforts (Reddy & Reinartz 2017). Given its pervasive impact on all business functions, data science is becoming an integral part of business, affecting marketing, supply chain management, logistics, human resource management, accounting, and finance (Verhoef et al. 2021b).

Consultancy agents typically report higher potential gains from data and data analytics than the more nuanced results of scientific publications (Gupta & George 2016), but both types of sources suggest that significant improvements in financial performance and market value are achievable (Brynjolfsson & McElheran 2016; Huang, Wang, & Huang 2020). Furthermore, academic research shows that the impact of data analytics is interdependent with other technologies such as social media (Dong & Yang 2020), and that the variety and the veracity of data, rather than just its volume, are crucial factors in driving these outcomes (Cappa et al. 2021). According to Mikalef et al. (2019), data and supporting technological resources are essential for achieving performance gains, and strong technical skills are necessary for converting data into actionable insights. In highly uncertain market conditions, managerial capabilities in problem-solving through analytics are essential contributors to high performance. Based on their experiences with many digital transformations, Davenport and Redman (2020) also identify having a process orientation and the capability for organizational change as key talent areas for a successful data-driven digital transformation.

However, there are also challenges associated with the use of data and data science in digital transformations. In a broad literature review, Sivarajah et al. (2017) distinguish between data challenges, which relate to the characteristics of the data itself (e.g., data volume, data quality, data volatility), process challenges, which refer to the issues that are encountered while processing the data (e.g., how to collect the data and how to analyze the data), and management challenges, such as privacy, security, governance, and ethical aspects. For this chapter, we will focus on the challenges that relate to privacy.

Privacy Concerns and Privacy Legislation

Privacy is a multifaceted concept that has been defined differently across various disciplinary perspectives. From a legal standpoint, privacy is viewed as the right to manage the flow of information concerning oneself, as expressed in regulations such as the "right to be forgotten" or the right to erasure (European Commission 2016). Beke, Eggers, and Verhoef (2018) distinguish physical privacy from informational privacy. Physical privacy refers to preventing intrusion into an individual's personal space, while informational privacy pertains to the monitoring and recording of an individual's behavior by others. This involves the collection and storage of information without the need for physical presence. In line with their conceptualization, we define privacy as the extent to which a consumer is aware of and has the ability to control the collection, storage, and use of personal information by a firm. In this definition, personal information refers to all information that relates to an individual consumer (European Commission 2016).

Consumers are increasingly worried about the growing collection, storage, and use of personal information, and are anxious about a lack of transparency or control over their personal data (Beke et al. 2018). As noted in the introduction section, privacy laws and regulations have been enacted in different parts of the world to address these privacy concerns.

In the European Union, the General Data Protection Regulation (GDPR) became effective on May 28, 2018, to protect consumers' data rights (Skiera et al. 2022). The GDPR includes key provisions such as data minimization and data anonymization. Data minimization involves only using data that is necessary for the agreed-upon purpose, and not retaining it longer than necessary to fulfill that purpose. Data anonymization refers among others to the process of ensuring that individuals cannot be identified based on their data. Public awareness of the GDPR has more than doubled since its introduction (DDMA 2023). However, while two-thirds of the population is aware of its existence, their practical knowledge of the regulation remains limited. Consumers consider financial (70 percent) and medical (69 percent) information to be the most personal, followed by IP and postal addresses while browsing behavior and passive data collection via apps or wearable devices receive an average score.

In addition to the GDPR, new legislation has emerged to create a safer and fairer digital space for businesses and users alike. The Digital Services Act and Digital Markets Act form a single set of rules that apply across the European Union, to protect the fundamental rights of digital service users and foster innovation, growth, and competitiveness. Meanwhile, the proposed Artificial Intelligence Act seeks to prohibit certain AI applications and designate high-risk uses of AI that will require stricter requirements for transparency, safety, and human oversight.

The United States does not have a singular law that covers the privacy of all types of data. Instead, it has several laws for specific types of data, and privacy regulation differs across states. Privacy protection is strongest in California where the California Consumer Privacy Act (CCPA) regulates how businesses handle the personal information of California residents. The CCPA grants Californian residents the right to know what personal information businesses collect about them, and whether their data are sold or disclosed and to whom. It also provides the right to say no to the sale of personal data and to request firms to delete their information, as well as the right not to be discriminated against for exercising their privacy rights. Following California's example, privacy regulation was expected to come into effect in 2023 in other states such as Colorado, Connecticut, Utah, and Virginia.

The increased attention for privacy concerns and the stricter privacy regulations may cause individuals to be less willing to share their data. They perceive the associated privacy risks as potential costs, which likely reduces their inclination to share data (Reddy & Reinartz 2017). At the same time, they also see benefits of sharing their data with organizations, such as gaining access to new products and services, greater convenience, more choice, new experiences, and lower prices. In the upcoming section, we will focus on how consumers weigh the costs and benefits of their privacy decisions. In the subsequent section, we will discuss the firm perspective.

Striking the privacy balance from the customer perspective

Both academic studies as well as professional literature conclude that consumers' response to privacy concerns is heterogeneous. For example, Aguirre et al. (2016) observe that consumers respond differently to personalization efforts, and the DDMA privacy monitor identifies three types of individuals, based on their willingness to share personal data. These are the pragmatics (the largest segment, representing approximately 40–50 percent) who are somewhat concerned about their online privacy but still willing to share their data, the unconcerned (about 30 percent) who are not very worried about their online privacy, and the skeptics (20–30 percent) who are highly concerned about their online privacy and are unwilling to share their data (DDMA 2023).

To better understand consumer privacy intentions and behavior, earlier studies focused on measuring privacy concern, which relates to the uneasiness or worries a consumer may have about the collection, storage, use, and control of personal information, as well as transparency issues. Beke et al. (2018) outline several operationalizations of privacy concern and related constructs that are studied in the literature, including privacy risk, perceived privacy, informational sensitivity, intrusiveness, and vulnerability. Smith, Dinev, and Xu (2011) review a number of scales, including the Concern for Information Privacy (CFIP) scale which is based on four data-related dimensions of privacy concerns (collection, errors, secondary use, and unauthorized access to information) and its adaptations to the Internet context (Malhotra, Kim, & Agarwal 2004). Ioannou, Tussyadiah, and Miller (2021) develop a scale specifically for the travel market that measures travelers' online privacy concerns. However, quantifying perceptions of privacy has proven to be difficult (Dinev et al. 2013).

While some of these constructs have been shown to successfully explain privacy intentions, they turn out not to be particularly useful in explaining the privacy-related behavior of consumers. For example, Tan et al. (2012) find that privacy concerns do not directly affect users' acceptance of social networking websites, but moderate the effects of perceived usefulness, and perceived ease of use, on users' intention to continue to use social networking sites. Spiekermann, Großklags, and Berendt (2001) observed that customers, irrespective of their specific privacy concerns, answered a majority of questions even if these were highly personal in an online shopping environment. Norberg, Horne, and Horne (2007) extend this finding and show that levels of actual disclosure significantly exceeded individuals' intentions to disclose. Such findings are in line with other studies that conclude that consumers' privacy attitudes or perceptions are inconsistent with their actual privacy-related behavior (Barth & de Jong 2017; Joinson et al. 2010). This discrepancy has been coined the privacy paradox (Gerber, Gerber, & Volkamer 2018; Kokolakis 2017; Norberg et al., 2007).

Researchers have proposed various explanations for this phenomenon (Acquisti, Brandimarte, & Loewenstein 2015; Dinev, McConnell, & Smith 2015). People often lack awareness of the information they are sharing and how it can be utilized. Even when individuals possess full knowledge of the consequences, they may still experience uncertainty regarding their privacy preferences. Other explanations suggest that certain aspects of consumer behavior are inherently inconsistent or affected by bounded rationality (Gigerenzer 2020). Furthermore, privacy concerns may not be triggered in low-involvement situations, such as online searches or mobile phone usage, where biases and heuristics can heavily influence decision-making. Additionally, individuals may be unaware that their information is being collected or used, lack control over privacy practices employed by companies, or have limited viable alternatives (Beke et al. 2018).

While these explanations might provide reasons for the existence of the privacy paradox, they are not necessarily helpful in the issue that we noted earlier: privacy concerns do not explain privacy-related behavior well, and specifically are not effective in explaining when and why consumers decide to share their personal information with a firm. Beke et al. (2022) take a different approach and consider the so-called privacy calculus as a possible explanation for the observed privacy behavior of customers.

The Privacy Calculus

The privacy calculus is based on the idea that consumers' privacy choices are shaped by an internal trade-off between positive and negative consequences of their decisions. In this view, privacy is defined as a commodity, encapsulating the idea of economic value and cost-trade benefit (Smith et al. 2011). Such a calculus perspective of privacy suggests that when requested to provide personal information to corporations, consumers perform a risk–benefit analysis to assess the outcomes they would face in return for the information and respond accordingly. This is in line with the 2023 edition of the European privacy monitor, where it is concluded that consumers consider the "What's in it for me" criterion as an important determinant of their privacy decisions (DDMA 2023).

Such cost–benefit analyses are broadly studied in the literature on risk-taking behavior, where it is noted that the trade-off between the costs and the benefits occurs in several dimensions. Beke et al. (2022) review the risk literature and identify six dimensions of risk: financial, performance, time, psychological, social, and physical safety. Building on these dimensions, they define six types of privacy consequences to conceptualize the privacy calculus, where physical safety is replaced by the broader, better-fitting construct security. Consequently, the consequences that they consider are:

1. Financial
2. Performance
3. Time
4. Psychological
5. Social
6. Security.

Financial consequences relate to the monetary gains or losses that consumers might face when sharing their data with a firm. Performance consequences refer to the improvements in products and services that firms provide to customers, based on insights that they derive from personal information shared by customers. Sharing personal data with firms may also have time consequences for customers. Allowing firms to collect, store, and use their information might reduce or increase the time they need to interact or transact with firms. Psychological consequences that consumers experience when sharing personal data pertain to the feelings (whether positive or negative) they have for the firm. Customers experience social consequences when their social status or their interpersonal relationships are affected by their data-sharing decisions.

The security consequences that Beke et al. (2022) consider pertain to the safety of consumers' information.

It is important to note that each of these consequences can take a positive and negative valence in their conceptualization of the privacy calculus. They also acknowledge that the likelihood of each of these consequences occurring may be context dependent.

The PRICAL Index

Beke et al. (2022) validate the theoretical conceptualization of the privacy calculus into these six types of consequences or dimensions with consumers and managers and develop a scale to quantify the privacy calculus. The resulting scale, which they label the PRICAL index, consists of 34 items that jointly measure the six theoretical dimensions that they identified. The scale is validated in four studies and passed the construct validity and the external validity tests.

One study in Beke et al. (2022) involves a field study on usage-based car insurance. Usage-based insurance offers customers a possible discount on their insurance fee in exchange for information about their driving behavior. The Dutch insurer that participated in this study invited a selection of their customers to join this program. These customers had to decide whether to accept or to refuse sharing their driving information in exchange for a possible reduction in their insurance fees, depending on a "safety score" of their driving. If they agreed to partake in the program, they also granted permission for the installation of an electronic device into their cars for the duration of the study, enabling a real-time data stream of their driving behavior to be transmitted to the insurer's data system. Each participating customer was given access to insights into their driving behavior via a web portal and an app, and this data was also used to calculate a safety score that determined the customer's reduction in the insurance fee. In total, 616 policyholders accepted the invitation to share their data, while 84 refused. Each of these 700 customers not only shared their decision with the insurer but also filled out a survey containing the items of the PRICAL index as well as some of the existing constructs to measure privacy concern that were discussed earlier in this section.

Figure 5.1 shows that the customers who decided to participate in the program had an average PRICAL score of 57.68, whereas the average PRICAL score of the customers who decided not to participate was −132.08. Table 5.1 shows a drill down of the participating and the non-participating customers, showing that 76 percent of the customers are on the diagonal of the 2x2 grid.

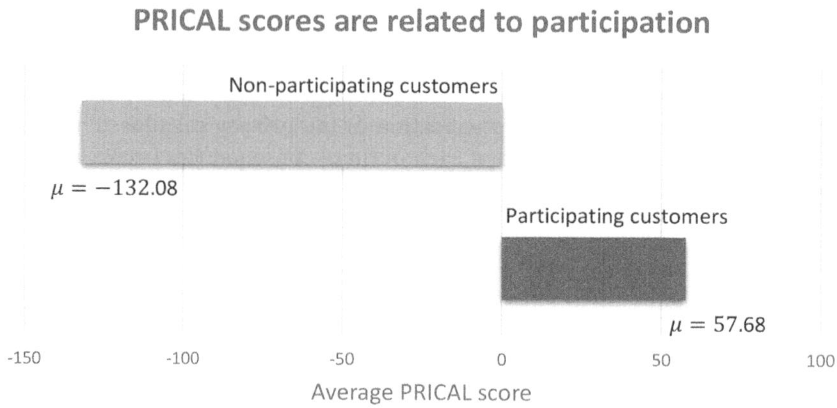

Source: Author.

Figure 5.1 Average PRICAL scores of customers that did and did not participate in the user-based insurance program

Table 5.1 Participating and non-participating customers according to the sign of the PRICAL score

	Negative PRICAL score	Positive PRICAL score	Total
Non-participating customers	74	10	84
Participating customers	158	458	616
Total	232	468	700

Figure 5.1 and Table 5.1 jointly suggest that the decision to participate in the program (and thus to share information) can be explained by the privacy calculus model, as measured by the PRICAL index. The potential reduction in insurance fees was apparently seen by the participating customers of the car insurance company as a benefit that outweighed the risks of sharing personal data on driving behavior.

The PRICAL index provides important insights into the privacy behavior of customers. Based on a sound conceptualization of the "privacy calculus," it offers valuable insights into the main drivers of how customers perceive the consequences of companies collecting personal information. Moreover, it shows that customers' decisions to share information are based on a trade-off of these consequences, such that consumers tend to share personal data with firms if the benefits outweigh the risks (Dinev & Hart 2006). Such a trade-off depends on the type of information and the ways the data are collected, stored, and processed, but also on attitudinal archetypes of customers (Plangger & Montecchi 2020). In some situations, this trade-off is a very deliberate process but, in others, this is a much faster, almost unconscious decision (Bilal, Wingreen, & Sharma, 2020).

The results of Beke et al. (2022) show that the privacy calculus is a versatile multidimensional tool for marketers to understand consumer privacy preferences and is better able to explain and predict customers' decisions to share data than existing privacy measures. Especially the latter provides a step forward in resolving the privacy paradox, in the sense that the PRICAL index is strongly related to the actual privacy behavior of customers, in contrast to other measures for privacy concern. Furthermore, brands can use the PRICAL index for diagnostic purposes to determine the factors that are the most relevant drivers of privacy concerns. In the applications that Beke et al. (2022) considered, the dimensions of "Security," "Performance," and "Psychological" turn out to be the most important factors that affected participants' decisions to share their data. Such diagnostics may provide guidance for firms when they have to decide on their privacy policies. We will further explore the firm perspective in the next section.

Striking the privacy balance from the firm perspective

To date, firms carry a great deal of responsibility for safeguarding customers' personal data. This responsibility is not only enforced by the privacy regulations we discussed earlier in this chapter but is also an expectation held by customers (Grewal, Gupta, & Hamilton 2021). Wieringa et al. (2021) argue that these responsibilities should ideally shift from companies to the owners of the personal information (i.e., the customers), but also note that this is not current practice. Hence firms typically are responsible for collecting, storing, and processing personal information in a responsible way (Wirtz et al. 2023).

For firms, this implies that they have to navigate the limitations of privacy actions while ensuring the sufficient profitability of analytics endeavors. However, it is impossible to ensure perfect privacy protection without compromising the utility of data. This leads to tensions between the marketing analytics function and legal or compliance departments (Martin & Palmatier 2020).

On the one hand, the legal or compliance departments tasked with the proper interpretation and application of regulations tend to prioritize the protection of individuals' privacy rights and the avoidance of any potential legal or reputational liabilities for the company. Despite good intentions to be as cooperative as possible, they are constrained by the regulations and must ensure that they are protecting the privacy rights of customers. Wedel and Kannan (2016) report that firms are increasingly likely to engage in self-policing, which may lead to additional restrictions on the use of sensitive data and being even more selective in combining data from different sources.

On the other hand, there are data scientists, marketing intelligence specialists, and business intelligence colleagues who are focused on using data to generate insights and drive revenue growth. They prefer to work with detailed data from many different sources, which allows them to develop a 360-degree view of the customer and make better business decisions. They see data as valuable assets that can help them gain a competitive edge and increase profitability. Consequently, they are focused on maximizing the value of the data and may view privacy restrictions as limiting their ability to innovate and create value for the company, as every increase in privacy protection is associated with a loss of analytical power (Gupta, Moutafis, & Schneider 2021). For example, Goldfarb and Tucker (2011) show how privacy regulation affects online advertising effectiveness negatively, and Campbell, Goldfarb, and Tucker (2015) show that small firms and new firms are most adversely affected. Conitzer, Taylor, and Wagman (2012) analyze how the anonymity of customers affects the costs of the firms. Liu and Mittal (2016) note that privacy concerns hinder the deployment of many real-world applications. Consequently, the typical view is that privacy limits the effectiveness of marketing analytics (Schäfer et al. 2022).

This section considers the trade-off between data utility and privacy protection. Wieringa et al. (2021) note that this balance is different for different types of data. They illustrate this in Figure 5.2, where for low-dimensional data the removal of certain attributes increases privacy protection considerably, as illustrated by the steep concavity of the curve in the top panel of Figure 5.2. However, for higher-dimensional data, the removal of detail in the data, leading to a reduction in data utility, has a different effect on privacy protection. In the lower panel of Figure 5.2, Barack Obama is still recognizable even in cases where a significant blur is added to the picture. Hence, it is important to navigate the balance between data utility and privacy protection with care. Certainly, a one-size-fits-all approach is not suited.

Existing Approaches for Protecting Privacy

To ensure privacy protection, organizations can resort to various anonymization approaches. Anonymization aims to prevent three types of privacy threats: the re-identification of individuals, the disclosure of attributes, and linking records that correspond to the same individual (D'Acquisto et al. 2015). According to Little (1993), data protection can be applied when:

- collecting the data
- processing the data (e.g., in analyses)
- presenting or using the insights that result from an analysis of the data.

Data protection methods that are applied when collecting data aim to provide privacy protection at the initial phases of any data project. If conducted properly, privacy protection is also ensured in the later stages of the data project. D'Acquisto et al. (2015) suggest data minimization as an important principle in this stage. It requires defining precisely what personal data are needed (and also what data are not needed) for further processing, as well as the data retention period (see Holtrop et al. 2017 for a recent application). Other possibilities are forms of local anonymization, which involve removing personal information before the data are released for analytics. An important example of this type of data protection is randomized response. This technique is especially useful when collecting potentially threatening data, or data that is potentially embarrassing (see de Jong, Pieters, & Fox 2010 for an interesting marketing application). The basic idea is to randomize whether a respondent answers a question truthfully or not, governed for example by a coin flip. This invokes a form of "plausible deniability," which makes it easier for respondents to share their sensitive data.

Privacy protection techniques that can be applied when processing data include k-anonymity and its extensions which we discuss later. Protecting a data set with k-anonymity prevents re-identification from an individual by ensuring that he or she cannot be distinguished from a group of k others. To ensure k-anonymity, first so-called identifiers need to be removed from the data. These are attributes that uniquely define an individual, such as a social security number. The remaining variables represent attributes that are shared by multi-

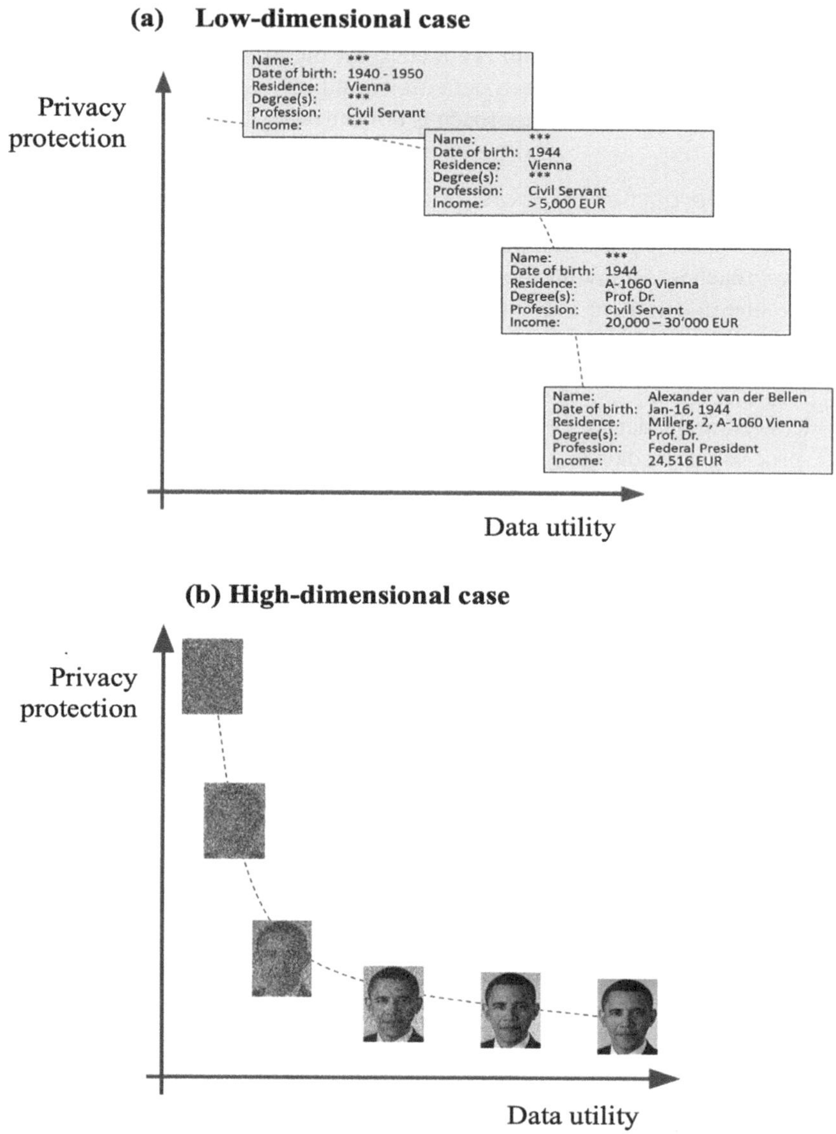

Source: Adapted from Wieringa et al. (2021) and Mostly.ai.

Figure 5.2 The relation between data utility and privacy protection for different types of data

ple individuals. These are called quasi-identifiers. Examples of quasi-identifiers are demographic variables such as age, gender, zip code, and so on. As all attributes of an individual in principle qualify as a quasi-identifier, they cannot all be removed in a data protection exercise because this would lead to an empty data set. In principle, knowledge of a quasi-identifier does not uniquely identify a single customer. However, combining several quasi-identifiers or combining quasi-identifiers with external data may allow for the re-identification of individuals. Consequently, to ensure *k*-anonymity it should be carefully assessed whether every distinct combination of quasi-identifiers involves at least *k* persons in the data. If this is not the case, attributes may be deleted from the data (i.e., suppression), specific values of attributes may be replaced by broader categories (i.e., generalization), or the values of some of the attributes may be changed (e.g., by adding noise, or by swapping values of attributes) to achieve *k*-anonymity. As an example of the latter, one may decide to replace a numerical attribute such as age with a broader ordinal attribute with levels "young," "middle-aged," and "senior."

While *k*-anonymity prevents re-identification, it does not prevent the disclosure of attributes, which is one of the other goals of anonymization. For example, all members of a group sharing a certain combination of quasi-identifiers may have the same level of another attribute (e.g., they may all live in the same city). To avoid disclosure of attributes, several extensions of *k*-anonymity have been developed, such as *p*-sensitive *k*-anonymity, *l*-diversity, *t*-closeness, and (*n*, *t*)-closeness (see D'Acquisto et al. 2015 for an overview).

The methods to achieve anonymity discussed thus far (suppression, generalization, adding noise, swapping) all involve some form of masking the data (Little 1993). An alternative approach is to generate artificial or synthetic data and analyze these data as if they were real. To be useful, the insights of these analyses should be the same or similar to those when analyzing real data. Anand and Lee (2023) develop a deep learning approach that samples artificial data that are close in distribution to data of real customers but are random on an individual level. Ponte, Wieringa, Boot, and Verhoef, (2024) train Generative Adversarial Networks (GANs) on data of real customers to generate artificial data of non-existing customers that, when analyzed, provide similar insights as those of the analysis of the real customer data.

Ensuring anonymity when presenting or using data insights typically involves some of the masking techniques to achieve anonymity that we described in the foregoing. For example, when customers are cross tabulated according to some attributes, cell counts can be deleted to prevent the inference of personal data.

Existing Privacy Protection Methods Are Un-private

A number of compelling examples in the literature demonstrate that the existing well-known privacy protection methods that we discuss above are inherently un-private. Kosinski, Stillwell, and Graepel (2013) show that a seemingly harmless data set consisting of Facebook likes of individuals can be used to automatically and accurately estimate a wide range of personal attributes that people would typically assume to be private, including ethnicity, sexuality, and religious and political background, as well as their drug, cigarette, and alcohol use. This is especially interesting since Facebook likes are publicly visible by default.

Another example concerns the data that Netflix released in 2006 containing more than 100 million ratings from over 480,000 randomly chosen anonymous subscribers on more than 17,000 movie titles. With this data set Netflix challenged the data mining, machine learning, and computer science communities to develop algorithms that outperformed their own recommendation system, Cinematch. The contest's grand prize was $1 million and was won by BellKor's Pragmatic Chaos team, who improved Netflix's recommendation performance by 10.06 percent. The data set that was used for this competition is still available on Kaggle.com today. By matching these data to film ratings on the Internet Movie Database (IMDb) of a very small sample of around 50 IMDb users, Narayanan and Shmatikov (2008) were able to identify individual Netflix customers. They conclude that removing identifying information is not sufficient to prevent the re-identification of individuals and that it only requires a very small amount of background knowledge about an individual to break this type of privacy protection.

Sweeney (2002) matched a data set containing individuals' medical details that was considered anonymous to voter registration data that was publicly available for purchase on three overlapping attributes: gender, zip code, and birth data. With the resulting data set, she was able to uniquely identify the governor of Massachusetts, including his medical details.

Such examples demonstrate that existing anonymization techniques do not provide sufficient protection against re-identification, especially if data sets are matched to other data based on shared attributes. But other forms of privacy protection prove to be unsafe as well. Fredrikson, Jha, and Ristenpart (2015) investigate facial recognition systems and are able to reconstruct with high accuracy the faces that the trained model is supposed to recognize. Similarly, Chen et al. (2020) show how intensive care unit patients can still be re-identified from synthetic data.

We conclude that firms that rely on existing data protection methods are at risk of complete reconstruction of their customers. This privacy risk is a direct consequence of Dinur and Nissim's (2003) Fundamental Law of Information Recovery (FLIR), which states that each time an analyst performs an analysis, this inevitably introduces privacy risk for the individuals included in the data set, and with enough analyses, every individual can be completely reconstructed (e.g., Garfinkel, Abowd, & Martindale 2018). This means that recent advanced data protection methods such as those developed by Anand and Lee (2023), Danaher and Smith (2011), or Schneider et al. (2018) are vulnerable to the re-identification of a firm's customers as well. The FLIR teaches us that there is an inherent trade-off between privacy and utility, and no method is available that provides full protection against privacy attacks without completely destroying the usefulness of the data.

On top of this important problem of existing privacy protection methods, there is also the issue that these approaches do not provide a quantification of the privacy risk that individuals face. The diversity of the principles they rely upon makes it difficult to assess the risks that anonymization tries to avoid, for immediate privacy threats or those that potentially occur later in time. This hampers a proper comparison of these anonymization methods and also hinders finding an appropriate balance between data utility and privacy protection in Figure 5.2.

We conclude that existing privacy protection methods do not protect against the complete reconstruction of individuals in the data. Furthermore, the existing methods do not provide a quantification of the privacy risk, which also does not provide an option to control the privacy risk an individual might incur when being subjected to data processing, now and in the future.

Differential Privacy

A privacy protection approach that explicitly takes the perspective of controlling privacy risk is differential privacy (Dwork & Roth 2014). It is based on a mathematical definition of privacy that provides protection by adding noise to data while maintaining data utility. Differential privacy considers two hypothetical scenarios: one in which a person is included in a data set versus one in which only this person is excluded from the data set. Informally, differential privacy adds noise (or uncertainty) to the possible outcomes (from both scenarios) of any analysis. By adding noise carefully, the overlap between the distributions of the outcomes of the two scenarios can be controlled. When more noise is added, the overlap will increase, and it becomes increasingly difficult to distinguish between the two scenarios based on the observed outcomes.

Consequently, privacy protection increases, as it becomes harder to infer whether an individual's data were used in the analysis. Formally, differential privacy is defined as follows:

A randomized algorithm $\mathcal{A}$: $\mathcal{D} \rightarrow \mathcal{O}$ defined on a certain domain of data sets $\mathcal{D}$ is (ε, δ)-differentially private if for any two adjacent data sets D and D' (D, $D' \in \mathcal{D}$) and for any subset $O \subseteq \mathcal{O}$ of outputs of $\mathcal{A}$ the following holds:

$$P[\mathcal{A}(D) \in O] \leq e^{\varepsilon} P[\mathcal{A}(D') \in O] + \delta,$$

where $P[\mathcal{A}(D) \in O]$ is the probability that the output of algorithm $\mathcal{A}$ using data set D is in O. In this definition, D and D' are adjacent data sets that differ at most for one individual (see Dwork & Roth 2014 for a textbook reference).

Dwork and Roth (2014) show that if an algorithm $\mathcal{A}$ is (ε, δ) is differentially private, this ensures that for adjacent data sets, the absolute value of the privacy loss of the algorithm will be bounded by ε with a probability of at least $1 - \delta$. The protection of (ε, 0) in differentially private algorithms is somewhat stricter: it ensures that, for every run of $\mathcal{A}$ on a given data set, the output observed is (almost) equally likely to be observed on every adjacent data set, simultaneously. Both forms of differential privacy offer learning about a population without learning about individuals.

An interesting aspect of differential privacy in the context of this chapter is that it provides a way to control the level of privacy protection by varying the amount of noise added to analyses. This means that the level of privacy protection can be "steered" by the level of noise added, which is an essential element in finding a good balance between data utility and privacy protection. The amount of noise that is added (and hence the level of privacy protection) is governed by ε, which makes ε a metric, a measurable quantity for privacy risk.

The mathematical definition of differential privacy also provides us with an interpretation of ε. The formula that is at the heart of the definition shows that a change in ε changes privacy risk with a factor of exp(ε). A related interpretation of ε is to view it as a privacy budget or privacy loss, as it quantitatively measures by how much the privacy risk of an individual may increase due to the inclusion of that individual's data in the inputs to the algorithm (Tang et al. 2017).

Consequently, the concept of differential privacy allows for controlling the level of privacy protection based on a mathematical definition, and it ensures protection against an increase in an individual's privacy risk, either now or in the future. Moreover, since ε can be considered as a metric for privacy risk, it enables a quantitative trade-off between privacy protection and data utility.

The latter point is particularly relevant in the discussions that take place between analysts and legal departments within organizations. These discussions are typically hindered by the fact that existing privacy protection methods do not provide an objective way to express the level of privacy risk. This makes it difficult for legal departments to set a privacy upper bound, and organizations may resort to conservative approaches that lead to over-protection and self-policing (Wedel & Kannan 2016). The measure of privacy risk that differential privacy provides may relieve the tensions between legal departments and analysts and allows for a discussion on the basis of objective arguments. Specifically, it may help in identifying points along the privacy–data-utility curve of Figure 5.2 that are acceptable for both parties: those that ensure acceptable levels of privacy protection while providing sufficient data utility.

Finding the Data Protection–Data Utility Balance

As a practical guideline for finding such feasible points, legal may start by choosing an appropriate level of ε. Subsequently, the data analysts can then evaluate the data utility at the selected level of privacy protection. If the outcome is such that the business case of the associated data science project is profitable, a feasible trade-off between privacy and data utility has been found. If the level of privacy protection proves to be too strict to allow for a positive return on investment (ROI) on the data science project, the legal department may want to reconsider and see whether it is possible to relax the privacy requirement. If this is not possible, the analyst will conclude that the data science project should not be executed. This approach is not limited to discussions that take place within organizations but can also benefit policymakers when developing industry-wide privacy guidelines. Together with industry representatives, policymakers can discuss the balance between data utility and privacy protection based on the objective criterion for privacy risk that differential privacy provides.

Because of its advantageous characteristics differential privacy is considered the gold standard for rigorous privacy guarantees (Chanyaswad et al. 2018). However, Gupta, Moutafis, and Schneider (2022) note that it can be challenging to implement, as several currently available differential privacy approaches can result in useless data for practical marketing applications. Ponte et al. (2024) illustrate this in an application where they use differentially private GANs to generate data for a churn application. They compare the distribution of real data of one of the variables (day calls) to data that is generated with increasing levels of privacy protection. Figure 5.3 illustrates that with lower levels of ε (i.e., higher privacy protection), the distribution of the artificial data deviates more from the distribution of the real data. The highest levels of privacy protection render the generated data useless because its distribution does not resemble that of the original variable.

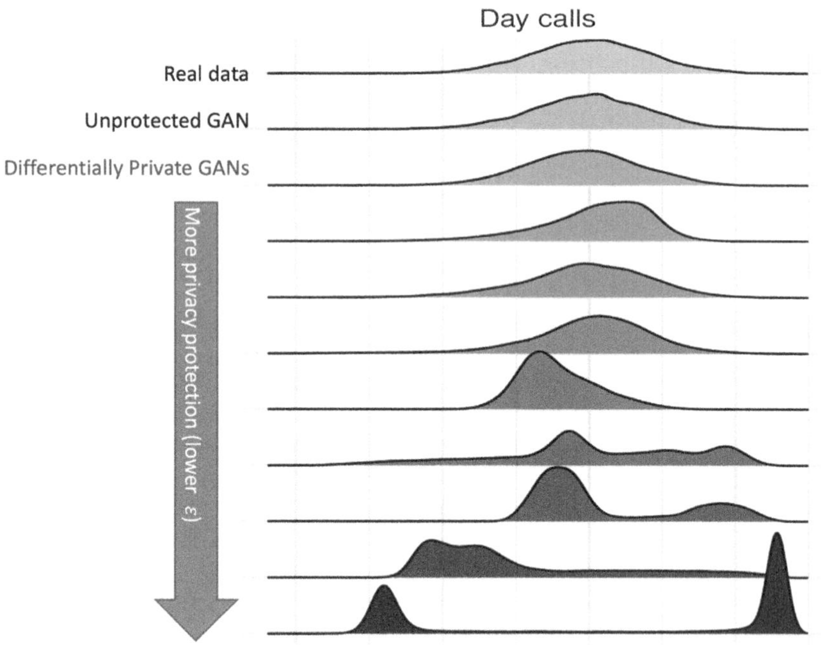

Source: Ponte et al. (2024).

Figure 5.3 The distribution of artificially generated data deviates stronger from that of the real data with higher levels of privacy protection

Despite the challenges when implementing differential privacy, we argue that this does not outweigh its potential for striking an appropriate balance between privacy protection and data utility. We see useful applications in all three phases of data projects that we discussed earlier in this section (i.e., data collection, data processing, and sharing or using data insights):

- In the context of data collection, differential privacy can help to ensure data protection "at the source." Differential privacy can for example be implemented via randomized response designs in survey data collection to protect respondents' identities while allowing for unbiased aggregate inferences (de Jong et al. 2010).
- When processing data, differential privacy can help prevent the disclosure of sensitive information by adding noise to the data in a way that preserves statistical accuracy. For example, Ponte et al. (2024) navigate the privacy–utility trade-off in two marketing applications and provide empirical evidence for a so-called "Where's Waldo?" effect. They show that increasing the sample size provides an opportunity to align the goals of legal departments and analysts that are typically opposing.
- When sharing data insights or making data-driven decisions, differential privacy can enable organizations to share or use information while protecting the privacy of individuals represented in the data. By obscuring the contribution of individual data points, differential privacy can prevent the identification of specific individuals while still allowing for meaningful usage of the data outcomes.

Local and Global Differential Privacy

If differential privacy is applied at the data collection stage, where noise is added to the data points before the data are stored or processed further, this is called local differential privacy. Such applications of differential privacy have the advantage that in each of the following phases the data are protected. This may stimulate individuals to share their data, especially if they do not trust data aggregators or data processors further down the data-value chain, or when data are collected from multiple sources, where combining data sets can increase the risk of re-identification. A downside of local differential privacy is that each of the data subjects adds noise to the data, which likely increases the total amount of noise. Consequently, more data subjects are typically needed to obtain a certain level of data utility. Some of the major tech companies have implemented local differential privacy. For example, Apple has deployed local differential privacy in their macOS operating system (Tang et al. 2017). Other interesting applications of local differential privacy involve Google and Microsoft (see Cormode et al. 2018 for an overview).

In contrast, if differential privacy is applied in the later stages of a data science project, for example before the data are shared with a third party, noise is only added once. This is called global differential privacy. In comparison to local differential privacy, the advantage is that less noise is required, which positively affects the data utility. However, a potential downside is the need for individuals who provide the data to trust the party responsible for protecting it, as the data must be brought together and processed before the data protection is applied. This can pose additional privacy risks, such as the possibility that the data protector's security is compromised and the data are leaked. A well-known application of this type of privacy protection is the 2020 decennial census, where the U.S. Census Bureau used global differential privacy to anonymize the data before publication (Abowd 2018).

Overall, while there are challenges in implementing differential privacy, we conclude that the concept of differential privacy provides an excellent basis for navigating the balance between data utility and privacy protection. It offers a mathematically guaranteed bound on privacy risk even under worst-case assumptions. Moreover, it allows for control of the level of privacy protection by varying the amount of noise and provides ε as a measurable quantity for privacy risk. In this section, we have argued that this helps organizations in defining their privacy strategies, but it has implications for policymakers as well, as they can use differential privacy to develop industry-wide privacy guidelines.

Joining the privacy balances: towards an integrated framework

In the foregoing sections, we have separately reviewed how consumers balance the perceived benefits of sharing data with the associated privacy risk and how companies make a trade-off between data utility and privacy risk. However, Kannan and Li (2017) raise the question of what kinds of mechanisms can be designed to benefit both firms and customers while safeguarding their privacy and security. This question can neither be answered by taking only the firm perspective into account, nor by investigating the customers' viewpoint in isolation. It requires the joint consideration of both sides of the market for privacy (Rust, Kannan, & Peng 2002; Rafieian & Yoganarasimhan 2021). For each of the two perspectives, there will be a trade-off between the costs or missed revenues/benefits due to privacy restrictions, and the benefits or utility of sharing and processing personal information.

As the foregoing sections illustrate, the privacy literature on each of the two types of balances is quite well developed. However, not much attention is devoted to how the elements of these balances interact across the two perspectives. There are a few exceptions: Beke et al. (2018) develop a conceptual framework that relates a firm's privacy practices to customers' perceptions or attitudes, which in turn drives their intentions and behaviors. Martin, Borah, and Palmatier (2017) develop two conceptual models, one that takes more the customer perspective and one that considers how customer data vulnerabilities affect firm performance. In this section, we want to link the elements of the balances that were discussed in the previous sections in a more detailed way. Figure 5.4 presents the framework that we propose.

Central in the conceptual model of Figure 5.4 are the building blocks that were discussed in the previous sections. The trade-off between the costs and the benefits that customers make when sharing data is depicted at the bottom of Figure 5.4, and the balance between privacy protection and data utility that is relevant for firms can be found at the top. The left-hand side of Figure 5.4 indicates that there are a number of direct links between the components of both privacy balances. The right-hand side of Figure 5.4 reflects that there are also indirect effects that connect the elements of the balances through outcome variables. Below we discuss these in turn. It should be noted that in this discussion we only focus on elements of the privacy balances that were discussed before, and we are abstracting away from other variables that may also be relevant in a privacy context. Examples of such variables at the firm level are transparency about the level of privacy control that the firm provides and (industry) reputation. Examples of such control variables at the customer level are general privacy concerns, innovativeness, propensity to trust, or prior experience (Eggers et al. 2023; Fortes, Rita, & Pagani 2017). Also, environmental variables such as culture, changes in legislation, and technology may be relevant but are not considered in this framework.

The left-hand side of Figure 5.4 postulates that privacy decisions made by firms, which impact their data utility, may affect both the costs and the benefits that consumers perceive. If a firm's increased data utility is employed by them only to their own benefit, consumers may perceive this as a cost. However, if the firm's benefit is partly transferred to their customers, they will likely consider this a benefit. Similarly, a firm's level of privacy protection can be perceived as a cost by consumers, for example when a firm has administrative procedures installed that involve authorization steps which take time or are a mental burden to their customers. But a firm's privacy protection can also be perceived as a benefit by consumers (e.g., from a security perspective). Note that these links illustrate how firms' privacy decisions directly affect the privacy balances of individual consumers. We propose that the reverse effects, the links between the privacy balances of individual customers and

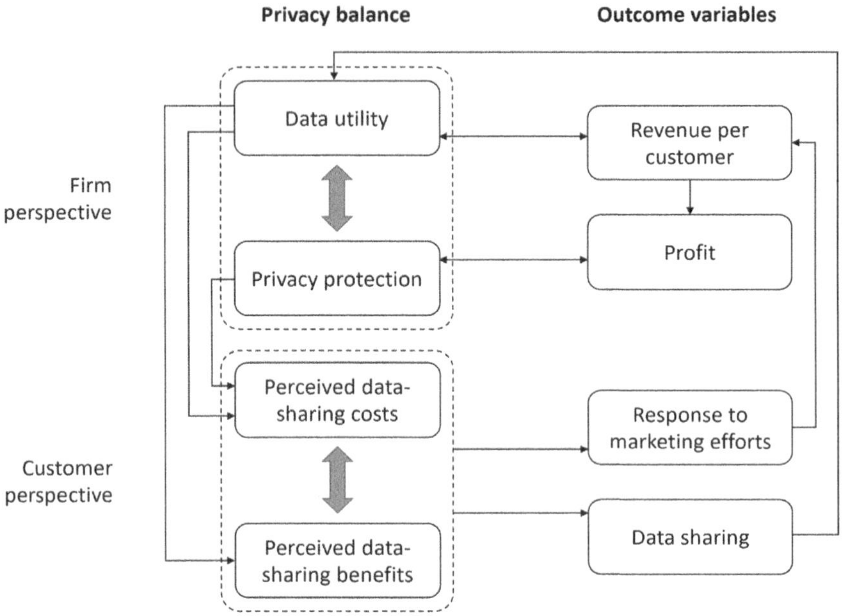

Source: Author.

Figure 5.4 Linking the privacy balances at the firm and the customer level

the privacy–data utility trade-off of firms, are less direct and are connected through outcome variables.

The bottom of Figure 5.4 depicts that a customer's decision to share their personal data is an important outcome variable of the privacy balance at the customer level. This decision affects the utility that firms can derive from their customer base (Varadarajan 2020), as more complete data likely leads to more revenue per customer and hence to higher profit levels. The contribution that consumer privacy evaluations potentially provide to a firm's bottom line makes it relevant for firms to investigate how their privacy policies affect the privacy calculus of individual customers. Eggers et al. (2023) show that companies can gain higher revenues and market shares by positively differentiating themselves in the "market for privacy," and actively promoting their privacy efforts. However, how companies can realize these advantages varies by industry. In information-sensitive contexts, data collection and use play an important role, while storage appears to be less important. When consumers have less frequent interactions with companies, transparency about privacy practices turns out to be a differentiator.

As customers become more aware of the value of their personal data to companies, they may view their data or privacy as a commodity or currency that can be exchanged for goods or services. This perspective is supported by Patil and Shyamasundar (2017) and Schwartz (2004), who highlight the growing recognition among consumers that their personal data is an asset with real economic value. However, this can have the unintended consequence of creating a two-tiered society where privacy is only attainable for the privileged few who can afford it. The "commodification of privacy" can lead to the creation of a market for privacy where only the wealthy can afford to protect their personal information (Allen & Mack 1991).

Another consequence of this could be that customers do not want firms to be in charge of this valuable resource. Much in line with the basic principles of the GDPR, customers are the owners of their data and should be sufficiently empowered to be in control of it. Consequently, there is a growing interest in the development of personal data pools, where individual users can configure their own decentralized personal data storage infrastructure (Wieringa et al. 2021). This enables consumers (in their roles as data owners) to have full control over whether and how their data may be used.

A final route through which the privacy balances of firms and customers are connected in Figure 5.4 runs via customers' responses to marketing efforts. As we reviewed earlier, there is ample evidence that customers' purchase intentions are affected by privacy concerns. For example, Eggers et al. (2023) show that a firm's revenues and market shares are positively affected by favorable customer perceptions of their privacy efforts. These effects are not entirely attributable to the route we described in the previous paragraphs, where a firm's privacy efforts lead to a higher intention for customers to share their data. Earlier research has shown that privacy concerns moderate the effectiveness of a firm's marketing efforts (Taylor, Davis, & Jillapalli 2009). For example, Tucker (2014) shows that when giving customers enhancement of perceived control over privacy, users were nearly twice as likely to click on personalized ads. Other examples are presented in table 3 of Martin and Murphy (2017). Together these earlier studies suggest that a firm's privacy efforts also affect customers' responses to their marketing mix variables, which in turn is related to the revenue per customer and, ultimately, to the firm's profit. Subsequently, this might affect the firm's privacy decisions. With Figure 5.4 we propose that such effects also result from balancing the costs and the benefits of a firm's privacy efforts. It would be therefore of interest to see to what extent the PRICAL index can explain differences in customers' responses to marketing mix variables, and how the resulting revenues and profits impact the firm's privacy balance.

Not all of the relationships in Figure 5.4 are investigated in earlier research. Future studies could uncover to what extent the proposed links between the elements of the trade-offs can be confirmed. By studying the two privacy balances and their interrelationships jointly, a more comprehensive understanding can be obtained of the role of privacy efforts of companies and the associated responses of consumers. From an academic perspective, this is interesting for scholars who want to further their knowledge of privacy. Also, this can be relevant for managers who want to optimize their privacy decisions taking consumers' responses into account. Finally, policymakers might also want to develop privacy guidelines that take both privacy balances into account.

Conclusions, managerial recommendations, and a research agenda

According to Wang, Lee, and Wang (1998), the balancing of beneficial uses of data sources with the privacy rights of individuals is one of the most challenging public policy issues of the information age. As a response, privacy legislation has been enacted at state, national, and international levels. In this chapter, we have reviewed this crucial issue which is highly relevant for organizations engaged in digital transformation from the standpoint of the customer and the firm.

Conclusions

For individual customers, we have taken the perspective that the decision to share their personal data depends on a trade-off of the associated perceived benefits and costs of doing so. This trade-off is in line with recent research that shows that Dutch consumers see both sides of the privacy coin: they are worried about the privacy consequences of sharing data but also acknowledge the benefits of data exchange. They feel more comfortable with the idea of sharing personal data with organizations than before (increase from 35 percent in 2018 to 43 percent in 2022; see DDMA 2023). In line with the basic principle of the privacy calculus, they consider "What's in it for me?" as the most important criterion for sharing their data. We have seen that the privacy trade-off that consumers make is a complex one that depends on multiple dimensions.

The PRICAL index that was developed to capture the trade-off on all of these dimensions proved to provide a better explanation of customers' behavior than other measures for privacy concern or related scales.

Organizations must also navigate a trade-off, but they are faced with the challenge of balancing their customers' privacy protection with the utility that customer data provides. This trade-off is not an easy one either and causes tensions between legal departments and analysts in many organizations. In the literature, there are various approaches available that aim to provide privacy protection, including anonymization, differential privacy, privacy-preserving data analysis, and machine learning algorithms. Among these, differential privacy is the only approach that provides a guaranteed upper bound on privacy risk, even under worst-case assumptions. Other approaches remain vulnerable to the re-identification of individuals, especially when data from multiple sources are combined. Differential privacy allows for an objective trade-off between data utility and privacy risk because it allows for controlling the privacy risk (or privacy budget) based on a numerical parameter ε. In theory, this makes differential privacy an ideal candidate for navigating the data-utility–privacy protection balance, but its applicability is hindered by the fact that in practical applications an acceptable level of privacy protection sometimes renders the data virtually useless. Fortunately, recent research is making progress in addressing this issue (see e.g., Ghazi et al. 2021) and notable exceptions exist where strong levels of data protection can be ensured while still providing data utility.

The two privacy balances do not operate in isolation but depend on each other. The privacy calculus of customers depends on the benefits and the costs that the privacy decisions of firms bring. In turn, these decisions are driven by the trade-off between the level of privacy protection that customers require and the utility that the customer data provide to firms. Consequently, both trade-offs should be jointly investigated, but the privacy literature is relatively silent on this topic. In this chapter, we have provided a model that conceptually links the elements of both privacy balances.

Studying the two privacy balances in conjunction provides a more comprehensive understanding of the privacy decisions of firms and consumers and should therefore be of interest to privacy scholars. But the framework also provides managers with a broader insight into the consequences of privacy decisions that they make, by considering both the direct associated effects that their decisions have for their company, together with the more indirect consequences that result from consumers' responses. This prevents them from making myopic choices in the privacy domain.

Managerial Recommendations

A number of managerial recommendations emerge from this chapter. First and foremost, we recommend that firms deepen their understanding of how their customers make privacy decisions. To this end, they can use the PRICAL index to analyze their clients' choices concerning data sharing. As discussed earlier in this chapter, having access to detailed and accurate data will greatly enhance the firm's potential for success when transitioning to a new digital business model.

We also suggest that firms engaged in digital transformation incorporate the PRICAL index as a diagnostic tool to identify the most relevant dimensions shaping privacy concerns. Such insights can provide invaluable guidance for firms when they are crafting or renewing their privacy policies. For example, we noted that in the contexts that were explored by Beke et al. (2022), the dimensions "Security," "Performance," and "Psychological" were the primary factors impacting consumers' decisions to share their data. However, their results also showed that these findings vary across the brands that were part of the study. Consequently, firms may want to (re)design their privacy policies to mitigate the firm-idiosyncratic privacy risks that customers experience when transacting with them.

Furthermore, following from our discussion of Figure 5.4, we recommend that organizations actively promote their privacy initiatives. A positive differentiation in the "market for privacy" provides new opportunities for obtaining higher revenues and increased market shares. It is crucial, however, that the privacy dimensions emphasized in the communications align with the organization's actual strengths and capabilities. Otherwise, this strategy may potentially backfire and may cause adverse effects. The PRICAL index can play a valuable role in pinpointing the dimensions in which the firm excels.

Another important managerial recommendation follows from our discussion on the privacy decisions that firms need to take. We suggest that firms base their data utility–privacy balance on metrics. While defining metrics for data utility can be relatively straightforward (e.g., based on key performance indicators that are already relevant in an organization), quantifying the level of privacy protection often proves challenging for organizations. Applying differential privacy may be a good idea in this respect, as one of its parameters, ε, serves as a numerical measure of privacy risk. Employing ε facilitates productive conversations between data analysts and legal teams, as it enables firms to make objective, data-driven trade-offs between data utility and the degree of privacy protection.

Moreover, applying differential privacy is an important managerial recommendation in its own right, as it provides a mathematically guaranteed upper bound on privacy risk, for now and for future data operations, even under worst-case assumptions. Given that this level of privacy assurance is not offered by other existing methods, we advise managers to delve into the possibilities of implementing differential privacy within their organizations. However, practical use cases have remained sporadic up to now.

When implementing differential privacy, we propose that firms set a company-wide threshold for ε. This ensures a consistent level of privacy protection that is the same across the entire data-value chain and contributes to establishing a uniform privacy policy within an organization. Furthermore, we suggest that firms collaborate with policymakers and industry stakeholders to define benchmark levels for privacy protection that are deemed appropriate for their sector. Such initiatives contribute to building customer trust for the sector as a whole. The financial sector for example could benefit greatly from implementing sector-wide agreements on a benchmark for ε. Such collaborations can be initiated bottom-up by cooperating firms, but they may also be orchestrated more top-down, with industry federations or regulators leading the way.

Finally, we recommend that firms adopt integral privacy decisions, taking their own privacy balance and that of their customers jointly into account. We firmly believe that a more holistic approach will enhance the alignment between the customer and the firm perspective on privacy. This alignment, in turn, will yield better decision-making and higher-quality data, two essential factors in driving digital transformation.

A Research Agenda

The framework in Figure 5.4 postulates that a firm's privacy trade-off has direct effects on the elements of the privacy trade-off of consumers. Vice versa, the privacy balancing act at the consumer level also affects data utility at the firm level. However, some of these effects are indirect and run through output variables. Not all relationships that the framework proposes are investigated in earlier research. Figure 5.4, therefore, identifies a number of directions for future privacy studies.

Regarding the direct relationships on the left-hand side of Figure 5.4, future research could investigate to what extent the utility that firms extract from customer data is perceived by customers as benefits or as costs. Similarly, privacy protection, the other side of a firm's privacy balance, can have positive consequences and negative consequences for customers. Future research can investigate the valence of these consequences. Furthermore, it would be of interest to learn whether these costs and benefits are perceived by customers mainly in monetary terms or also in nonmonetary terms, such as norms and values.

Turning to the right-hand side of the framework in Figure 5.4, it would be of interest to observe to what extent the privacy calculus can explain differences in customers' responses to marketing mix variables. Earlier research that we reviewed in this chapter has already shown that general privacy concerns affect the efficacy of marketing efforts. Future research could build on this by providing a more detailed investigation into the dimensions that are driving such moderation effects. The PRICAL index which was developed as a comprehensive scale to capture the privacy calculus of consumers may be helpful in this respect. Its multidimensional nature allows future studies to identify which privacy dimensions most critically affect marketing effectiveness. We believe this is an intriguing question because it is unclear whether such positive effects of a firm's privacy protection measures outweigh the negative effects that are typically associated with them. We hope that this part of the conceptual model in Figure 5.4 stimulates research that investigates the net performance effects of a firm's privacy policy by taking not only the negative direct effects into account but also considering the potential positive marketing consequences of their privacy efforts.

Another interesting avenue for future research concerns possible contingency effects on the relationships that are depicted in Figure 5.4. Such contingencies may be caused by variables that we did not explicitly include in the conceptual model. As noted before, we abstracted away from relevant firm variables such as the transparency about privacy control and (industry) reputation. Also, several customer variables were not considered, such as general privacy concerns, innovativeness, propensity to trust, or prior experience, and environmental variables such as culture, changes in legislation, and technology were also not taken into account. However, these variables likely affect several relations in Figure 5.4 or impose boundary conditions on their effects. We hope that new studies enhance our understanding of how privacy balances operate under various conditions in the market for privacy. To this end, it may also be of interest to investigate how the effects of the privacy balances on the outcome are mediated by intermediate variables such as satisfaction or other customer feedback constructs.

In addition to the research cues that stem from the conceptual model depicted in Figure 5.4, we would like to draw attention to a number of other specific aspects that warrant scholarly attention. Firstly, as we strongly believe that differential privacy could potentially play a significant role in devising effective privacy strategies at both the organizational and higher aggregation levels, it is imperative to address the major limitations associated with its implementation. Thus, future studies should concentrate on developing implementations of differential privacy that offer improved data utility at specific levels of data protection.

Second, the emergence of personal data vaults – secure, encrypted digital spaces where individuals can store and manage their personal data – is likely to have a significant impact on consumers' willingness to share their data with firms. With personal data vaults, individuals would have greater control over their personal data, and they would be able to selectively grant access to firms based on their specific preferences and privacy concerns. By allowing individuals to decide which data they want to share, with whom, and for what purpose, personal data vaults may increase consumers' trust in firms and encourage them to share their data more freely. Additionally, since personal data vaults can help consumers keep their data secure and reduce the risk of data breaches, they may feel more confident in sharing their data with firms, knowing that their information is protected. Therefore, personal data vaults have the potential to shift the power balance between individuals and firms, putting individuals in control of their data and making them more comfortable with sharing them for mutual benefit. This likely will have sizable effects on both privacy balances that we consider in this chapter.

Finally, in an increasingly digital and interconnected world, privacy is becoming a crucial factor for customers when choosing which firms to trust and engage with. We expect that firms who recognize this shift and take proactive measures to ensure robust data protection can gain a substantial competitive edge. However, further research is needed into how firms can leverage privacy to differentiate themselves from their competitors. We hope that the research agenda outlined in this chapter provides useful guidance in this regard, ultimately benefiting both firms and their privacy-conscious customers.

References

Abowd, J. M. (2018). The U.S. Census Bureau adopts differential privacy. *Proceedings of the 24th ACM SIGKDD International Conference on Knowledge Discovery & Data Mining*, 2867. https://doi.org/10.1145/3219819.3226070.

Acquisti, A., Brandimarte, L., & Loewenstein, G. (2015). Privacy and human behavior in the age of information. *Science*, 347(6221), 509–514. https:// doi .org/ 10 .1126/ science.aaa1465.
Aguirre, E., Roggeveen, A. L., Grewal, D., & Wetzels, M. (2016). The personalization-privacy paradox: Implications for new media. *Journal of Consumer Marketing*, 33(2), 98–110. https://doi.org/10.1108/JCM-06-2015-1458.
Allen, A., & Mack, E. (1991). How privacy got its gender. *Northern Illinois University Law Review*. https://scholarship.law.upenn.edu/faculty_scholarship/1309.
Anand, P., & Lee, C. (2023). Using deep learning to overcome privacy and scalability issues in customer data transfer. *Marketing Science*, 42(1), 189–207. https://doi.org/ 10.1287/mksc.2022.1365.
Barth, S., & de Jong, M. D. T. (2017). The privacy paradox: Investigating discrepancies between expressed privacy concerns and actual online behavior. A systematic literature review. *Telematics and Informatics*, 34(7), 1038–1058. https://doi.org/10.1016/ j.tele.2017.04.013.
Beke, F. T., Eggers, F., & Verhoef, P. C. (2018). Consumer informational privacy: Current knowledge and research directions. *Foundations and Trends® in Marketing*, 11(1), 1–71. https://doi.org/10.1561/1700000057.
Beke, F. T., Eggers, F., Verhoef, P. C., & Wieringa, J. E. (2022). Consumers' privacy calculus: The PRICAL index development and validation. *International Journal of Research in Marketing*, 39(1), 20–41. https://doi.org/10.1016/j.ijresmar.2021.05.005.
Bilal, A., Wingreen, S., & Sharma, R. (2020). Virtue ethics as a solution to the privacy paradox and trust in emerging technologies. *Proceedings of the 3rd International Conference on Information Science and System*, 224–228. https:// doi .org/ 10 .1145/ 3388176.3388196.
Brei, V. (2020). Machine learning in marketing: Overview, learning strategies, applications, and future developments. *Foundations and Trends® in Marketing*, 14(3), 173–236. https://doi.org/10.1561/1700000065.
Brynjolfsson, E., & McElheran, K. (2016). The rapid adoption of data-driven decision-making. *American Economic Review*, 106(5), 133–139. https:// doi .org/ 10 .1257/aer.p20161016.
Campbell, J., Goldfarb, A., & Tucker, C. (2015). Privacy regulation and market structure. *Journal of Economics & Management Strategy*, 24(1), 47–73. https://doi.org/10 .1111/jems.12079.
Cappa, F., Oriani, R., Peruffo, E., & McCarthy, I. (2021). Big data for creating and capturing value in the digitalized environment: Unpacking the effects of volume, variety, and veracity on firm performance. *Journal of Product Innovation Management*, 38(1), 49–67. https://doi.org/10.1111/jpim.12545.
Chanyaswad, T., Dytso, A., Poor, H. V., & Mittal, P. (2018). MVG mechanism: Differential privacy under matrix-valued query. *Proceedings of the 2018 ACM SIGSAC Conference on Computer and Communications Security*, 230–246. https:// doi.org/10.1145/3243734.3243750.
Chen, D., Yu, N., Zhang, Y., & Fritz, M. (2020). GAN-leaks: A taxonomy of membership inference attacks against generative models. *Proceedings of the 2020 ACM SIGSAC Conference on Computer and Communications Security*, 343–362. https:// doi.org/10.1145/3372297.3417238.
Conitzer, V., Taylor, C. R., & Wagman, L. (2012). Hide and seek: Costly consumer privacy in a market with repeat purchases. *Marketing Science*, 31(2), 277–292. https://doi.org/10.1287/mksc.1110.0691.

Cormode, G., Jha, S., Kulkarni, T., Li, N., Srivastava, D., & Wang, T. (2018). Privacy at scale: Local differential privacy in practice. *Proceedings of the 2018 International Conference on Management of Data*, 1655–1658. https://doi.org/10.1145/3183713.3197390.

D'Acquisto, G., Domingo-Ferrer, J., Kikiras, P., Torra, V., de Montjoye, Y.-A., & Bourka, A. (2015). Privacy by design in big data: An overview of privacy enhancing technologies in the era of big data analytics. https://doi.org/10.2824/641480.

Danaher, P. J., & Smith, M. S. (2011). Modeling multivariate distributions using copulas: Applications in marketing. *Marketing Science*, 30(1), 4–21. https://doi.org/10.1287/mksc.1090.0491.

Davenport, T. H., & Redman, T. C. (2020). Digital transformation comes down to talent in 4 key areas. *Harvard Business Review*. https://hbr.org/2020/05/digital-transformation-comes-down-to-talent-in-4-key-areas (accessed April 10, 2023).

DDMA (2023). DDMA privacy monitor 2023. https://ddma.nl/download/31396/ (accessed April 10, 2023).

de Jong, M. G., Pieters, R., & Fox, J.-P. (2010). Reducing social desirability bias through item randomized response: An application to measure underreported desires. *Journal of Marketing Research*, 47(1), 14–27. https://doi.org/10.1509/jmkr.47.1.14.

Dinev, T., & Hart, P. (2006). An extended privacy calculus model for e-commerce transactions. *Information Systems Research*, 17(1), 61–80. https://doi.org/10.1287/isre.1060.0080.

Dinev, T., McConnell, A. R., & Smith, H. J. (2015). Research commentary—informing privacy research through information systems, psychology, and behavioral economics: Thinking outside the "APCO" box. *Information Systems Research*, 26(4), 639–655. https://doi.org/10.1287/isre.2015.0600.

Dinev, T., Xu, H., Smith, J. H., & Hart, P. (2013). Information privacy and correlates: An empirical attempt to bridge and distinguish privacy-related concepts. *European Journal of Information Systems*, 22(3), 295–316. https://doi.org/10.1057/ejis.2012.23.

Dinur, I., & Nissim, K. (2003). Revealing information while preserving privacy. *Proceedings of the 22nd ACM SIGMOD-SIGACT-SIGART Symposium on Principles of Database Systems*, 202–210. https://doi.org/10.1145/773153.773173.

Dong, J. Q., & Yang, C.-H. (2020). Business value of big data analytics: A systems-theoretic approach and empirical test. *Information & Management*, 57(1), 103124. https://doi.org/10.1016/j.im.2018.11.001.

Dwork, C., & Roth, A. (2014). The algorithmic foundations of differential privacy. *Foundations and Trends® in Theoretical Computer Science*, 9(3–4), 211–407. https://doi.org/10.1561/0400000042.

Eggers, F., Beke, F. T., Verhoef, P. C., & Wieringa, J. E. (2023). The market for privacy: Understanding how consumers trade off privacy practices. *Journal of Interactive Marketing*. https://doi.org/10.1177/10949968221140061.

European Commission (2016). *General Data Protection Regulation (GDPR) – Official Legal Text*. https://gdpr-info.eu/.

Fortes, N., Rita, P., & Pagani, M. (2017). The effects of privacy concerns, perceived risk and trust on online purchasing behaviour. *International Journal of Internet Marketing and Advertising*, 11. https://doi.org/10.1504/IJIMA.2017.10007887.

France, S. L., & Ghose, S. (2019). Marketing analytics: Methods, practice, implementation, and links to other fields. *Expert Systems with Applications*, 119, 456–475. https://doi.org/10.1016/j.eswa.2018.11.002.

Fredrikson, M., Jha, S., & Ristenpart, T. (2015). Model inversion attacks that exploit confidence information and basic countermeasures. *Proceedings of the 22nd ACM*

SIGSAC Conference on Computer and Communications Security, 1322–1333. https://doi.org/10.1145/2810103.2813677.
Garfinkel, S., Abowd, J. M., & Martindale, C. (2018). Understanding database reconstruction attacks on public data: These attacks on statistical databases are no longer a theoretical danger. *Queue*, 16(5), 28–53. https://doi.org/10.1145/3291276.3295691.
Gerber, N., Gerber, P., & Volkamer, M. (2018). Explaining the privacy paradox: A systematic review of literature investigating privacy attitude and behavior. *Computers & Security*, 77(August), 226–261. https://doi.org/10.1016/j.cose.2018.04.002.
Ghazi, B., Golowich, N., Kumar, R., Manurangsi, P., & Zhang, C. (2021). Deep learning with label differential privacy. https://doi.org/10.48550/arXiv.2102.06062.
Gigerenzer, G. (2020). What is bounded rationality? In R. Viale (Ed.), *Routledge Handbook of Bounded Rationality* (pp. 55–70). Routledge.
Goldfarb, A., & Tucker, C. (2011). Online display advertising: Targeting and obtrusiveness. *Marketing Science*, 30(3), 389–404. https://doi.org/10.1287/mksc.1100.0583.
Grewal, R., Gupta, S., & Hamilton, R. (2021). Marketing insights from multimedia data: Text, image, audio, and video. *Journal of Marketing Research*, 58(6), 1025–1033. https://doi.org/10.1177/00222437211054601.
Gupta, M., & George, J. F. (2016). Toward the development of a big data analytics capability. *Information & Management*, 53(8), 1049–1064. https://doi.org/10.1016/j.im.2016.07.004.
Gupta, S., Moutafis, P., & Schneider, M. J. (2021). To protect consumer data, don't do everything on the Cloud. *Harvard Business Review*. https:// hbr .org/ 2021/ 06/ to -protect -consumer -data -dont -do -everything -on -the -cloud (accessed April 10, 2023).
Gupta, S., Moutafis, P., & Schneider, M. J. (2022). The marketer at the privacy table. *Impact at JMR* (March). https:// www .ama .org/ 2022/ 03/ 17/ the -marketer -at -the -privacy-table/.
Holtrop, N., Wieringa, J. E., Gijsenberg, M. J., & Verhoef, P. C. (2017). No future without the past? Predicting churn in the face of customer privacy. *International Journal of Research in Marketing*, 34(1), 154–172. https://doi.org/10.1016/j.ijresmar.2016.06.001.
Huang, C.-K., Wang, T., & Huang, T.-Y. (2020). Initial evidence on the impact of big data implementation on firm performance. *Information Systems Frontiers*, 22(2), 475–487. https://doi.org/10.1007/s10796-018-9872-5.
Ioannou, A., Tussyadiah, I., & Miller, G. (2021). That's private! Understanding travelers' privacy concerns and online data disclosure. *Journal of Travel Research*, 60(7), 1510–1526.
Joinson, A., Reips, U.-D., Buchanan, T., & Paine Schofield, C. (2010). Privacy, trust, and self-disclosure online. *Human–AI Computer Interaction*, 25, 1–24. https://doi.org/10.1080/07370020903586662.
Kannan, P. K., & Li, H. (2017). Digital marketing: A framework, review and research agenda. *International Journal of Research in Marketing*, 34(1), 22–45. https://doi.org/10.1016/j.ijresmar.2016.11.006.
Kokolakis, S. (2017). Privacy attitudes and privacy behaviour: A review of current research on the privacy paradox phenomenon. *Computers & Security*, 64, 122–134. https://doi.org/10.1016/j.cose.2015.07.002.
Kosinski, M., Stillwell, D., & Graepel, T. (2013). Private traits and attributes are predictable from digital records of human behavior. *Proceedings of the National Academy of Sciences*, 110(15), 5802–5805. https://doi.org/10.1073/pnas.1218772110.

Little, R. J. A. (1993). Statistical analysis of masked data. *Journal of Official Statistics*, 9(2), 407–426.

Liu, C., & Mittal, P. (2016). LinkMirage: Enabling privacy-preserving analytics on social relationships. http://dx.doi.org/10.14722/ndss.2016.23277.

Malhotra, N., Kim, S., & Agarwal, J. (2004). Internet users' information privacy concerns (IUIPC): The construct, the scale, and a causal model. *Information Systems Research*, 15(4), 336–355. https://doi.org/10.1287/isre.1040.0032.

Martin, K. D., Borah, A., & Palmatier, R. W. (2017). Data privacy: Effects on customer and firm performance. *Journal of Marketing*, 81(1), 36–58. https://doi.org/10.1509/jm.15.0497.

Martin, K. D., & Murphy, P. E. (2017). The role of data privacy in marketing. *Journal of the Academy of Marketing Science*, 45(2), 135–155. https:// doi .org/ 10 .1007/s11747-016-0495-4.

Martin, K. D., & Palmatier, R. W. (2020). Data privacy in retail: Navigating tensions and directing future research. *Journal of Retailing*, 96(4), 449–457. https://doi.org/10.1016/j.jretai.2020.10.002.

Mikalef, P., Boura, M., Lekakos, G., & Krogstie, J. (2019). Big data analytics and firm performance: Findings from a mixed-method approach. *Journal of Business Research*, 98(2), 261–276. https://doi.org/10.1016/j.jbusres.2019.01.044.

Narayanan, A., & Shmatikov, V. (2008). Robust de-anonymization of large sparse datasets. *2008 IEEE Symposium on Security and Privacy*, 111–125. https://doi.org/10.1109/SP.2008.33.

Norberg, P. A., Horne, D. R., & Horne, D. A. (2007). The privacy paradox: Personal information disclosure intentions versus behaviors. *Journal of Consumer Affairs*, 41(1), 100–126. https://doi.org/10.1111/j.1745-6606.2006.00070.x.

Patil, V. T., & Shyamasundar, R. K. (2017). Privacy as a currency: Un-regulated? *Proceedings of the 14th International Joint Conference on E-Business and Telecommunications – SECRYPT*, 2, 586–595. https:// doi .org/ 10 .5220/0006478705860595.

Petrescu, M., Krishen, A., & Bui, M. (2020). The internet of everything: Implications of marketing analytics from a consumer policy perspective. *Journal of Consumer Marketing*, 37(6), 675–686. https://doi.org/10.1108/JCM-02-2019-3080.

Plangger, K., & Montecchi, M. (2020). Thinking beyond privacy calculus: Investigating reactions to customer surveillance. *Journal of Interactive Marketing*, 50(1), 32–44. https://doi.org/10.1016/j.intmar.2019.10.004.

Ponte, G., Wieringa, J. E., Boot, T., & Verhoef, P. C. (2024). Where's Waldo? A framework for quantifying the privacy-utility trade-off in marketing applications. *International Journal of Research in Marketing*, forthcoming. https://doi.org/10.1016/j.ijresmar.2024.05.003

Rafieian, O., & Yoganarasimhan, H. (2021). Targeting and privacy in mobile advertising. *Marketing Science*, 40(2), 193–218. https://doi.org/10.1287/mksc.2020.1235.

Reddy, S. K., & Reinartz, W. (2017). Digital transformation and value creation: Sea change ahead. *GfK Marketing Intelligence Review*, 9(1), 10–17. https:// doi .org/ 10.1515/gfkmir-2017-0002.

Rust, R. T., Kannan, P. K., & Peng, N. (2002). The customer economics of internet privacy. *Journal of the Academy of Marketing Science*, 30(4), 455–464. https:// doi.org/10.1177/009207002236917.

Schäfer, F., Gebauer, H., Gröger, C., Gassmann, O., & Wortmann, F. (2022). Data-driven business and data privacy: Challenges and measures for product companies. *Business Horizons*, S0007681322001288. https://doi.org/10.1016/j.bushor.2022.10.002.

Schneider, M. J., Jagpal, S., Gupta, S., Li, S., & Yu, Y. (2018). A flexible method for protecting marketing data: An application to point-of-sale data. *Marketing Science*, 37(1), 153–171. https://doi.org/10.1287/mksc.2017.1064.

Schwartz, P. M. (2004). Property, privacy, and personal data. *Harvard Law Review*, 117(7), 2056–2128.

Sheth, J. (2021). New areas of research in marketing strategy, consumer behavior, and marketing analytics: The future is bright. *Journal of Marketing Theory and Practice*, 29(1), 3–12. https://doi.org/10.1080/10696679.2020.1860679.

Sheth, J., & Kellstadt, C. H. (2021). Next frontiers of research in data driven marketing: Will techniques keep up with data tsunami? *Journal of Business Research*, 125, 780–784. https://doi.org/10.1016/j.jbusres.2020.04.050.

Sivarajah, U., Kamal, M. M., Irani, Z., & Weerakkody, V. (2017). Critical analysis of Big Data challenges and analytical methods. *Journal of Business Research*, 70, 263–286. https://doi.org/10.1016/j.jbusres.2016.08.001.

Skiera, B., Miller, K., Jin, Y., Kraft, L., Laub, R., & Schmitt, J. (2022). *The Impact of the GDPR on the Online Advertising Market*. leanpub.com.

Smith, H. J., Dinev, T., & Xu, H. (2011). Information privacy research: An interdisciplinary review. *MIS Quarterly*, 35(4), 989–1015. https://doi.org/10.2307/41409970.

Spiekermann, S., Großklags, J., & Berendt, B. (2001). Stated privacy preferences versus actual behaviour in EC environments: A reality check. In H. U. Buhl, N. Kreyer, & W. Steck (Eds.), *e-Finance* (pp. 129–148). Springer. https://doi.org/10.1007/978-3-642-59504-2_8.

Statista (2022). Big data market size revenue forecast worldwide from 2011 to 2027. https://www.statista.com/statistics/254266/global-big-data-market-forecast/.

Sweeney, L. (2002). k-anonymity: A model for protecting privacy. *International Journal of Uncertainty, Fuzziness and Knowledge-Based Systems*, 10(5), 557–570. https://doi.org/10.1142/S0218488502001648.

Tan, X., Qin, L., Kim, Y., & Hsu, J. (2012). Impact of privacy concern in social networking websites. *Internet Research*, 22(2), 211–233. https://doi.org/10.1108/10662241211214575.

Tang, J., Korolova, A., Bai, X., Wang, X., & Wang, X. (2017). Privacy loss in Apple's implementation of differential privacy on MacOS 10. https://doi.org/10.48550/arXiv.1709.02753.

Taylor, D. G., Davis, D. F., & Jillapalli, R. (2009). Privacy concern and online personalization: The moderating effects of information control and compensation. *Electronic Commerce Research*, 9(3), 203–223. https://doi.org/10.1007/s10660-009-9036-2.

Tucker, C. (2014). Social networks, personalized advertising, and privacy controls. *Journal of Marketing Research*, 51(5), 546–562.

Varadarajan, R. (2020). Customer information resources advantage, marketing strategy and business performance: A market resources based view. *Industrial Marketing Management*, 89, 89–97. https://doi.org/10.1016/j.indmarman.2020.03.003.

Verhoef, P. C., Broekhuizen, T., Bart, Y., Bhattacharya, A., Dong, J. Q., Fabian, N., & Haenlein, M. (2021a). Digital transformation: A multidisciplinary reflection and research agenda. *Journal of Business Research*, 122, 889–901. https://doi.org/10.1016/j.jbusres.2019.09.022.

Verhoef, P. C., Kooge, E., Walk, N., & Wieringa, J. E. (2021b). *Creating Value with Data Analytics in Marketing: Mastering Data Science* (2nd edition). Routledge. https://doi.org/10.4324/9781003011163.

Wang, H., Lee, M. K. O., & Wang, C. (1998). Consumer privacy concerns about Internet marketing. *Communications of the ACM*, 41(3), 63–70. https://doi.org/10.1145/272287.272299.
Wang, S., Beatty, S. E., & Foxx, W. (2004). Signaling the trustworthiness of small online retailers. *Journal of Interactive Marketing*, 18(1), 53–69. https://doi.org/10.1002/dir.10071.
Wedel, M., & Kannan, P. K. (2016). Marketing analytics for data-rich environments. *Journal of Marketing*, 80(6), 97–121. https://doi.org/10.1509/jm.15.0413.
Wieringa, J. E., Kannan, P. K., Ma, X., Reutterer, T., Risselada, H., & Skiera, B. (2021). Data analytics in a privacy-concerned world. *Journal of Business Research*, 122, 915–925. https://doi.org/10.1016/j.jbusres.2019.05.005.
Wirtz, J., Kunz, W. H., Hartley, N., & Tarbit, J. (2023). Corporate digital responsibility in service firms and their ecosystems. *Journal of Service Research*, 26(2), 173–190. https://doi.org/10.1177/10946705221130467.

6 Retail platformization in digital transformation

Julian R. K. Wichmann and Werner J. Reinartz

Introduction

The past decades of digital transformation have brought about a dominant new force in the economy, the digital platform (Verhoef et al., 2021). Today, five out of the world's ten most valuable companies feature a platform at the core of their business model (Forbes, 2022). Their core characteristics—a focus on mediation, autonomy of participants, network effects, and digital infrastructure—allow them to grow rapidly on both market sides—demand and supply—while incurring low cost of sales (Reinartz, Wiegand, & Wichmann, 2019). After all, a platform like eBay does not stock any products, Airbnb owns no hotels, homes, or beds, and Uber does not employ a single driver. Instead, they act as intermediaries that bring together demand and supply, enabling and facilitating their exchange. Consequently, "platform by birth" eBay became profitable almost instantly after its inception in 1995 (Tarnoff, 2022) whereas "retailer by birth" Amazon only became profitable in 2002—eight years after being founded and two years after platformizing with the launch of its marketplace (CNN Money, 2002). Platformization is thus one of the major changes in today's marketplace and requires important strategic challenges for firms. In the following, we first discuss the strategic impact of platformization and present and structure the vast academic platform literature presenting an overview of the most common platform types. Subsequently, we describe the retailing market and the effects that platformization had on retailers' traditional core competencies of distribution, assortment size, assortment curation, service, and experience. Thereafter, we present the three generic platformization strategies for established retailers illustrated by multiple case studies. Finally, we present implications to managers and future research directions for academics.

Impact of platformization

Given their dominance, platforms have profoundly impacted *industries*, *value-creation chains*, *modes of work*, and *consumer demands and habits*. For example, ride-hailing platforms Uber and Lyft have disrupted the business-to-business (B2B) and business-to-consumer (B2C) ground transportation industries resulting in substantial revenue losses among taxi and rental car companies (Muller, 2020).

In addition, digital platforms have reshaped the traditional value-creation chain as value creation on platforms is fundamentally shaped by consumers and the value they draw from the platform (crowdsourcing) and create for it (crowdsending; Wichmann, Wiegand et al., 2022a). Consequently, entirely new value types emerge on platforms (e.g., consumer social value through the psychological benefits provided by other platform participants; Wichmann et al., 2022) while others increase in importance (e.g., inter-consumer influence and referrals; Kumar & Reinartz, 2016). Moreover, manufacturers increasingly use platform structures to circumvent the traditional intermediation through retailers in favor of direct interactions (and transactions) with consumers (Wichmann, Wiegand et al., 2022a). Consequently, the traditional pipeline model (manufacturer → retailer → consumer) is increasingly dismantled in favor of a value-creation orchestration among multiple stakeholders (Alstyne et al., 2016). Hence, manufacturers and new "online-born" entrants have much to gain from the accelerating platformization of the market as it allows them to challenge retailers' direct interface to consumers (Reinartz, Wiegand, & Imschloss, 2019).

Furthermore, digital platforms have reshaped established modes of work by making consumers the central part of the value-creation process. Hence, consumers do not only create the demand for platforms but often also the supply (Wichmann, Uppal et al., 2022). On Uber, Lyft, and BlaBlaCar, for example, consumers are not only passengers but also offer rides; on Airbnb consumers take on the roles of guests as well as hosts; and on Etsy consumers sell as well as buy self-made products. As part of the sharing (and gig) economy, platforms have also normalized highly flexible work arrangements (Eckhardt et al., 2019) that create financial opportunities for many workers (Chen et al., 2019) while also raising new issues in terms of, for example, labor rights, unionization, and accountability (Vallas & Schor, 2020).

At the same time, platformization shapes consumer demands and habits. Brand aggregation platforms (or "aggregator platforms" for brevity's sake from here on out) like Amazon, JD.com, or OTTO are digital marketplaces that focus on aggregating and enabling commercial transactions of branded products, which distinguishes them from, for instance, services-oriented platforms (e.g., Uber, TaskRabbit) and other types of interpersonal matchmakers (e.g., Tinder, Glassdoor) (Wichmann, Wiegand et al., 2022a). These aggregator platforms offer virtually endless digital shelves stocked with a staggering number and variety of brands. They typically pair their immense assortments with convenient buying processes, quick delivery to consumers' doorsteps, and competitive prices as multiple vendors of the same products underprice each other (Reinartz, Wiegand, & Wichmann, 2019, p. 24). Consequently, the majority of consumers now begin their online shopper journey directly on an aggregator platform (depending on the study, 37 percent, 61 percent, or 57 percent) rather than on a search engine (34 percent, 23 percent, 30 percent), not to mention at a retailer or brand website (24.5 percent, 16 percent, 18 percent) (Attest, 2019; eMarketer Editors, 2020; Wunderman Thompson Commerce, 2022).

Hence, aggregator platforms have been exercising immense pressure on traditional retailers and, as a consequence, many retailers have lost market share, gone bankrupt, or been relegated to become suppliers for platforms. In Germany, for example, the two major department store chains Galeria Kaufhof and Karstadt were forced to merge, were bailed out by the government, and closed down a large share of their stores (EHI, 2023). In the U.S.A., JCPenney had been struggling since the early 2010s and declared bankruptcy in 2020 (Meyersohn, 2022).

However, as we show in this work, the poison can also be the antidote. That is, in order to deal with the growing threat from aggregator platforms, traditional retailers may embrace digital transformation by platformizing themselves (Verhoef et al., 2021). That is, they may establish their own digital platform that orchestrates value-creating interactions among its stakeholders—usually consumers and suppliers (Boudreau, 2017; Wichmann, Wiegand et al., 2022a). Examples of such platformized or platformizing retailers can be found in Walmart in the U.S.A., Kaufland in Germany, and Bol.com in the Netherlands. Importantly, we argue that not all thus-emerging retail platforms are created equal. Instead, retailers have different strategic options in terms of how they platformize and in what type of retail platform they turn into. Consequently, retailers are not doomed to copycat established aggregator platforms but, as we show, can choose among three distinct paths towards retail platformization. Hence, managers can strategically select the path that best suits the retailer's underlying competitive environment and idiosyncratic strengths. Our work thus shows how retailers can respond to the challenges presented by the digital transformation of the marketplace, in the form of increasingly dominant aggregator platforms, through their own digital transformation into one of three retail platform types.

Naturally, further strategies to oppose aggregator platforms may exist that embrace or forego an own digital transformation. For example, recent work argues that providing small but focused and competitively priced assortments in traditional brick-and-mortar retail formats such as Trader Joe's effectively wards off competitors (Steenkamp & Sloot, 2018). Also, physical retailers may emphasize the experiential character and service focus in their stores to set themselves apart from the online competition such as German owner-operated fashion retailer L&T which not only features an extensive food court but also an indoor pool with a standing wave for surfing (Reinartz & Hudetz, 2019). In addition, traditional retailers may embrace the various efficiency gains that a digital transformation may bring about such as grab-and-go systems that allow for cashierless stores through AI-powered camera tracking systems, self-service counters, service AI, or replenishment robots (Shankar et al., 2021). Finally, aggregator platforms may also serve as an attractive additional sales channel for retailers because of their large, often global customer base (Maier & Wieringa, 2021). Hence, instead of platformizing themselves, retailers may simply join an existing platform. C&A, a major European clothing retailer, for example, has joined aggregator platforms Amazon and Zalando.

Covering all the potential strategies to compete or collaborate with aggregator platforms in depth would exceed the scope of this research. Therefore, we focus firmly on platformization-related strategies and encourage future research to explore those strategies that relate to other facets of digital transformation or those that forego it completely in favor of strengthening or reconfiguring traditional retail competencies.

A brief overview of the academic platform literature

Platforms have a rich history in academic research going back to the 1980s with Katz and Shapiro's (1985) seminal work on network effects and later Rochet and Tirole's (2003) work on two-sided markets. While this early research originated in economics, marketing entered the research stream at the end of the 1990s with work by Padmanabhan and colleagues (1997) on technology platforms.

Drawing on Rietveld and Schilling's (2021) systematic literature review, we observe that research on platforms has experienced steady growth up to 2016;

since then, work in the field across disciplines has grown exponentially, with an explosion of publications in the past two years. Specifically, the number of published papers in the major journals across economics, information systems, management, and marketing has almost doubled between 2016 and 2020 from 21 to 40 publications. And over the subsequent two years, research output has again more than doubled with 107 publications in 2022, 20 percent of those in marketing journals. To date, the marketing discipline counts a total of 86 publications on platforms across the major marketing journals. Marketing research on platforms has an especially strong interface with economics with more than half of the papers cited in marketing publications coming from economics (Rietveld & Schilling, 2021).

From this rich academic background, a vast nomenclature for platforms has evolved leading to a fragmented and unclear landscape with often fuzzy and inconsistent definitions such as platforms, ecosystems, and branded apps. In the following, we will give an overview of the most often-used platform terms which we summarize in Table 6.1 along with their definitions, defining characteristics, and examples.

An *ecosystem* describes the loose network of the direct and indirect connections between a focal firm and its relevant stakeholders (Gawer & Cusumano, 2008). A prominent example is Apple's iPhone ecosystem which directly and indirectly connects a whole range of parties with each other and the consumer; for example, app developers through the app store, musicians and labels through iTunes, and third-party accessory manufacturers through the physical and digital interfaces. To manage this network, a *platform* can connect the company with one or more of its stakeholders and/or stakeholders with each other (Altman & Tushman, 2017). Hence, platforms represent the digital infrastructure that mediates the interactions within a company's ecosystem (e.g., the app store as a marketplace platform within the iPhone ecosystem). The involved parties fall into four categories: (a) the platform owner, who owns the intellectual property of the platform, (b) the platform provider, running the platform and controlling its interface with the user, (c) platform producers that offer products, services, and content, and (d) platform consumers that consume the offerings (Alstyne et al., 2016). Importantly, the parties can take on several roles, that is, the same company may be the platform owner and provider while consumers can also take on the role of producers (Alstyne et al., 2016; Eckhardt et al., 2019). "Platform" is an exceedingly broad term that includes a vast range of different manifestations. In the following, we present, explain, and provide examples of some of the commonly used terms and platform types from the academic literature. Please note that some of these platform types have partial overlaps so that individual examples may fit multiple platform terminologies.

Multisided platforms (MSPs) represent a specific group of platforms that connect two or more *distinct* sides to enable *direct* interactions between them (Altman & Tushman, 2017; Hagiu & Wright, 2015). This definition implies that, first, the platform does not interfere in interactions but focuses on providing the infrastructure that allows parties to find and directly interact with one another. Hence, the parties retain control over central components of the interaction such as product presentation or pricing (Hagiu & Wright, 2015). Second, the demand and supply sides are clearly distinguishable during the exchange. *Digital marketplaces*, *matchmaking platforms*, and *knowledge exchange platforms* are common varieties of MSPs that meet this definition. Digital marketplaces are MSPs that strictly focus on commercial transactions between platform producers and platform consumers (Täuscher & Laudien, 2018). Besides obvious examples like China's Amazon-equivalent Alibaba, Apple's App Store, or Google's Play Store, this also includes consumer-to-consumer (C2C) platforms like eBay or Craigslist as well as B2B platforms like online advertising exchange Google Ad Manager. Matchmaking platforms are MSPs whose value proposition rests upon providing matches between demand and supply sides with a focus on human actors (Wu et al., 2018). As such, matchmaking platforms typically center on service providers (e.g., ride-hailing app Uber, freelance labor platform TaskRabbit), interpersonal connections (e.g., dating app Tinder), or professional connections (e.g., job search on Glassdoor). All platforms need to engage in matchmaking to some degree to ensure that consumers find the offering within an often-vast assortment that best suits their needs. In the case of dedicated matchmaking platforms, however, the entire business model rests on algorithmically creating optimal matches (Wu et al., 2018). Finally, knowledge exchange platforms like Stack Overflow firmly focus on knowledge sharing among users (Kuang et al., 2019).

Perren and Kozinets (2018) introduce another group of platforms denoted *lateral exchange markets* (LEMs), which partly overlap with MSPs. They define LEMs as markets created by a "platform that facilitates exchange activities among a network of equivalently positioned economic actors" (p. 21), that is, regular consumers can assume the role of producers as well as consumers. For example, on eBay or Craigslist, actors are equivalently positioned because consumers may act as both sellers and buyers of products. The authors identify four distinct architectures of LEMs: Matchmakers simply connect consumers and producers, which interact directly with each other. Contrary to the previously discussed matchmaking platforms, matchmakers in the LEM context only feature equivalently positioned actors, as is the case for services from the *sharing economy* (Eckhardt et al., 2019). Hence, Uber or BlaBlaCar would constitute matchmakers while Glassdoor would not as a company providing a job offer is not equally positioned to a job seeker. Enablers focus on providing platform producers with the tools to exchange their offerings with consumers as on C2C platforms like eBay for second-hand products or Etsy for handmade products. Beyond product sales, enablers can also foster consumer-backed investments as on Kickstarter or online learning as on Skillshare. Exchanges in hubs are largely controlled by the platform, and the extent of direct interactions between consumers and producers is limited. In the financial community Lending Club, for example, consumers can borrow as well as lend money but only interact anonymously and in a highly intermediated fashion through Lending Club. In contrast, forums allow direct interaction between consumers and producers without any platform intermediation. Contrary to knowledge exchange platforms, they may also feature commercial transactions as on Craigslist (Perren & Kozinets, 2018).

While MSPs and LEMs focus on orchestrating interactions between different stakeholders in the focal brand's ecosystem, there are also platform types that focus on direct interactions between the brand and its customers. For example, *branded apps* are mobile applications provided by a brand designed to engage consumers in self-service activities, shopping, and brand-related social interactions (Boyd et al., 2019). German beauty care brand Nivea, for example, operates an app featuring a skin guide and opportunities to collect and redeem loyalty points, similar to the Starbucks app. *Online brand communities* are often owned and managed by brands connecting consumers around "the lifestyle, activities, and ethos of the brand" (Fournier & Lee, 2009, p. 2) as in the case of motorcycle manufacturer Harley Davidson or beauty care brand Sephora. Such communities enable consumers to share their knowledge of the brand, its products, and applications (Huang et al., 2018; Schau et al., 2009). *Virtual customer environments* (VCEs) represent various platform designs that involve customers in the brand's product development process, for example in terms of product testing, co-innovation, and co-design (Nambisan & Baron, 2009). German software firm SAP, for example, uses VCEs to co-develop products with their business clients and partners leading to quicker prototyping and turnarounds into market-ready solutions.

Ramaswamy and Ozcan (2016, 2018) introduce a novel, marketing-focused perspective on platforms. Their concept of *brand engagement platforms* (BEPs) describes a platform type that allows and encourages consumers to interact with each other, the brand, and third parties in a joint creation of experience and value (Ramaswamy & Ozcan, 2016). On L'Oréal's Style My Hair, for example, consumers can virtually try out new haircuts, share them with the community, and search for hairdressers in their vicinity. In their concept of *digitalized interactive platforms* (DIPs), Ramaswamy and Ozcan (2018) enhance this notion, arguing that DIPs allow brands to extend their activities beyond a simple "exchange of a fixed offering between a firm and its customers" (p. 19). Instead, DIPs create value through interactions between the various platform components which consist of artifacts (data), persons (platform participants), processes (mechanisms and algorithms), and interfaces (digital and physical touchpoints like apps, websites, wearables) (Ramaswamy & Ozcan, 2018). For example, Apple Watch Nike+ and the accompanying app (interfaces) allow consumers (persons) to collect, analyze, and share (processes) their workout data (artifacts). Recent technological advances have affected and will continue to affect each of the four platform components, further enhancing the creation of value: Today's brands can collect, store, analyze, and transmit a myriad of data points (artifacts), personalize interactions through algorithms (processes), connect with consumers through ambient devices (interfaces), and allow integration of participants through standardized application programming interfaces (APIs) (persons).

Recently, Wichmann, Wiegand et al. (2022a) have expanded on previous relational platform conceptualizations (Ramaswamy & Ozcan, 2016, 2018) by differentiating *brand aggregation platforms* from *brand flagship platforms*. Brand aggregation platforms are similar to digital marketplaces, enabling commercial transactions of branded products between consumers and sellers (e.g., Amazon Marketplace, JD.com). In contrast, brand flagship platforms are manufacturer-operated platforms that foster interactions with consumers beyond mere transactions by offering complementary products, services, and content beyond the core offering within a broader need category. Nike and Adidas, for example, both offer flagship platforms that allow consumers a range of workout tracking features, social functionalities to engage with a community of peers, access to third-party offerings (e.g., professional coaching, Spotify playlists, or guided running with Headspace), and access to the brands' product assortments. Bosch DIY applies the brand flagship platform concept to the DIY space with a community forum, build guides, expert advice, and more.

Of course, more platform types exist such as the hardware-software platforms as described in Binken and Stremersch (2009) and Stremersch and colleagues (2007). These, however, have more technical and operational foci and thus are less important in this research context. In addition, other platform subtypes exist such as the online-to-offline service platforms described by Zhang et al. (2019). These are more specific versions of the overarching platform types described above and thus are subsumed in these definitions. For example, online-to-offline service platforms are a subtype of matchmaking platforms that focus on local, almost instant service provision (e.g., online food delivery platforms) (Zhang et al., 2019).

The academic platform literature to date reflects the enormous variety of platforms. It also illustrates the complexity that retailers face when assessing the platformization in their market and evaluating how to best leverage platform structures for their own business. Therefore, the following sections develop several concrete paths to platformization for retailers by leveraging different platform types.

The platformization of the retailing sector

Especially the retailing sector has been deeply affected by the accelerating platformization with profound consequences for its competitive environment. To illustrate the development, we focus on the German e-commerce market in the following.

Platforms have become major competitors to retailers and outperform them, especially in the online space. In Germany, for example, the top three online shops (retailers and platforms) by revenue are platforms (Amazon, OTTO, Zalando; see EHI Retail Institute, 2021). Total revenues for online marketplaces amount to more than €45 billion, considerably exceeding the €27 billion of online retailers (bevh, 2023). With 46 percent online marketplaces make up almost half of the entire online retailing revenues (HDE & IFH Köln, 2022). While the online share of revenues in the overall retail industry in Germany is only 14.7 percent of the total €588 billion—demonstrating that stationary retailing is still a dominant market force—the share of online revenues has been growing rapidly by an average 12.7 percent annually since the early 2010s (HDE & IFH Köln, 2021, 2022). Importantly, there are substantial differences among retail sectors. That is, in clothing, toys, and consumer electronics, the majority of sales (>50 percent) are already generated online, while sectors like furniture (<20 percent), DIY (<10 percent), and fast-moving consumer goods (FMCG) (<5 percent) are still trailing behind (HDE & IFH Köln, 2022). Also, stationary retailers have steadily increased the share of products sold online over the past decades. Interestingly, however, the share of products sold via their own online shops has fallen from 77 percent in 2010 to 60 percent in 2021, suggesting the growing importance of online marketplaces as digital sales channels for traditional retailers (HDE & IFH Köln, 2022).

Table 6.1 Overview of platform concepts

Terminology	Definition	Core characteristics	Example
Ecosystem	"Ecosystems organize and leverage external entities, which are frequently complementors and have interdependencies between them" (Altman & Tushman, 2017, p. 180).	Loosely organized web of interdependent and interacting parties.	Apple's iPhone ecosystem
Platform	"Platforms sit at the nexus of a multiple relationships to orchestrate value-creating interactions" (Boudreau, 2017, p. 228).	A central organ that orchestrates value-creating interactions.	Any of the examples below
Multisided platform (MSP)	"[...] MSPs have two key features [...]: • They enable direct interactions between two or more distinct sides. • Each side is affiliated with the platform" (Hagiu & Wright, 2015, p. 163).	Enables direct interactions between two or more distinct market sides.	Alibaba, TaskRabbit, Stack Overflow
Digital marketplace	"Marketplaces [...] enable and support transactions between independent supply- and demand-side participants" (Täuscher & Laudien, 2018, p. 319).	Platform focused on enabling commercial transactions.	Alibaba, Craigslist, Google Ad Manager
Matchmaking platform	A two-sided market that "provide[s] matchmaking services that help customers find compatible partners" (Wu et al., 2018, p. 406).	Matchmaking (bringing together two human actors) as the platform's key value proposition.	TaskRabbit, Tinder, Glassdoor
Knowledge exchange platform	"[I]ndividuals can simultaneously share their knowledge, experience, and expertise by answering questions and posting articles" (Kuang et al., 2019, p. 290).	Exchange of knowledge between equally positioned actors.	Stack Overflow, Quora.com

Terminology	Definition	Core characteristics	Example
Lateral exchange market (LEM)	"[A] market that is formed through an intermediating technology platform that facilitates exchange activities among a network of equivalently positioned economic actors" (Perren & Kozinets, 2018, p. 21).	Platform producers and consumers are equivalently positioned.	Craigslist, Airbnb, Skillshare
Sharing economy	"[A] technologically enabled socioeconomic system with five key characteristics (i.e., temporary access, transfer of economic value, platform mediation, expanded consumer role, and crowd-sourced supply)" (Eckhardt et al., 2019, p. 5).	Ownership is temporary and mediated by a matchmaker; consumers are also producers.	BlaBlaCar, LendingClub
Branded app	"[S]oftware downloadable to a mobile device which prominently displays a brand identity [...] throughout the user experience" (Bellman et al., 2011, p. 191).	Enables direct interactions between brand and customers.	Nivea app, Starbucks app
Online brand community	"[A] group of ardent consumers organized around the lifestyle, activities, and ethos of the brand" (Fournier & Lee, 2009, p. 2).	Brand-related knowledge sharing among customers.	Harley-Davidson, Sephora
Virtual customer environment (VCE)	"[P]rovide services ranging from online discussion forums to virtual design and prototyping centers, enable firms to involve their customers in product design, product testing, and product support activities" (Nambisan & Baron, 2009, p. 389).	Firm-operated platform interacting with customers to co-innovation.	SAP Co-Innovation Lab
Brand engagement platform (BEP)	"[A]ny physical/digital interactional assemblage of persons [...], artifacts (including data), interfaces, and processes, whose design intensifies agencial engagement" (Ramaswamy & Ozcan, 2016, p. 96).	Designed to intensify consumers' brand engagement.	L'Oréal Style My Hair

Terminology	Definition	Core characteristics	Example
Digitalized interactive platform (DIP)	"[A]n evolving digitalized networked arrangement of artifacts, persons, processes, and interfaces [...] where value is created through interactions, versus [...] the exchange of a fixed offering" (Ramaswamy & Ozcan, 2018, p. 19).	Creates value through interactions on the platform instead of commercial transactions.	Apple Watch Nike+
Brand aggregation platform	"Platform-brand-owned digital platform that mediates discrete transactions between buyers and commercial sellers of branded products" (Wichmann, Wiegand, et al., 2022a, p. 112).	Focus on aggregating and enabling commercial transactions of branded products.	Amazon Marketplace, JD.com, OTTO
Brand flagship platform	"Product-brand-owned digital platform that mediates versatile interactions between participants within the brand-related category space" (Wichmann, Wiegand, et al., 2022a, p. 112).	Product-brand-owned platform fostering intimate and ongoing interactions with consumers.	Nike Run Club, Adidas Runtastic, Bosch DIY

Threats to Traditional Retailer's Core Competencies

Digitalization has put substantial pressure on the traditional brick-and-mortar retailing format attacking some of its core competencies as we show in Figure 6.1 and explicate in the following.

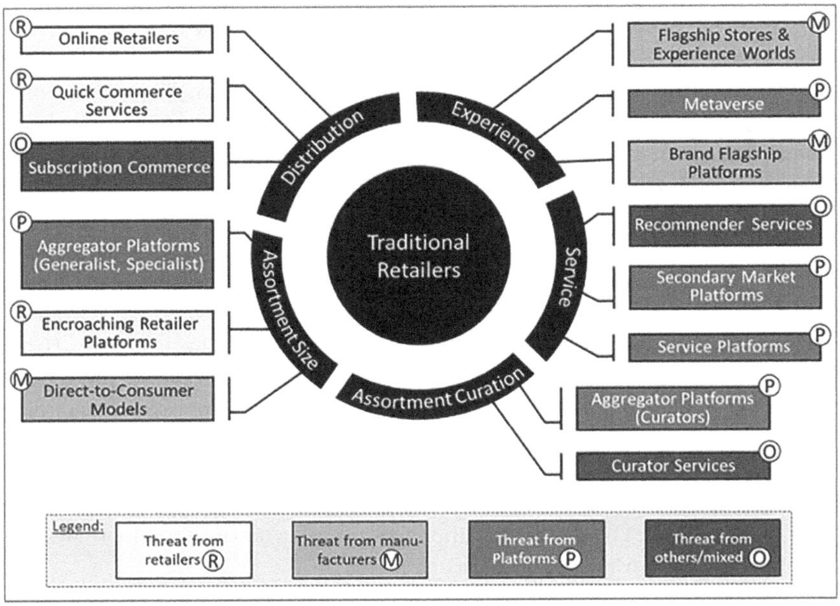

Source: Authors.

Figure 6.1 Traditional retailers' core competencies and their challengers

Distribution

For the competence of distribution, traditional retailers face several challenges from within the retailing sector such as the still-growing online retailing. Offering convenient delivery modes, *online retailers* have permeated into virtually any market segment including the initially sluggish FMCG and furniture markets. While online shares are still low in these categories, they exhibit extraordinary annual growth rates of more than 35 percent in Germany (HDE & IFH Köln, 2022).

Recently, *quick commerce services* such as Gorillas, Flink, Getir, and Grab have introduced a new distribution format that allows ultrafast delivery times of around ten minutes typically by (e-)bike or scooter in larger cities. Thereby, these services challenge stationary retailers on their ability to make products immediately available to consumers which is a major reason for consumers to shop offline (National Retail Federation, 2022). Importantly, however, it remains unclear whether these new contenders can become profitable in the long term. Their early business was strongly driven by steep price promotions to drive growth and, therefore, difficult to maintain long-term in the low-margin FMCG market, especially with rising labor costs and decreasing labor supply (Ellett et al., 2022). While German Gorillas reports that a quarter of its delivery centers operate profitably today and expects to achieve group-level profitability in 2023, the company is also cutting jobs and collaborating with larger retailers (Humphries et al., 2022).

Subscription commerce also plays an increasingly important role in distribution as it offers convenience to consumers and a more steady and reliable income stream to companies by increasing consumer loyalty (Hauck & Mlynarski, 2022). Today, an average U.S. consumer is subscribed to four services (Choi et al., 2021). For a long time, subscription models were limited to some main categories such as magazines and paid circulations, software products, or club memberships. Nowadays, however, subscription models are also increasingly employed for regular product offerings by platforms such as Amazon's Subscribe & Save option, various food box deliverers (e.g., HelloFresh), and manufacturers like Gillette and Philips who offer subscriptions for their consumables (e.g., razor blades, toothbrush heads).

Interestingly, even retailers like The Home Depot and Bed Bath & Beyond are offering subscription models which is an intriguing development considering that retailers have a long tradition of influencing consumer decision-making at the point-of-sale through, for example, shelf placement, tasting booths, displays, and banners (e.g., Chandon et al., 2009; Shankar et al., 2011). Hence, when traditional retailers use subscription models, consumers likely become less susceptible to those in-store marketing stimuli because the initial decision to set up a specific subscription is probably more conscious and involved compared to a regular in-store purchase while subsequently changing a subscription comes with inertia (Henderson et al., 2021). Hence, for retailers introducing subscription models interesting new dynamics emerge, especially for in-store marketing and manufacturers' advertising allowances.

Assortment size

In terms of retailers' competence assortment size, *aggregator platforms* have put considerable pressure on traditional retailers. Through (indirect) network effects, they can attract a large number of consumers and suppliers through positive feedback loops in which additional consumers draw more producers to the platform and vice versa (Chu & Manchanda, 2016; Katz & Shapiro, 1994). Digitization considerably boosts these network effects because it lifts physical and temporal constraints. After all, platforms do not have to offer own storage but can function as mere matchmakers, allowing them to accommodate a virtually infinite number of consumers and producers and a practically endless shelf irrespective of their physical location (Alba et al., 1997). As a case in point, Airbnb offers more accommodation than the major hotel chains combined (Hartmans, 2017). The substantial assortment size of aggregator platforms gives rise to "the long tail" (Anderson, 2004), allowing consumers to find precisely the offering they are looking for, thus minimizing the need to compromise (Brynjolfsson, 2003; Hoch et al., 1999). Aggregator platforms thus become one-stop shops that minimize consumers' transaction costs (Messinger & Narasimhan, 1997). Such aggregator platforms can take a generalist approach, offering products from virtually any product category such as Alibaba or Google Shopping, or they can take a more specialized approach, focusing on an individual product category such as StockX, a platform for reselling sneakers.

However, traditional retailers are not only challenged by aggregator platforms like eBay but increasingly also by *encroaching retailer platforms* entering their market. These are "retailers by birth" that either fully transform into a platform or follow a hybrid approach by combining their retailing and marketplace such as Amazon, OTTO, or Bol.com. By substantially increasing their assortment size through platformization, these retailers extend their assortment into further product categories and enter adjacent markets. Thereby, they encroach upon retailers that are native to the respective market and that they were not competing with before. For example, German fashion retailer Zalando launched its marketplace in 2018 through which it now provides a vast assortment covering beauty products, consumer electronics, and sports equipment. Hence, Zalando does not only compete in the fashion space any longer but also with perfumeries, drugstores, consumer electronics retailers, and sporting goods retailers. Accordingly, the necessary competencies for encroaching retailers increasingly shift: assortment and product expertise are "outsourced" to the platform suppliers while technological excellence becomes crucial to provide smooth, reliable, and convenient discovery and buying processes for consumers (e.g., through collaborative filtering, one-click shopping), and value-adding interfaces for platform suppliers (e.g., providing data and insights on page visits and purchases).

Finally, manufacturers are increasingly competing with traditional retailers, too, by employing *direct-to-consumer (DTC) models*. Thereby, they offer their complete assortments directly to consumers through their own physical stores (Wang et al., 2009), own online shops (Chiang et al., 2003), or platforms (Reinartz, Wiegand, & Imschloss, 2019). In this way, especially loyalists of the manufacturer brands profit from the direct interaction with the brand and the deep brand-specific assortment (Tahirov & Glock, 2022). For manufacturers, the direct sales channel offers significant revenue potential with higher margins and a greater level of control over the product presentation (Chiang et al., 2003). Nike, for example, has been able to build a substantial direct sales channel that has doubled its revenues since 2017 and now accounts for more than $18 billion annually or around 40 percent of its revenues (Nike, 2022). Importantly, the direct channel does not necessarily require own infrastructure (e.g., own stores, an online shop, or a platform) but brands may also join existing aggregator platforms. On Amazon, for example, brands can choose between one-party versus third-party modes. In the one-party mode, the manufacturer acts as a traditional wholesaler to the platform resulting in the classical indirect sales channel from the perspective of the manufacturer. In contrast, in the third-party setting, manufacturers can establish a direct sales channel to consumers in which they retain full control over pricing, presentation (within the confines of the general platform layout and capabilities), and fulfillment. However, as interactions are still mediated by the platform, manufacturers do forego data sovereignty and typically incur some transaction fees (Bei & Gielens, 2023).

Assortment curation

An important competence of retailers is not only offering consumers choice through a large assortment but also curating the offering to reduce choice overload and buyer's remorse and ensure quality (Gourville & Soman, 2005; Xu et al., 2013).

This competence is challenged by *aggregator platforms* that are less concerned with offering broad (generalist) or deep (specialist) assortments but instead curate an assortment around a central theme. Take Avocadostore as an example of a curating aggregator platform. This online marketplace offers products from various categories but only as long as they are ecologically produced. Marketplace EarthHero takes it a step further by allowing consumers to "shop by values," that is, filtering the assortment based on values such as "made in USA," "Black owned," or "Zero-waste packaging." Hence, these platforms tend to curate their offerings around ideals, thereby, addressing consumers' increasing desire to "vote with their wallets," that is, buying products and brands that align with their values (Becchetti & Salustri, 2019; StrategyOne, 2010). *Curator services* put an even stronger emphasis on assortment curation by offering highly customized selections of products. Outfittery, Maison365, and Stitch Fix are examples from the fashion industry that regularly send customers preselected outfits based on their individual tastes and desired look following a personal style consultation. Similarly, FabFitFun sends its members curated boxes covering a variety of product categories such as beauty care, fitness, and home and consumer electronics. And home and living platform Westwing offers individualized interior design counseling based on which it constructs a personalized shop with a tailored selection of products.

Service

Service is another core competence of traditional retailers, especially given their neutral role as vendors of different brands. During the pre-purchase stage retailers typically provide consumers with important product information and personalized recommendations (Lamey et al., 2021). During the post-purchase phase, retailers have also traditionally offered additional services related to product returns and maintenance (Homburg et al., 2002).

Regarding these competencies, traditional retailers get competition from *recommender services* such as comparison platforms like Shopzilla, PriceGrabber, and Check24 which offer a broad range of filters and aggregated product reviews and ratings that guide consumers in the pre-purchase stage. For the post-purchase stage, *secondary market platforms* have emerged that allow consumers to resell their purchased products. In some cases, these platforms directly buy the products from consumers such as Zalando's pre-owned service or Refurbed for consumer electronics. In other cases, the platform acts as a marketplace helping consumers to find buyers and setting an appropriate price as is the case for eBay and StockX. *Service platforms* act as matchmakers between consumers and freelance workers of any type. Some of these platforms compete with retailers by offering repairs, assemblies, and other post-purchase services such as Jafix, MyHammer, and TaskRabbit.

Experience

Finally, in the domain of experiences traditional retailers have been competing for a while with brands' own *flagship stores and experience worlds* that are highly focused on offering an exciting and unique experience (Bell et al., 2018; Keller, 2010). Apple, for example, plans to launch so-called "town squares" where consumers are able to experience and apply their products and enjoy community through joint sharing and learning (Wichmann, Uppal et al.,

2022). A novel development in the domain of shopping experience is the nascent *metaverse* which describes technology platforms to create interactive and highly immersive virtual worlds (Hennig-Thurau et al., 2022). Creating virtual retail environments, the metaverse has the potential to adopt and significantly expand on many of the experiential functions of traditional brick-and-mortar retailing, potentially leading to yet unseen and unknown shopping experiences (Yoo et al., 2023). Finally, *brand flagship platforms* have allowed manufacturers to establish direct interfaces to consumers by offering intimate interactions and experiences around their core offering (Wichmann, Wiegand et al., 2022b). That is, a brand like Nike does not only offer a direct sales channel through its apps but also provides functionalities such as run tracking, challenges, workout playlists, and a community of fellow enthusiasts. These functionalities foster unique and novel experiences and allow Nike to connect and interact with consumers along the entire purchase process and even independently from it. In doing so, brand flagship platforms mitigate the importance of manufacturers' indirect consumer channels through retailers.

Three Paths for the Platformization of Retailers

Analyzing the market by means of desk research reveals that retailers pursue a variety of strategies when embracing digital transformation in the form of platformization. Importantly, these transformations are rarely complete. Instead, the large majority of retailers add platform elements to their existing retailing business. Amazon, for example, has a sizable marketplace but also still carries its own product assortment. In the following, we present three archetypical paths for the platformization of retailers—assortment expansion, assortment specialization, and service focus.

Naturally, these strategies are not exhaustive. Instead, as mentioned earlier, other strategies that do not relate to an own platformization (and, therefore, are out of scope of this work) may exist for retailers to compete with aggregator platforms. Such strategies may embrace other facets of digital transformation beyond platformization (e.g., lower costs and prices through technological efficiency gains) or forego digital transformation completely and instead focus on traditional retailing competencies (e.g., service excellence, shopping experience, curation, supply chain excellence).

In addition, our proposed three retail platformization paths are not mutually exclusive. Instead, they can be combined into hybrid platformization approaches. And, of course, retailers may also decide to collaborate with existing platforms instead of platformizing themselves (Maier & Wieringa, 2021). German online pharmacy Disapo, for example, not only sells its assortment through its own webshop but also through beauty care retailer Douglas. Similarly, home décor and furniture retailer Butlers sells its assortment through its own physical stores, its webshop, and various marketplaces such as OTTO, Westwing, and Home24 as well as other retailers such as C&A and Galeria Karstadt Kaufhof.

After presenting each of the three paths, we discuss their managerial implications and argue how each path relates to a distinct mode of competition with major aggregator platforms in the market. Figure 6.2 summarizes our discussions.

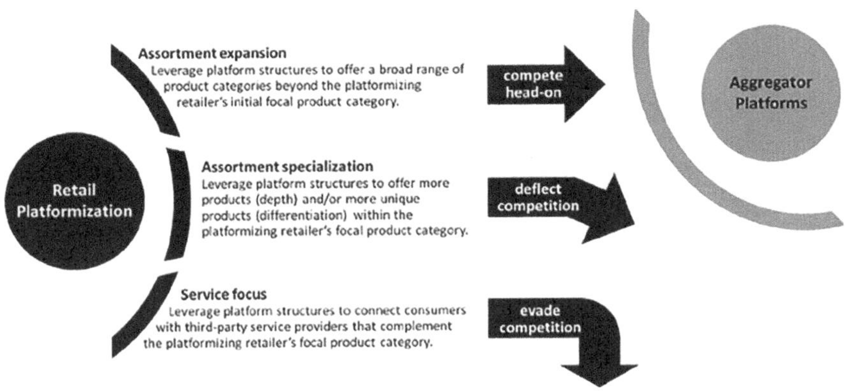

Source: Authors.

Figure 6.2 Paths to retail platformization and their competitive implications

Assortment expansion

One of the most common approaches to platformization is assortment expansion. A retailer uses platform structures to expand its own product offering. Thereby, assortments usually grow considerably in breadth extending into new product categories. Examples of this strategy are plentiful. Most prominently, Amazon initially started its business in 1994 as a retailer of books before introducing its marketplace in 2000 (Amazon, 2001). Today, it pursues a hybrid strategy acting as both a one-party and a third-party marketplace. That is, as part of the one-party platform, Amazon acts as a common online retailer, buying products from manufacturers and reselling them via its platform. In contrast, as part of its third-party marketplace, Amazon acts merely as a middleman for transactions between manufacturers (and other vendors) and consumers (Bei & Gielens, 2023). Currently, third-party sales via Amazon make up 59 percent of its total unit sales on the platform and revenues generated from third-party seller services amount to more than €36 billion; roughly half of its first-party sales revenues (Amazon, 2023).

Such a transformation is not limited to an online-born retailer like Amazon. In fact, stationary retailing behemoth Walmart underwent a similar metamorphism launching its online shop in 2000 and its marketplace in 2009 (Vusirikala, 2021). Through its initial marketplace launch alone, it was able to add around one million items to its assortment (Walmart, 2009), illustrating the substantial assortment expansion that platformization allows for. Currently, Walmart's marketplace features an estimated 100,000 sellers which, however, still dwarves Amazon's estimated 6.3 million sellers (Perez, 2021).

Similar to Walmart, OTTO started out in Germany as a mail-order retailer in 1949 and became a major online retailer over the past decades before platformizing in 2020. Despite its rather late transformation, OTTO is Germany's third-largest marketplace in terms of transaction volume (behind Amazon and eBay) featuring 3,500 vendors. And with more than €6.5 billion in revenues, its marketplace business is already twice the size of its traditional retailing business (OTTO Group, 2022).

While these companies already had vast assortments covering various product categories as retailers, others have opted to substantially expand their product category coverage by platformizing. This leads to an interesting imbalance between these retailers' stationary and platform businesses in that their brick-and-mortar stores usually still carry their traditional, much more specialized assortment while their online platform takes a generalist approach. Take Kaufland as an example, the German hypermarket chain and part of retailing giant Schwarz Gruppe which also owns Lidl. In its physical stores, Kaufland offers the typical assortment of a hypermarket with a strong focus on FMCG products and a small assortment of durables. With its online marketplace, however, it considerably expanded its assortment to virtually all product categories including furniture, consumer electronics, DIY, gardening, home appliances, and much more. Similarly, Douglas sells its traditional perfumery assortment in its stationary stores, while it has expanded its online assortment to rather distal product categories such as home décor, accessories, fashion, toys, and pet care. Interestingly, the two sides—the traditional (online and offline) retailing business and the platform business—are still separated rather strictly in most cases. For instance, neither Kaufland nor Douglas allows consumers to send or return articles from third-party vendors via their stationary stores. So while these retailers have indeed managed to create online-offline-channel synergies for their *retailing* business, they—like most others—have not yet found omnichannel solutions that also integrate their *platform* business. As such, the current early days of retail platformization are reminiscent of the early days of e-commerce in which retailers' online and offline channels were still largely separate and independent entities. However, this is bound to change as we already see retailers like Walmart leveraging their stationary store locations as fulfillment centers for their platform orders. Fulfillmenttools, a daughter company of German FMCG retailer Rewe, pursues a similar approach in its fulfillment solutions that it sells to retailers.

Assortment specialization

Instead of expanding the assortment in breadth, retailers may also use platform structures to become even more specialized in their core category. Such specialization may not only lead to greater assortment depth but also a more differentiated and curated offering as we show in the following.

Depth. French sporting goods retailer Decathlon introduced platform structures in 2021 to invite other retailers as well as manufacturers to sell sporting goods through their marketplace. In doing so, Decathlon can offer an ever-deeper assortment within the category of sporting goods. Compared to those retailers pursuing assortment expansion, Decathlon illustrates the much more focused and specialized approach of assortment specialization—since launch, it has grown the offered assortment by approximately 50 percent to 62,000 products with 300 partners (Javorovic, 2023). Hence, compared to OTTO, Walmart, and Amazon, Decathlon's marketplace is smaller by a factor of 10, 1,000, and 10,000, respectively.

German maternal and baby care retailer babymarkt follows a similar strategy. After starting out as a stationary retailer in 1989 and launching an online shop in 2004, babymarkt transformed into a marketplace in 2021 through which it provides a deeper assortment in its central product category (babymarkt, 2023).

Differentiation. British clothing retailer Asos pursues a different strategy with its marketplace. While its main online shop follows a typical retailing approach, Asos launched a marketplace in 2010 that firmly focuses on offering vintage clothing and independent brands. Asos achieves this by carefully curating the marketplace members to select small boutiques and labels from across the globe including countries like Austria, Australia, Belarus, and Bulgaria (Asos, 2023). In doing so, Asos can offer an assortment that is not merely deeper within the fashion category but also much more unique and differentiated from its competitors. Similarly, lingerie retailer Victoria's Secret recently launched its marketplace VS&Co-Lab on which it curates brands that are female-led, -owned, or -founded (Howland, 2022). Naturally, Asos and Victoria's Secret also deepen their assortment by adding these curated offerings. However, assortment depth and differentiation are not perfect correlates but tend to exhibit an inverted U-shaped relationship (Hamilton & Richards, 2009). Past research on the retailing sectors shows that assortment differentiation is a viable strategy to fend off large generalists like Walmart (Seenivasan & Talukdar, 2016). As such, leveraging platform structures to create a unique, differentiated assortment may be an especially valuable strategy in a market dominated by major generalist aggregator platforms.

Service focus

Finally, as a third platformization strategy, retailers may extend their service offering by leveraging platform structures. German DIY retailers OBI and Hagebaumarkt, for example, first help consumers plan their home renovation projects and then support the execution by acting as a matchmaker between consumers and tradespeople (Hagedoo, 2023; OBI, 2023). Thus, these DIY retailers went from merely offering tools and materials for consumers' projects to providing the entire solution, from planning to execution. Similarly, furniture manufacturer and retailer IKEA acquired TaskRabbit—a matchmaking platform for freelance workers—in 2017 to provide an assembly service to consumers (Dickey, 2017).

Pet food retailer Fressnapf uses platform structures in a variety of ways such as connecting pet owners to veterinarians, finding dog parlors and animal shelters, and providing personalized health advice through a smart dog collar and an accompanying app. Consumers can even plan and book pet-friendly holidays via Fressnapf's platform. Fressnapf thus becomes a one-stop shop for all needs related to pet ownership akin to the brand flagship platforms described in Wichmann, Wiegand et al. (2022a).

Hence, instead of offering products across a product category (assortment expansion) or specializing in a product category (assortment specialization) these service-focused platformized retailers seek to cover a need category through additional services that complement their product offering. In doing so, retailers can also differentiate themselves from platforms (and other platformized retailers) that have broader and deeper assortments by offering personalization. That is, the service focus is able to address consumers' very individual needs and personal projects, akin to the integrated consumer solutions described in prior literature (e.g., Epp & Price, 2011; Tuli et al., 2007).

Competitive implications of the three paths to retail platformization

As presented in Figure 6.2, each of the three paths to retail platformization has distinct implications for the competition with aggregator platforms.

For the *assortment expansion strategy*, the competitive implication is rather straightforward as this strategy essentially copies the common brand aggregator approach. As such, retailers platformizing through assortment expansion *compete head-on* with aggregator platforms. Nonetheless, retailers that still also operate physical locations may have some unique advantages as they may leverage their stationary store network for platform-offline synergies. While this is not the norm yet, Walmart, for example, already leverages its stores as fulfillment centers for its platform allowing for rapid deliveries. In addition, brick-and-mortar stores may also function as showrooms for products sold through the platform—similar to a store-within-store system—which may be especially relevant for product categories with a high need for touch (Wichmann, Uppal et al., 2022). B8ta pursued a similar approach by providing retail spaces to manufacturers in which they could showcase their products while retaining a great degree of control over the product presentation and receiving data on consumer interactions with their products.

In terms of *assortment specialization*, a *deep assortment* may still overlap with that of major generalist platforms. Hence, such an approach may merely *deflect competition* with aggregator platforms as competitive pressure would still be intense in the shallower, more generic parts of the assortments while it decreases in the deeper parts of the assortment. *Differentiated assortments*, in contrast, are less likely to be covered by generalists because their uniqueness requires careful curation and a closer relationship with the platform suppliers. This opposes the generalist platform approach which necessitates a greater openness towards suppliers and more distant, authoritative relationships (Broekhuizen et al., 2019). Hence, assortment specialization through differentiation may be a more potent strategy to deflect competition with major aggregator platforms than assortment specialization through depth.

When pursuing the *service focus* path, retailers move away from simply offering products towards addressing consumer needs more holistically through complementary services. As a result, retailers pursuing this platformization path may *evade competition* with generalist aggregator platforms. That is, by targeting entire consumer projects (e.g., renovating a kitchen) and providing integrated consumer solutions for these projects from start to finish (e.g., in the case of OBI planning the kitchen, providing materials, providing craftspeople, and overseeing the execution of the renovation), the locus of value creation shifts form an individual product or purchase occasion to a bundle of interlocking products and service encounters. In addition, a stronger focus on services also implies that a retailer's offering gradually moves from a search good towards an experience or even credence good. This, in turn, may make these retailers and their offerings less susceptible to simple comparisons of price and quality (e.g., through ratings and reviews) (Lu & Rui, 2018), thereby, decreasing competitive pressure. Take, for example, an integrated consumer solution such as a complete kitchen renovation. For consumers, it is difficult to evaluate and compare this service to other offerings a priori. And even a posteriori, the quality is difficult to judge because it remains unclear whether a competitor would have come up with a better design, a smoother execution, or a quicker completion. As a result, platformizing through a service focus shifts a retailer furthest from the competitive pressure of aggregator platforms.

Managerial implications and future research directions

Retailers are under substantial pressure from the effects of digitalization and especially platformization which has birthed new competitors and intensified the competition with existing ones, especially in terms of *distribution*, *assortment size*, *assortment curation*, *service*, and *experience*. To weather this challenging new market environment, we present three paths for retailers to leverage digital transformation through platformization to *compete head-on* with aggregator platforms through *assortment expansion*, *deflect competition* through *assortment specialization*, or *evade competition* through *service focus*.

Managerial Implications

Evidently, the three paths towards retail platformization present managers of traditional retailers with plentiful opportunities to remain competitive in the platform era.[1] However, they must carefully consider the market environment as well as their internal conditions to select the best-suited platformization approach.

In terms of *assortment expansion*, venturing into distal product categories through assortment expansion can be beneficial as retailers do not need to convince direct competitors to join the platform. However, as retailers branch out into other product categories, they must consider how this affects their brand positioning. A broad shotgun approach may dilute a carefully crafted brand and confuse consumers, especially, when the stationary stores are still confined to the original product category and brand positioning as is common for most retailers that we analyzed. Hence, managers must decide whether they want to position their brand around a large assortment or whether they want to stand for something beyond that. In the case of the latter, a more gradual and curated approach to assortment extension and selection of platform suppliers may be fruitful to ensure quality and alignment with the platform branding. However, such an approach naturally also slows platform growth.

In addition, managers must find ways to harmonize their stationary and platform approaches for a coherent shopping experience, brand positioning, and communication (Swaminathan et al., 2020). Allowing for in-store orders and returns is a start but hardly sufficient. Instead, in-store ordering kiosks or virtual shelves that display the extended platform offering may further synergize both channels.

Managers must further consider that the more product categories they enter, the higher the potential to encounter competing platforms. As such, fragmented markets with many low-power suppliers may be better suited to enter than highly concentrated markets as the incumbents would be less likely to join the platform or pull out of it quickly. Take the gaming market as an example. Epic Games—one of the major game developers (e.g., Fortnite, Unreal Tournament)—initially joined the Steam platform to sell its games only to leave it in 2018 to launch its own competing game distribution platform.

In terms of *assortment specialization*, retailers remain in their core product category and thus must convince direct competitors to join their platform. Again, this is easier in highly fragmented markets and for smaller suppliers with low bargaining power who would clearly profit from a larger retailer's size and reach. If this is not the case, managers may opt to join forces with competitors to launch a platform. This proved useful to Goldman Sachs who attempted to launch a platform for financial products. While clients were eager to join, the intended platform suppliers—that is, Goldman Sachs' rivals such as JP Morgan Chase—remained reluctant. Ultimately, however, Goldman Sachs still managed to reel in its competitors by spinning off its platform business and selling shares in it to its major competitors.

Finally, the *service focus* approach lends itself to retailers that have strong relationships with third-party service providers. In addition, integrating and leveraging stationary retail locations may be more straightforward and seamless for service-focused platforms. Fressnapf, for example, provides spaces for pet salons in its stationary stores. And when consumers want to renovate their home or garden at OBI, they can set up an appointment online to get a personal consultation in its physical stores where the service encounter is supported through virtual reality (VR) technologies. However, the service focus is also the most removed from traditional retailing as the retailer now not only curates products but also services and service providers. Hence, consumers may be skeptical at first regarding a retailer's competencies in this context. Therefore, managers must find ways to instill trust in consumers, for example, through communication campaigns or by providing guarantees.

Future Research Directions

Our research is only a first foray into retailers' platformization strategies. As such, there are still plentiful future research opportunities.

First and foremost, more research is needed on successful strategies for retailers to compete with aggregator platforms. Such research may focus on platformization-related strategies as this work, look at other digital transformation strategies, or consider strategies that forego digital transformation. Especially empirical results in this context are scarce and could add significantly to the existing literature by answering questions such as: When should a retailer platformize or pursue a different digital transformation strategy? Can retailers even still afford to forego digital transformation while staying competitive? Also, which organizational structures does a successful platformization necessitate? And how can a retailer best steer the platformization process and communicate it to consumers?

Future research could also analyze whether and when retailers should pursue a full versus partial platform transformation and explore how each of these approaches can succeed. Also, what role do contingency factors play, such as the industry, existing brand associations, or the speed of transformation?

Second, future research should also take a closer look at the specific platformization strategies to test whether our proposed relationships indeed hold. That is, are service-focused retailers and assortment specialists indeed better equipped to escape the competitive pressure from major aggregator platforms? And are these platform types thus more likely to coexist in a given market than multiple generalist platforms (including retailers that have platformized through assortment expansion)? Also, how effective are hybrid approaches?

Furthermore, when engaging in assortment extension, some product categories may have vastly different characteristics than others in terms of the competitive landscape but also in terms of their complexity and sensitive nature (e.g., pharmaceuticals, alcoholic beverages). Hence, future research should analyze how retailers can identify particularly delicate product categories, how to best integrate credible third parties for these product categories, and how to present them to consumers. Future research should also consider the role of a platformizing retailer's established brand and brand associations. More specifically, many retailers have a brand heritage tied to their core product offering. Hence, for the assortment expansion strategy, the question arises if and how far a retailer can believably expand its retailing brand to other product categories. It is notable, for example, that perfumery Douglas has expanded its assortments into all kinds of product categories but within the more distal product categories (e.g., consumer electronics or pet care) the assortment remains rather shallow and centers on lifestyle-focused products. In this way, the assortment is still loosely connected to Douglas' traditional retail brand context of health and beauty. Hence, future research may explore how a retailer's existing brand may function as the connective tissue for an ever-expanding assortment breadth providing credibility and consistency for consumers.

Similar issues may also arise in the service focus strategy in which a retailer remains in its core product category but extends its core capabilities (e.g., capabilities related to matchmaking, integrated consumer solutions, orchestrating multiple service providers, overseeing the service execution). Hence, the question arises of how a retailer can convince consumers of its proficiency in these new capabilities and which organizational transformations are needed to become a capable service provider and orchestrator.

Another important future research area pertains to the field of offline-online-platform integration which is still largely unexplored. Should retailers integrate their platform offerings into their existing offline and online business and, if so, how can they do it successfully? What do we know and can we adopt from the omnichannel literature? How can a retailer bring its platform offering into its stationary retailing business? And which role does the stationary retailing business still play when the retailer has established a thriving platform? Can platformizing retailers leverage synergies with their existing stationary stores? And can the existing brick-and-mortar locations provide a competitive advantage over online-born aggregator platforms? Current examples from the industry paint an inconclusive picture. For example, online-born Zalando has opened multiple brick-and-mortar outlet stores (Zalando, 2023). In contrast, Amazon just recently closed a large share of its physical retail locations (Dastin, 2022; Isidore, 2023).

Finally, future research should also consider the role of a platformizing retailer's established brand and brand associations. More specifically, many retailers have a brand heritage tied to their core product offering. Hence, for the assortment expansion strategy, the question arises if and how far a retailer can believably expand its retailing brand to other product categories. It is notable, for example, that perfumery Douglas has expanded its assortments into all kinds of product categories but within the more distal product categories (e.g., consumer electronics or pet care) the assortment remains rather shallow and centers on lifestyle-focused products. In this way, the assortment is still loosely connected to Douglas' traditional retail brand context of health and beauty. Hence, future research may explore how a retailer's existing brand may function as the connective tissue for an ever-expanding assortment breadth providing credibility and consistency for consumers.

Note

1. As we focus on platformization, we only cover one type of a myriad of potential digital transformation strategies. Therefore, we refer to Verhoef et al. (2021) for a more general discussion of implications for companies that seek to digitally transform.

References

Alba, J., Lynch, J., Weitz, B., Janiszewski, C., Lutz, R., Sawyer, A., & Wood, S. (1997). Interactive Home Shopping: Consumer, Retailer, and Manufacturer Incentives to Participate in Electronic Marketplaces. *Journal of Marketing, 61*(3), 38–53. https://doi.org/10.2307/1251788.

Alstyne, M. W. V., Parker, G. G., & Choudary, S. P. (2016). Pipelines, Platforms, and the New Rules of Strategy. *Harvard Business Review, 94*(4), 9.

Altman, E. J., & Tushman, M. L. (2017). Platforms, Open/User Innovation, and Ecosystems: A Strategic Leadership Perspective. In J. Furman, A. Gawer, B. S. Silverman, & S. Stern (Eds.), *Advances in Strategic Management* (Vol. 37, pp. 177–207). Emerald Publishing.

Amazon (2001). Amazon Marketplace a Winner for Customers, Sellers and Industry; New Service Grows over 200 Percent in First Four Months. Press Center. https://press.aboutamazon.com/2001/3/amazon-marketplace-a-winner-for-customers-sellers-and-industry-new-service-grows-over-200-percent-in-first-four-months.

Amazon (2023). Amazon.com Announces Fourth Quarter Results. Amazon.com, Inc. https://s2.q4cdn.com/299287126/files/doc_financials/2022/q4/Q4–2022-Amazon-Earnings-Release.pdf.

Anderson, C. (2004). The Long Tail. *Wired.* https://www.wired.com/2004/10/tail/.

Asos (2023). What Is ASOS Marketplace? Asos_marketplace. https://marketplace.asos.com/help/what-is-asos-marketplace?ctaref=mktp|footer|aboutus.

Attest (2019). Shopper Journey: Where Do You Start Your Online Shopping? Statista. https://www.statista.com/statistics/1041281/starting-point-online-shopping-uk-consumers/.

babymarkt (2023). Unsere Historie. babymarkt.de. https:// corporate .babymarkt .de/ inside/historie/.
Becchetti, L., & Salustri, F. (2019). The Vote with the Wallet Game: Responsible Consumerism as a Multiplayer Prisoner's Dilemma. *Sustainability, 11*(4), 1109. https://doi.org/10.3390/su11041109.
Bei, Z., & Gielens, K. (2023). The One-Party Versus Third-Party Platform Conundrum: How Can Brands Thrive? *Journal of Marketing, 87*(2), 253–274. https://doi.org/10 .1177/00222429221116803.
Bell, D. R., Gallino, S., & Moreno, A. (2018). Offline Showrooms in Omnichannel Retail: Demand and Operational Benefits. *Management Science, 64*(4), 1629–1651. https://doi.org/10.1287/mnsc.2016.2684.
Bellman, S., Potter, R. F., Treleaven-Hassard, S., Robinson, J. A., & Varan, D. (2011). The Effectiveness of Branded Mobile Phone Apps. *Journal of Interactive Marketing, 25*(4), 191–200.
bevh (2023). Umsatz im Online-Handel mit Waren nach Versendertyp in Deutschland in den Jahren 2020 bis 2022 (in Millionen Euro). Statista. https:// de .statista .com/ statistik/ daten/ studie/ 534414/ umfrage/ umsatz -im -online -handel -nach -versendertyp-in-deutschland/.
Binken, J. L. G., & Stremersch, S. (2009). The Effect of Superstar Software on Hardware Sales in System Markets. *Journal of Marketing, 73*(2), article 2. https:// doi.org/ 10 .1509/jmkg.73.2.88.
Boudreau, K. J. (2017). Platform Boundary Choices & Governance: Opening-Up While Still Coordinating and Orchestrating. In J. Furman, A. Gawer, B. S. Silverman, & S. Stern (Eds.), *Advances in Strategic Management* (Vol. 37, pp. 227–297). Emerald Publishing. https://doi.org/10.1108/S0742-332220170000037009.
Boyd, D. E., Kannan, P. K., & Slotegraaf, R. J. (2019). Branded Apps and Their Impact on Firm Value: A Design Perspective. *Journal of Marketing Research, 56*(1), 76–88. https://doi.org/10.1177/0022243718820588.
Broekhuizen, T. L. J., Emrich, O., Gijsenberg, M. J., Broekhuis, M., Donkers, B., & Sloot, L. M. (2019). Digital Platform Openness: Drivers, Dimensions and Outcomes. *Journal of Business Research, 122*. https://doi.org/10.1016/j.jbusres.2019.07.001.
Brynjolfsson, E. (2003). Consumer Surplus in the Digital Economy: Estimating the Value of Increased Product Variety at Online Booksellers. *Management Science, 49*(11), 18.
Chandon, P., Hutchinson, J. W., Bradlow, E. T., & Young, S. H. (2009). Does In-Store Marketing Work? Effects of the Number and Position of Shelf Facings on Brand Attention and Evaluation at the Point of Purchase. *Journal of Marketing, 73*(6), 1–17. https://doi.org/10.1509/jmkg.73.6.1.
Chen, M. K., Chevalier, J. A., Rossi, P. E., & Oehlsen, E. (2019). The Value of Flexible Work: Evidence from Uber Drivers. *Journal of Political Economy, 127*(6), 2735–2794. https://doi.org/10.1086/702171.
Chiang, W. K., Chhajed, D., & Hess, J. D. (2003). Direct Marketing, Indirect Profits: A Strategic Analysis of Dual-Channel Supply-Chain Design. *Management Science, 49*(1), 1–20. https://doi.org/10.1287/mnsc.49.1.1.12749.
Choi, M., Moss, S., Reasor, E., Nading, J., & Remley, D. (2021). Sign Up Now: Creating Consumer—and Business—Value with Subscriptions. McKinsey & Company. https://www.mckinsey.com/capabilities/growth-marketing-and-sales/our-insights/ sign-up-now-creating-consumer-and-business-value-with-subscriptions.
Chu, J. H., & Manchanda, P. (2016). Quantifying Cross and Direct Network Effects in Online Consumer-to-Consumer Platforms. *Marketing Science, 35*(6), 870–893.

CNN Money (2002). Amazon Posts a Profit. CNN Money. https://money.cnn.com/2002/01/22/technology/amazon/.

Dastin, J. (2022). Amazon to Shut Its Bookstores and Other Shops as Its Grocery Chain Expands. Reuters. https://www.reuters.com/business/retail-consumer/exclusive-amazon-close-all-its-physical-bookstores-4-star-shops-2022-03-02/.

Dickey, M. R. (2017). IKEA Has Bought TaskRabbit. TechCrunch. https://techcrunch.com/2017/09/28/ikea-buys-taskrabbit/.

Eckhardt, G. M., Houston, M. B., Jiang, B., Lamberton, C., Rindfleisch, A., & Zervas, G. (2019). Marketing in the Sharing Economy. *Journal of Marketing, 83*(5), 5–27. https://doi.org/10.1177/0022242919861929.

EHI (2023). *Galeria Karstadt Kaufhof*. EHI Handelsdaten.de. https://www.handelsdaten.de/unternehmensportraets/galeria-karstadt-kaufhof.

EHI Retail Institute (2021). Marktplätze: Umsatztreiber des Onlinehandels. EHI News. https://www.ehi.org/news/marktplaetze-umsatztreiber-des-onlinehandels/.

Ellett, L., Martin, P., & Hwata, T. (2022). Quick Commerce: Who Will Turn It into a Profitable Long-Term Play? KPMG. https://kpmg.com/uk/en/blogs/home/posts/2022/07/quick-commerce.html.

eMarketer Editors (2020). Where Do US Consumers Begin Their Product Searches? Insider Intelligence. https://www.insiderintelligence.com/content/where-do-us-consumers-begin-their-product-searches.

Epp, A. M., & Price, L. L. (2011). Designing Solutions around Customer Network Identity Goals. *Journal of Marketing, 75*(2), 36–54.

Forbes (2022). The 100 Largest Companies in the World by Market Capitalization in 2022 (in Billion U.S. Dollars). Statista. https://www.statista.com/statistics/263264/top-companies-in-the-world-by-market-capitalization/.

Fournier, S., & Lee, L. (2009). Getting Brand Communities Right. *Harvard Business Review*, 11. https://hbr.org/2009/04/getting-brand-communities-right.

Gawer, A., & Cusumano, M. A. (2008). How Companies Become Platform Leaders. *MITSloan Management Review, 11*. https://sloanreview.mit.edu/article/how-companies-become-platform-leaders/.

Gourville, J. T., & Soman, D. (2005). Overchoice and Assortment Type: When and Why Variety Backfires. *Marketing Science, 24*(3), 382–395. https://doi.org/10.1287/mksc.1040.0109.

Hagedoo (2023). *Erfahrene Handwerker in Deiner Nähe finden*. Hagedoo. https://hagedoo.de/.

Hagiu, A., & Wright, J. (2015). Multi-Sided Platforms. *International Journal of Industrial Organization, 43*, 162–174. https://doi.org/10.1016/j.ijindorg.2015.03.003.

Hamilton, S. F., & Richards, T. J. (2009). Product Differentiation, Store Differentiation, and Assortment Depth. *Management Science, 55*(8), 1368–1376. https://doi.org/10.1287/mnsc.1090.1032.

Hartmans, A. (2017). Airbnb's Total Worldwide Listings Is More than the Top 5 Hotel Brands Combined—Business Insider Deutschland. https://www.businessinsider.de/airbnb-total-worldwide-listings-2017-8?r=UK.

Hauck, A., & Mlynarski, W. (2022). Why More Companies Could Benefit from a Subscription-Based Model. Bank of America. https://business.bofa.com/content/dam/flagship/global-transaction-services/benefits-of-subscription-based-business-model/subscription-based-business-models.pdf.

HDE, & IFH Köln (2021). *Online Monitor 2021*. HDE Handelsverband Deutschland. https://einzelhandel.de/index.php?option=com_attachments&task=download&id=1057.

HDE, & IFH Köln (2022). *Online Monitor 2022*. HDE Handelsverband Deutschland. https://einzelhandel.de/index.php?option=com_attachments&task=download&id=10659.

Henderson, C. M., Steinhoff, L., Harmeling, C. M., & Palmatier, R. W. (2021). Customer Inertia Marketing. *Journal of the Academy of Marketing Science, 49*(2), 350–373. https://doi.org/10.1007/s11747-020-00744-0.

Hennig-Thurau, T., Aliman, D. N., Herting, A. M., Cziehso, G. P., Linder, M., & Kübler, R. V. (2022). Social Interactions in the Metaverse: Framework, Initial Evidence, and Research Roadmap. *Journal of the Academy of Marketing Science, 51*. https://doi.org/10.1007/s11747-022-00908-0.

Hoch, S. J., Bradlow, E. T., & Wansink, B. (1999). The Variety of an Assortment. *Marketing Science, 18*(4), 527–546. https://doi.org/10.1287/mksc.18.4.527.

Homburg, C., Hoyer, W. D., & Fassnacht, M. (2002). Service Orientation of a Retailer's Business Strategy: Dimensions, Antecedents, and Performance Outcomes. *Journal of Marketing, 66*(4), 86–101. https://doi.org/10.1509/jmkg.66.4.86.18511.

Howland, D. (2022). Victoria's Secret Launches Online Marketplace Dominated by Women-Led Brands. Retail Dive. https://www.retaildive.com/news/victorias-secret-launches-online-marketplace-women-led-brands/624466/.

Huang, P., Tafti, A., & Mithas, S. (2018). Platform Sponsor Investments and User Contributions in Knowledge Communities: The Role of Knowledge Seeding. *MIS Quarterly, 42*(1), 213–240. https://doi.org/10.25300/MISQ/2018/13490.

Humphries, C., Schimroszik, N., & Farr, E.-V. (2022). Fast Grocery Group Gorillas Eyes Collaborations in Profitability Push. Reuters. https://www.reuters.com/business/retail-consumer/german-gorillas-grocery-app-seeks-big-retail-partners-boost-profit-2022-06-22/.

Isidore, C. (2023). Amazon Closing Some of Its Cashier-Free Stores. CNN Business. https://www.cnn.com/2023/03/06/business/amazon-closing-some-amazon-go-stores/index.html.

Javorovic, M. (2023). Rekordbilanz: Decathlon Deutschland mit 28 percent Umsatzplus. *TextilWirtschaft*. https://www.textilwirtschaft.de/business/sports/rekordbilanz-decathlon-deutschland-mit-28-umsatzplus-239492.

Katz, M. L., & Shapiro, C. (1985). Network Externalities, Competition, and Compatibility. *American Economic Review, 75*(3), 424–440.

Katz, M. L., & Shapiro, C. (1994). Systems Competition and Network Effects. *Journal of Economic Perspectives, 8*(2), 93–115. https://doi.org/10.1257/jep.8.2.93.

Keller, K. L. (2010). Brand Equity Management in a Multichannel, Multimedia Retail Environment. *Journal of Interactive Marketing, 24*(2), 58–70.

Kuang, L., Huang, N., Hong, Y., & Yan, Z. (2019). Spillover Effects of Financial Incentives on Non-Incentivized User Engagement: Evidence from an Online Knowledge Exchange Platform. *Journal of Management Information Systems, 36*(1), 289–320. https://doi.org/10.1080/07421222.2018.1550564.

Kumar, V., & Reinartz, W. J. (2016). Creating Enduring Customer Value. *Journal of Marketing, 80*(6), 36–68. https://doi.org/10.1509/jm.15.0414.

Lamey, L., Breugelmans, E., Vuegen, M., & ter Braak, A. (2021). Retail Service Innovations and Their Impact on Retailer Shareholder Value: Evidence from an Event Study. *Journal of the Academy of Marketing Science, 49*(4), 811–833. https://doi.org/10.1007/s11747-021-00777-z.

Lu, S. F., & Rui, H. (2018). Can We Trust Online Physician Ratings? Evidence from Cardiac Surgeons in Florida. *Management Science, 64*(6), 2557–2573. https://doi.org/10.1287/mnsc.2017.2741.

Maier, E., & Wieringa, J. (2021). Acquiring Customers through Online Marketplaces? The Effect of Marketplace Sales on Sales in a Retailer's Own Channels. *International Journal of Research in Marketing, 38*(2), 311–328. https://doi.org/10.1016/j.ijresmar.2020.09.007.

Messinger, P. R., & Narasimhan, C. (1997). A Model of Retail Formats Based on Consumers' Economizing on Shopping Time. *Marketing Science, 16*(1), 1–23.

Meyersohn, N. (2022). JCPenney Was Once a Shopping Giant: Can It Make a Comeback? CNN Business. https://www.cnn.com/2022/11/27/business/jcpenney-stores-ceo-marc-rosen/index.html.

Muller, E. (2020). Delimiting Disruption: Why Uber Is Disruptive, but Airbnb Is Not. *International Journal of Research in Marketing, 37*(1), 43–55. https://doi.org/10.1016/j.ijresmar.2019.10.004.

Nambisan, S., & Baron, R. A. (2009). Virtual Customer Environments: Testing a Model of Voluntary Participation in Value Co-Creation Activities. *Journal of Product Innovation Management, 26*(4), 388–406. https://doi.org/10.1111/j.1540-5885.2009.00667.x.

National Retail Federation (2022). Leading Reasons Why Consumers Worldwide Shop in Stores in 2021. Statista. https://www.statista.com/statistics/1300788/main-reasons-to-shop-in-store-world/.

Nike (2022). Form 10-K. https://s1.q4cdn.com/806093406/files/doc_downloads/2022/399556(1)_27_Nike-Inc._NPS_Combo_Form-10-K_WR.pdf.

OBI (2023). Machbar Macher. OBI Baumarkt und Online-Shop. https://www.obi.de/beratung-und-planung/machbarmacher.

OTTO Group (2022). Geschäftsbericht 2021/22. OTTO Group. https://static.ottogroup.com/medien/cached/docs/de/bpk/2021-22/otto_group_geschaeftsbericht_2021_22.pdf.

Padmanabhan, V., Rajiv, S., & Srinivasan, K. (1997). New Products, Upgrades, and New Releases: A Rationale for Sequential Product Introduction. *Journal of Marketing Research, 34*(4), 456–472. https://doi.org/10.1177/002224379703400404.

Perez, S. (2021). Walmart to Sell Its E-Commerce Technologies to Other Retailers. TechCrunch. https://techcrunch.com/2021/07/28/walmart-to-sell-its-e-commerce-technologies-to-other-retailers/.

Perren, R., & Kozinets, R. V. (2018). Lateral Exchange Markets: How Social Platforms Operate in a Networked Economy. *Journal of Marketing, 82*(1), 20–36. https://doi.org/10.1509/jm.14.0250.

Ramaswamy, V., & Ozcan, K. (2016). Brand Value Co-Creation in a Digitalized World: An Integrative Framework and Research Implications. *International Journal of Research in Marketing, 33*(1), 93–106. https://doi.org/10.1016/j.ijresmar.2015.07.001.

Ramaswamy, V., & Ozcan, K. (2018). Offerings as Digitalized Interactive Platforms: A Conceptual Framework and Implications. *Journal of Marketing, 82*(4), 19–31. https://doi.org/10.1509/jm.15.0365.

Reinartz, W. J., & Hudetz, K. (2019). Attraktiv auf der Fläche. *Harvard Business Manager, 07.* https://www.harvardbusinessmanager.de/heft/artikel/erfolgreiche-onlinehaendler-a-1274446.html.

Reinartz, W. J., Wiegand, N., & Imschloss, M. (2019). The Impact of Digital Transformation on the Retailing Value Chain. *International Journal of Research in Marketing, 36*(3), 350–366. https://doi.org/10.1016/j.ijresmar.2018.12.002.

Reinartz, W. J., Wiegand, N., & Wichmann, J. R. K. (2019). *The Rise of (Digital) Retail Platforms* (Selected Publications of the IFH Sponsors, No. 9). Gesellschaft zur Förderung des Institut für Handelsforschung an der Universität zu Köln e.V.

Rietveld, J., & Schilling, M. A. (2021). Platform Competition: A Systematic and Interdisciplinary Review of the Literature. *Journal of Management, 47*(6), 1528–1563. https://doi.org/10.1177/0149206320969791.

Rochet, J.-C., & Tirole, J. (2003). Platform Competition in Two-Sided Markets. *Journal of the European Economic Association, 1*(4), 990–1029. https:// doi .org/ 10 .1162/ 154247603322493212.

Schau, H. J., Muñiz, A. M., & Arnould, E. J. (2009). How Brand Community Practices Create Value. *Journal of Marketing, 73*(5), 30–51. https://doi.org/10.1509/jmkg.73 .5.30.

Seenivasan, S., & Talukdar, D. (2016). Competitive Effects of Wal-Mart Supercenter Entry: Moderating Roles of Category and Brand Characteristics. *Journal of Retailing, 92*(2), 218–225. https://doi.org/10.1016/j.jretai.2015.09.003.

Shankar, V., Inman, J. J., Mantrala, M., Kelley, E., & Rizley, R. (2011). Innovations in Shopper Marketing: Current Insights and Future Research Issues. *Journal of Retailing, 87, Supplement 1*, S29–S42. https://doi.org/10.1016/j.jretai.2011.04.007.

Shankar, V., Kalyanam, K., Setia, P., Golmohammadi, A., Tirunillai, S., Douglass, T., Hennessey, J., Bull, J. S., & Waddoups, R. (2021). How Technology Is Changing Retail. *Journal of Retailing, 97*(1), 13–27. https://doi.org/10.1016/j.jretai.2020.10.006.

Steenkamp, J.-B. E. M., & Sloot, L. M. (2018). *Retail Disruptors: The Spectacular Rise and Impact of the Hard Discounters* (1st edition). Kogan Page.

StrategyOne (2010). Voting with their Wallets: New Research Finds Younger Americans, Liberals and West Coast Consumers Most Likely to Report Boycotting and "Buycotting" Based on Values. Cision PR Newswire. https://www.prnewswire .com/ news -releases/ voting -with -their -wallets -new -research -finds -younger -americans -liberals -and -west -coast -consumers -most -likely -to -report -boycotting -and-buycotting-based-on-values-91533949.html.

Stremersch, S., Tellis, G. J., Franses, P. H., & Binken, J. L. G. (2007). Indirect Network Effects in New Product Growth. *Journal of Marketing, 71*(3), 52–74.

Swaminathan, V., Sorescu, A., Steenkamp, J.-B. E. M., O'Guinn, T. C. G., & Schmitt, B. (2020). Branding in a Hyperconnected World: Refocusing Theories and Rethinking Boundaries. *Journal of Marketing, 84*(2), 24–46. https://doi.org/10.1177/ 0022242919899905.

Tahirov, N., & Glock, C. H. (2022). Manufacturer Encroachment and Channel Conflicts: A Systematic Review of the Literature. *European Journal of Operational Research, 302*(2), 403–426. https://doi.org/10.1016/j.ejor.2021.12.006.

Tarnoff, B. (2022). 'Wallets and Eyeballs': How eBay Turned the Internet into a Marketplace. *The Guardian*. https://www.theguardian.com/technology/2022/jun/ 16/wallets-and-eyeballs-how-ebay-turned-the-internet-into-a-marketplace.

Täuscher, K., & Laudien, S. M. (2018). Understanding Platform Business Models: A Mixed Methods Study of Marketplaces. *European Management Journal, 36*(3), 319–329. https://doi.org/10.1016/j.emj.2017.06.005.

Tuli, K. R., Kohli, A. K., & Bharadwaj, S. (2007). Rethinking Customer Solutions: From Product Bundles to Relational Processes. *Journal of Marketing, 71*(3), 1–17.

Vallas, S., & Schor, J. B. (2020). What Do Platforms Do? Understanding the Gig Economy. *Annual Review of Sociology, 46*(1), 273–294. https:// doi .org/ 10 .1146/ annurev-soc-121919–054857.

Verhoef, P. C., Broekhuizen, T. J. L., Bart, Y., Bhattacharya, A., Qi Dong, J., Fabian, N., & Haenlein, M. (2021). Digital Transformation: A Multidisciplinary Reflection and Research Agenda. *Journal of Business Research, 122*, 889–901. https://doi.org/10.1016/jbusres.2019.09.022.

Vusirikala, N. (2021). Marketplace: What Makes It the Holy Grail of E-Tail. Walmart Global Tech. https://tech.walmart.com/content/walmart-global-tech/en_us/news/articles/Marketplace.html.

Walmart (2009). Walmart.com Adds Nearly One Million New Items with the Launch of Walmart Marketplace. Walmart Corporate. https://corporate.walmart.com/newsroom/2009/08/30/walmart-com-adds-nearly-one-million-new-items-with-the-launch-of-walmart-marketplace.

Wang, Y., Bell, D. R., & Padmanabhan, V. (2009). Manufacturer-Owned Retail Stores. *Marketing Letters, 20*(2), 107–124.

Wichmann, J. R. K., Reinartz, W. J., & Venkatesan, R. (2022). Conceptualizing Value Creation in the Platform Era. *Journal of Creating Value, 8*(2), 184–203. https://doi.org/10.1177/23949643221121887.

Wichmann, J. R. K., Uppal, A., Sharma, A., & Dekimpe, M. G. (2022). A Global Perspective on the Marketing Mix across Time and Space. *International Journal of Research in Marketing, 39*(2), 502–521. https://doi.org/10.1016/j.ijresmar.2021.09.001.

Wichmann, J. R. K., Wiegand, N., & Reinartz, W. J. (2022a). The Platformization of Brands. *Journal of Marketing, 86*(1), 109–131. https://doi.org/10.1177/00222429211054073.

Wichmann, J. R. K., Wiegand, N., & Reinartz, W. J. (2022b). Building Your Own Brand Platform. *Harvard Business Review, 100*(5), 47–53.

Wu, Y., Zhang, K., & Padmanabhan, V. (2018). Matchmaker Competition and Technology Provision. *Journal of Marketing Research, 55*(3), 396–413. https://doi.org/10.1509/jmr.16.0423.

Wunderman Thompson Commerce (2022). Leading Online Sources Where Consumers Worldwide Search for Products in 2022. Statista. https://www.statista.com/statistics/1034209/global-product-search-online-sources/.

Xu, J., Jiang, Z., & Dhar, R. (2013). Mental Representation and Perceived Similarity: How Abstract Mindset Aids Choice from Large Assortments. *Journal of Marketing Research, 50*(4), 548–559.

Yoo, K., Welden, R., Hewett, K., & Haenlein, M. (2023). The Merchants of Meta: A Research Agenda to Understand the Future of Retailing in the Metaverse. *Journal of Retailing, 99*. https://doi.org/10.1016/j.jretai.2023.02.002.

Zalando (2023). Outlets—In deiner Stadt. Zalando Outlet. https://www.zalando-outlet.de/outlets/.

Zhang, S., Pauwels, K., & Peng, C. (2019). The Impact of Adding Online-to-Offline Service Platform Channels on Firms' Offline and Total Sales and Profits. *Journal of Interactive Marketing, 47*(3), 115–128. https://doi.org/10.1016/j.intmar.2019.03.001.

7 Open innovation in digital transformation

Chee-Wee Tan and Bingqing Xiong

Open innovation refers to "the use of purposive inflows and outflows of knowledge to accelerate internal innovation, and expand the markets for external use of innovation, respectively" (Chesbrough, 2006, p. 1). As a catalyst for accelerating the digital transformation, creating and realizing value in open innovation has remained a prominent topic of discussion. Although extant literature on open innovation spans across individual, business, and platform levels, there exists a dearth of research on the realization of value through open innovation in scenarios where multifaceted actors co-create and co-realize value within open innovation platforms. Notably, recent developments indicate that the focus of value creation is shifting from businesses to clusters of businesses and individuals operating within these platforms.

An open innovation platform is a digital space that facilitates open innovation initiatives by connecting various stakeholders such as companies, developers, researchers, and individuals. This diversity fosters a rich environment for generating a wide array of ideas. Unlike traditional research and development (R&D), which often requires significant investment, open innovation platforms are digital and globally accessible, frequently featuring low or no entry barriers, thus democratizing access to value creation opportunities. For example, GitHub serves as an open innovation platform where developers and learners from around the world can collaborate on projects, contribute to open-source software, and even solve issues for rewards. Another example is Kaggle, a Google-owned platform that hosts data science competitions where companies and researchers post their data and statisticians and data miners from all over the world compete to produce the best models. In essence, open innovation platforms are specialized digital platforms designed to facilitate collaborative problem-solving and value co-creation among diverse parties.

Although open innovation platforms offer vast potential for value creation, recent practices and research have revealed substantial weaknesses that could threaten the sustainability of these platforms. For open innovation platforms to strive, it is imperative to realize and sustain value creation over time, while ensuring continued commitment and contribution from platform participants. Particularly, one of the primary obstacles to the ongoing growth of such platforms is maintaining the flow of the value creation process, which demands a continuous exchange of ideas between creators and distributors of innovation.

At their core, platforms are multisided markets that create value through open innovation and distribution processes. From a platform standpoint, it is essential to facilitate these processes through digital resource provision. Given that digital resources form an integral part of open innovation platforms, their product-agnostic nature introduces a high degree of uncertainty, necessitating increased flexibility in adaptation for platform growth. Furthermore, the interdependent relationship between value co-creation and co-realization must be viewed through a dynamic and evolutionary lens. For instance, platforms can offer resources like application programming interfaces (APIs) to complementors to help them create better innovation. Additionally, platforms provide a channel for continuous updates, engaging different sides of the market through diverse resource offerings.

This chapter presents an opinion on how platforms can sustain growth through the interplay between value co-creation and value co-realization processes. First, we explore the origins of open innovation platforms to gain a historical perspective on why they came into existence. Examining their emergence allows us to understand the changing needs they were designed to meet, from accelerating the pace of innovation to making opportunities more accessible to a broader audience. Then we use the perspective of a virtuous cycle of growth of digital co-creation and co-realization to understand the sustainability of open innovation platforms. The following section explores the resources and engagement models that characterize sustainable open innovation platforms. We also suggest potential avenues for future development in this domain.

Emergence of open innovation platforms

The flow of value creation is the essence of innovation. Novel products and services are derived from the creation of new value for target consumers. This idea transcends disciplines. While a prevailing assumption in innovation research is that firms carry out the process of value creation (Mahr & Lievens, 2012), emerging digital innovation research recognizes that firms are not the only actors creating and distributing innovations (Trischler et al., 2017). Instead, there is a growing importance of multisided markets in the value creation as individuals, be they amateurs or professionals, are becoming increasingly involved. The emergence of open innovation platforms has led to a growing awareness among firms that their products and services will be co-created with different parties within such multisided markets.

In an era when digital resources are readily editable (Kallinikos et al., 2013), reprogrammable (Yoo et al., 2010), and reusable through the (re-)combination of modular functions (Eaton et al., 2015; Henfridsson et al., 2014), the firm-centric view of value creation is extended to include a multisided view of value co-creation. For value co-creation, the focus should be on reinventing the value-creating system itself, where various actors – suppliers, business partners, allies, and customers – collaborate in the process of creating value. Innovation is no longer confined to traditional businesses with defined boundaries, but rather a collection of multidisciplinary digital resources that are assembled into a whole from scratch (Yoo et al., 2010). Individual users can, for instance, develop and publish their own products by integrating third-party plug-ins or extensions provided by open innovation platforms. As part of an open innovation initiative, platforms serve as the core value-generating systems that allow multifaceted actors to contribute to the value creation process. In this context, we employ the term 'value co-creation' to refer to the process of creating innovative value by connecting digital resources from multifaceted actors on open innovation platforms. Both businesses and individuals partake in the process of co-creating value. Value co-creation processes on open innovation platforms stand in contrast to traditional value creation processes that generate value paths without incorporating other actors, such as individual users, into the process. Value is typically created by businesses operating on top of other actors as stand-alone entities.

The framework for value co-creation proposed by Saarijärvi et al. (2013) contains three components: value, resources, and mechanisms. The value component identifies what types of value are provided to customers and service providers. The resource component includes the actors and the resources that are available to participate in the co-creation process. Different types of interactions exist between actors (e.g., consumers and businesses), namely business-to-business (B2B), business-to-consumer (B2C), consumer-to-business (C2B), and consumer-to-consumer (C2C). Resource component pertains to customers and firms. Finally, the mechanism component discusses the myriad processes by which actors co-create, such as co-design, co-development, and co-conception.

Value Co-creation

Value co-creation in open innovation platforms is often associated with the concept of recombination, which involves reimagining how diverse functions could be integrated into novel ways (Henfridsson et al., 2018; Schillebeeckx et al., 2021). Value co-creation is characterized by interactions of exteriority, meaning that its generation is influenced by relationships with multifaceted actors. Compared to the modular system in which there is a logically necessary relationship between parts, such as in a hierarchy-of-parts framework, the relationships between actors in open innovation platforms are contingent. In traditional value creation, parts and the whole are regarded as a bounded entity, each of which possesses certain characteristics that are necessary for its placement and function within a business scheme (Clark, 1985). Usually, it has a ready-made shape, provided as a discrete entity by a firm to a customer for adoption or rejection. Contingent relationships among multifaceted actors in open innovation platforms imply that any value, when provided as part of an offering, may become a constituent of many different value-generating processes as it is recombined and rendered meaningful by different actors. In this regard, innovation emerges from the utilization of digital rendered resources by individual users, businesses, and platforms. These actors will also gain different benefits from the co-creation process.

Individual value

In the context of co-creation, individual value refers to the motivational drivers that drive an individual's participation (Trischler et al., 2017). One of the main reasons individuals participate in these platforms is to have their problems solved, which ultimately leads to improved customer experience and satisfaction with the service (Shamim et al., 2017; Vega-Vazquez et al., 2013). As well as intrinsic benefits, individuals may also enjoy extrinsic benefits in the form of economic rewards, including bonus points, monetary awards, discounts, or even promotion by connecting new customers with service providers (Fernandes & Remelhe, 2016; Rashid et al., 2019). Additionally, individuals may benefit from social networking by forming friendships with other customers who share similar interests and exchanging experiences with them (Ranjan & Read, 2019), as well as establishing connections with businesses and platforms. A customer's status can also be determined via networks both within the open innovation platform and across external social media platforms (Quach & Thaichon, 2017; Verleye, 2015).

Business value

Customer co-creation provides businesses with economic value, innovation, competencies, and other desired outcomes in open innovation platforms (Aquilani et al., 2020; Oertzen et al., 2018; Tu et al., 2018). Three types of business value can be distinguished: economic, social, and cognitive (Xie et al., 2016). Economic benefits refer to profits gained, social benefits relate to improving customer relationships and value creation, and cognitive benefits come from a deeper understanding of customer knowledge and experience, ultimately contributing to value creation (Xie et al., 2016). Customer knowledge and skills are widely recognized as a crucial source of innovation and service improvement (Angeren et al., 2016; Rashid et al., 2019).

Platform value

In open innovation, a platform serves as the central hub for value co-creation (Thomas et al., 2014). As a central hub on which other actors can develop innovation, platforms can create opportunities and facilitate the distribution of innovation among these actors (Bogers et al., 2017). In this way, they provide a way for these actors to share knowledge, resources, and expertise, leading to the creation of new products, services, or processes that benefit all participants. Increasingly, digital firms are engaging with the crowd to leverage external resources (Bogers, 2011; Lavie & Rosenkopf, 2006). As platforms for open innovation, these digital firms engage users and resources as external resources to participate actively in value co-creation processes with other actors.

Digital Resources

As part of the open innovation platforms, value co-creation supports the open-ended nature of value, by which the value of specific innovations must be viewed over time as fluid rather than fixed, as a function of connections to assemblages of digital resources, as well as the degree of engagement among individuals, businesses, and platforms. Digital resources refer to entities that act as fundamental components in the creation and realization of value from information (Henfridsson et al., 2018). By substituting digital resources for the products and services (Barrett et al., 2015; Fosfuri & Giarratana, 2009) that are widely used in traditional value creation, the emergence of open innovation platforms is able to create and realize value at a more granular level.

Open innovation platforms provide digital resources which are not self -contained units with fixed meaning and relations. By leveraging the advantages of digital resources, the platforms allow multifaceted actors to simultaneously participate in multiple value paths through the value co-creation process. Open innovation research needs to better investigate the interrelationships among all these multifaceted actors and how they contribute to value creation collaboratively, thus contributing to a novel and much needed level of analysis of digital resources that contrasts with conventional product or service focus. The shift in focus to digital resources and their connections is also necessary because they are product-agnostic in the context of open innovation. An agnostic view of digital resources is that their function in the use situation is largely determined by their relationships to other resources and how they are leveraged by different actors. Rather than being defined by predefined functions, digital resources are agnostic, making these relationships and usage scenarios contingent on context (Henfridsson et al., 2018).

Actor interrelationships trends

Recent studies have demonstrated that the interrelationships between these three actors (individuals, businesses, and platforms) have changed. Past studies have concentrated on the importance of businesses to businesses and how they impact individuals through the creation of value and the consumption of resources (Galvagno & Dalli, 2014). In recent years, however, a number of studies have observed discrepancies in interrelationships: the way in which platforms, businesses, and individuals can leverage digital resources in conjunction with one another (Oertzen et al., 2018). As an example, co-creation often occurs between individuals when creating and sharing content (Rashid et al., 2019). Additionally, idea creation platforms allow businesses and individuals with similar interests to exchange their expertise and knowledge (Huang et al., 2018; Lee et al., 2012; Rashid et al., 2019). These platforms enable customers to share their knowledge and experience with others who share similar interests. These platforms often facilitate the value co-creation among a variety of individuals.

Interrelationships among actors fluctuate over time. Relationships are dynamic and are affected by a variety of factors, including the agnostic nature of digital resources, changes in actors' priorities, and technological advancements. Over the course of time, the relationships between actors on open innovation platforms may evolve as they collaborate on different projects and initiatives. As priorities change or market conditions change, actors may form new partnerships and collaborations. For example, long-term value can be derived from direct and ongoing interactions between customers and service providers (Grissemann & Stokburger-Sauer, 2012; Vega-Vazquez et al., 2013).

Virtuous cycle of growth: co-creation and co-realization

Platforms are capable of adding tremendous value to open innovation environments, but recent studies have suggested that current practices may have notable shortcomings that might pose a challenge to the sustainability of such platforms over time (Flak et al., 2022). According to a study of sharing accommodation platforms, Airbnb, for example, provides an effective solution to the spare accommodation needs of individuals (Miller & Breton-Miller, 2021). The downside of Airbnb is that as more people started using the service, agencies and hotels began to flock to the platform, and while this has resulted in an increase in the number of tourists on the platform, it has also led to significant erosion of revenue for hotels and individual accommodations.

A similar scenario has occurred in open innovation environments where GitHub has revolutionized software development by providing a platform for collaborative coding. The influx of large corporations into GitHub has led to increased competition, potentially marginalizing individual contributors and smaller developers. While this has resulted in a concentration of high-quality projects on GitHub, it raises questions about the long-term sustainability and inclusivity of the platform. Such scenarios highlight the paradox in open innovation platforms, where initial winners may reap vast profits but could undermine the broader value chain in the long run. The paradox has been emphasized in information systems research that discussion is required regarding the sustainability of open innovation platforms (e.g., Han et al., 2012).

The topic of value co-creation has been extensively deliberated in the context of open innovation platforms. However, there remains a paucity of studies concerning the transformation of such co-created value into a form that is readily applicable and beneficial to the end users. Existing perspectives such as the layered-modular architectpure (Kazan et al., 2018; Yoo et al., 2010), architectural frames (Henfridsson et al., 2014), the co-creation of value (Füller et al., 2009, 2013; Kohler et al., 2011; Panico & Cennamo, 2022), and network effects (Grange & Benbasat, 2018), these studies offer valuable insights on how to address the co-creation process to achieve the open innovation landscape. According to the framework proposed by Flak et al. (2022), platforms need to adopt co-creative and co-realizing process to enable a vision of how selected resources can assist cooperating partners in appropriating value effectively. It is essential to think of co-creation and co-realization in open innovation platforms concurrently, rather than tilting too much toward the value co-creation. Henceforth, it would be beneficial for open innovation platforms, with the objective of attaining enduring growth, to contemplate the amalgamation of value co-creation and value co-realization processes through the provision of digital resources to the multifaceted actors involved.

It is imperative to acknowledge that the concept of value co-creation is not confined to the manufacturing process, but rather extends to the consumers' individual consumption contexts (Figueiredo & Scaraboto, 2016; Vargo & Lusch, 2004, 2008). Consumers are not mere passive recipients of marketing efforts but are instead regarded as active and integral resources that are capable of generating and distributing value in their diverse co-realization processes. In open innovation platforms, consumers have the ability to reconfigure their roles from being mere contributors and creators (Saarijärvi et al., 2013) to that of value realizers. However, despite the consensus regarding the active role of consumers and the subjective and process-driven nature of customer value, theoretical discussions have encountered controversy, particularly as the emphasis shifts from value creation to value co-creation.

In furtherance of the objectives outlined above, we proffer an opinion of virtuous cycle of growth, predicated upon the reciprocal relationship between value co-creation and value co-realization for open innovation platforms, as an integral component of an integrated approach. Figure 7.1 depicts a representation of the key elements and process. As we can see from Figure 7.1, the platform facilitates a collaborative environment where value creators – such as developers, researchers, and innovators – can interact seamlessly with value distributors, which may include end-consumers, enterprises, or even governmental organizations. Value creators contribute innovative ideas, technologies, or solutions, while value distributors provide the necessary channels, market access, or financial resources to bring these innovations to fruition. Consumers or end users also play a crucial role by providing feedback, thereby refining the value proposition and contributing to the iterative process of innovation creation and distribution. Together, they engage in a dynamic process of value co-creation and value co-realization.

Moreover, open innovation platforms are not static entities; they continually evolve in response to the interactions and contributions of the different parties involved. This evolution may manifest in various ways, such as the introduction of new features, adaptation to emerging technologies, or shifts in governance models. Such ongoing evolution ensures that the platform remains responsive to changing market needs and technological advancements, thereby sustaining its relevance and efficacy in fostering innovation in a sustainable way. This framework affords a superior comprehension of the processes involved in value creation and realization within the context of open innovation, while highlighting the significance of their interdependence, and its potential to engender sustainable growth in the long term.

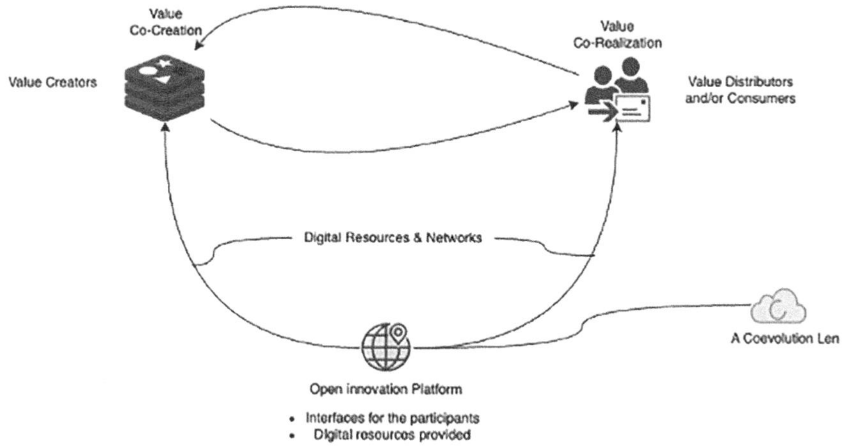

Source: Authors.

Figure 7.1 Key components and relationships in open innovation platforms

Interdependence and Overlap between Co-creation and Co-realization

By using new products and services created in the previous value creation process, value realization enables multifaceted actors to actualize one or more things of great value. In the context of open innovation platforms that facilitate the provision of digital resources, digital value co-creation occurs at the back-end stages of implementation where values are being created and functions are being incorporated and captured. It pertains to the collaborative interactions that occur during the implementation of products and services. The aim is to enhance the capture of co-created value and measure the joint fulfillment of multifaceted actors within the platform.

Within extant literature on innovation, a significant perspective posits that "a firm's offerings are not embedded with value (value-in-exchange), but rather value occurs when the offering is useful to the customer or beneficiary (value-in-use)" (Lusch & Nambisan, 2015, p. 159). In order to reconcile the paradoxical impediments that hinder the sustainable development of open innovation platforms, it is imperative to endeavor to reach the equitable dissemination and practical application of the generated value.

In the method of agile system development, prototypes are iteratively demonstrated to beneficiaries/stakeholders and, if unmet needs remain, the systems are quickly adjusted by returning to creation processes to enhance quality. Similarly, the phenomena of value co-creation and value co-realization reflect dynamic processes that are fittingly descriptive of the expected patterns in open innovation platforms. By virtue of the value co-creation process, the products and digital services have been iteratively delivered in order to exercise their capabilities. The digital resources proffered by open innovation platforms facilitate thc innovation process by virtue of their modular and evolutionary features. The deployment of successive iterations of created products and digital services to end users, which includes both individuals and businesses, serves as the basis for the value co-realization process. Through this process, feedback is solicited from end users regarding the degree to which their goals are being fulfilled, and subsequently relayed to the relevant parties. The timely receipt of this feedback not only expedites the iterative process, but also facilitates the refinement of digital products and services in actual use. As is the case with open innovation platforms, the feedback emanating from diverse sources, including multifaceted actors, further enhances the value co-realization process.

Over time, the co-creative process, which involves the active collaboration of multiple actors to generate new ideas and solutions, reaches its peak in terms of intensity and effectiveness. This is due in part to the fact that the initial benefits of co-creation become more apparent and are fully accepted by the market. As the value co-creation process matures, it becomes more refined and efficient, with the participants working together more seamlessly and effectively. This can lead to a greater sense of trust and cooperation among the parties involved, as they develop a deeper understanding of each other's strengths, weaknesses, and perspectives. Moreover, the co-realization process, which refers to the implementation and commercialization of the co-created products and services, also reaches its fullest potential as the co-creation process begins to wind down. At this point, the ideas and solutions generated through co-creation have been thoroughly tested, refined, and optimized, and are ready for implementation and commercialization. The co-realization process involves a range of activities, including prototyping, testing, marketing, and distribution. It requires a high degree of coordination and collaboration among the parties involved, as well as a deep understanding of the needs and preferences of the target market.

In open innovation platforms, the value co-creation process and value co-realization process are two distinct concepts that require careful consideration. Failure to recognize any process or the differences between these two processes can impede the sustainable growth of such platforms. Co-realization highlights the jointly experienced outcomes by the actors involved in the co-creation process. While this is the end result of the value co-creation process, it is important to note that the co-realization process of organizing and managing the potential benefits arising from co-creation must occur in parallel, as argued by Ward and Daniel (2006). In the literature on benefits management, the distinction between benefits realization (outcome) and benefits management (process) has often been conflated, with the terms used interchangeably (Flak et al., 2022). This conflation is similar to the conflations of creation and appropriation discussed earlier. Therefore, it is crucial to differentiate between the two processes to ensure effective management of the benefits arising from co-creation. Our initial opinion of co-realization encompasses activities related to value realization, which involves the realization of benefits. However, it is important to note that while the co-creation and co-realization processes occur in parallel, they require varying degrees of time and effort from both developers and users. As one process waxes, the other process wanes.

The concepts of co-creation and co-realization are two interrelated yet distinct processes that both compete with and complement each other in the context of value creation. These two processes occur simultaneously and are characterized by the gradual accumulation of value. Therefore, the value co-realization process is a critical component of open innovation platforms and must be carefully managed to ensure the sustainable growth and success of such initiatives. By recognizing the importance of balancing and coordinating these processes, platforms can maximize the potential benefits of open innovation and drive innovation forward in a virtuous cycle and sustainable manner.

Value Aggregation from Multifaceted Actors

Furthermore, the effectiveness of open innovation platforms is contingent upon the ability of businesses to develop sophisticated measures of the performance of the entire network of businesses, rather than single business performance or simplistic aggregations of single business performance metrics. This is in line with the arguments made by Straub et al. (2004), who suggest that businesses engaged in networks have an imperative to develop such measures. In other words, the success of open innovation initiatives and open innovation platforms is not determined solely by the performance of individual businesses. Rather, it is the collective performance of the network of individuals and businesses that ultimately determines the success or failure of the initiative. This requires a shift in focus from individual business metrics to network-level metrics that capture the interactions and interdependencies between all parties within the network.

The aggregated value generated by multifaceted actors is crucial for the sustainable growth of open innovation platforms. By pooling their resources and expertise, individuals and businesses can achieve more than they could individually, creating a mutually beneficial relationship that drives innovation and creates value for all involved. By adopting this approach, all related actors in the platforms can more effectively leverage the power of co-creation and co-realization to drive innovation and the platform can therefore achieve sustainable competitive advantage in the long term.

Our argument is that aggregated value emanating from multifarious actors can be construed as an accumulated value for open innovation platforms. A well-governed value co-creation and co-realization process can culminate in superior outcomes for all actors involved. Each efficacious product and service that emerges from this process can furnish benefits at both project and platform levels. Consequently, networks and digital resources, when implemented in conjunction, can ultimately lead to value realization at the platform level over the major stages of the project. Furthermore, the accruement of benefits across the entire platform will engender sustainable growth.

Platform sustainable growth: a co-evolution paradigm

In the context of open innovation, the sustainable growth of such platforms through the integration of digital resources, co-creation and co-realization processes, and value aggregation is closely tied to the evolution of their constituent components in relation to one another. This phenomenon, known as coevolution, is a concept derived from the field of complexity science, with its origins in biology. Coevolution refers to the evolutionary process by which different species adapt to each other and their surrounding environment over time (Ehrlich & Raven, 1964). The intricacy of coevolving relationships renders them indeterminate and reactive, rather than causal and predictable. Consequently, the objective of coevolution in open innovation platforms is to explicate how continuous adaptations facilitate sustainable growth of these platforms over an extended period, rather than making anticipations based on presumed cause-and-effect relationships.

A coevolutionary paradigm has been put forward as fitting for exploring the link between digital platform architecture, governance, and environmental factors (Tiwana et al., 2010). Drawing from the aforementioned studies, we posit that the coevolutionary paradigm offers a promising approach towards achieving sustainable growth for open innovation platforms. This paradigm provides a multifaceted perspective of the open innovation phenomenon, enabling the identification and conceptualization of diverse coevolution mechanisms. In contrast to previous studies that have primarily focused on mechanisms of platform infrastructure evolution (Henfridsson et al., 2014), coevolution considers the reciprocal changes between different parties, thus providing a more holistic perspective. Notably, open innovation platforms present a distinct phenomenon from digital infrastructures in general, which are typically characterized as being more open and decentralized (Hanseth & Lyytinen, 2010).

In this regard, the application of coevolution theory is particularly relevant to the sustainable growth of open innovation platforms in view of the fact that they involve multiple parties. This theoretical framework affords us the opportunity to scrutinize how changes between these parties transpire over time as a continual process. Specifically, this lens sheds light on the evolution of diverse digital resources over time and how interactions between different actors result in reciprocal changes.

Platform Mechanisms

The mechanisms illustrate the importance of innovation management in stimulating customer engagement. In open innovation platforms, mechanism refers to how different actors in the platform can participate in value generation activities, which can be used to build trust for individuals and businesses to engage.

Open innovation platforms provide individuals with a greater range of roles in co-creating values than previous contexts. An individual may contribute to service innovation by taking on the role of an ideator, as well as designing advancements in digital service or serving as an intermediary for the exchange of knowledge in the business ecosystem (Xie et al., 2016). Additionally, the role of individuals can also be observed in associations with the business community, especially in certain industries such as health and fitness (e.g., Quach & Thaichon, 2017). The studies of Oertzen et al. (2018) and Pellicano et al. (2019) outline the different roles that individuals can play, such as co-innovation, co-valuation, co-test, co-launch, co-experience, co-consumption, co-investment, and co-production.

Viewed through the lens of the coevolution paradigm, open innovation platforms require careful attention to the design and implementation of various mechanisms to achieve sustainable growth. Within this context, various mechanisms and platform design elements have been pinpointed as prospective avenues for both platform development and the corresponding research questions.

The adoption of a modular platform architecture has emerged as a promising mechanism for achieving sustainable growth in open innovation platforms. This architecture enables collaboration among developers and individual contributors to build and integrate different platform components and functionalities. While digital resources are often modular and provided by existing open innovation platforms, they are primarily at the micro level rather than the macro level. Adopting a modular approach to platform architecture development can enable value co-creation by generating new products and services, while also allowing for the seamless integration of existing ones to make the co-realization process more efficient. From a coevolutionary perspective, this modular approach can facilitate the ongoing adaptation of the platform to changing user needs and requirements. This is because it provides a flexible and dynamic framework for coevolving relationships between different actors in the platform ecosystem. As such, this approach can enhance the platform's ability to evolve over time and keep up with the changing demands of its users. Consequently, several research questions emerge for scholarly consideration: How do relationships among diverse actors – such as developers, and consumers – evolve within the context of a modular platform ecosystem? Additionally, how do modular open innovation platforms compare with their non-modular counterparts in metrics of performance, adaptability, and user engagement?

One crucial mechanism that is deemed fundamental for open innovation platforms is an impartial collaborative model. Such a model fosters the involvement of a diverse array of contributors and advances a platform ecosystem that is equitable and inclusive. To accomplish this objective, platforms may deploy lucid and transparent standards for participation, along with mechanisms for scrutinizing and endorsing the value co-creation and value co-realization processes. The impartial collaborative model facilitates the perpetuation of coevolutionary processes between the platform and its multifarious stakeholders, allowing for the continuous enhancement and adjustment of the platform to fulfill the users' requirements. Consequently, this results in the establishment of a more sustainable growth trajectory for the platform. Similarly, research questions can be formulated as follows: What are the fundamental components that define an impartial collaborative model within open innovation platforms, and how do these elements foster an equitable and inclusive ecosystem? Additionally, how does an impartial collaborative model facilitate the coevolutionary dynamics between the platform and its diverse stakeholders?

Finally, timely supply-side scaling is another critical mechanism for sustainable growth in open innovation platforms. Platforms must be able to effectively scale their supply side to meet demand from value creators and value realizers. To achieve this, platforms can set up mechanisms that allow for timely supply-side scaling. One such mechanism involves instituting a community-driven feedback system that empowers contributors to request new features and services in real time. Furthermore, platforms have the ability to form strategic alliances with supplementary services and digital resources offered by third-party providers, which can aid in addressing the hurdles associated with scaling. When viewed through the lens of coevolution, such measures enable continual adjustments in accordance with evolving user demands and platform prerequisites. Future research endeavors may consider exploring the following questions: First, what role do strategic alliances with third-party service and digital resource providers play in mitigating the challenges associated with scaling? Second, how does effective supply-side scaling influence the experiences and contributions of both value creators and value realizers within the open innovation platform?

Engagement Amplification

In addition to the aforementioned platform mechanisms, open innovation platforms have the capacity to facilitate increased engagement among users and support co-creation and co-realization processes, thus contributing to a virtuous cycle of growth. These platforms can offer a range of additional features and strategies that serve to further enhance user involvement and foster collaborative innovation. By leveraging these approaches, open innovation platforms can effectively cultivate an environment conducive to co-creation and co-realization.

One approach to increase engagement is to facilitate greater communication and collaboration among users. This can be achieved through various tools and features, such as discussion forums, chat rooms, and virtual workspaces. Such tools can help users share ideas, collaborate on projects, and provide feedback to one another, which can promote greater engagement and participation in the co-creation and co-realization processes. Research questions pertinent to this design approach may encompass the following: First, do communication and collaboration tools contribute to fostering a sense of community among platform users, and, if so, through what mechanisms? Second, how do enhanced communication and collaboration functionalities influence the processes of value co-creation and co-realization within the platform? Lastly, is the impact of communication and collaboration tools on user engagement sustained over an extended period, or is it transient in nature?

Feedback loops and iterative development can also be provided as an addition. Platforms can create an instant feedback loop where users can quickly see the impact of their contributions, whether it's through upvotes, comments, implementation into ongoing projects, or gamification features that reward users for contributing ideas, collaborating on projects, or achieving milestones. Evaluating the efficacy of real-time feedback mechanisms in stimulating user participation constitutes a pertinent research question. Discovering methodologies for evaluating user feedback and the subsequent presentation of these features within the open innovation platform also merits further investigation.

Platforms can serve as a vital resource for enhancing users' knowledge and skills by providing an adaptive learning and skill development, enabling them to participate more effectively in co-creation and co-realization processes. Platforms can integrate an adaptive learning system that offers tutorials, webinars, or courses based on the current needs and skill levels of the customers, covering a wide range of topics such as collaboration tools, project management, and platform features. Furthermore, the platform may offer virtual helpers or interactive tutorials, designed to assist newcomers in developing a deeper understanding of the value co-creation and value co-realization processes. To promote greater user engagement, platforms may also incorporate gamification features such as ranking boards and badges. By leveraging such resources, users can acquire the skills and knowledge needed to participate in the co-creation and co-realization process more fully within the platform ecosystem. Potential avenues for scholarly investigation encompass the following: First, how do virtual helpers and interactive tutorials shape newcomers' comprehension of the value co-creation and co-realization processes? Second, to what extent do the skills and knowledge garnered through the platform's resources translate into efficacious participation in co-creation and co-realization endeavors? Third, what are the economic implications – both advantageous and disadvantageous – of incorporating adaptive learning systems and skill development resources within open innovation platforms?

Furthermore, platforms can harness the potential of social networks to bolster engagement and participation. This can be accomplished by integrating social media functionality, which enables users to disseminate their contributions and engage with others across diverse social media platforms. By leveraging the potency of social networks, platforms can expand their reach, enhance visibility, and foster greater participation and co-creation processes. This not only amplifies the platform's reach and visibility but also creates a conducive environment for enhanced participation and co-creation processes. As such, investigating the impact of social media integration and the role of social networks in co-creation activities becomes a salient research direction, offering valuable insights into the optimization of user engagement strategies within open innovation platforms.

Conclusion

In summary, the coevolution paradigm, when viewed through the lens of digital transformation, offers a robust framework for conceptualizing mechanisms that underpin sustainable growth in open innovation platforms. It provides a nuanced understanding of how open innovation platforms and their diverse stakeholders can adapt and coevolve to meet rapidly changing market conditions and user needs.

For decision-makers involved in the development and operation of such platforms, digital transformation serves as a catalyst for fostering an agile environment. From the coevolution perspective, the priority should be to create a digitally agile ecosystem that is responsive to evolving market conditions and user needs. This involves leveraging digital technologies to facilitate the development of novel products and services while enabling rapid scaling. Achieving this requires a flexible architectural design underpinned by digital capabilities, as well as efficient resource allocation strategies that are aligned with digital transformation objectives.

Adopting a learning perspective, platforms should also offer comprehensive training and support mechanisms. These digital resources empower users to participate more effectively in co-creation and co-realization processes, thereby enhancing overall user engagement. Moreover, the integration of communication and collaboration tools serves to bolster user engagement and facilitate value co-creation and co-realization processes. This integration is not limited to person-to-person interactions but also extends to interactions between individuals and generative artificial intelligence (Gen AI) systems. When coupled with the incorporation of open communities such as social media, these multifaceted communication channels significantly amplify both user engagement and the value process. By leveraging the inherent potential of social networks, platforms can expand their digital reach and visibility, thereby fostering a more vibrant and engaged user ecosystem.

By strategically implementing these digital transformation initiatives, open innovation platforms can establish a thriving ecosystem of digitally engaged users who actively contribute to value co-creation and co-realization. This not only enhances the platform's digital value proposition but also lays the foundation for a sustainable model of long-term growth.

References

Angeren, J. van, Alves, C., & Jansen, S. (2016). Can we ask you to collaborate? Analyzing app developer relationships in commercial platform ecosystems. *Journal of Systems and Software, 113*, 430–445.

Aquilani, B., Piccarozzi, M., Abbate, T., & Codini, A. (2020). The role of open innovation and value co-creation in the challenging transition from Industry 4.0 to Society 5.0: Toward a theoretical framework. *Sustainability, 12*(21), 8943. https://doi.org/10.3390/su12218943.

Barrett, M., Davidson, E., Prabhu, J., & Vargo, S. L. (2015). Service innovation in the digital age: Key contributions and future directions. *MIS Quarterly, 39*(1), 135–154. https://doi.org/10.25300/misq/2015/39:1.03.

Bogers, M. (2011). The open innovation paradox: Knowledge sharing and protection in R&D collaborations. *European Journal of Innovation Management, 14*(1), 93–117. https://doi.org/10.1108/14601061111104715.

Bogers, M., Zobel, A.-K., Afuah, A., Almirall, E., Brunswicker, S., Dahlander, L., Frederiksen, L., Gawer, A., Gruber, M., & Haefliger, S. (2017). The open innovation research landscape: Established perspectives and emerging themes across different levels of analysis. *Industry and Innovation, 24*(1), 8–40.

Clark, K. B. (1985). The interaction of design hierarchies and market concepts in technological evolution. *Research Policy, 14*(5), 235–251. https://doi.org/10.1016/0048-7333(85)90007-1.

Chesbrough, H. (2006). Open innovation: A new paradigm for understanding industrial innovation. In H. Chesbrough, W. Vanheverbeke & W. Haas (Eds.), *Open Innovation: Researching a New Paradigm* (pp. 1–13). Oxford University Press.

Eaton, B., Elaluf-Calderwood, S., Sørensen, C., & Yoo, Y. (2015). Distributed tuning of boundary resources: The case of Apple's iOS service system. *MIS Quarterly, 39*(1), 217–243. https://doi.org/10.25300/misq/2015/39.1.10.

Ehrlich, P. R., & Raven, P. H. (1964). Butterflies and plants: A study in coevolution. *Evolution, 18*(4), 586. https://doi.org/10.2307/2406212.

Fernandes, T., & Remelhe, P. (2016). How to engage customers in co-creation: Customers' motivations for collaborative innovation. *Journal of Strategic Marketing, 24*(3–4), 311–326. https://doi.org/10.1080/0965254x.2015.1095220.

Figueiredo, B., & Scaraboto, D. (2016). The systemic creation of value through circulation in collaborative consumer networks. *Journal of Consumer Research, 43*(4), 509–533. https://doi.org/10.1093/jcr/ucw038.

Flak, L. S., Solli-Sæther, H., & Straub, D. W. (2022). A theory of multi-realization of IT value: Toward construct clarity in the co-development of large platforms. *MIS Quarterly, 46*(3), 1739–1758.

Fosfuri, A., & Giarratana, M. S. (2009). Masters of war: Rivals' product innovation and new advertising in mature product markets. *Management Science, 55*(2), 181–191. https://doi.org/10.1287/mnsc.1080.0939.
Füller, J., Mühlbacher, H., Matzler, K., & Jawecki, G. (2009). Consumer empowerment through internet-based co-creation. *Journal of Management Information Systems, 26*(3), 71–102. https://doi.org/10.2753/mis0742-1222260303.
Füller, J., Schroll, R., & Hippel, E. von (2013). User generated brands and their contribution to the diffusion of user innovations. *Research Policy, 42*(6–7), 1197–1209. https://doi.org/10.1016/j.respol.2013.03.006.
Galvagno, M., & Dalli, D. (2014). Theory of value co-creation: A systematic literature review. *Managing Service Quality, 24*(6), 643–683. https://doi.org/10.1108/msq-09-2013-0187.
Grange, C., & Benbasat, I. (2018). Opinion seeking in a social network-enabled product review website: A study of word-of-mouth in the era of digital social networks. *European Journal of Information Systems, 27*(6), 629–653. https://doi.org/10.1080/0960085x.2018.1472196.
Grissemann, U. S., & Stokburger-Sauer, N. E. (2012). Customer co-creation of travel services: The role of company support and customer satisfaction with the co-creation performance. *Tourism Management, 33*(6), 1483–1492. https://doi.org/10.1016/j.tourman.2012.02.002.
Han, K., Oh, W., Im, K. S., Chang, R. M., & Pinsonneault, A. (2012). Value cocreation and wealth spillover in open innovation alliances. *MIS Quarterly, 36*(1), 291. https://doi.org/10.2307/41410418.
Hanseth, O., & Lyytinen, K. (2010). Design theory for dynamic complexity in information infrastructures: The case of building internet. *Journal of Information Technology, 25*(1), 1–19. https://doi.org/10.1057/jit.2009.19.
Henfridsson, O., Mathiassen, L., & Svahn, F. (2014). Managing technological change in the digital age: The role of architectural frames. *Journal of Information Technology, 29*(1), 27–43. https://doi.org/10.1057/jit.2013.30.
Henfridsson, O., Nandhakumar, J., Scarbrough, H., & Panourgias, N. (2018). Recombination in the open-ended value landscape of digital innovation. *Information and Organization, 28*(2), 89–100. https://doi.org/10.1016/j.infoandorg.2018.03.001.
Huang, P., Tafti, A., & Mithas, S. (2018). Platform sponsor investments and user contributions in knowledge communities: The role of knowledge seeding. *MIS Quarterly, 42*(1), 213–240. https://doi.org/10.25300/misq/2018/13490.
Kallinikos, J., Aaltonen, A., & Marton, A. (2013). The ambivalent ontology of digital artifacts. *MIS Quarterly, 37*(2), 357–370. https://doi.org/10.25300/misq/2013/37.2.02.
Kazan, E., Tan, C.-W., Lim, E. T. K., Sørensen, C., & Damsgaard, J. (2018). Disentangling digital platform competition: The case of UK mobile payment platforms. *Journal of Management Information Systems, 35*(1), 180–219. https://doi.org/10.1080/07421222.2018.1440772.
Kohler, T., Fueller, J., Matzler, K., Stieger, D., & Füller, J. (2011). Co-creation in virtual worlds: The design of the user experience. *MIS Quarterly, 35*(3), 773–788. https://doi.org/10.2307/23042808.
Lavie, D., & Rosenkopf, L. (2006). Balancing exploration and exploitation in alliance formation. *Academy of Management Journal, 49*(4), 797–818. https://doi.org/10.5465/amj.2006.22083085.

Lee, S. M., Olson, D. L., & Trimi, S. (2012). Co-innovation: Convergenomics, collaboration, and co-creation for organizational values. *Management Decision*, *50*(5), 817–831. https://doi.org/10.1108/00251741211227528.

Lusch, R. F., & Nambisan, S. (2015). Service innovation: A service-dominant logic perspective. *MIS Quarterly*, *39*(1), 155–175. https://doi.org/10.25300/misq/2015/39.1.07.

Mahr, D., & Lievens, A. (2012). Virtual lead user communities: Drivers of knowledge creation for innovation. *Research Policy*, *41*(1), 167–177. https://doi.org/10.1016/j.respol.2011.08.006.

Miller, D., & Breton-Miller, I. L. (2021). Paradoxical resource trajectories: When strength leads to weakness and weakness leads to strength. *Journal of Management*, *47*(7), 1899–1914. https://doi.org/10.1177/0149206320977901.

Oertzen, A.-S., Odekerken-Schröder, G., Brax, S. A., & Mager, B. (2018). Co-creating services: Conceptual clarification, forms and outcomes. *Journal of Service Management*, *29*(4), 641–679. https://doi.org/10.1108/josm-03-2017-0067.

Panico, C., & Cennamo, C. (2022). User preferences and strategic interactions in platform ecosystems. *Strategic Management Journal*, *43*(3), 507–529. https://doi.org/10.1002/smj.3149.

Pellicano, M., Calabrese, M., Loia, F., & Maione, G. (2019). Value co-creation practices in smart city ecosystem. *Journal of Service Science and Management*, *12*(1), 34–57. https://doi.org/10.4236/jssm.2019.121003.

Quach, S., & Thaichon, P. (2017). From connoisseur luxury to mass luxury: Value co-creation and co-destruction in the online environment. *Journal of Business Research*, *81*, 163–172. https://doi.org/10.1016/j.jbusres.2017.06.015.

Ranjan, K. R., & Read, S. (2019). Bringing the individual into the co-creation of value. *Journal of Services Marketing*, *33*(7), 904–920. https://doi.org/10.1108/jsm-02-2019-0056.

Rashid, Y., Waseem, A., Akbar, A. A., & Azam, F. (2019). Value co-creation and social media. *European Business Review*, *31*(5), 761–784. https://doi.org/10.1108/ebr-05-2018-0106.

Saarijärvi, H., Kannan, P. K., & Kuusela, H. (2013). Value co-creation: Theoretical approaches and practical implications. *European Business Review*, *25*(1), 6–19. https://doi.org/10.1108/09555341311287718.

Schillebeeckx, S. J. D., Lin, Y., George, G., & Alnuaimi, T. (2021). Knowledge recombination and inventor networks: The asymmetric effects of embeddedness on knowledge reuse and impact. *Journal of Management*, *47*(4), 838–866. https://doi.org/10.1177/0149206320906865.

Shamim, A., Ghazali, Z., & Albinsson, P. A. (2017). Construction and validation of customer value co-creation attitude scale. *Journal of Consumer Marketing*, *34*(7), 591–602. https://doi.org/10.1108/jcm-01-2016-1664.

Straub, D. W., Rai, A., & Klein, R. (2004). Measuring firm performance at the network level: A nomology of the business impact of digital supply networks. *Journal of Management Information Systems*, *21*(1), 83–114. https://doi.org/10.1080/07421222.2004.11045790.

Thomas, L. D. W., Autio, E., & Gann, D. M. (2014). Architectural leverage: Putting platforms in context. *Academy of Management Perspectives*, *28*(2), 198–219. https://doi.org/10.5465/amp.2011.0105.

Tiwana, A., Konsynski, B., & Bush, A. A. (2010). Research commentary—platform evolution: Coevolution of platform architecture, governance, and environmental dynamics. *Information Systems Research, 21*(4), 675–687. https://doi.org/10.1287/isre.1100.0323.

Trischler, J., Pervan, S. J., & Scott, D. R. (2017). Exploring the "black box" of customer co-creation processes. *Journal of Services Marketing, 31*(3), 265–280. https://doi.org/10.1108/jsm-03-2016-0120.

Tu, Y., Neuhofer, B., & Viglia, G. (2018). When co-creation pays: Stimulating engagement to increase revenues. *International Journal of Contemporary Hospitality Management, 30*(4), 2093–2111. https://doi.org/10.1108/ijchm-09-2016-0494.

Vargo, S. L., & Lusch, R. F. (2004). Evolving to a new dominant logic for marketing. *Journal of Marketing, 68*(1), 1–17. https://doi.org/10.1509/jmkg.68.1.1.24036.

Vargo, S. L., & Lusch, R. F. (2008). Service-dominant logic: Continuing the evolution. *Journal of the Academy of Marketing Science, 36*(1), 1–10. https://doi.org/10.1007/s11747-007-0069-6.

Vega-Vazquez, M., Revilla-Camacho, M. Á., & Cossío-Silva, F. J. (2013). The value co-creation process as a determinant of customer satisfaction. *Management Decision, 51*(10), 1945–1953. https://doi.org/10.1108/md-04-2013-0227.

Verleye, K. (2015). The co-creation experience from the customer perspective: Its measurement and determinants. *Journal of Service Management, 26*(2), 321–342. https://doi.org/10.1108/josm-09-2014-0254.

Ward, J., & Daniel, E. (2006). *Benefits Management: Delivering Value from IS & IT Investments*. John Wiley & Sons.

Xie, K., Wu, Y., Xiao, J., & Hu, Q. (2016). Value co-creation between firms and customers: The role of big data-based cooperative assets. *Information & Management, 53*(8), 1034–1048. https://doi.org/10.1016/j.im.2016.06.003.

Yoo, Y., Henfridsson, O., & Lyytinen, K. (2010). Research commentary—the new organizing logic of digital innovation: An agenda for information systems research. *Information Systems Research, 21*(4), 724–735. https://doi.org/10.1287/isre.1100.0322.

8 Supply chain and logistics in digital transformation

Ilke Bakir, Marjolein Aerts-Veenstra, Kees Jan Roodbergen and A. Berfu Ünal

1. Introduction

The logistics sector is facing major challenges. The Paris Agreement sets out a global framework to limit global warming, with the European Union now aiming to reach a 55 percent reduction of greenhouse gas emissions by 2030, compared with 1990 (European Union, 2020). At the same time, demand for truck drivers is increasing, while the amount of available labor is decreasing due to demographic developments (Anderhofstadt & Spinler, 2020). In the longer run, autonomous vehicles may partly resolve this issue; however, for the short term this is not viable, for among other reasons, remaining safety concerns (Zhao et al., 2021). Moreover, many of the more environmentally friendly options for road transport are actually more labor-intensive. Increasingly, for example, transport of goods in cities is performed using cargo bikes, which typically can deliver fewer parcels per time unit than a delivery van with a combustion engine (Arnold et al., 2018).

These developments may require the logistics sector to overhaul to a large extent the habits and systems that have been developed over past decades. Many transport systems that are in existence now can be seen as variants of the hub-and-spoke network (see Fleischmann, 1998). A typical hub-and-spoke network has a central hub that receives goods from suppliers, and from which the goods are transported to satellite hubs. In turn, customers' goods are delivered from the satellite hubs. Three major changes to current network designs are imminent. Due to the smaller driving range of electric trucks compared to trucks with a combustion engine, hub locations will need to be reconsidered, extra hubs may be needed, and charging stations must be added (Macrina et al., 2019; Kchaou-Boujelben, 2021). Second, many cities are introducing zero-emission zones requiring typically smaller electric vehicles for delivery, while long-distance traffic is most usually in large combustion-engine trucks.

This requires hubs where goods can be transferred between vehicle types (De Bok et al., 2022). Third, many small suppliers are currently making deliveries using the cheapest possible means of transportation, for example a secondhand van running on diesel. This will not be permissible in many cities in the near future, but electric vehicles may not be economical for these companies due to the high purchasing prices. This situation is likely to increase the viability of bundling concepts (Lozano et al., 2013), that is, transporting goods of different suppliers in the same vehicle.

At the same time, digital technologies, such as artificial intelligence, cloud computing, blockchain, and Internet of Things, are increasingly deployed by companies as core components of innovative strategies, and leading to new business models (Ardolino et al., 2018; Hanelt et al., 2021). These new digital technologies cause a change in competition, which has resulted in a transfer of sales to young digital firms, and in competition becoming more global (Verhoef et al., 2021). In the logistics sector this is visible, for example, from a relatively new player like Amazon, which now operates from 2,373 facilities worldwide for order fulfillment and distribution (MWPVL, 2023), with Amazon Air operating 110 cargo planes to transport parcels (McLoughlin, 2022). Furthermore, especially in cities, a rapid increase in new delivery formats can be observed, such as delivery by cargo bicycles (Wicaksono et al., 2022). Since companies often promise to deliver orders within a day after the customer places the order, logistics processes are subject to high fluctuations, which makes it increasingly challenging to design a resilient network, to determine adequate staffing levels, and to make an effective operational planning. The importance of this is significantly increased as a result of the fact that the logistics sector has become a main factor determining the perceived service level by customers (Hekimoğlu et al., 2024). The delivery process is now an integral part of the value proposition of many companies (Daugherty et al., 2019; Nguyen et al., 2019). Digital technologies are increasingly deployed to cope with these challenges, leading to digital supply chains, that is, "intelligent best-fit technological system[s] that [are] based on the capability of massive data disposal and excellent cooperation and communication for digital hardware, software, and networks to support and synchronize interaction between organizations by making services more valuable, accessible and affordable with consistent, agile and effective outcomes" (Büyüközkan & Göçer, 2018).

In this chapter, we explore the landscape of digital transformation in the logistics sector, where we specifically focus on the setting of food distribution in densely populated cities. We have selected food distribution for a number of reasons (see also Sections 3 and 4). First, food distribution forms one of the largest goods flows into cities, supplying hotels, restaurants, and bars.

Second, a majority of new (environmental) requirements for logistics, such as zero-emission zones, arise currently in cities, not in rural areas. Because food distribution occurs predominantly in cities, changes in logistics requirements impact the entire company, in turn leading to a higher need for innovations. Third, in food distribution still many small suppliers exist that deliver their goods, for example only cheese or only wine, directly to their customers. Many of these small suppliers can be seen to deploy a single truck for making all their deliveries, using very limited technology for ordering and planning. Buying an electric truck might be too expensive for these suppliers; hence, to comply with upcoming zero-emission regulations, they are likely to be open to innovative concepts like bundling, where a number of suppliers collaborate to make their combined deliveries. The introduction of bundling, however, requires these suppliers to adopt new digital technologies (see Section 2).

The added value of our work is threefold. First, to the best of our knowledge, we are the first to present a comprehensive view on digital transformation from the viewpoint of the food logistics sector. We demonstrate how food suppliers may navigate the transition toward digitization and environmentally friendly logistics concepts. Related earlier studies have focused on, for example, logistics service providers in general (Cichosz et al., 2020) and maritime logistics (Jovic et al., 2022). Second, we thoroughly analyze the opportunities that arise for a food supplier to initiate a digitally enabled bundling concept for jointly delivering goods, investigating consequential changes in communication, logistics concepts, agreements with customers on service levels, collaboration between suppliers, and planning concepts. Numerous studies on bundling and other collaborative logistics frameworks have been published (e.g., Asgharieh Ahari et al., 2024; Fernandez et al., 2018). To the best of our knowledge, however, none fully describes the large dimensionality of the organizational impact from the involved digital transformation. We deploy a multi-methods approach that combines (1) quantitative modeling of logistics processes to estimate the new business model's financial viability with (2) a qualitative analysis of stakeholders' views on the digital transformation, as obtained through in-depth interviews. In general, research focusing on quantitative modeling to determine the costs of collaborative logistics is long-standing and abundant (e.g., Ergun et al., 2007), as are qualitative analyses of logistics innovations (e.g., Reinecke et al., 2023). Fewer logistics studies, however, exist in the context of digital transformation, and to the best of our knowledge, our work is unique in the fact that we can provide an integral and coherent view on both aspects since all results relate to the same case company. Third, from a practical perspective, we highlight how the opportunity for introducing a bundling concept can make the business model of a food supplier shift toward a logistics service provider, and hence induce a digital transformation.

In the next section, we introduce basic terminology, position the developments in the logistics sector in the context of digital transformation, and discuss challenges the logistics sector is facing in this respect. We then zoom in on the logistics of food distribution, explaining how these logistics processes are typically organized. The attitudes of food suppliers toward novel logistics concepts that are enabled by digital technologies are investigated after, with an emphasis on bundling. Quantitative insights into the advantages and disadvantages of bundling as a new business model for a food distributor are presented. Finally, conclusions are provided.

2. Digital transformation in logistics

Digital transformation is defined by Verhoef et al. (2021) as "a change in how a firm employs digital technologies, to develop a new digital business model that helps to create and appropriate more value for the firm." In the digital transformation process, companies often move to organizational designs that enable continuous adaptation, and tend to build a business ecosystem to obtain a good value proposition (Hanelt et al., 2021). In such a business ecosystem, a set of partners interacts for a value proposition to materialize (Adner, 2017), which is essential for a firm's strategy because it forms a firm's decisions about where and how to compete (Jacobides et al., 2018). This process toward developing new organizational designs and building ecosystems can be clearly observed in the logistics sector, albeit there are many challenges (Seghezzi et al., 2023). We describe the ongoing process at logistics companies, using the multidimensional framework for digital transformation of Hanelt et al. (2021), consisting of three main categories: *contextual conditions*, *mechanisms*, and *outcomes*.

Contextual conditions mark the beginning of innovation trajectories, when changes occur in one or more elements of technological innovation—artifacts, beliefs, and evaluation routines (Henfridsson & Yoo, 2014). *Artifacts* perform specific functions that can be seen in action (Baldwin & Clark, 2000), which for the digital transformation is found to include so-called SMACIT technologies (social, mobile, analytics, cloud, and Internet of Things) (Hanelt et al., 2021). Although we consider the artifacts for the digital transformation in the logistics sector to be quite similar to those for digital transformations in other sectors, the change in *beliefs* (i.e., how opinions about the role of logistics in a company's strategy have developed) are assumed to exhibit unique aspects. Traditionally, logistics companies tended to have a cost focus leading to the offering of a fairly standardized set of services, while over time logistics has been evolving toward a high degree of customer adaptation (Hertz & Alfredsson, 2003). With the emergence of e-commerce, the ongoing increase in strategic importance of logistics has been accelerated. The logistics sector now finds itself at the forefront of customer service, and forms a main determinant for customer satisfaction (Daugherty et al., 2019; Hong et al., 2019; Nguyen et al., 2019). Additionally, the redesign of logistics processes is increasingly acknowledged to provide opportunities for companies to improve sustainability, which is increasingly valued by customers (Melkonyan et al., 2020; Ignat & Chankov, 2020; Rai et al., 2021). These changes in beliefs about the role and importance of logistics are considered to be core triggers for initiating changes in companies' business strategy. Consequently, *evaluation routines*, which serve as standards for determining the value of an innovation, have also shifted from reducing costs to increasing value and reducing environmental impact (Evangelista et al., 2017; Hertz & Alfredsson, 2003).

Mechanisms, primarily innovation and integration, are used by companies to realize a digital transformation (Hanelt et al., 2021). *Innovation* concerns the introduction of new approaches, and *integration* concerns the synthesis of these new approaches with existing approaches. Triggered by the various contextual conditions, the logistics sector has been introducing numerous innovations in recent years. Many of these innovations have—at least initially—been focused on the business-to-consumer market. We name a few of the relevant developments. Logistics systems are increasingly innovating their organization to be more adaptive and to enable faster delivery (i.e., to enable a shorter time between ordering and delivery of a product) (Leung et al., 2018). This has led to adoption of logistics concepts enabling next-day delivery (Hekimoğlu et al., 2024), and in recent years concepts enabling instant delivery (Altay et al., 2022), which generally results in delivery within 20 minutes after ordering. Also, more attention is paid to the environmental consequences in these concepts, even though consumers tend to have a preference for free, next-day delivery at an address of their choice (Rai et al., 2019). Crowdsourced delivery systems have emerged that leverage networks of nonprofessional persons for making deliveries to consumers' homes (Castillo et al., 2018). A long-standing trend in logistics innovations is various forms of collaboration between companies in supply chains (Cao & Zhang, 2011). Interestingly, collaborations can—in turn—serve as a stimulus for further innovations when collaborators share knowledge and processes, and subsequently engage in joint investing in improved supply chain operations (Soosay et al., 2008).

There are a multitude of innovative forms of logistics collaboration (see Pan et al., 2019). A shared future perspective on collaboration in the logistics sector is the *physical internet*, which foresees an open network for collaboratively organizing goods' flows (Sternberg & Norrman, 2017; Crainic & Montreuil, 2016). We highlight here a number of current concepts, namely order sharing, resource sharing, and bundling. *Order sharing* is a framework where logistics companies collaborate by exchanging customer orders. That is, any company may be serving its own customers, but also customers of other companies, whichever is considered most effective (Buijs et al., 2016; Gansterer & Hartl, 2018; Fernandez et al., 2018). Each company uses only its own vehicles in the order sharing framework. In contrast, in *resource sharing*, logistics companies collaborate by borrowing and lending each other's vehicles, while each company remains to deliver exclusively to its own customers (Asgharieh Ahari et al., 2024). *Bundling* occurs when a number of suppliers collaborate to make their combined deliveries to their combined customers via a common distribution network (Lozano et al., 2013). There are various forms in which bundling may take shape. For example, suppliers may outsource their logistics activities via a freight marketplace to logistics companies (Huang & Xu, 2013), or suppliers may actively collaborate to coordinate and align their transport tasks (Ergun et al., 2007). Alternatively, a supplier with its own fleet of vehicles may incorporate deliveries of other suppliers into its own delivery routes. It is the latter form of bundling that we focus on in this chapter. In all forms of bundling, an essential requirement for success is the creation of an ecosystem (i.e., bringing together a group of companies that are willing to collaborate and have the ability to create value together) (Adner, 2017; Jacobides et al., 2018). Bundling can also be a viable option, for example, when regulations require deliveries within city limits to occur with electric trucks, while long-distance transport from suppliers is performed by trucks with a combustion engine (Breunig et al., 2019).

Another identified main *mechanism* toward realizing a digital transformation is *integration* (i.e., merging innovations and preexisting approaches into a common organizational format). Generally, large firms tend to have an advantage initially when adopting innovations due to their available resources, but they tend to have to overcome inertia in later stages (Zhu et al., 2006). For example, Roodbergen and Kolman (2016) describe the challenges of a retailer to integrate logistics operations for their brick-and-mortar stores with logistics operations for their e-commerce sales channel. Online retailers may even set up innovative logistics concepts themselves, instead of collaborating with a logistics company, thus avoiding the issues involved with integration that traditional logistics companies would face. In this respect, order fulfillment by an online retailer like Amazon, which performs a majority of its logistics processes itself, can be seen to outperform other online retailers (Zhang et al., 2019). However, many of the contextual conditions likely lead naturally to the integration of innovations with existing processes. For example, environmental regulations and sustainability considerations invite logistics companies to add electric trucks to their fleet, which must be fully integrated into the existing planning alongside combustion-engine trucks (Dönmez et al., 2022) to ensure all customers are delivered according to schedule. Electric trucks, however, have different requirements with respect to the logistics network design, because of their shorter driving range and the need to recharge intermittently (Zhang et al., 2018).

Outcomes constitute the third category in the multidimensional framework for digital transformation of Hanelt et al. (2021). This relates to the composition and structure of the company itself, its surroundings, and economic effects. Of specific interest to us are the structures and activities involved in acquiring and processing of large amounts of data, and how these can support making better operational decisions and developing innovative logistics solutions (Del Giudice et al., 2021). Verhoef et al. (2021) consider three levels of outcomes: digitization, digitalization, and digital transformation.

Digitization concerns the conversion of analog to digital information or tasks in a technical sense (Loebbecke & Picot, 2015). In the logistics sector, digitization is an ongoing effort that evolves with the technical capabilities and organizational requirements. For example, Chhabra et al. (2022) illustrate a performance monitoring system that digitizes logistics activities to support environmental improvement efforts. Many other digitization processes have been proposed and introduced in the logistics sector (Vanderroost et al., 2017; Sanders et al., 2019). There are also significant challenges for digitization in the logistics sector. Because a major component of logistics involves the movement of physical goods across borders between countries worldwide, part of the digitization process in logistics is dependent on international agreements between countries. Notably, the consignment note, which is the main document in international transport and serves as proof of the conclusion of the contract of carriage, is still frequently used in analog format (i.e., paper-based). The first international shipment ever that used an electronic consignment note only occurred in 2017 (Tomicová et al., 2021), using the Dutch IT system of TransFollow. Furthermore, digitization in logistics and supply chain management is still considered in its early stages of development among academics (Büyüközkan & Göçer, 2018). From the authors' own observations, this also applies to many companies, which may result in relevant data not being stored in IT systems. For example, only start times of activities may be registered in an IT system, which makes it difficult or impossible to distinguish processing times from waiting times (Larco et al., 2017).

Digitalization considers the change in methods and processes under the influence of digital technologies (Verhoef et al., 2021; Leviäkangas, 2016), which may, for example, allow for a more efficient coordination between processes. Numerous approaches have been introduced in the logistics sector that were only possible due to the advent of digital technologies. The availability of data in digital format enables car drivers to find available parking slots (Chauhan et al., 2020), warehouse workers to determine their next activity (Schrotenboer et al., 2017), maintenance activities to be better scheduled (Bakir et al., 2021), and infrastructure usage to be estimated (Toole et al., 2015). In the transport of food, analysis of data can reveal patterns of food quality losses due to different transport conditions, which may in turn be used to improve conditions by redesigning the logistics network (Chaudhuri et al., 2018). Collaborative logistics, where multiple companies work together to improve the efficiency of their logistics processes (Gansterer & Hartl, 2018), is made possible by the availability of data and digital technologies. Jointly working on data storage, data exchange, and supply synchronization can reduce inventories, enhance synergies, improve service quality, and provide more flexibility (Cao & Zhang, 2011). When companies collaborate in a bundling concept, they need to exchange data digitally for testing and quantifying the synergies to determine the most profitable collaboration opportunities (Lozano et al., 2013).

Digital transformation goes beyond digitalization and affects the whole company or even the industry, leading to new business models (Verhoef et al., 2021; Kane et al., 2015). As such, digital technologies can be instrumental in achieving a competitive advantage by developing new competencies. Ardolino et al. (2018) investigate how three digital technologies (Internet of Things, cloud computing, and predictive analytics) can be key in digital transformation. Of specific importance to the logistics sector are the strategic opportunities that can arise when data is used for algorithmic decision-making (Newell & Marabelli, 2015). For example, the new business model of instant grocery delivery (Altay et al., 2022) is significantly dependent on the logistics processes, which have to ensure timely retrieval of the requested product from the warehouse and timely delivery to the consumers' homes. The effectiveness of these logistics processes in turn are dependent on available data and data processing, such as demand prediction, personnel planning, inventory management, warehouse process optimization, and delivery route planning (Melacini et al., 2018). Other new business models in logistics are crowdsourced delivery and related concepts; for example, for meal delivery (Castillo et al., 2018; Yildiz & Savelsbergh, 2019). The success of these concepts depends on a digital transformation that enables the company to bring together real-time interaction with the customers for ordering and delivery timing, real-time GPS information from delivery agents, and real-time operational decision-making for efficiency (Mao et al., 2022).

3. Food distribution logistics

Food distribution logistics consists of many interconnected processes that hinge on moving products both at a hub level and between hubs and end customers, often with cooled vehicles in order to adhere with food safety regulations. Typically, products that are destined for an end customer leave their origin hubs, travel through a network of hubs to reach the destination hub, get consolidated into a single shipment at the destination hub, and get transported to the end customer, potentially in the same vehicle as other end customers' shipments. Figure 8.1 is a graphical representation of this network. We focus here on the last mile logistics, which is from the hub to the end customers.

In last mile food logistics, specific challenges due to (i) the locations of end customers, typically in city centers that are subject to strict transport limitations and regulations, (ii) cooling and food safety considerations, (iii) customers' rising service expectations (e.g., adjusting orders for the following day until late at night, as explained in detail in Section 1), and (iv) uncertainties in transport volumes and timing, are prevalent. Additionally, the time margins are very tight, since the customers must receive their food products as freshly as possible. Customer orders can (digitally) arrive very late in the evening, which means that hub-to-hub deliveries, which may also arrive late at night or very early in the morning, must be consolidated very quickly and leave early in the morning to adhere to stringent customer and emission zone time windows. To address this timing challenge, food distributors have to start the consolidation process before all customer orders are known and hub-to-hub deliveries have arrived. In order to ensure timely and fresh deliveries, a food distributor can start the consolidation process according to a *tactical plan*, which is a blueprint derived from historical ordering behavior of the end customers, typically through both descriptive and prescriptive data analytics methods.

There is usually a large number of dock doors in a food distributor's warehouse, and products can be staged near each dock door before they are loaded onto the delivery vehicle that will later depart for its last mile delivery route to the end customers. In the *tactical plan*, customers are, via the assignment to route numbers, associated with dock doors (e.g., the order of customer 1 will be loaded onto the vehicle that is to depart from dock door 2). By using the tactical plan, the distributor can start staging the customer orders next to dock

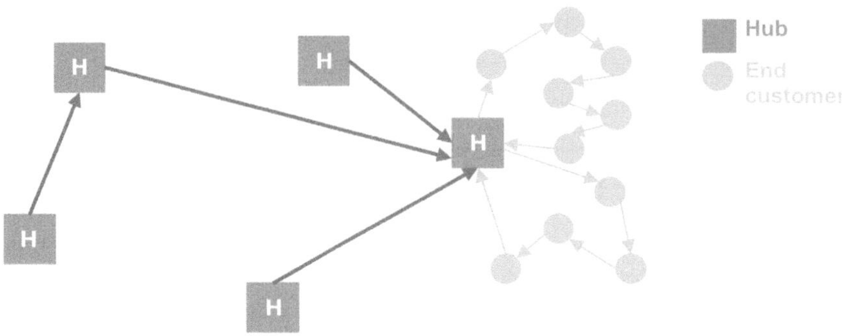

Source: Authors.

Figure 8.1 Illustrative example of a food distribution logistics network

doors before all customers have placed their final orders for the next day, and all hub-to-hub deliveries have arrived. This way, the distributor can ensure that consolidation and loading can be feasibly completed before the vehicles need to depart to arrive at the customers on time.

After the staging starts according to the tactical plan, the actual customer orders arrive. The actual customer orders can deviate from the tactical plan; for example, customers can order different products or volumes, or irregular customers who do not order frequently enough to be assigned a dock door in the tactical plan can decide to place an order. These last-minute order alterations require the *operational plan*, which defines the actual assignment of customers to dock doors and the corresponding vehicle routes, to deviate from the tactical plan (e.g., the order of customer 1 will now have to be loaded onto the vehicle of dock door 3, because it no longer fits into that of dock door 2). These changes might require goods to be moved between the staging areas of dock doors, which requires additional handling. Once staging and loading is completed according to the operational plan, the vehicles depart the warehouse and start their planned routes.

Many end customers of food distributors (e.g., restaurants, hotels) are located within city centers. Numerous distributors bring products to these customers, which contributes to increased driven kilometers, emissions, noise, and traffic congestion. A way to limit the flow of distribution vehicles into city centers and therefore partially eliminate the aforementioned adverse effects is consolidating deliveries of multiple suppliers. As briefly introduced in Section 1, *bundling* envisions a big distributor to receive goods from smaller distributors at their destination hub, where they consolidate these goods with their own, and deliver to the end customers. This way, the end customers receive their products in one delivery from the big distributor, henceforth referred to as the *bundler*, instead of numerous smaller deliveries from the bundler and each one of the smaller distributors, referred to as the *suppliers* from this point onward. This approach, which is graphically illustrated in Figure 8.2, has the potential to increase vehicle utilization and reduce the driven kilometers and the number of vehicles in city centers, which can contribute to reducing the environmental impact of the last mile. We analyze different aspects of bundling in Sections 4 and 5.

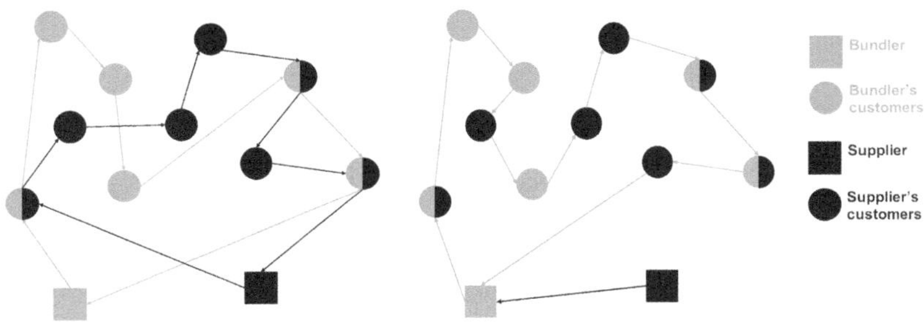

(a) No bundling; the bundler and the supplier serve their own customers

(b) Bundling; the supplier brings the goods to the bundler and the bundler serves all customers

Source: Authors.

Figure 8.2 Typical delivery routes for the bundler (gray) and the supplier (black)

The challenges in the logistics processes in the warehouse of a food distributor, mainly stemming from stringent timing requirements and the uncertainty of customer orders, are exacerbated by the implementation of bundling. With bundling, there are more strict timing requirements because (i) there are more suppliers that bring goods to the warehouse at varying times, (ii) there is more handling because larger product volumes need to be processed, and (iii) there are more customers who may require products at varying times. There is also more uncertainty in the logistics processes under the bundling scheme due to the uncertain timing and volumes of a larger number of suppliers.

Bundling also brings up new questions in digitization (e.g., whether the suppliers store the necessary data digitally at all, and, if so, whether it is stored in a format that is compatible with the bundler's) and digitalization (e.g., how big of an undertaking the integration of the bundler's and the supplier's relevant IT and data infrastructures will be, or whether there will be data privacy issues to be considered). These questions are also brought up by several involved stakeholders (see Section 4). Adoption of the envisioned bundling framework requires a digital transformation for the company by integrating logistics services into their business model. Adding the capability of delivering on behalf of other companies, rather than only delivering their own goods, invites the company to rethink and redesign their entire digital infrastructure to enable proper handling of suppliers' and customers' demands, and in addition to reap logistics benefits from the integrated logistics by means of advanced planning systems. In a sense, bundling envisions the bundler to act as a logistics service provider to other (smaller) companies, in addition to satisfying its own customers' orders.

As mentioned throughout this section, bundling comes with its unique set of challenges and opportunities. We conducted several interviews with practitioners in the field to get insights on the perceived challenges and opportunities of this new concept (see Section 4). Some of the challenges described above were tackled by means of a quantitative study (see Section 5) carried out in conjunction with our partner, Bidfood.

Bidfood is a wholesale food distributor that supplies cafeterias, restaurants, hotels, and medical institutions (Bidfood, 2023). Bidfood currently operates in 35 different countries worldwide. There are 17 Bidfood branches in the Netherlands. Bidfood has a history of initiating innovation trajectories to reduce environmental impact, for example, by improving sustainability of their product packaging (Bidfood, 2019a) and by reducing food waste (Bidfood, 2019b). In recent years, Bidfood has been active to investigate new opportunities aimed at reducing their CO2 emissions by rethinking their logistics network design. For this purpose, Bidfood collaborates with several knowledge institutions, companies, and policymakers to work toward this goal. For the research project described in this chapter, we have analyzed the current and projected situation of the Bidfood branch in Groningen. Bidfood has completed and ongoing projects regarding, for example, estimating the number of electric delivery vehicles needed under various bundling scenarios, deliveries into city centers via electric boats, innovative vehicles (light electric vehicles, mobile hubs), the effect of time windows on emissions, and bundling. Research collaborations, as well as collaborations with stakeholders in the supply chain, are actively built to achieve sustainability goals.

The aforementioned emphasis of Bidfood on sustainability and collaboration makes them suitable as a unit of analysis for studying a bundling concept. Moreover, they have the resources (suitable warehouse and fleet), customer base in the inner city, and data that can benefit the digitalization phase. In the next sections, the details and results of the analysis related to bundling are shared.

4. Stakeholder perspectives on bundling concepts

In this section, we present the results of the qualitative research we conducted with regard to the bundling concept introduced in Section 3. We focus on the city of Groningen, where we envision Bidfood as the bundler. In this envisioned setting, several other small suppliers deliver their products to Bidfood's hub, after which Bidfood consolidates the products and delivers them to the customers in one delivery. We conducted several interviews with suppliers and customers to investigate their view on the bundling concept. All interviews took place in the fall of 2021. In total, 22 interviews are conducted with customers in the hospitality sector and with suppliers to the hospitality sector. Among these interviewees, 16 are customers, including 11 customers of Bidfood and five customers in the hospitality sector that weren't customers of Bidfood at the time the interviews took place. All customers interviewed are located in the inner city of Groningen within the zero-emission zone. Six interviews are conducted with suppliers who perform deliveries toward customers located in the zero-emission zone of Groningen.

First, the attitude toward the bundling concept is investigated from the perspective of customers and suppliers either located or active in the zero-emission zone. Second, the conditions that need to be in place for the concept to be successful are identified. Both the *must-haves*, conditions that need to be in place for the concept to work, and the *nice-to-haves*, additional conditions that will make the concept more attractive, are investigated. Finally, data is gathered on the product and transportation flows of the customers and suppliers. The purpose of this data collection is to get a deeper understanding of the current situation, and to obtain first estimates for the quantitative analyses (see Section 5).

The results of the interviews show interesting insights into the attitude of the customers and suppliers toward the bundling concept. All interviewees are very open to the bundling concept; there are no interviewees with a negative attitude toward the concept. All customers are at worst neutral toward the concept, but most of them are positive or very positive. Some of them call the concept an "ideal situation." The customers mention that they like the concept of only one vehicle that delivers to them, since it is environmentally friendly and practical, leading to, for example, less handling during the day and less administration (i.e., less digitization on their end). There are customers that already decided to order at fewer suppliers to prevent multiple deliveries, showing that this idea fits well with the wishes from the customers. However, there are also some concerns about the bundling concept from the customers' view with regard to *feasibility*, *sustainability*, and a possible *monopoly position* for the bundler. Although customers have not explicitly mentioned the exact words "digital transformation" during the interviews, when asked to contemplate about the feasibility of the concept, they indicate to expect significant logistical challenges in practice. These remarks do not pertain to the physical processes in the warehouse or the movement of goods in trucks, but rather concern the challenges in information flows and synchronization of the logistics planning between participating companies. Additional packaging, resulting from merging multiple separate shipments for combined handling and delivery, could have a negative impact on sustainability, which customers argue could actually reduce sustainability in practice. Also the position of the bundler is questioned: since the bundler acting as the key player in the process might get a *monopoly position*, some customers give preference to a white label concept. In that sense, customers wonder whether the bundler's position in the food supply chain, and notably its access to relevant data, will mostly benefit the bundler itself, rather than the supply chain's sustainability or other stakeholders. For the digital transformation to become successful, transparent information must be created for stakeholders to gauge the benefits of the bundling concept for all involved parties.

The suppliers are also open toward the bundling concept. Most of the interviewed suppliers are positive, mentioning that it would be a lot easier for them compared to doing their own deliveries to customers, and it would save them time and probably also money. One of the suppliers is not open toward the bundling concept for their own business, since customer contact is part of their core business and therefore it is too important to them to outsource, however this supplier sees the potential for the concept in general. The *contact* and *service* aspects are something to be considered in general, since other suppliers also mention that the service level should not be affected by bundling. Possible negative consequences of bundling mentioned by the suppliers are the loss of their own identity and loss of control over the process. Making agreements, performing evaluations, and giving feedback are possible tools that are mentioned to keep some control over the process. The development, integration, and coordination of these contact and service aspects should be considered in the digitalization phase. We expect this may be a challenging task, as this implies a centralized digitization and digitalization effort for food delivery, while maintaining brand image and personalized service offerings from participating suppliers.

There are some preconditions mentioned by the interviewees that need to be in place in order to make the concept work. First of all, the *timing issue* is emphasized. Customers mention that they need their deliveries before a specific time, for example to ensure that they can start preparing their meals. This means that when all products are delivered at once by the bundler, they need to be delivered before the earliest time at which a product needs to be available at the customer location (e.g., if the customer needs meat at 07:00 and vegetables at 09:00, the bundler must deliver everything before 07:00). Arriving at customer locations on time becomes even more important in the bundling scenario, since it's a more serious problem when all products are too late instead of only one supplier being late. The suppliers also mention that the products need to be delivered before the time agreed upon with the customers.

A related precondition highlighted by the interviewees is the *delivery frequency*. If, in the current situation, a supplier delivers to a customer on a day that the bundler does not, it should still be possible for the bundler to deliver to that customer on that day in the bundling scenario. This would imply that the delivery frequency of the bundler increases for customers in this scenario.

The *cost aspect* is mentioned by many of the interviewees. The customers mention that the products should not become more expensive, and suppliers mention that the operations should either be equally costly or cheaper than current operations. Hence many stakeholders wonder about the bundler's business model, which is evidently relevant for making the digital transformation feasible, and which is analyzed in detail in Section 5.

As the bundling concept under consideration involves parties in food distribution, *quality requirements* are of high importance. Both the customers and the suppliers mention that (i) the quality of the products needs to be guaranteed, (ii) products need to be cooled and remain fresh, and (iii) food safety regulations, such as the Hazard Analysis Critical Control Points (HACCP), should be in place during the entire process including the phases of consolidation and temporary storage. One way of ensuring food safety is continuously and accurately monitoring food temperature conditions, which is a digitization effort. Such digitization cannot reasonably be expected to be affordable for smaller suppliers individually, but a bundler may provide the operational scale to make this economically feasible.

Service is one of the aspects that is mentioned quite frequently during the interviews. Customers mention that the products need to be delivered neatly and in an orderly fashion. Agreements should be made on how the bundler unpacks the products and where he stores it at the customer location. Some of the customers mention that Bidfood brings the products into the freezer at the customers', which is a service that these customers want to keep. It would be nice, one of the customers mentions, that he gets a phone call about the exact delivery time, so that he can ensure to be present to receive the products. The suppliers also mention that the service is of very high importance. It should be guaranteed that everything will be delivered in the correct way.

Both the customers and suppliers mention the *return flows* that need to be incorporated into this concept. For example, crates that need to be returned to the suppliers should be taken care of. *Local partners* are mentioned by the customers: it is important that they feel seen and heard, and the possibilities to order local products should remain. The *market position* of both the bundler and the supplier(s) is also mentioned by the interviewees. One of the customers mentions that there should not be one bundler having all the rights and reaping all benefits from the concept. There is a need for transparency to ensure that this will not happen when executing the bundling concept. It is also important to think about the visibility of the other suppliers, one of them also mentions that their name and brand should still be visible.

Communication is one of the keywords that arises throughout the interviews; good communication is a must-have for this process to work in practice. Clear agreements should be made about the consolidation and distribution processes, and where specific responsibilities lie. Relatedly, it needs to be clear for the customers with whom to communicate regularly, and whom to contact in different (unexpected) situations, such as when products are missing or in case of complaints.

Findings indicate that there are several preconditions that need to be met and barriers that need to be removed for a successful implementation of the bundling concept. These preconditions are mainly related to ensuring the convenience of the customers while using bundling (e.g., timing and frequency of delivery, ease of communication) as well as the quality of the service. For suppliers, status-related factors, such as being visible for the customer despite the use of bundling, seem to be key. Digitization could act as a major enabler to address these preconditions and barriers. Although not explicitly mentioned by the interviewees, the bundling concept requires joint data storage, exchange, and synchronization mechanisms between the bundler and the suppliers. The economical and sustainability benefits of the bundling concept are analyzed in Section 5; however, the feasibility of these joint digitalization efforts, as well as potential privacy issues that may arise, must be considered before bundling can be implemented in food logistics.

5. Financial viability of the bundling concept

For a digital transformation from food supplier into a bundler to succeed, the need for a sound business model is imperative. Benefits will be reaped largely from increased efficiencies in the logistics processes, while costs will mostly come from one-time investments to develop the needed digitization and digitalization capabilities. Other costs, like purchasing costs for trucks, largely scale with the size of the operation in a near-linear fashion. We analyze data to design the envisioned logistics network of the bundler and predict the expected efficiency gains of bundling. Such predictive analytics are considered key in digital transformations (Ardolino et al., 2018). Digitization and digitalization efforts will partly be similar to those of any platform that aims at connecting suppliers and customers. The setting of a bundler requires, however, specific capabilities to enable real-time alignment of customers' orders and logistics execution. Bidfood is currently not yet in the phase to request price quotes for developing the IT systems, hence we have no data available about this aspect. We can, however, quantitatively showcase the benefits that can be derived from bundling (Section 5.1), identify some system parameters that impact bundling success (Section 5.2), and highlight the importance of coordination between the bundler and the supplier(s) (Section 5.3). The numerical results presented here are based on Binder (2022) and Bloemhard (2022).

5.1 Quantifying the Bundling Benefits

Bundling has the potential to improve network-wide performance, due to reducing the total kilometers driven and the number of vehicles used. However, receiving other suppliers' products, possibly storing them, and consolidating them into a single shipment may result in additional handling and storage costs for the bundler. Thus, the trade-off between reduced driving distance and additional handling/storage costs must be thoroughly analyzed.

While bundling has the potential to reduce the direct cost of transport (e.g., fuel expenses and drivers' wages) compared to a non-collaborative approach, it likely increases the bundler's handling/storage costs, which may consist of (i) the wages of the loading/unloading workforce, (ii) the cost of additional storage space that might be necessary to store the suppliers' products, and (iii) cooling costs that might be incurred to keep the suppliers' products at appropriate temperatures. Additionally, limitations regarding the capacity for storage at the depot, workforce sufficiency, and fleet transport capacity may restrict the practicality of bundling. Therefore, when examining the profitability of bundling, these implications must be taken into consideration, and the research perspective must exceed that of transport cost savings only.

We analyze bundling from a cost–benefit perspective by examining empirical data from Bidfood. The costs and benefits of bundling are quantified through solving the vehicle routing problems of Bidfood (i.e., the bundler) and potential bundling partners (i.e., the suppliers) with and without bundling. Specifically, attention is paid to observing (i) when the bundling benefits in terms of driven kilometers outweigh the additional costs of storage and handling, and (ii) what kind of bundling partnerships result in the largest savings.

The costs and benefits are analyzed from the perspective of the bundler (Bidfood). The bundler's costs are decomposed into three cost components, as listed in detail below (Binder, 2022):

1. *Warehouse handling cost*: Based on the data provided by Bidfood, the number of labor hours necessary to handle the freight is calculated. Multiplying this number by the wages paid in the warehouse delivers a realistic cost measure.
2. *Storage cost*: This cost component provides a unit (per roll-container) cost estimate for storing cooled or frozen products.
3. *Transport cost*: This cost component includes the total driving cost (total distance driven by the fleet of the bundler times the average cost per kilometer) and the wages paid to the drivers.

In order to quantify the impact of bundling to the costs of the bundler, a supplier that is smaller than the bundler is considered. In this setting, the supplier has approximately half as many customers as the bundler, each having the same demand volume as the bundler, on average. Furthermore, about half of the supplier's customers are also the bundler's customers. Overall system performance is computed for the bundler's base scenario, where the bundler only delivers to its own customers, and for the bundling scenario, where the bundler consolidates its own and the supplier's shipments, and delivers to both its own and the supplier's customers. The aforementioned system performance measures are presented in Table 8.1.

The particular setting, whose results are presented in Table 8.1, quantifies the effect of bundling in a hypothetical partnership where bundling increases the bundler's shipment volumes by 50 percent, but the increase in the number of customers that the bundler must visit is less than 50 percent (since some of the suppliers' and the bundler's customers are mutual). It can be clearly observed in Table 8.1 that even though bundling increases the bundler's shipment volumes by 50 percent, the total driven distance increases only by 4.9 percent. This marginal increase in driven distance highlights the very rationale behind bundling. Furthermore, the increase in transport costs introduced by bundling amounts to 33.6 percent, which is significantly less than the 50 percent increase in the bundler's shipment volume.

Table 8.1 The bundler's base case vs. bundling (from the bundler's perspective)

Metric	Base scenario	Bundling	Change %
Total driven distance	299 km	313 km	+4.9
Total driving time	1,646 min	2,325 min	+39.7
Total shipped volume	140.30 roll-containers	207.3 roll-containers	+50.0
Total shipped weight	15,729 kg	23,569 kg	+50.0
Number of used vehicles	4.95 trucks	7.18 trucks	+45.0
Total utilization (volume)	85.32%	88.90%	+4.2
Warehouse cost	€796	€1,175	+47.6
Storage cost	€1,055	€1,581	+49.9
Transport cost	€822	€1,098	+33.6
Total costs	€2,673	€3,864	+44.6

Note: The numbers in the table are averages of 23 days.

The marginal increase in the total driving distance, even when bundling substantially increases the number of customers and shipment volumes that the bundler must serve, demonstrates the potential benefit of this collaborative approach. In what follows, we dive deeper into some characteristics of a bundling partnership (e.g., the number and locations of the supplier's customers) and their effects on bundling performance.

5.2 Potential Predictors of Bundling Success

This subsection evaluates bundling success under different bundler–supplier partnerships by quantifying the effects of the following three supplier characteristics on bundling performance: (i) size of the supplier's customer base, (ii) the proportion of the supplier's customers that are mutual with the bundler, and (iii) the average distance of the supplier's customers from the bundler's customers.

First, the effect of varying number of customers for the supplier is evaluated on the bundler's warehouse, storage, driving, and total costs. To that end, the supplier's number of customers is gradually increased from 0 percent (i.e., there is no bundling; the bundler only delivers to its own customers) of the number of customers of the bundler to 100 percent (i.e., the supplier has as many customers as the bundler). In this experimental setting, the supplier has equal shipment weights and volumes to the bundler, on average, and approximately 50 percent of the supplier's customers are mutual with the bundler. The resulting costs are illustrated in Figures 8.3 and 8.4.

Figure 8.3 demonstrates the total cost increase with a growing customer base for the supplier, and Figure 8.4 zooms into only the driving cost in the same setting. It can be clearly observed that both the driving cost and the total cost increase at a slower rate than the increase in the supplier's customer base. For example, when the supplier's customer base is 25 percent of that of the bundler, bundling increases the bundler's driving cost by 16.5 percent and total cost by 22.0 percent, whereas when the supplier has equally as many customers as the bundler, the increase in the driving cost and the total cost of the bundler are 67.0 percent and 88.3 percent, respectively. These findings hint at economies of scale with growing supplier customer base. To approach economies of scale from a slightly different perspective, an additional experiment is performed, where the supplier's customer base is kept constant at 50 percent of the bundler's customer base, but the average shipment volume of the supplier's customers is gradually increased. This additional experiment resulted in very similar findings regarding economies of scale (i.e., the bundler's driving cost and total cost increase at a slower rate than the increase in the total shipment volume); therefore, its results are not presented in detail, for brevity of exposition.

Another clear indication of economies of scale can be observed in Figure 8.5, where the total cost (sum of warehousing, storage, and driving costs) per delivered roll-container is depicted for a growing customer base for the supplier. Here, cost per roll-container shows a steady decline for a growing customer base. Thus, it can be concluded that the cost per roll-container incurred by the bundler gets smaller when the collaboration is formed with larger suppliers.

The bundler and the supplier can have varying degrees of mutual customers. The following analysis quantifies the potential efficiency gains with increasing

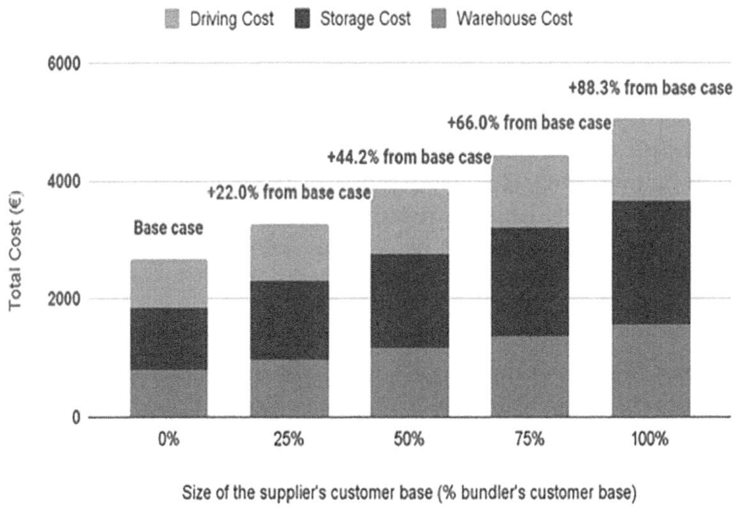

Source: Authors.

Figure 8.3 Bundler's total cost with growing supplier customer base

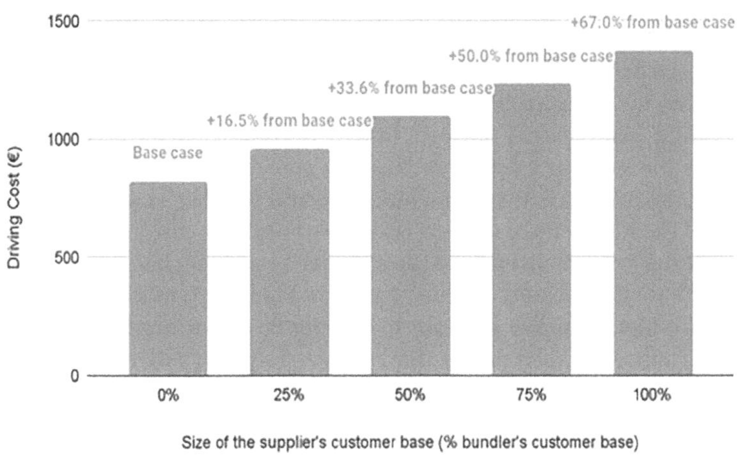

Source: Authors.

Figure 8.4 Bundler's driving cost with growing supplier customer base

overlap between the customer bases of the bundler and the supplier. Figure 8.6 demonstrates the bundler's driving costs when the overlap between the bundler's and supplier's customer bases increases (0 percent overlap means that the bundler and the supplier have no mutual customers; 100 percent overlap means that all customers of the supplier are also customers of the bundler). As could be expected, increasing degrees of overlap between the customer bases reduce the driving cost, since a high degree of overlap means that the bundler simply needs to deliver larger shipment volumes to the customers it is already visiting along its delivery routes, whereas a small degree of overlap means that the bundler needs to visit more customers. A 25 percent overlap of customer bases results in an 8.4 percent reduction in driving cost compared to no overlap, and a 100 percent overlap results in a 27.3 percent reduction in driving cost.

The positive effect of overlap on driving costs can be attributed to efficiency gains stemming from the drivers delivering two orders (the bundler's and the supplier's) at once, and therefore putting in the time and effort for parking and administrative tasks only once. For example, if a customer requests one roll-container from the bundler and one roll-container from the supplier, bundling does not double the driver's service time at the customer (i.e., if delivering one roll-container takes five minutes, delivering two would take less than ten minutes).

The locations of the bundler's and the supplier's customers are likely to impact bundling success: if the customers of the bundler and the supplier are geographically close to each other, the increase in the driving distance (and therefore the driving cost) due to bundling is expected to be small. To quantify the effect of the distance between the bundler's and the supplier's customers on bundling performance, an experiment is conducted. In this experiment, the size of the supplier's customer base (50 percent of the bundler's customer base) and the overlap between the bundler's and supplier's customer bases (50 percent of the supplier's customers is also the bundler's customers) is kept constant, and the average distance of the supplier's customer base to the bundler's customer base is increased. As can be seen in Figure 8.7, this distance increase results in a much smaller increase in driving cost. For example, tripling the average distance between the customer bases results in a driving cost increase of only 33 percent. This finding can be explained by the high density observed in city centers, where the average distance between locations is well below 1 km. Thus, even tripling the distance between locations in dense city centers ultimately does not add much to the driving costs. This is a good indication that the concept of bundling is particularly effective in dense regions with city center characteristics.

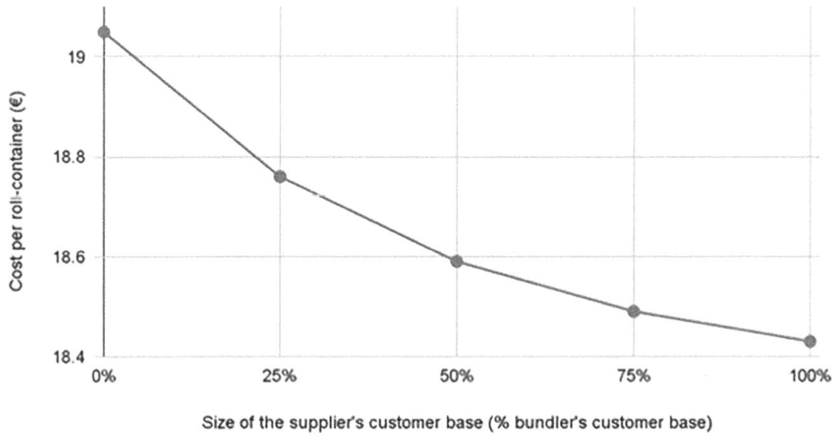

Source: Authors.

Figure 8.5 Bundler's cost per roll-container with growing supplier customer base

In this subsection, we aimed to shed some light on how various partnership characteristics may affect the success of bundling, and under which circumstances bundling has the potential to benefit the partaking stakeholders the most. First and foremost, we demonstrate that scaling effects are fundamental for the feasibility of bundling. Since the bundler's overall costs increase at a slower rate than that of the growth in the supplier's customer base and shipment volumes, it is beneficial to initiate bundling partnerships with relatively large suppliers. This way, due to the economies of scale, the bundler can have lower marginal costs.

Secondly, we identify the overlap in the bundler's and supplier's customer bases as a critical success predictor. When a large percentage of the supplier's customers are already customers of the bundler, we observe a significant positive effect on the cost-effectiveness of bundling. Thus, it can be inferred that creating bundling partnerships with suppliers that have a considerably overlapping customer base with the bundler can be beneficial.

Thirdly, we observe that there are numerous factors affecting the cost-effectiveness of bundling. Although a supplier with a relatively large customer base that largely overlaps with the bundler's is ideal, it might not always be possible to

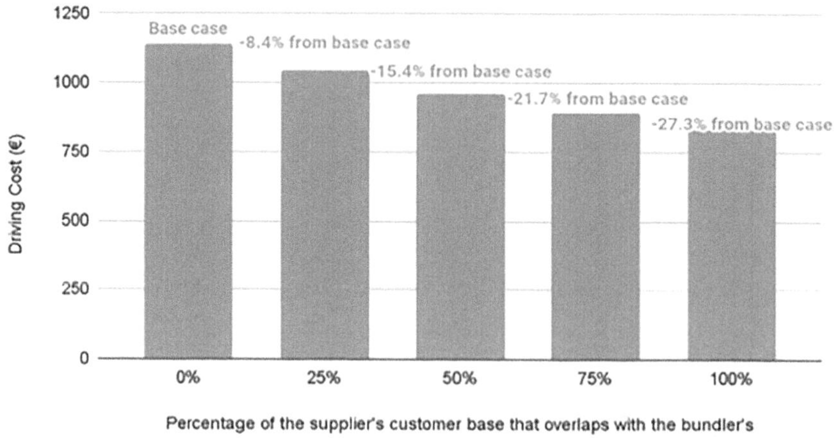

Source: Authors.

Figure 8.6 Bundler's driving cost with increasing overlap in customer bases

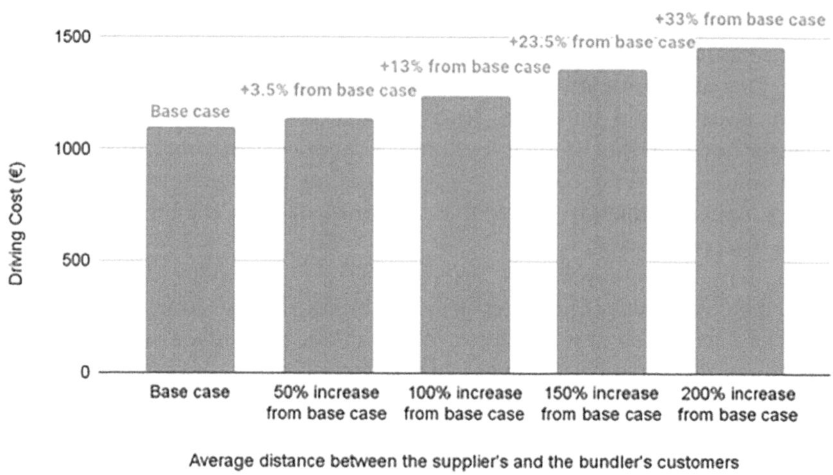

Source: Authors.

Figure 8.7 Bundler's driving cost with increasing distance between the bundler's and the supplier's customers

find such bundling partners. In that case, we recommend not disregarding, for example, suppliers with a relatively high average distance to the bundler's customers, as we illustrated that the negative effect of longer distances between the bundler's and supplier's customer bases can be insignificant in city center settings.

Finally, it is important to note that this subsection focused on operational costs in evaluating bundling success, however, operational cost is not the only area where bundling can offer benefits. Investment costs can also be of paramount importance in motivating collaborative approaches such as bundling. For example, with emissions regulations in city centers becoming tighter and tighter, smaller suppliers may not be able to justify purchasing new (electric) delivery vehicles that would comply with the regulations. In such cases, the advantage of a large bundler such as Bidfood hinges not only on the economies of scale in operational costs, but also on its ability/willingness to invest in the necessary (electric) vehicles to cater to new regulations. Thus, besides the apparent advantage of scale, we can conclude that other resources, such as specific vehicles or transport permits, can make bundling a profitable undertaking as it mitigates investment costs in addition to operational costs.

5.3 Coordination of Bundling Activities

Bundling can only be effective under strict timing requirements. In order to comply with customers' time windows and the time windows of the zero-emission zone, vehicles cannot leave the bundler's depot too late. Therefore, suppliers need to arrive at the depot before a certain time, and late arrivals might have a huge impact on the effectiveness of bundling, as also pointed out by the interviewees in Section 4. In this subsection, we will look into bundling with multiple suppliers, and we will specifically focus on the effects of supplier timing and coordination.

The bundling scenarios in this subsection involve Bidfood (the bundler) and three other suppliers. The data of Bidfood is provided by the company itself. Data for the three suppliers is generated based on the information gathered from interviews (see Section 4). It is important to note that for an even more accurate analytics, the suppliers would also need to share their data. This demonstrates that even in the exploratory phase toward a digital transformation, the storage and exchange of data between the bundler and the suppliers can be valuable.

The first supplier, which we refer to as supplier A, resembles a small vegetable supplier that only delivers fresh products. This supplier has a customer base of around 13 percent of the size of Bidfood's customer base. The second supplier, which we refer to as supplier B, resembles a medium-size supplier of beverages. This supplier only delivers fresh products, where the order size is on average approximately twice as large as for supplier A. This supplier has a customer base of around 17 percent of the size of Bidfood's customer base. The third supplier, which we refer to as supplier C, resembles a fish and meat supplier. This supplier delivers both fresh and frozen products. This is the largest supplier with regard to its customer base, which is around 19 percent of the size of Bidfood's customer base. For all suppliers, the number of customers in common with Bidfood is between 75 percent and 80 percent.

We consider different bundling scenarios: three scenarios where the bundler collaborates with one of the suppliers A, B, or C, and the other suppliers perform their own deliveries, and one scenario where all of the suppliers A, B, and C collaborate with the bundler. We compare these scenarios against the scenario without bundling (i.e., Bidfood and suppliers A, B, and C all perform their routes separately). For each of these scenarios, we compute the total number of vehicles and the total distance traveled for the total system (i.e., Bidfood and the three suppliers). Table 8.2 shows the results of the different scenarios, where we report the total number of vehicles (*Nr. of vehicles*), the percentage difference in number of vehicles as a comparison of the scenario against the scenario without bundling (Δ *Nr. of vehicles (percent)*), the distance traveled in kilometers (*Distance (km)*), and the percentage difference in driving distance as a comparison of the scenario against the scenario without bundling (Δ *Distance (percent)*). All of these results are daily averages, based on results over a set of different days.

As can be seen in Table 8.2, both the number of vehicles and the driving distance decrease under all bundling scenarios compared to the scenario without bundling. The maximum decrease in the number of vehicles and the distance is 6.6 percent and 9.1 percent, respectively, when bundling with one supplier. A larger decrease in both the number of vehicles and distance traveled can be obtained when bundling with more suppliers; that is, a reduction of 18.0 percent in the number of vehicles used and a reduction of 21.5 percent in driving distance when bundling with all three suppliers.

Table 8.2 Bundling vs. no bundling from the total system's perspective

Scenario	Nr. of vehicles	Δ Nr. of vehicles (%)	Distance (km)	Δ Distance (%)
No bundling	9.69	-	160.54	-
Bundling with supplier A	9.28	-4.2	146.64	-8.7
Bundling with supplier B	9.05	-6.6	149.20	-7.1
Bundling with supplier C	9.05	-6.6	145.90	-9.1
Bundling with all suppliers (A, B, and C)	7.95	-18.0	126.11	-21.5

The above results show the clear benefits of bundling. However, as mentioned earlier, bundling happens under very strict timing requirements. Therefore, the benefits can only be obtained when suppliers bring their products to the bundler's warehouse early enough. In this setting, the suppliers must deliver their products early enough to ensure that the vehicles can be dispatched at 06:50 at the latest. This would ensure that the products of the suppliers can be delivered together with the bundler's products in a single visit to the customer. When the supplier does not deliver its products to the bundler's warehouse on time, the bundler's vehicles cannot wait and therefore have to be dispatched before the supplier arrives, in order to meet the customers' time windows. In that case, additional routes are needed to deliver the products of the late supplier separately. When allowing for these additional routes, the *latest feasible dispatch time* for a late supplier (i.e., the latest time at which the additional routes need to depart the bundler's warehouse to ensure that the customers' time windows are met) can be computed. These additional routes give more flexibility in arrival times for the suppliers; however, they require extra vehicles and an increase in driving distance.

We created four scenarios in which either supplier A, B, or C is late or all of the suppliers A, B, and C are late, and compare them against the scenario where all suppliers are on time (i.e., they arrive at the bundler's warehouse before 06:50). Table 8.3 shows for the different scenarios for a busy day and an average day, the latest feasible dispatch time (*Latest dispatch time*), the percentage difference in number of vehicles as a comparison of the scenario against the scenario without late arrivals (*Δ Nr. of vehicles (percent)*), and the percentage difference in driving distance as a comparison of the scenario against the scenario without late arrivals (Δ *Distance (percent)*). As can be seen in the results, there is slightly more flexibility on an average day compared to a busy day; that is, for the scenarios where either supplier B or C or all suppliers are late, the latest dispatch time on a busy day is 07:50 compared to 08:20 on an average day. Supplier A can arrive latest; the latest dispatch time is 09:50. However, this comes at a high cost; that is, the percentage increase in the number of vehicles and driving distance is 20 percent and 9 percent, respectively, for a busy day, and 43 percent and 24 percent, respectively, for an average day.

Table 8.3 The effects of late supplier arrivals at the bundler's warehouse

Late arrival of supplier	Busy day			Average day		
	Latest dispatch time	Δ Nr. of vehicles (%)	Δ Distance (%)	Latest dispatch time	Δ Nr. of vehicles (%)	Δ Distance (%)
	06:50	-	-	06:50	-	-
A	09:50	20	9	09:50	43	24
B	07:50	10	7	08:20	14	11
C	07:50	10	3	08:20	0	13
A, B, and C	07:50	10	14	08:20	14	19

When a supplier is late, the time of arrival of the supplier heavily influences the number of vehicles and driving distance. The later the supplier arrives, the less flexibility there is to ensure that the products arrive at the customers' locations on time, and therefore the larger the number of vehicles and driving distance. The latest possible dispatch time is heavily influenced by the time windows of the customers. Relaxing the time windows of the customers results in later feasible dispatch times. In the next experiment, the time windows of the city zone customers are extended. Figure 8.8 shows the results for different dispatch times in the scenario where supplier B is late on a busy day under the extended customer time windows.

Figure 8.8 shows that relaxing the time windows results in a latest dispatch time for supplier B of 11:30, which is much later than the original dispatch time of 08:20. The results also show how the dispatch time influences the number of vehicles used and the total driving distance. Comparing a dispatch time of 11:30 with a dispatch time of 06:50 we see that the number of vehicles increases by 80 percent and the driving distance increases by 38 percent. Hence, this experiment shows that if the customers' time windows are extended, there is much more flexibility in how late the suppliers are allowed to deliver to the bundler's warehouse, however, this comes at the cost of a substantial increase in both the number of vehicles and the driving distance.

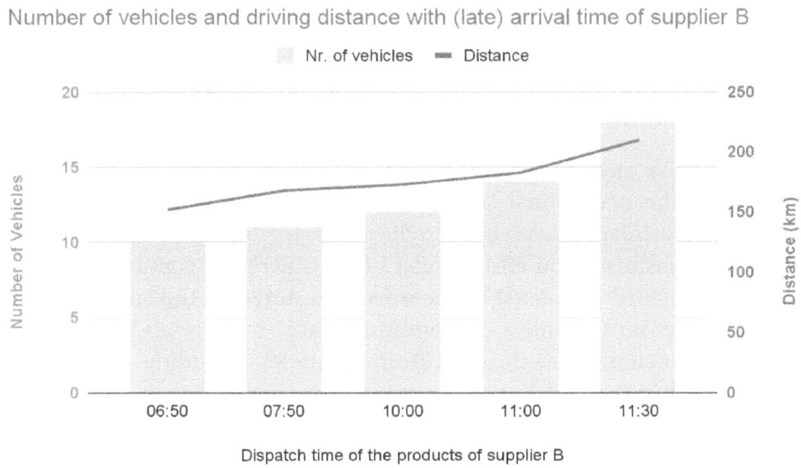

Source: Authors.

Figure 8.8 Effect of dispatch time (for extended customers' time windows)

In this subsection, we further emphasized the benefits of bundling, by quantifying the benefits of bundling not only with one supplier, but also with multiple suppliers simultaneously. We demonstrated another layer of economies of scale by showing that the benefits for the collaborating parties in terms of number of vehicles and driving distance increase with an increasing number of suppliers. Furthermore, we computationally tested the importance of supplier timing on system performance. To that end, we illustrated that the most beneficial setup in terms of the system-wide number of vehicles and driving distance is when all collaborating suppliers bring their products to the bundler's warehouse at an early, previously agreed-upon time, so that the bundler can consolidate the products of all suppliers destined for each customer and deliver everything with a single visit. It is also possible, when one or more suppliers are late, that the bundler makes additional trips to the customers of the late supplier(s). Although these additional trips introduce some flexibility into the system in terms of latest feasible dispatch times, it also comes at the cost of increased number of vehicles and driving distance.

Finally, we identified the customers' restrictive time windows as a factor that restricts suppliers' latest feasible dispatch times. We illustrate this impact by widening the customers' time windows and observing that the latest feasible dispatch time can be significantly later for more relaxed time windows. Although wider time windows allow additional flexibility in the suppliers' latest feasible dispatch times, the later dispatch times lead to a growing detriment to both the number of vehicles and total driving distance.

The quantitative analyses presented in this section provide insights into the benefits and the operational costs of bundling. To implement bundling in reality, the investment costs related to the necessary digitization, digitalization, and digital transformation efforts must be considered in conjunction. At the lower level, detailed data must be recorded and stored by the bundler and the suppliers. To ensure seamless collaboration, data exchange and synchronization should be considered in detail from all angles, including investment in digital technologies and data privacy regulations. Furthermore, clear communication protocols must be established and real-time communication must be ensured between the bundlers, customers, and suppliers. Likely, a comprehensive digital platform should be established that enables secure communication and payment between the suppliers and the bundler. To ensure bundling success, continuous efforts should be made in developing and maintaining digital tools that support advanced analytics modules. These modules can include demand prediction, real-time algorithmic decision-making tools for delivery route planning, and continuous improvement in the design of the delivery network.

6. Conclusion

In upcoming years, many cities are expected to instate zero-emission zones, that is, to define parts of the city (usually the downtown area and its immediate vicinity) where vehicles with a combustion engine may no longer drive. In preparation for this situation, logistics companies are purchasing electric trucks. However, electric trucks are significantly more expensive, and they have a smaller driving range. As a consequence, logistics companies must reconsider their logistics network design and their methods of operation. Companies that have a small number of deliveries in zero-emission zones may even find themselves in a situation where the purchase of electric trucks is not considered economical. Bundling, a concept in which a number of suppliers collaborate to jointly deliver goods to customers, is increasingly considered.

Our overview of literature, with a focus on the logistics sector, describes the contextual conditions, the process of innovation and integration, and the resulting outcomes in digitization, digitalization, and digital transformation. The logistics sector tended to have a cost focus leading to the offering of a fairly standardized set of services, but has evolved in past decades toward a high degree of customer adaptation. The sector now is at the forefront of customer service, and forms a main determinant for customer satisfaction. Innovations have been realized that enable ever faster response times, crowdsourced delivery systems, and various forms of collaboration between companies in supply chains. Digitization in logistics and supply chain management is still in its early stages of development, for example, resulting in the storage of less data than would be desirable for performing advanced data analytics. Digitalization is clearly observable in logistics collaborations, where participating companies need to exchange data digitally for testing and quantifying the synergies to determine the most profitable collaboration opportunities. Digital transformation has occurred in some areas of logistics, such as meal delivery, while in other areas companies are still developing toward new business models. Bundling concepts, where one company transports goods on behalf of other companies rather than only their own goods, are impending in many cities.

Our results provide insights into the innovations and accompanying digitization and digital transformation processes which are ongoing in the logistics sector. We especially provide a detailed view of the situation in food distribution (i.e., the logistics of delivering food and related goods to hotels, restaurants, and bars). Food distribution faces many planning challenges, some of which are in practice already addressed by means of advanced data analytics, while others still have room for improvement. As an example of the latter, we note that process planning in the warehouse is extremely challenging due to the prevalent focus on customer satisfaction, which allows customers to order until very late in the evening. The processes in the warehouse take a significant time, which necessitates starting with these processes before all customer orders are known. Only once all orders have been received, can all truck routes be finalized, and can all warehousing processes be adjusted accordingly. The consequence is that often part of the work in the warehouse has to be "reverted" after all orders are known. For example, a customer's order that was positioned for loading into one truck has to be repositioned for loading into another truck. Smart data analytics could possibly provide enhanced solutions to this planning problem.

Based on a series of interviews with suppliers and customers in the hospitality and food sector, we found that the general attitude toward an innovative approach such as bundling is very positive. Customers explain their opinion by, among others, the convenience of receiving all goods in one delivery. Importantly, interviewed customers indicate that adequate timing of deliveries is crucial. They request to receive their deliveries before a specific time, for example, to ensure that they can start preparing their meals in a timely manner. If bundling all deliveries, this implies that all goods must be delivered before the first product is needed. This increases the pressure on the logistics system. Furthermore, interviewees point out that transparency is desirable about the sharing of additional profits that may arise due to the concept. Cost reduction can be expected because of reduced travel, whereas cost increases can be expected because more handling is needed at the hub. Suppliers explain their positive attitude from the convenience of bundling, as well as saving time and money. Hesitations of suppliers include fear for loss of customer contact, and loss of control over the delivery process. Comments of both customers and suppliers appear to be related to a need for good communication of detailed information, such as costs per shipment, and real-time status updates about truck routes and delivery times. In this sense, bundling induces the need for more digitalization, or reversely digitalization can be regarded as an enabler for a bundling concept.

A quantitative analysis from a cost–benefit perspective revealed several relevant insights, based upon data made available to us by the food supplier Bidfood. We demonstrate that efficiency gains of bundling are higher if the participating suppliers have more customers in common. Driving distances are lowered when bundling, even if there are no overlapping customers between suppliers, although higher overlap helps to decrease driving distances. However, a significant part of a truck driver's time is spent on unloading the truck and bringing the goods into the customers' buildings. This component of transport cost is only reduced if a customer is receiving goods from multiple suppliers, in which case, for example, the time and effort for parking and administrative tasks is incurred only once. Besides such operational efficiency gains, collaboration is also stimulated because it mitigates investment costs for purchasing electric trucks, which is especially of interest for suppliers with few customers in zero-emission zones. Our analyses emphasize the value and knowledge that can be obtained provided that companies have the relevant data available, which in turn depends on having reached an adequate level of digitization. Furthermore, our research shows that a digital transformation may provide a new business model for a food supplier, if such food supplier starts to serve other, collaborating suppliers by bundling their goods for joint delivery to customers.[1]

Note

1. This work is part of the project Shared connectivity in Mobility and Logistics Enable Sustainability (SMiLES) and was partially supported by the Dutch Research Council (NWO), the Ministry of Infrastructure and Water Management, and the Dutch Institute for Advanced Logistics (TKI Dinalog) under grant 439.18.459. This support is gratefully acknowledged. The authors also acknowledge the contributions of Marinus Hol (Operations Manager & CO2-Coördinator at Bidfood Groningen, at the time of conducting the referenced research), Sahand Asgharieh Ahari (PhD student), Ilse Attema and Inger Zeevalkink (junior researchers, at the time of conducting the referenced research), and Jakob Binder and Channah Bloemhard (MSc students, at the time of conducting the referenced research).

References

Adner, R. (2017). Ecosystem as structure: An actionable construct for strategy. *Journal of Management*, 43, 39–58.

Altay, B. C., Okumuş, A., & Adıgüzel Mercangöz, B. (2022). An intelligent approach for analyzing the impacts of the COVID-19 pandemic on marketing mix elements (7Ps) of the on-demand grocery delivery service. *Complex & Intelligent Systems*, 8(1/2), 129–140.

Anderhofstadt, B., & Spinler, S. (2020). Preferences for autonomous and alternative fuel-powered heavy-duty trucks in Germany. *Transportation Research Part D: Transport and Environment*, 79, 102232.

Ardolino, M., Rapaccini, M., Saccani, N., Gaiardelli, P., Crespi G., & Ruggeri, C. (2018). The role of digital technologies for the service transformation of industrial companies. *International Journal of Production Research*, 56(6), 2116–2132.

Arnold, F., Cardenas, I., Sorensen, K., & Dewulf, W. (2018). Simulation of B2C e-commerce distribution in Antwerp using cargo bikes and delivery points. *European Transport Research Review*, 10(1), 2.

Asgharieh Ahari, S., Bakir, I., & Roodbergen, K. J. (2024). A new perspective on carrier collaboration: Collaborative vehicle utilization. *Transportation Research Part C: Emerging Technologies*, 163, 104647.

Bakir, I., Yildirim, M., & Ursavas, E. (2021). An integrated optimization framework for multi-component predictive analytics in wind farm operations & maintenance. *Renewable & Sustainable Energy Reviews*, 138(6–7), 110639.

Baldwin, C. Y., & Clark, K. B. (2000). *Design Rules: The Power of Modularity*. MIT Press, Cambridge, MA.
Bidfood (2019a). Bidfood gaat verpakkingen in foodservice verduurzamen. https://www.bidfood.nl/over/nieuws/2019_2/bidfood_verduurzaamt_verpakkingen_huismerk_artikelen.jsp.
Bidfood (2019b). Bidfood en Voedselbanken Nederland bestrijden voedselverspilling met landelijke samenwerking. https://www.bidfood.nl/over/nieuws/2019_2/samenwerking_bidfood_en_voedselbank_nederland.jsp.
Bidfood (2023). Bidfood, dé online groothandel voor foodprofessionals. https://www.bidfood.nl/over/wie_we_zijn.jsp.
Binder, J. (2022). Last-mile delivery bundling: A cost-benefit analysis of one-sided, urban transport consolidation. Master's thesis. University of Groningen, the Netherlands.
Bloemhard, C. (2022). Supplier timing in collaborative last-mile food deliveries: A multi-compartment vehicle routing problem with time windows. Master's thesis. University of Groningen, the Netherlands.
Breunig, U., Baldacci, R., Hartl, R. F., & Vidal, T. (2019). The electric two-echelon vehicle routing problem. *Computers & Operations Research*, 103, 198–210.
Buijs, P., Lopez Alvarez, J. A., Veenstra, M., & Roodbergen, K. J. (2016). Improved collaborative transport planning at Dutch logistics service provider Fritom. *Interfaces*, 46(2), 119–132.
Büyüközkan, G., & Göçer, F. (2018). Digital supply chain: Literature review and a proposed framework for future research. *Computers in Industry*, 97, 157–177.
Cao, M., & Zhang, Q. Y. (2011). Supply chain collaboration: Impact on collaborative advantage and firm performance. *Journal of Operations Management*, 29(3), 163–180.
Castillo, V. E., Bell, J. E., Rose, W. J., & Rodrigues, A. M. (2018). Crowdsourcing last mile delivery: Strategic implications and future research directions. *Journal of Business Logistics*, 39(1), 7–25.
Chaudhuri, A., Dukovska-Popovska, I., Subramanian, N., Chan, H. K., & Bai, R. B. (2018). Decision-making in cold chain logistics using data analytics: A literature review. *International Journal of Logistics Management*, 29(3), 839–861.
Chauhan, V., Patel, M., Tanwar, S., Tyagi, S., & Kumar, N. (2020). IoT-enabled real-time urban transport management system. *Computers & Electrical Engineering*, 86, 106746.
Chhabra, D., Singh, R. K., & Kumar, V. (2022). Developing IT-enabled performance monitoring system for green logistics: A case study. *International Journal of Productivity and Performance Measurement*, 71(3), 775–789.
Cichosz, M., Wallenburg, C. M., & Knemeyer, A. M. (2020). Digital transformation at logistics service providers: Barriers, success factors and leading practices. *International Journal of Logistics Management*, 31(2), 209–238.
Crainic, T. G., & Montreuil, B. (2016). Physical internet-enabled hyperconnected city logistics. *Transportation Research Procedia*, 12, 383–398.
Daugherty, P. J., Bolumole, Y., & Grawe, S. J. (2019). The new age of customer impatience: An agenda for reawakening logistics customer service research. *International Journal of Physical Distribution & Logistics Management*, 49(1), 4–32.
De Bok, M., Tavasszy, L. A., & Thoen, S. (2022). Application of an empirical multi-agent model for urban goods transport to analyze impacts of zero emission zones in the Netherlands. *Transport Policy*, 124, 119–127.

Del Giudice, M., Chierici, R., Mazzucchelli, A., & Fiano, F. (2021). Supply chain management in the era of circular economy: The moderating effect of big data. *International Journal of Logistics Management*, 32(2), 337–356.
Dönmez, S., Koc, C., & Altiparmak, F. (2022). The mixed fleet vehicle routing problem with partial recharging by multiple chargers: Mathematical model and adaptive large neighborhood search. *Transportation Research Part E: Logistics and Transportation Review*, 167(4), 102917.
Ergun, O., Kuyzu, G., & Savelsbergh, M. (2007). Reducing truckload transportation costs through collaboration. *Transportation Science*, 41(2), 206–221.
European Union (2020). Communication from the commission to the European parliament, the council, the European economic and social committee and the committee of the regions. https://eur-lex.europa.eu/legal-content/EN/TXT/?uri=CELEX:52020DC0562.
Evangelista, P., Colicchia, C., & Creazza, A. (2017). Is environmental sustainability a strategic priority for logistics service providers? *Journal of Environmental Management*, 198(1), 353–362.
Fernandez, E., Roca-Riu, M., & Speranza, M. G. (2018). The shared customer collaboration vehicle routing problem. *European Journal of Operational Research*, 265(3), 1078–1093.
Fleischmann, B. (1998). Design of freight traffic networks. In B. Fleischmann, J. A. E. E. Nunen, M. G. Speranza, P. Stähly (Eds.), *Advances in Distribution Logistics* (pp. 56–81). Springer, Berlin.
Gansterer, M., & Hartl, R. F. (2018). Collaborative vehicle routing: A survey. *European Journal of Operational Research*, 268(1), 1–12.
Hanelt, A., Bohnsack, R., Marz, D., & Marante, C. A. (2021). A systematic review of the literature on digital transformation: Insights and implications for strategy and organizational change. *Journal of Management Studies*, 58(5), 1159–1197.
Hekimoğlu, M. H., Park, J. H., & Kazaz, B. (2024). Service at risk in delivery operations. *Decision Sciences*, *55*(1), 33–56.
Henfridsson, O., & Yoo, Y. (2014). The liminality of trajectory shifts in institutional entrepreneurship. *Organization Science*, 25(3), 932–950.
Hertz, S., & Alfredsson, M. (2003). Strategic development of third party logistics providers. *Industrial Marketing Management*, 32(2), 139–149.
Hong, W., Zheng, C., Wu, L., & Pu, X. (2019). Analyzing the relationship between consumer satisfaction and fresh e-commerce logistics service using text mining techniques. *Sustainability*, 11(13), 3570.
Huang, G. Q., & Xu, S. X. (2013). Truthful multi-unit transportation procurement auctions for logistics e-marketplaces. *Transportation Research Part B: Methodological*, 47, 127–148.
Ignat, B., & Chankov, S. (2020). Do e-commerce customers change their preferred last-mile delivery based on its sustainability impact? *International Journal of Logistics Management*, 31(3), 521–548.
Jacobides, M., Cennamo, C., & Gawer, A. (2018). Towards a theory of ecosystems. *Strategic Management Journal*, 39(8), 2255–2276.
Jovic, M., Tijan, E., Vidmar, D., & Pucihar, A. (2022). Factors of digital transformation in the maritime transport sector. *Sustainability*, 14(15), 9776.
Kchaou-Boujelben, M. (2021). Charging station location problem: A comprehensive review on models and solution approaches. *Transportation Research Part C: Emerging Technologies*, 132, 103376.

Kane, G. C., Palmer, D., Philips, A. N., Kiron, D., & Buckley, N. (2015). Strategy, not technology, drives digital transformation. *MIT Sloan Management Review and Deloitte University Press*, 14, 1–25.

Larco, J. A., De Koster, R., Roodbergen, K. J., & Dul, J. (2017). Managing warehouse efficiency and worker discomfort through enhanced storage assignment decisions. *International Journal of Production Research*, 55(21), 6407–6422.

Leung, K. H., Choy, K. L., Siu, P. K. Y., Ho, G. T. S., Lam, H. Y., & Lee, C. K. M. (2018). A B2C e-commerce intelligent system for re-engineering the e-order fulfilment process. *Expert Systems with Applications*, 91, 386–401.

Leviäkangas, P. (2016). Digitalisation of Finland's transport sector. *Technology in Society*, 47(1), 1–15.

Loebbecke, C., & Picot, A. (2015). Reflections on societal and business model transformation arising from digitization and big data analytics: A research agenda. *Journal of Strategic Information Systems*, 24(3), 149–157.

Lozano, S., Moreno, P., Adenso-Diaz, B., & Algaba, E. (2013). Cooperative game theory approach to allocating benefits of horizontal cooperation. *European Journal of Operational Research*, 229(2), 444–452.

Macrina, G., Di Puglia Pugliese, L., Guerriero, F., & Laporte, G. (2019). The green mixed fleet vehicle routing problem with partial battery recharging and time windows. *Computers & Operations Research*, 101, 183–199.

Mao, W. Z., Ming, L., Rong, Y., Tang, C. S., & Zheng, H. (2022). On-demand meal delivery platforms: Operational level data and research opportunities. *Manufacturing & Service Operations Management*, 24(5), 2535–2542.

McLoughlin, J. (2022). Amazon adds 10 planes to its air cargo fleet. *Logistics Manager*. https://www.logisticsmanager.com/amazon-adds-10-planes-to-its-air-cargo-fleet/.

Melacini, M., Perotti, S., Rasini, M., & Tappia, E. (2018). E-fulfilment and distribution in omni-channel retailing: A systematic literature review. *International Journal of Physical Distribution & Logistics Management*, 48(4), 391–414.

Melkonyan, A., Gruchmann, T., Lohmar, F., Kamath, V., & Spinler, S. (2020). Sustainability assessment of last-mile logistics and distribution strategies: The case of local food networks. *International Journal of Production Economics*, 228(2), 107746.

MWPVL (2023). Amazon global supply chain and fulfillment center network. https://www.mwpvl.com/html/amazon_com.html.

Newell, S., & Marabelli, M. (2015). Strategic opportunities (and challenges) of algorithmic decision-making: A call for action on the long-term societal effects of 'datification'. *Journal of Strategic Information Systems*, 24(1), 3–14.

Nguyen, D. H., de Leeuw, S., Dullaert, W., & Foubert, B. P. J. (2019). What is the right delivery option for you? Consumer preferences for delivery attributes in online retailing. *Journal of Business Logistics*, 40(4), 299–321.

Pan, S., Trentesaux, D., Ballot, E., & Huang, G. Q. (2019). Horizontal collaborative transport: Survey of solutions and practical implementation issues. *International Journal of Production Research*, 57(15–16), 5340–5361.

Rai, H. B., Broekaert, C., Verlinde, S., & Macharis, C. (2021). Sharing is caring: How non-financial incentives drive sustainable e-commerce delivery. *Transportation Research Part D: Transport and Environment*, 93(2), 102794.

Rai, H. B., Verlinde, S., & Macharis, C. (2019). The 'next day, free delivery' myth unravelled: Possibilities for sustainable last mile transport in an omnichannel environment. *International Journal of Retail & Distribution Management*, 47(1), 39–54.

Reinecke, P. C., Wrona, T., Rueckert, N., & Fischer, K. (2023). A typology of the collaboration willingness of carriers in hinterland logistics. *International Journal of Physical Distribution & Logistics Management*, 53(9), 967–984.
Roodbergen, K. J., & Kolman, I. B. (2016). Order fulfillment and logistics considerations for multichannel retailers. In W. H. M. Zijm, M. Klumpp, V. Clausen, & M. Ten Hompel (Eds.), *Logistics and Supply Chain Innovation: Bridging the Gap between Theory and Practice* (pp. 183–196). Lecture Notes in Logistics. Springer.
Sanders, N. R., Boone, T., Ganeshan, R., & Wood, J. D. (2019). Sustainable supply chains in the age of AI and digitization: Research challenges and opportunities. *Journal of Business Logistics*, 40(3), 229–240.
Schrotenboer, A. H., Wruck, S., Roodbergen, K. J., Veenstra, M., & Dijkstra, A. (2017). Order picker routing with product returns and interaction delays. *International Journal of Production Research*, 55(21), 6394–6406.
Seghezzi, A., Mangiaracina, R., & Tumino, A. (2023). E-grocery logistics: Exploring the gap between research and practice. *International Journal of Logistics Management*, 34(6), 1675–1699.
Soosay, C. A., Hyland, P. W., & Ferrer, M. (2008). Supply chain collaboration: Capabilities for continuous innovation. *Supply Chain Management: An International Journal*, 13(2), 160–169.
Sternberg, H., & Norrman, A. (2017). The physical internet: Review, analysis and future research agenda. *International Journal of Physical Distribution & Logistics Management*, 47(8), 736–762.
Tomicová, J., Poliak, M., & Zhuravleva, N. A. (2021). Impact of using e-CMR on neutralization of consignment note. *Transportation Research Procedia*, 55(3), 110–117.
Toole, J. L., Colak, S., Sturt, B., Alexander, L. P., Evsukoff, A., & González, M. C. (2015). The path most traveled: Travel demand estimation using big data resources. *Transportation Research Part C: Emerging Technologies*, 58, 162–177.
Vanderroost, M., Ragaert, P., Verwaeren, J., De Meulenaer, B., De Baets, B., & Devlieghere, F. (2017). The digitization of a food package's life cycle: Existing and emerging computer systems in the logistics and post-logistics phase. *Computers in Industry*, 87, 15–30.
Verhoef, P. C., Broekhuizen, T., Bart, Y., Bhattacharya, A., Dong, J. Q., Fabian, N., & Haenlein, M. (2021). Digital transformation: A multidisciplinary reflection and research agenda. *Journal of Business Research*, 122, 889–901.
Wicaksono, S., Lin, X., & Tavasszy, L. A. (2022). Market potential of bicycle crowdshipping: A two-sided acceptance analysis. *Research in Transportation Business and Management*, 45(A), 100660.
Yildiz, B., & Savelsbergh, M. (2019). Service and capacity planning in crowd-sourced delivery. *Transportation Research Part C: Emerging Technologies*, 100(10), 177–199.
Zhang, J. R., Onal, S., Das, R., Helminsky, A., & Das, S. (2019). Fulfilment time performance of online retailers: An empirical analysis. *International Journal of Retail & Distribution Management*, 47(5), 493–510.
Zhang, X., Rey, D., & Waller, S. T. (2018). Multitype recharge facility location for electric vehicles. *Computer-Aided Civil and Infrastructure Engineering*, 33(11), 943–965.
Zhao, C., Li, L., Pei, X., Li, Z., Wang, F.-Y., & Wu, X. (2021). A comparative study of state-of-the-art driving strategies for autonomous vehicles. *Accident Analysis & Prevention*, 150, 105937.
Zhu, K., Kraemer, K. L., & Xu, S. (2006). The process of innovation assimilation by firms in different countries: A technology diffusion perspective on e-business. *Management Science*, 52(10), 1557–1576.

PART III

Implementation and impact of digital transformation

9 Change management for digital transformation

Albert Boonstra

Digital transformation involves deploying digital technologies to develop new business models for value creation (Leinwand and Mani, 2021). This process can include optimizing business processes, enhancing customer experiences, digitizing existing products and services, developing new products or services, and expanding into new markets (Francis and Bessant, 2005). By embracing digital technologies, organizations can unlock opportunities for development and growth.

However, achieving the full benefits of a digital transformation requires more than simply adopting new technologies. It necessitates a radical reorganization of established companies. Organizations must adjust and align all their organizational dimensions to fully exploit the advantages of digital technologies, hence the term "digital transformation" (Verhoef et al., 2021; Baiyere et al., 2020). Incumbent organizations often find themselves forced by competitors and digital disruptors within their industry to adopt digital technologies. Failing to do so puts them at risk of losing market share and can even jeopardize their survival (McKendrick, 2019). Uber, Amazon, Alibaba, Booking.com, Tesla, Netflix, and Airbnb are prime examples of digital disruptors that have revolutionized industries and cornered incumbents.

Consequently, managers of established companies, whether driven by external pressures or their own strategic choices, are faced with the challenge of digitally transforming their organizations. They are responsible for adapting business strategies, supply chains, processes, customer relationships, the workforce, IT deployment, organizational structure, and culture to ensure the success of the digital transformation. Established skills and ingrained processes that have formed the bedrock of such organizations ("how we do things here"), despite having been instrumental to their past success, become obsolete in the face of digital transformations (Baptista et al., 2020). This complex endeavor constitutes a multifaceted, layered, and multi-stakeholder process of corporate change (Hanelt et al., 2020).

Many established companies struggle to make these changes happen (Chanias, 2019; Ditsche et al., 2022; Deloitte, 2020). They often fail to deliver the desired benefits and sometimes lead to complete failure. Corrie Block, a council member of Forbes, claims an alarming 84 percent failure rate for digital projects (Block, 2022). This statistic aligns with studies from leading consulting organizations such as McKinsey, BCG, KPMG, and Bain & Company, who estimate failure risks ranging from 70 percent to 95 percent.

While a systematic overview of the causes of failed attempts at digital transformation is lacking, it is evident that many failures stem from a naive or flawed approach to change. The change management literature consistently shows that major digitalization projects fail due to underestimating the social, cultural, political, process, and technical complexities (Alderman and Ivory, 2007; Boonstra and van Offenbeek, 2011; Constantinides and Barrett, 2006; Doolin, 2004; Greenhalgh et al., 2009; Jensen and Aanestad, 2007; Lapointe and Rivard, 2005). Bent Flyvjbjerg, known for his research on large-scale projects (Flyvjbjerg, 2017), acknowledges this underestimation. He found that many comprehensive projects fail due to oversimplification and a bias toward optimism. Optimistic proponents of digital transformation often overestimate the benefits while underestimating the organizational and technical challenges. As a result, digital transformation initiatives that initially appear promising only reveal their true complexity and comprehensiveness in later stages.

The mainstream business literature and major consultancies often present generic "one best way" procedures for managing digital transformations (McKinsey, 2017). These formulas for change management originate in the classical school of management, commonly referred to as Taylorist, Unitarist, or Scientific Management. They are characterized by linear, deterministic, and staged processes (Collins, 1998; Smith et al., 2020) that view digital transformation as a series of logical and sequential goal-directed activities. These activities are intended to get digital technology right and working. They are based on a unitarist perspective that views management and staff members as sharing a common goal through their loyalty toward the organization (Collins, 1998). Third parties are viewed as irrelevant while employees and employers mutually cooperate (Fox, 1966). This assumes that all key stakeholders share the same digital transformation objectives, that the necessary resources are readily available, and that there is a high degree of certainty. The approach advocates a rational diagnosis of the desired digital transformation and a sequential approach to achieving it. The steps within these classical, linear prescriptions for digital transformation can be summarized as follows: (1) clearly define and communicate the digital transformation goals, (2) analyze the initial situation, (3) identify and allocate the required resources to achieve the goals, (4) plan and sequence the activities to achieve the goals, (5) implement the digital technology and associated new business processes and provide employee training, and (6) evaluate and communicate the outcomes. Many proponents of this classical linear approach assert its universal validity, suggesting that all organizations embarking on a digital transformation should adopt this change approach under the "one size fits all" notion (Shenhar, 2001). While this approach's simplicity is appealing, it underestimates the real complexity of digital transformations. It overlooks the variations in initial situations, the diversity of contextual factors that impact change, and the dualities faced by implementers of a digital transformation.

This chapter presents an alternative approach to managing a digital transformation that, by adopting a duality perspective, recognizes and embraces the inherent complexity. Dualities refer to the interplay of contrasting or complementary forces that contribute to a balanced understanding. Managers and other organizational members can better understand the tensions that arise during digital transformations by acknowledging the existence of relevant dualities. Duality thinking will enable them to identify opposing poles and recognize the significance of simultaneously managing and harnessing these dualities. In managing a digital transformation, there is no universal way to deal with these dualities. Based on a systematic diagnosis, those responsible for a digital transformation should recognize the dualities when developing an effective context-dependent change strategy that takes into account the organization's characteristics, challenges, and the available digital technology for a successful digital transformation.

This chapter aims to provide insights into the diversity of initial situations encountered in digital transformations and the corresponding change strategies that can align with them. In contrast to the classical linear approach, which follows predefined step-by-step formulas (Collins, 1998), this chapter explores how combining seemingly contradictory elements can result in situation-specific change strategies. As such, the chapter aims to accomplish three objectives: (1) demonstrate how organizations can analyze digital initiatives; (2) identify change strategies that are appropriate for these initiatives; and (3) combine these change strategies in a duality framework for a digital transformation. This framework facilitates a balanced understanding of the digital transformation process by addressing the most common dualities that may arise. Before delving into the specifics of conducting a diagnosis and developing a change strategy for a digital transformation, we briefly overview the theoretical foundations upon which this chapter is built.

Theoretical background

The duality framework for digital transformations presented in this chapter draws on three key perspectives: duality theory, contingency theory, and complexity. By integrating these perspectives, we offer a comprehensive framework that should enable implementers to recognize complexities and manage the hurdles associated with digital transformation. In this section, we provide a concise introduction to each of these three perspectives.

Duality Theory

In the context of change management, duality theory suggests that complex change projects, such as a digital transformation, are inherently ambiguous. Duality thinking asserts that seemingly opposing perspectives are not necessarily mutually exclusive, and can even complement each other and coexist (Smith et al., 2020; Seo et al., 2004; Pich et al., 2002). As a result, those who adopt the duality theory take a pluralistic approach (Söderlund, 2011). They acknowledge the multiple views and interests, and strive to combine and complement them.

An example of duality in digital transformation is the tension between implementing it through a top-down approach or embracing a participatory bottom-up path. The classical linear change strategy emphasizes a top-down approach in which influential managers direct the change process. However, in certain circumstances, it can be more effective to actively engage staff members by seeking their input and empowering them to drive the digital transformation. By leveraging their internal insights, organizations can achieve a more intelligent and inclusive change process that encourages adoption. Another example is the choice over the change approach: whether to follow a 'planned approach' with well-defined goals and means, or to complement this with an 'emergent approach.' The classical linear strategy advocates a planned approach, emphasizing clarity and structure. However, an emergent approach may provide the flexibility to rapidly address evolving technologies and environmental uncertainties, allowing organizations to adapt and respond effectively to changing circumstances.

The duality framework for digital transformation presented in this chapter demonstrates how digital transformation projects can effectively integrate contrasting approaches to address the comprehensive, multifaceted, and complex nature of the transformation process. Digital transformation inherently leads to duality, and tensions, regarding its what, where, and how

(Boonstra et al., 2017). For example, within the same organization, one unit may wholeheartedly embrace digitalization, while another continues to adhere to established practices. A duality approach can effectively address such divergent perspectives on the desired digital transformation within organizational units and also the uncertainty surrounding digital advancements in the external environment. Managing these tensions is a critical responsibility for change managers involved in digital transformation.

Contingency Theory

In the context of a digital transformation, contingency theory recognizes that there is no generic change approach that can be universally applied to all change initiatives. Traditionally, organizational change, particularly in the context of technological change, has followed a classical linear approach, viewing change as a sequential series of planned activities driven from the top and aimed at achieving predetermined goals. However, in the 1970s and 1980s, it became evident that this approach no longer suited the practice of complex change projects. New strategies emerged, such as agile and scrum (Fernandez and Fernandez, 2016), emphasizing experimentation, learning, and participation. Some proponents of these new approaches were so enthusiastic that they believed they could entirely replace traditional change strategies.

Others, in line with contingency theory (Lawrence and Lorsch, 1967; Woodward, 1958; Burns and Stalker, 1961; Thompson, 1967), argued that a change strategy should align with both the internal and external contexts in which the change occurs (Burnes and Jackson, 2011). This perspective suggests that different organizational change strategies can be effective depending on the organization, the content of the change, and the surrounding environment. Scholars in the field of contingency thinking in organizational change, such as Dunphy and Stace (1993), Plowman et al. (2007), and Balogon and Hailey (2008), have developed typologies that consider these contextual factors in determining the most appropriate change strategy. The fundamental question here is to identify which situational factors in an organizational change should influence the choice of a change strategy. In the duality framework for digital transformation, as outlined in this chapter, we assume that the degree and the kind of complexity of the digital transformation are the main contingency factors that should determine the change approach. We distinguish dynamic and structural complexities, as explained in the next paragraph.

Complexity

When selecting a digital transformation strategy, assessing the complexity is crucial. A misjudgment in estimating the complexity can result in an inappropriate change management approach. Complexity can be characterized by structural and dynamic dimensions (Morcov et al., 2021). Structural complexity pertains to the intricacy of the digital technology and the prevailing sociopolitical environment, both internally and externally. Moreover, the dynamic complexity escalates with the speed of technological and contextual changes in the digital transformation process, the novelty of the situation, limited technical and commercial maturity, and the changing power, interests, and attitudes of stakeholders.

In distinguishing the key domains in digital transformation, we draw on Winch (2014), Pettigrew and Whipp (1991), Greenhalgh et al. (2017), and Damschroeder et al. (2009). These domains correspond with the well-known technology–organization–environment (TOE) framework (Oliveira and Martins, 2011). The domains include: (1) the digital technology, (2) the organization undergoing digital transformation, and (3) the surrounding environment. Each of these domains can exhibit varying degrees of complexity. Digital technology is the central enabler of digital transformation and can vary in complexity. Factors such as the maturity of the technology, the options for its deployment (turnkey or customized), and its proven track record play a role. The organization must adapt, deploy, and implement this technology to achieve a successful digital transformation. For some organizations, incorporating and deploying digital technology is routine but, for others, it represents a significant disruption.

Additionally, the organization's environment, encompassing stakeholders including customers, suppliers, competitors, and technology providers, is affected by the digital transformation and can either support or resist the digital transformation. Thus, these three domains span a spectrum from simple through complicated to complex (Greenhalgh et al., 2017). In diagnosing and developing a change strategy, the level of complexity within each dimension becomes crucial in determining an appropriate, context-specific, and adaptive change strategy. Recognizing and effectively managing complexity is essential for achieving a successful digital transformation.

Diagnosing change toward digital transformation

An analysis of the current state is necessary to develop an effective change strategy for a successful digital transformation. This analysis involves assessing the complexity of the environment, the organization, and the digital technology (Figure 9.1).

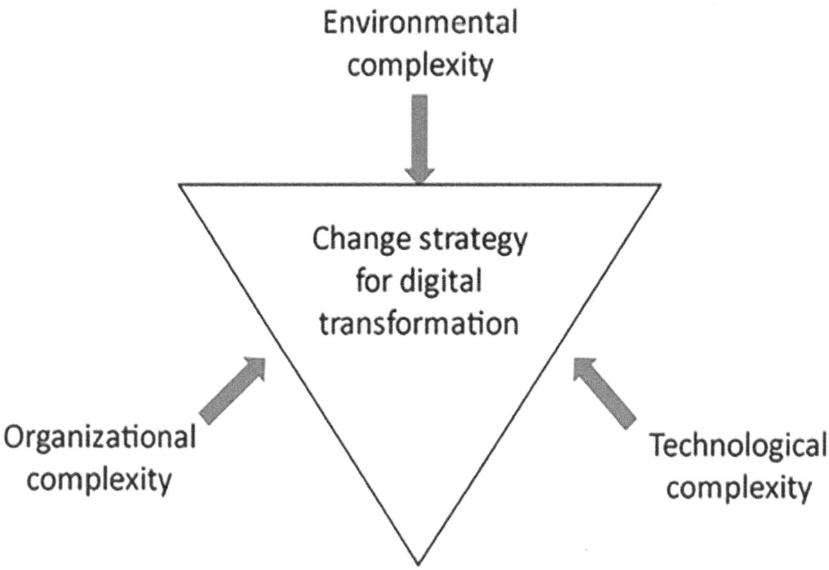

Source: Author.

Figure 9.1 Diagnosis of a change strategy for digital transformation

Environment

In the context of an organization's digital transformation, the external environment comprises various stakeholders. To conduct a diagnosis, it is essential to identify which external stakeholders are affected by the digital transformation. Estimating how these stakeholders are connected, and how they may respond to the organization's digital transformation, is required. External stakeholders include customers, suppliers, shareholders, competitors, government agencies, and technology partners. Once all these parties are identified, it becomes possible to assess and map how they relate to the focal firm's digital transformation. The matrix presented in Table 9.1 can be used for estimating this relationship. This table, based on an example situation (Tessler, 2017), indicates the sociopolitical complexity in terms of the level of support or resistance toward the digital transformation and dynamic complexity in terms of the extent of certainty or uncertainty in their attitudes and anticipated responses.

A long-established newspaper (Tessler, 2017) aims to transform digitally, which entails phasing out newspaper production and distribution while delivering personalized news to subscribers and other readers. This transformation also involves developing a new revenue model and business model. An assessment of the external environment revealed the following. News agencies delivering content to the newspaper were generally satisfied with this envisioned digital transformation as it aligns with their existing work practices [1]. The newspaper's technology partner is willing to support this change, although the newspaper's management is unsure about the partner's competences and capabilities in terms of providing technical support for personalized news [3]. Many online advertisers view the further digitalization of the newspaper positively, as it allows for more targeted advertising. However, the advertising market is recognized as uncertain and volatile [4]. Some traditional advertisers express concerns and may consider switching to other newspapers once the transformation takes place [2]. The opinions among subscribers and readers are divided. Some support the change and are accustomed to consuming digital news. The newspaper hopes to entice older readers to embrace digital news through price reductions and a dedicated help desk. However, the speed at which this change will be accepted remains uncertain [5, 7]. Shareholders' views are fluid and subject to uncertainty. Certain shareholders support the digital transformation process, while others doubt the significant investments required and the unproven business model's ability to generate sufficient returns [6, 8].

Table 9.1 illustrates how the surrounding parties relate to digital transformation in this particular example (Stacey, 1996). A change context can be considered as straightforward when surrounding parties are united in their support. Conversely, the change context becomes complex when faced with both resistance and uncertainty. In other scenarios, with both favorable and hostile parties, the change context may be considered complicated.

Table 9.1 Complexity of the environment in the example

		Structural complexity	
		External support for the digital transformation	*External resistance to the digital transformation*
Dynamic complexity	*Certain environmental context*	1. News agencies	2. Some of the offline advertisers
	Uncertain environmental context	3. Technology partner 4. Online advertisers 5. Online subscribers and other readers 6. Groups of shareholders	7. Offline subscribers and other readers 8. Groups of shareholders

However, the CFO [4] and the CM [5] were ambivalent: while they acknowledged the conventional newspaper's non-viability, they feared the high start-up costs and the potential loss of traditional subscribers and advertisers. Typical questions that can guide the diagnosis of the environment of the digital transformation are:

- From which external stakeholders is cooperation and support required to achieve a successful digital transformation?
- Is there consensus or disagreement among external stakeholders regarding the digital transformation?
- What interests do these stakeholders have in this digital transformation?
- Is there any interest in impeding its success?
- Are there any incentives in place to encourage cooperation from these stakeholders? Are they willing to cooperate?
- How stable is the support or resistance from these stakeholders, is it subject to change? Under what circumstances might their attitudes or positions change?
- Are competitors successfully undergoing digital transformations?
- Is a comprehensive and rapid digital transformation necessary from a competitive perspective, or can a gradual or partial approach be adopted?
- What are the political, legislative, and institutional contexts in which this digital transformation will occur?
- Is there societal support for the chosen digital transformation? How stable is this support or resistance?

Answering these questions will provide a deeper understanding of the environment surrounding the digital transformation and enables one to make informed decisions.

Organization

Undergoing a digital transformation has significant implications for the organization as it entails a strategic realignment affecting both its hard and soft sides (Chanias et al., 2019). The hard side encompasses the organization's structure, business processes, and systems. The soft side includes organizational culture, communication practices, and leadership approaches. When choosing a change strategy, assessing the organization's internal context is imperative. This should address the experience and the ability of the organization to innovate and change, the support from and capability of the top management, the competence of the project team, the availability of resources, and the willingness and preparedness of employees to acquire new skills relevant to the digital transformation (Armenakis et al., 1993). Additionally, the persuasiveness of the business case should also be considered in this diagnostic process (Greenhalgh et al., 2017). Relating this to the earlier example:

During the newspaper's digital transformation, various groups of employees held distinct perceptions and attitudes toward the change process. One group, consisting of motivated journalists and online production staff, embraced the digital transformation as necessary and believed it would result in a future-proof product. They firmly believed that the future of news will be entirely online, in real-time, and on-demand [1]. On the other hand, a more traditional group, including conventional journalists, printing house employees and distribution staff, perceived limited benefits and significant risks associated with digital transformation. Their preference was to continue to cater for a specific group of loyal readers who can choose between an online or a print version of a standardized product. These employee groups were highly unionized [4]. The IT staff within the newspaper also exhibited divided opinions: some viewed digital transformation as an exciting and necessary challenge [3], while others were hesitant and perceived it as a high-risk threat. The top management also exhibited differing perspectives. The innovation manager and the CEO [2] supported the proposed digital transformation, recognizing its value. However, the CFO and CMO [4] were ambivalent: while they acknowledged the conventional newspaper's nonviability, they feared the high start-up costs and the potential loss of traditional subscribers and advertisers.

Table 9.2 illustrates how the organizational stakeholders relate to digital transformation in the example.

Table 9.2 Complexity of the organization in the example

		Structural complexity	
		Internal support for the digital transformation	*Internal resistance to the digital transformation*
Dynamic complexity	*Certain organizational context*	1. Supporting staff members, including journalists and online production employees 2. CEO and innovation manager	3. Traditional journalists, printing and distribution workers
	Uncertain organizational context	4. CFO	5. CMO

In assessing the readiness of the organization for digital transformation, the following questions can be considered:

- How compelling is the business case for digital transformation?
- What is the capacity and experience of the organization to change?
- How capable and experienced is the project team assigned to lead the transformation?
- Does the team possess the necessary skills to execute the required changes?
- Can sufficient financial, human, and technical resources be provided to support the digital transformation initiative?
- From which internal stakeholders are cooperation and support needed to ensure a successful digital transformation?
- Is there agreement on the digital transformation among the internal stakeholders?
- Which stakeholders are willing to cooperate and what are their interests in this digital transformation?
- Are there parties with vested interests who may try to impede the digital transformation and is there a possibility to gain their support and overcome any potential obstacles?
- How stable is the level of support or resistance?
- Can attitudes change and, if so, when might this happen?

Digital Technology

Any digital transformation is reliant on a well-functioning digital technology or a mix of technologies. To develop an appropriate change strategy, it is necessary to determine the technology needed for this transformation, and assess whether it is available and deployable. If the technology is off-the-shelf and proven, such that the organization can implement it immediately, the digital transformation can be considered as "simple" from the technological perspective (Greenhalgh et al., 2017).

However, there is greater complexity if the technology is still in the development or testing phase, requires customization, or necessitates education and training processes. It is essential to distinguish between hard and soft technologies. Hard technology refers to the software and hardware required for the digital transformation, including applications for big data, AI systems, operating systems, network infrastructure, and servers. Soft technology refers to the organization's capability to effectively use this technology. Returning to the example:

In the digital transformation of the newspaper, technology was available and was already being used to make the paper newspaper available to readers in digital form [1]. Data on reader interactions, such as clicks on digital articles and advertisements were being collected, although systematic analysis of these data was lacking [2]. The technology partner was anticipating shortly developing an application utilizing push messages to enable targeted delivery to readers based on their profiles [4]. However, the payment model for this service had not been finalized [3]. The newspaper was also focusing on retraining employees to ensure their proficiency in managing an on-demand digital newspaper that primarily relies on online ads and push messages.

Table 9.3 illustrates the complexity of the hard and soft technologies in the digital transformation described in this example. The complexity is categorized along two dimensions: the structural complexity and the dynamic complexity of the digital technology (Brady and Davies, 2014; Boonstra and Reezigt, 2023). The structural complexity is considered low when standard digital technology can easily replace legacy systems, and off-the-shelf solutions are available and proven. Structural complexity is high if, among other things: (1) the legacy systems are difficult to replace, (2) multiple interfaces need to be integrated with existing systems, (3) complex adjustments are necessary, (4) new software has to be developed, and (5) advanced and scarce expertise is required (Greenhalgh et al., 2017; Boonstra and van Offenbeck, 2023).

The dynamic complexity of the digital technology is low when the digital technology remains relatively stable and does not require frequent adaptation to changing circumstances (Geraldi et al., 2011; Daniel and Daniel, 2018). However, the dynamic complexity increases if the organization or the environment imposes challenging requirements or desires that necessitate continuous technological adaptation. (Greenhalgh et al., 2017; Boonstra and van Offenbeek, 2023).

Table 9.3 Complexity of the technology in the example

		Structural complexity	
		Low	*High*
Dynamic complexity	*Stable technology, few adaptations*	1. Existing online newspaper	
	Unstable technology, frequent changes	2. Big data analysis and use 3. Payment model	4. Personalized news delivery

Typical questions that can aid in assessing the hard digital technology include:

- What legacy technology currently exists, and does it align with the new digital technology?
- What are the essential technological features required for achieving the digital transformation?
- How new or proven is this technology?
- Is it necessary to design, customize, or reconfigure it, or is it readily available as an off-the-shelf solution?

Further, typical questions that can guide the assessment of the soft digital technology are:

- What knowledge is necessary to deploy this technology effectively, and do we possess that knowledge?
- How challenging or straightforward is it to apply this technology effectively?
- Does the organizational culture embrace digitization?
- Do work processes need to be modified, or can they be integrated with existing processes?
- Are there competent and dependable technology partners available to provide support?

An overview of the complexity involved in the change process can be made to conclude the analysis of a digital transformation. This can be visually represented, as demonstrated in Figure 9.2 for the given example.

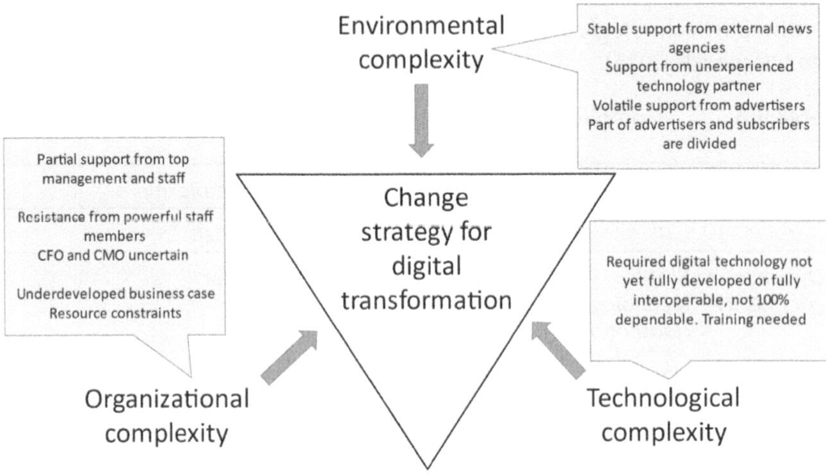

Source: Author.

Figure 9.2 Analysis of the complexity of digital transformation

In the next section, we explain how a change strategy can be developed by leveraging the analysis of the environmental, organizational, and technological complexities outlined above.

A duality framework for change management for digital transformation

An analysis of the organization and its environment is a necessary starting point for developing an informed change strategy for a digital transformation. In this section, we show how this facilitates the development of an organizational change strategy.

To achieve this, we use a framework consisting of two dimensions: (1) structural complexity in terms of the frame of reference for a digital transformation, and (2) dynamic complexity in terms of the degree of uncertainty surrounding

Table 9.4 Duality framework for digital transformation

			Structural complexity (in terms of a frame of reference for digital transformation)	
			Unitarist	Pluralist
			Simple change	*Complicated change*
Dynamic complexity (in terms of the degree of uncertainty surrounding a digital transformation)	*Low uncertainty*	Approach	*Planned* support, guidance, and resources	*Emergent* assess power and interests
		Scope	*Integrated* blueprint, goals, best practices	*Partial* limit scope, slow down
		Style	*Directive* communicate, train, and educate	*Adjustive* negotiate, compromise, incentivize
		Pace	*Big bang* bold strokes, radical	*Incremental* deploy pilots, long marches
			QUADRANT 1	QUADRANT 2
			QUADRANT 3	QUADRANT 4
	High uncertainty	Approach	*Emergent* experiments, self-organization	*Emergent* future scenarios, experiments, ongoing
		Scope	*Partial* evolve, quick wins	*Partial* experiments, evolve
		Style	*Collaborative* empowering consultative/learning/agile	*Debates and dialogues* encourage dissent and pluralism
		Pace	*Incremental* scrum, lenient, flexible planning	*Incremental* ambidexterity, alternative paths of action
			Complicated change	*Complex change*

a digital transformation. The duality framework for digital transformation shown in Table 9.4 illustrates this.

In the next section, we further explain the two dimensions of the framework and in the following one the change dualities in the approach, scope, style, and pace.

Dimensions of the Duality Framework for Digital Transformation

Dimension 1 – structural complexity: unitarist or pluralist frame of reference for digital transformation

In the unitarist frame of reference (Collins, 1998), a digital transformation is perceived as a change that enjoys robust support. Both internal and external stakeholders support the goals and provide the necessary resources. The main stakeholders view the digital transformation as a shared interest that benefits the entire organization, ensuring long-term survival and short-term advantages. Significant conflicts regarding the goals and the means of digital transformation are not expected and, if they do arise, they will be seen as undesirable. Objecting to or resisting the digital transformation is seen as counterproductive and not aligned with the organization's best interests. It is assumed that all parts of the organization will cooperate harmoniously, and criticism will not be encouraged.

The pluralist frame of reference (Collins, 1998) originates from political theory and posits that organizations are comprised of groups with diverse interests, whose consent and cooperation are necessary. Consequently, organizational change is inherently a political process. In this context, the role of management is to identify interest groups and make compromises to garner sufficient support for change. A digital transformation affects the interests of various parties, resulting in winners and perceived losers. Implementers of such a digital transformation acknowledge that conflict and resistance are common, and elements to address in achieving a widely accepted change. They are expected to be receptive to objections and criticism. Debates arise regarding the nature, pace, and approach of the digital transformation. Negotiations take place, and concessions may be made to ensure an adequate transformation. Initial plans may also undergo modifications or be only partially implemented.

When selecting an appropriate change strategy for a digital transformation, it is important to consider which frame of reference best aligns with the overall diagnosis. If there is support from both internal and external stakeholders, a unitarist frame of reference may prove effective. However, one should be aware that, during the change process, the attitudes of stakeholder groups may evolve, making the process more, or less, unitarian or pluralistic. In cases where the stakeholder landscape is divided, a pluralist frame of reference is more suitable. In the example presented earlier, both support and resistance to the digital transformation can be observed within the internal and external environments. Therefore, adopting a pluralist, rather than a unitarist, frame of reference would be more appropriate in this particular scenario.

Dimension 2 – dynamic complexity: degree of certainty about the digital transformation

This dimension refers to the level of adaptability of the intended digital transformation. In contexts with a high degree of certainty, the goals and required resources are well defined, and there is sufficient knowledge and experience to implement it (Boonstra and Reezigt, 2023). Furthermore, the technology necessary for the digital transformation is straightforward, standardized, and proven in similar situations. Key stakeholders are well acquainted with digital transformation, and their preferences remain stable, while stakeholder relationships and power dynamics undergo minimal changes. In essence, there are few surprises in such scenarios.

In high-uncertainty digital transformations, the goals are not fixed and often require adjustment or development over time. These transformations involve ongoing and constantly evolving interactions with both internal and external stakeholders (Brady and Davies, 2014; Daniel and Daniel, 2018; Maylor et al., 2008). Such interactions are influenced by changing attitudes and varying degrees of support. The uncertainty in the digital transformation is further compounded by unexpected challenges arising from a lack of experience. These challenges can emerge from new insights provided by internal interest groups, shifts in power dynamics, or an inexperienced technology partner operating in a changing environment with limited information. Additionally, determining the necessary resources for a successful execution of the digital transformation can be unclear. It is not uncommon for internal and external stakeholders to change attitudes during such a project due to a lack of an initial understanding of the project and its implications (Brady and Davies, 2014).

The example case discussed above demonstrates an environment characterized by uncertainty. The qualities and capabilities of the technology partner are uncertain, adding to the overall uncertainty. Furthermore, there are concerns about the behavior of advertisers, subscribers, and shareholders, which further contributes to the uncertain landscape. Internally, the level of support from the board is ambivalent and uncertain. Furthermore, the dynamic nature of the digital transformation introduces complexity and further diminishes the level of certainty. Overall, these factors indicate a relatively low level of certainty in the example's context.

The following section focuses on tensions that commonly surface in change management when dealing with digital transformations. Depending on the chosen frame of reference (unitarist or pluralist) and the level of uncertainty surrounding the digital transformation, various dualities arise concerning the approach, scope, style, and pace. Below, we will discuss these dualities.

Change Management Dualities in Digital Transformation

This subsection focuses on the primary dualities that are likely to arise during a digital transformation. These dualities have been extensively highlighted and discussed in the change management literature (Boonstra et al., 2017, Smith et al., 2020; Burnes 2017; Senior and Swailes, 2020). However, it is important to note that, in the practice of digital transformation within organizations, additional or distinct dualities may emerge.

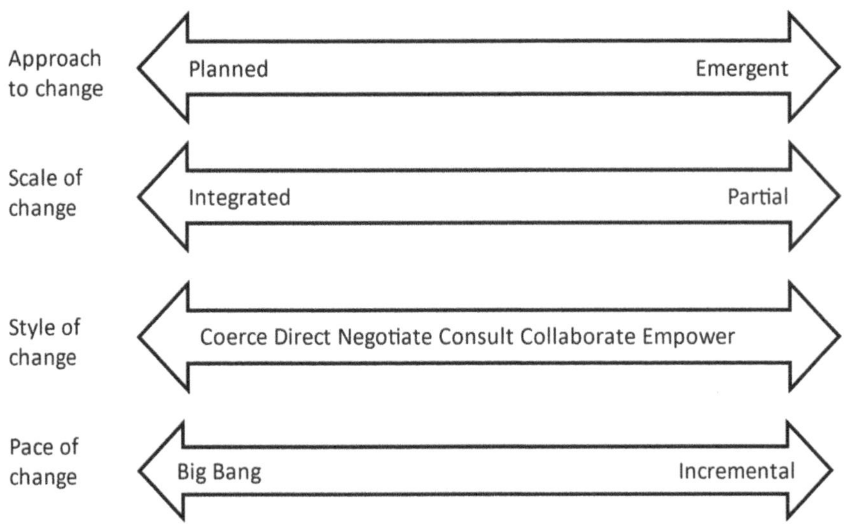

Source: Author.

Figure 9.3 Commonly reported change management dualities in digital transformation

Below we establish relationships between the two dimensions previously and four prevalent change management dualities (Smith et al., 2020; Senior and Swailes, 2020) that pertain to the approach, scale and scope, style, and pace of change (Figure 9.3).

Approach to change: balancing between planned and emergent digital transformations

A planned digital transformation is characterized by having established clear start and end points, which includes defining the change path or "gap" (Rajagoplalan and Spreitzer, 1997). This approach involves deliberate adjustments to the structure, processes, and systems in order to achieve the transformation. The change process is typically managed in a top-down approach by senior change managers and implemented through a systematic, staged approach. It assumes that there is agreement on goals and means, and sufficient certainty about the available technology and the organizational environment. This planned approach to organizational change is often referred to as "teleological" because it assumes that organizations act purposefully (Van de Ven and Poole, 2005). In the context of digital transformation, it is primarily driven by senior managers who perceive it necessary and aim to implement it in a rational and linear manner.

Emergent digital transformations, as described by Chanias et al. (2019), assume that digital transformation is an ongoing, open-ended, and unpredictable process that continuously strives to align the organization with the changing environment (Burnes, 2017). Unlike a planned transformation, emergent change is not the result of intentional or planned interventions but rather emerges organically and spontaneously from an organization's collective behavior. Mitchell (2009) sees emergent change as the occurrence of new and unexpected patterns and behaviors at the system level that arise from the actions and interactions among components in a complex system. This phenomenon is often referred to as the "butterfly effect." Emergent change is not easily predictable or manageable, but it has the potential to foster creative and innovative solutions. In the context of organizational change, an emergent change offers a bottom-up alternative to traditional, top-down approaches by acknowledging that successful innovations can originate from local sources rather than being driven solely by a central authority.

Based on Table 9.4, the planned change strategy fits well in Quadrant 1, representing a unitarist frame of reference and a high level of certainty regarding the digital transformation. However, when there is pluralism and uncertainty, an emergent strategy may be more appropriate as observed in Quadrants 2–4.

During the diagnosis, a digital transformation is differentiated across three dimensions: environment, organization, and technology. These dimensions can align with different quadrants. For instance, a planned strategy may be appropriate for implementing a technology if it is a standard, off-the-shelf solution with a proven track record (Burnes, 2004; Edwards et al., 2020). On the other hand, if there is disagreement within the organization or the external environment, an emergent style of change may fit better.

Scope of change: balancing between integral (corporate) and partial (unit) digital transformations

The scope of a digital transformation can vary, with one option being for organizations to undertake a comprehensive organization-wide journey. In such cases, the entire organization's systems, processes, and structures change to facilitate the transformation. This approach is known as integral digital transformation, and focuses on developing a fundamentally different 'digital' organization, characterized by a radical shift in structure, culture, and processes. Many of the employees will require completely different competences and skills. Integral digital transformations often involve planned initiatives led by senior leaders within the organization (Rogers, 2016). This approach is most suitable when there is a unitarist frame of reference, a relatively high level of certainty about the desired direction, and manageable technical complexity. Such comprehensive digital transformations have been observed in the transition of numerous major banks from traditional banking models to "fintech" platforms (Wewege and Thomsett, 2020).

Organizations seeking a digital transformation can also opt for a partial approach, such as through implementing living labs. In these living labs, initiatives are allowed to fail, and successful outcomes can serve as inspiration. The achievements in these labs can convince skeptics about the direction of the transformation, leading to increased enthusiasm. Partial digital transformations align with a pluralist frame of reference as they are a compromise that avoids an 'all-or-nothing' integral approach. To illustrate, in the newspaper example discussed earlier, the organization could choose to continue with a printed newspaper while simultaneously experimenting with various forms of online news delivery and new payment models. However, partial transformations can also occur within a unitarist frame of reference. For example, when faced with high technological or environmental uncertainty, a rational decision may be to pursue a partial digital transformation (Boonstra et al., 2017).

Leadership style tension: balancing between coercive/directive and consultative/collaborative digital transformations

In a transformation, the style of governance can vary significantly, ranging from highly top-down to bottom-up processes. Dunphy and Stace (1993) identify four styles that differ in the level of stakeholder involvement: (1) coercive: change is imposed from the top down under immense pressure, (2) directive: senior managers use their positions to implement change from the top down, (3) consultative: employees are consulted and involved to a limited extent in setting goals and choosing the means of digital transformation, and (4) collaborative: the participation and active involvement of employees shape the course of digital transformation. A fifth style, empowerment, has also been identified where stakeholders actively participate in digital transformation and possess decision-making authority. Triplett et al. (2022) highlight that stakeholder engagement can vary throughout a digitalization project. It may start with a coercive or directive approach but later move toward a more consultative or collaborative approach. They emphasize that collaborative leadership styles foster higher levels of support and engagement.

When the diagnosis of the intended digital transformation reveals a high degree of agreement and certainty about the desired direction, a directive leadership style may be appropriate. In such cases, there is a shared understanding and consensus on the necessary steps to be taken. The organization is aligned and ready to collectively move forward. However, in situations of uncertainty, participation, empowerment, and stakeholder engagement all become crucial. By involving stakeholders and empowering them, their available knowledge and expertise can be effectively mobilized. This active engagement helps reduce uncertainty by incorporating diverse perspectives and fostering collaboration.

Within a pluralistic frame of reference, where different viewpoints and interests exist, change strategies based on deliberation, negotiation, and concessions tend to be more effective than imposing change from above. Rather than a top-down approach, a collaborative and inclusive process encourages dialogue, compromise, and finding common ground among stakeholders.

Pace of change: balancing between big bang and incremental digital transformations

Big bang digital transformations involve a sudden and rapid change in an organization's processes, systems, and structures rather than a gradual or incremental approach. The primary objective is to achieve quick results, often driven by the need to catch up with competitors or respond swiftly to changing circumstances. While big bang transformations can deliver rapid improvements, they also carry significant risks as they can disrupt the organization if not properly executed. Successful big bang digital transformations require careful planning, execution, and the involvement of knowledgeable and engaged stakeholders. The COVID-19 pandemic highlighted examples of big bang and organization-wide digital transformations. For instance, many organizations swiftly transitioned to remote working, schools adopted online education, and hospitals offered online consultations. These were rapid and comprehensive changes implemented in response to the urgent demands of the situation.

On the other hand, incremental digital transformations follow a gradual and cumulative approach. They involve implementing small and iterative digitalization steps, evaluating each step before moving to the next. The goal is to gradually transform the organization digitally, focusing on achieving 'quick wins' to gain support and convince opponents. Incremental digital transformation allows the organization to incrementally adapt and respond to feedback and evaluations, mitigating the risks of failure. Incremental digital transformation can be an effective strategy for organizations that do not want to fall behind but want to minimize the risks of failure.

Incremental digital transformation can be an effective strategy for organizations that want to avoid falling behind while minimizing the risks associated with large-scale changes. It provides flexibility and the opportunity to learn from each step, gradually building support for the digital transformation within the organization.

The four dualities discussed above are presented in Table 9.4 in the duality framework for digital transformation. Our intention behind producing this framework is to provide guidance to those responsible for digital activities within established companies. By diagnosing the environment, the organization, and the digital technology, as discussed previously, the degree of complexity in these three domains can be assessed. This assessment enables the identification of the most appropriate frame of reference, either unitarist or pluralist. Furthermore, the level of certainty within these three domains can be evaluated as relatively high or low.

This categorizes a digital transformation into one or more quadrants within the framework. It is important to note that the three domains need not align with the same quadrant. For instance, while the digital technology might be relatively simple and stable, the organization or environment could be complex. In such cases, distinct change strategies could be employed for each domain. Additionally, the emphasis may shift throughout the digital transformation process. As support for the change process gradually develops, the frame of reference could become more unitarist. The degree of certainty can also increase or decrease. This is why the change strategy should be flexible and not stick to one approach.

Discussion and conclusion

This chapter has argued that the classical linear approach to enabling a digital transformation fails to capture the reality's complexity. Rather, we argue that digital transformation within organizations is a dynamic and multidimensional change process. This complexity stems primarily from the various interest groups that hold different perceptions of digital transformation, the technology itself that is not always off-the-shelf, and the uncertain environment surrounding the organization undergoing the digital transformation. In reality, leading a change process within this complexity requires a deep understanding of its nature and the dualities that arise within it. We contribute to this understanding by addressing the following aspects: (1) how organizations can analyze a change toward digital transformation, (2) what change strategies can fit these initiatives, and (3) how these change strategies can be combined within a duality framework for a successful digital transformation.

This chapter explored how managing change for a digital transformation can be approached from three theoretical perspectives: contingency theory, duality theory, and complexity. Adopting these perspectives, the environment, the organization, and the technology can all be analyzed to develop a change strategy in terms of its approach, scope, style, and pace of change. Using this approach, we propose a coherent, theory-based, duality framework to establish an appropriate context-specific digital transformation strategy based on well-known change management dualities. This framework can help shape the change management of digital transformation in a new and more profound way.

The duality framework for digital transformation highlights the importance of managing and reconciling apparent contradictions. On the one hand, it is crucial that management establishes clear goals for a digital transformation, assembles a project team, allocates available resources, and then achieves tangible outcomes. At the same time, a digital transformation is an iterative learning process that involves navigating uncertainties and overcoming resistance. The developed diagnostic approach demonstrates that balancing dualities, such as solid leadership versus fostering participation, and planned actions versus emergent adaptations, is essential. Effective change leadership in digital transformation requires a blend of both rigid and adaptable qualities. While there may well be instances where directive and planned measures are required, they should be combined with consultation, learning, and experimentation. Engaging in consultation and negotiation with stakeholders is essential if one is to sustain momentum along the digital transformation journey.

The proposed change framework for digital transformation serves as a guide for those involved in realizing digital transformation initiatives. By developing the framework, we demonstrate how one can analyze the digital transformation technology, the organization, and its environment, including support, resistance, certainty, and structural and dynamic complexity. Through this diagnosis, it becomes possible to determine the focal points of the change strategy by considering factors such as approach, scope, style, and pace of the transformation efforts.

The framework can be applied in various contexts depending on the stage, type of digital transformation, and stakeholders' attitudes. Before embarking on the transformation journey, the framework can be used to assess the complexity associated with the digital transformation. As the change process unfolds, the framework can be used to investigate the various project domains and facilitate productive dialogue among the key stakeholders. This will foster the development of an appropriate approach that embraces the inherent dualities of digital transformation. These activities will further foster a shared understanding of the nature of digital transformation. Subsequently, the management team will be able to make informed decisions based on the insights gained from the project diagnosis when selecting and adjusting digital transformation strategies. The framework remains applicable throughout the digital transformation process, enabling the identification of potential problems and providing insight into necessary adjustments to the change strategy.

In terms of the next step, the proposed framework can be further validated both theoretically and practically. Research efforts should be directed at examining both successful and failed digital transformation endeavors to identify the specific circumstances within which certain change strategies proved effective. This analysis will help establish a theory-based relationship between the diagnosis of the desired transformation and the appropriate change strategy, as indicated in Table 9.4, and assess its practical validity. Further, research could usefully seek to understand how seemingly contradictory change strategies can complement each other in a digital transformation. This understanding will enable managers to make informed decisions regarding the optimal combination of strategies, determining when and how they should be employed.

Our hope is that the duality framework outlined in this chapter will assist those responsible for digital transformations to develop a deeper understanding of the change management challenges they face at an early stage, resulting in tailored, duality-aware, and flexible change management strategies.

References

Alderman, N., & Ivory, C. (2007). Partnering in major contracts: Paradox and metaphor. *International Journal of Project Management*, *25*(4), 386–393.

Armenakis, A. A., Harris, S. G., & Mossholder, K. W. (1993). Creating readiness for organizational change. *Human Relations*, *46*(6), 681–703.

Baiyere, A., Salmela, H., & Tapanainen, T. (2020). Digital transformation and the new logics of business process management. *European Journal of Information Systems*, *29*(3), 238–259.

Balogun, J., & Hailey, V. H. (2008). *Exploring Strategic Change*. Pearson Education.

Baptista, J., Stein, M. K., Klein, S., Watson-Manheim, M. B., & Lee, J. (2020). Digital work and organisational transformation: Emergent digital/human work configurations in modern organisations. *Journal of Strategic Information Systems*, *29*(2), 101618.

Block, C. (2022). 12 reasons your digital transformation will fail. https:// www .forbes .com/ sites/ f orbescoach escouncil/ 2022/ 03/ 16/ 12 -reasons -your -digital -transformation-will-fail/?sh=a0af331f1eea.

Boonstra, A., & Reezigt, C. (2023). A complexity framework for project management strategies. *Project Management Journal*, *54*(3), 253–267.

Boonstra, A., & van Offenbeek, M. A. G. (2011). Towards consistent modes of e-health implementation: Structurational analysis of a telecare programme's limited success. *Information Systems Journal*, *20*(6), 537–561.

Boonstra, A., & van Offenbeek, M. A. G. (2023). Tailoring the implementation of digital business: A diagnostic framework. In B. S. Baalmans, T. L. J. Broekhuizen & N. Fabian (Eds.), *Digital Transformation: A Guide for Managers* (pp. 90–119). Groningen Digital Business Centre, University of Groningen.

Boonstra, A., van Offenbeek, M. A. G., & Vos, J. F. J. (2017). Tension awareness of stakeholders in large technology projects: A duality perspective. *Project Management Journal*, *48*(1), 19–36.

Brady, T., & Davies, A. (2014). Managing structural and dynamic complexity: A tale of two projects. *Project Management Journal*, *45*(4), 21–38.

Burnes, B. (2004). Emergent change and planned change—competitors or allies? The case of XYZ construction. *International Journal of Operations & Production Management*, *24*(9), 886–902.

Burnes, B. (2017). *Managing Change*. Pearson.

Burnes, B., & Jackson, P. (2011). Success and failure in organizational change: An exploration of the role of values. *Journal of Change Management*, *11*(2), 133–162.

Burns, T., & Stalker, G. M. (1961). *The Management of Innovation.* Tavistock Publications.
Chanias, S., Myers, M. D., & Hess, T. (2019). Digital transformation strategy making in pre-digital organizations: The case of a financial services provider. *Journal of Strategic Information Systems, 28*(1), 17–33.
Collins, D. (1998). *Organisational Change: Sociological Perspectives.* Routledge.
Constantinides, P., & Barrett, M. (2006). Large-scale ICT innovation, power, and organizational change: The case of a regional health information network. *Journal of Applied Behavioral Science, 42*(1), 76–90.
Damschroder, L. J., Aron, D. C., Keith, R. E., Kirsh, S. R., Alexander, J. A., & Lowery, J. C. (2009). Fostering implementation of health services research: A consolidated framework for advancing implementation science. *Implementation Science, 4*, 50.
Daniel, P. A., & Daniel, C. (2018). Complexity, uncertainty and mental models: From a paradigm of regulation to a paradigm of emergence in project management. *International Journal of Project Management, 36*(1), 184–197.
Deloitte (2020). Why companies struggle with digital disruption. *The Wallstreet Journal.* https://deloitte.wsj.com/cmo/2020/02/14/why-companies-struggle-with-digital-disruption/?reflink=desktopwebshare_permalink.
Ditsche, J., Rohrhirsch, D., Grunow, S., & Fritze, R. (2022). The digital dilemma: Why companies struggle to master digital transformation. RolandBerger.com. https://content.rolandberger.com/hubfs/07_presse/Roland_Berger_Focus_Digital_Dilemma_N3XT_2022.pdf.
Doolin, B. (2004). Power and resistance in the implementation of a medical management information system. *Information Systems Journal, 14*(4), 343–362.
Dunphy, D., & Stace, D. (1993). The strategic management of corporate change. *Human Relations, 46*(8), 905–921.
Edwards, K., Prætorius, T., & Nielsen, A. P. (2020). A model of cascading change: Orchestrating planned and emergent change to ensure employee participation. *Journal of Change Management, 20*(4), 342–368.
Fernandez, D. J., & Fernandez, J. D. (2016). Agile project management: Agilism versus traditional approaches. *Journal of Computer Information Systems, 49*(2), 10–17. https://doi.org/10.1080/08874417.2009.11646044.
Flyvbjerg, B. (2017). Introduction: The iron law of megaproject management. In B. Flyvbjerg (Ed.), *The Oxford Handbook of Megaproject Management* (pp. 1–18). Oxford University Press.
Fox, A. (1966). Managerial ideology and labour relations. *British Journal of Industrial Relations, 4*(1–3), 366–378.
Francis, D., & Bessant, J. (2005). Targeting innovation and implications for capability development. *Technovation, 25*(3), 171–183.
Geraldi, J., Maylor, H., & Williams, T. (2011). Now, let's make it really complex (complicated): A systematic review of the complexities of projects. *International Journal of Operations & Production Management, 31*(9), 966–990.
Greenhalgh, T., Potts, H. W., Wong, G., Bark, P., & Swinglehurst, D. (2009). Tensions and paradoxes in electronic patient record research: A systematic literature review using the meta-narrative method. *Milbank Quarterly, 87*(4), 729–788.
Greenhalgh, T., Wherton, J., Papoutsi, C., Lynch, J., Hughes, G., A'Court, C., Hinder, S., Fahy, N., Procter, R., & Shaw, S. (2017). Beyond adoption: A new framework for theorizing and evaluating nonadoption, abandonment, and challenges to the scale-up, spread and sustainability of health and care technologies. *Journal of Medical Internet Research, 19*(11), 1–21.

Hanelt, A., Bohnsack, R., Marz, D., & Antunes, C. (2020). A systematic review of the literature on digital transformation: Insights and implications for strategy and change management. *Journal of Management Studies, 58*(5), 1159–1197.
Jensen, T. B., & Aanestad, M. (2007). Hospitality and hostility in hospitals: A case study of an EPR adoption among surgeons. *European Journal of Information Systems, 16*(6), 672–680.
Lapointe, L., & Rivard, S. (2005). A multilevel model of resistance to information technology implementation. *MIS Quarterly, 29*(3), 461–491.
Lawrence, P. R., & Lorsch, J. W. (1967). *Organization and Environment: Managing Differentiation and Integration.* Harvard Business Press.
Leinwand, P., & Mani, M. M. (2021). The 7 imperatives for a successful digital transformation. *Harvard Business Review,* 27 October. https://hbr.org/webinar/2021/10/the-7-imperatives-for-a-successful-digital-transformation.
Maylor, H., Vidgen, R., & Carver, S. (2008). Managerial complexity in project-based operations: A grounded model and its implications for practice. *Project Management Journal, 39*(S1), S15–S26.
McKendrick, J. (2019). Digital transformation is risky, but not transforming is even riskier. https:// www .forbes .com/ sites/ joemckendrick/ 2019/ 05/ 27/ digital -transformation-is-risky-but-not-transforming-is-even-riskier/?sh=6e4808c03f3a.
McKinsey (2017). A roadmap for a digital transformation. https://www.mckinsey.com/industries/financial-services/our-insights/a-roadmap-for-a-digital-transformation.
Mitchell, M. (2009). *Complexity: A Guided Tour.* Oxford University Press.
Morcov, S., Pintelon, L., & Kusters, R. (2021). Definitions, characteristics, and measures of IT project complexity: A systematic literature review. *International Journal of Information Systems and Project Management, 8*(2), 5–21.
Oliveira, T., & Martins, M. F. (2011). Literature review of information technology adoption models at the firm level. *Electronic Journal of Information Systems Evaluation, 14*(1), 110–121.
Pettigrew, A., & Whipp, R. (1991). *Managing Change for Competitive Success.* Blackwell Publishing.
Pich, M., Loch, C. H., & De Meyer, A. (2002). On uncertainty, ambiguity, and complexity in project management. *Management Science, 48*(8), 1008–1023.
Plowman, D. A., Baker, L. T., Beck, T. E., Kulkarni, M., Solansky, S. T., & Travis, D. V. (2007). Radical change accidentally: The emergence and amplification of small change. *Academy of Management Journal, 50*(3), 515–543.
Rajagoplalan, N., & Spreitzer, G. M. (1997). Toward a theory of strategic change: A multi lens perspective and integrative framework. *Academy of Management Review, 22*(1), 48–79.
Rogers, D. (2016). *The Digital Transformation Playbook.* Columbia University Press.
Senior, B., & Swailes, S. (2020). *Organizational Change.* Pearson.
Seo, M., Putnam, L. L., & Bartunek, J. M. (2004). Dualities and tensions of planned organizational change. In M. S. Poole & A. H. Van de Ven (Eds.), *Handbook of Organizational Change and Innovation* (pp. 73–107). Oxford University Press.
Shenhar, A. J. (2001). One size does not fit all projects: Exploring classical contingency domains. *Management Science, 47*(3), 394–414.
Smith, A. C. T., Skinner, J., & Read, D. (2020). *Philosophies of Organizational Change: Perspectives, Models and Theories for Managing Change.* Edward Elgar Publishing.
Söderlund, J. (2011). Pluralism in project management: Navigating the crossroads of specialization and fragmentation. *International Journal of Management Reviews, 13*(2), 153–176.

Stacey, R. D. (1996). *Complexity and Creativity in Organizations.* Berrett-Koehler Publishers.
Tessler, E. (2017). How digital transformation will change a 90-year old newspaper. Innovation in News Media. https://innovation.media/insights/how-digital-transformation-will-change-a-90-year-old-newspaper.
Thompson, J. D. (1967). *Organizations in Action: Social Science Bases of Administrative Theory.* McGraw-Hill.
Triplett, N. S., Woodard, G. S., Johnson, C., Nguyen, J. K., AlRasheed, R., Song, F., Storddard, S., Mugisha, J. C., Sievert, K., & Dorsey, S. (2022). Stakeholder engagement to inform evidence-based treatment implementation for children's mental health: A scoping review. Implementation Science Communications, *3*. https://doi.org/10.1186/s43058-022-00327-w.
Van de Ven, A. H., & Poole, M. S. (2005). Alternative approaches for studying organizational change. *Organization Studies, 26*(9), 1377–1404.
Verhoef, P., Broekhuizen, T. L. J., Bart, Y., Bhattacharya, A., Dong, J. Q., Fabian, N., & Haeinlein, M. (2021). Digital transformation: A multidisciplinary reflection and research agenda. *Journal of Business Research, 122*, 889–901.
Wewege, L., & Thomsett, M. C. (2020). *The Digital Banking Revolution: How Fintech Companies Are Transforming the Retail Banking Industry through Disruptive Financial Innovation.* De Gruyter.
Winch, G. M. (2014). Three domains of project organising. *International Journal of Project Management, 32*(5), 721–731. https://doi.org/10.1016/j.ijproman.2013.10.012.
Woodward, J. (1958). *Management and Technology.* Her Majesty's Stationery Office.

10 Cybersecurity management for digital transformation

Guy Alain Sylvanus Kouyo, Rohit Nishant and Hager Khechine

Through a strong convergence of the physical and digital worlds, digital transformation (DT) – the use of a collection of digital technology resources to digitize an organization's procedures and operations (Tan et al., 2020; Wessel et al., 2020) – has substantially altered the daily lives of humans since the early 2000s (Zeadally & Tsikerdekis, 2020). It happens when the use of digital technology alters a company's business model, resulting in new products, structures, or automated processes (Hess et al., 2016). DT should not be confused with IT-enabled organizational transformation (ITOT) because they differ in two key ways: (1) DT activities help organizations redefine their value proposition using digital technology, whereas ITOT activities help organizations support their value proposition using digital technology, and (2) DT results in the appearance of a new organizational identity, whereas ITOT improves an existing organizational identity (Wessel et al., 2020).

Professional and academic discussions around DT are growing (Gurbaxani & Dunkle, 2019). The rapid proliferation of digital technologies has provided organizations with unprecedented benefits, putting them under pressure to digitally improve their procedures to better meet their customers' needs (Vial, 2019). As a result, our era is more reliant on digital technology than ever (Sarker et al., 2021). For example, digital technologies enabled television companies to offer innovative products and services such as video-on-demand, gaming content related to television content, and movie production. In the organizational context, connected devices such as the internet of things (IoT) provide opportunities for logistics, warehouse, and shipment organizations to be more productive by redefining stock management strategy and product traceability using 24/7 connected devices (Kumar et al., 2020; Zeadally & Tsikerdekis, 2020).

However, DT is also increasing cybersecurity threats for various reasons, including broadening the scope of vulnerabilities, increasing the financial stakes, and enhancing cyber criminals' capacity. Thus, the context of the emerging DT paradigm has increased cybersecurity management challenges and threats (Mendhurwar & Mishra, 2021). Cybersecurity management refers to comprehensive, safe, and secure operation management structures and practices for information security (Li et al., 2019; Soomro et al., 2016). It is one of the most pressing technological challenges confronting organizations today (Mou et al., 2022). For example, in 2021, companies in the United States lost more than USD6.9 billion due to cybersecurity breaches, and over 847,376 cyberattack complaints were reported (FBI, 2021). Furthermore, cyberattacks have a high financial cost worldwide; the annual estimated cost of cybercrime to the global economy is more than USD400 billion (Sarker et al., 2021).

As threats become more complex and dynamic, sophisticated tools for gathering, processing, and analyzing evidence to guide strategic and operational cybersecurity measures are increasingly developed (Naseer et al., 2018). Organizations are increasingly exploring artificial intelligence-based approaches to face cybersecurity threats. Artificial intelligence (AI) is a branch of computer science which aims to create intelligent machines that think and behave like humans (Sarker et al., 2021). The literature on the use of AI for cybersecurity has several scientific and practitioner studies addressing technical aspects such as threat identification (Ebrahimi et al., 2022; Samtani et al., 2022), cryptography, digital forensics (Kabanov & Madnick, 2021), and incident response (Naseer et al., 2021). Building on these studies, we propose a more human–AI collaboration approach to improving cybersecurity management. It is worth noting that humans (employees) have been identified as a firm's weakest point in cybersecurity (Kweon et al., 2021). Accordingly, we propose in this chapter, new approaches to use AI in cybersecurity management in the areas of policy specifications and compliance; and a security education, training, and awareness (SETA) recommendation system. Hence, the approaches we propose are essentially based on three principles: improving human–machine interaction by striking a balance between increasing AI users' capabilities and automating some tasks; next, focusing on the needs of the users when using AI so that it can better respond to their expectations; finally, using AI as a management tool rather than a replacement for managers.

For research, we emphasize a human–machine collaborative approach in which the human uses the machine as a tool rather than as a separate entity that makes decisions for them. Furthermore, we combine AI characteristics such as speed, accuracy, reliability, and scalability with human competencies like creativity, empathy, judgment, and critical thinking to exploit the aspects of human–AI hybrid concepts (Rai et al., 2019). By emphasizing the increased capabilities of managers and employees using AI for cybersecurity management, we contribute to the concept of a symbiotic relationship between augmentation and automation rather than the automation–augmentation paradox. In particular, we seek a dynamic integration of humans and AI, fostering an assemblage type of interdependence as they function as a cohesive unit (Rai et al., 2019). According to the literature, users are often seen as the weakest link in organizational cybersecurity. Therefore, it's crucial to involve them in developing cybersecurity solutions. Users need systems that can provide them with personalized and relevant cybersecurity policy suggestions by analyzing their data to understand individual tasks and challenges. Therefore, we suggest a different application of recommendation systems. Recommendation systems are widely used in commerce and services; however, we discuss their application inside organizations to help managers make strategic decisions about human resource management.

In practice, the approaches outlined in this chapter will allow managers to save time and money on investments in educating employees about cybersecurity. Managers will also have more autonomy and less reliance on outside resources such as costly consultants. Finally, managers will save time, effort, and human resources because of optimized cybersecurity policy design and implementation.

The rest of this chapter is organized as follows: the next section presents cybersecurity management in which we discuss DT and the human factor role in cybersecurity management challenges. We then present AI for cybersecurity management. We discuss AI involvement in cybersecurity policy specifications, an AI-based system to improve policy compliance, and an AI-based SETA recommendation system. Finally, we present the conclusion.

Cybersecurity management

Digital Transformation Role in Cybersecurity Challenges

For several reasons, DT implementation poses cybersecurity risks to organizations. DT has enabled system interconnectivity, allowing systems on different continents to exchange information in seconds, improving organization efficiency (Gurbaxani & Dunkle, 2019). However, if one of the network's systems is breached, all of them are vulnerable, even if they are geographically distant (Zeadally & Tsikerdekis, 2020). In 2021, the U.S. cloud-based video surveillance company Verkada was hacked, giving criminals access to live feeds from over 150,000 cameras in factories, hospitals, schools, and prisons (Turton,

2021). Thus, organizations need assistance securing their interconnected systems in increasingly complex networks (Pan & Yang, 2018).

Next, DT has enabled organizations to reinvent their products and services to serve customers better, resulting in an explosion of personal data (Weill & Woerner, 2018). This personal data is valuable and critical in some organizations' activities, resulting in data-driven business (Hartmann et al., 2016). As a result, the more DT an organization experiences, the more data it generates (Dremel et al., 2017). However, large amounts of valuable data in an organization attract inside and outside hackers (Pang & Tanriverdi, 2022). Hackers are interested in organizations with customer data to steal, exploit, and resell on the dark web (Samtani et al., 2022). For example, the Internal Revenue Service (IRS) of the United States is a frequent target of cyberattacks because it holds sensitive information about taxpayers' income tax filings and refunds (Taylor & Associated Press, 2017).

DT requires significant financial investment from organizations, which not all small to medium-sized businesses can afford (Vial, 2019). As a result, organizations turn to third-party vendors for software, platform, and infrastructure as a service (Pang & Tanriverdi, 2022). However, the security of their information depends on the service providers, and when a security breach occurs, all organizations that use their services are automatically targeted (Al Nafea & Almaiah, 2021). Dependence on third-party providers for technology services opens the door to vulnerabilities to which these providers are vulnerable.

DT involves technical and managerial skills that are scarce and costly in some countries, leading organizations to hire experts abroad (Weill & Woerner, 2018). Hence, this introduces additional security challenges because organizations must look for ways to authenticate remote workers correctly and segregate their potentially conflicting access privileges (Sipior, 2021).

By providing cyber criminals with multiple access points to organizations' systems and fostering their skills, DT has increased their capacity. Hackers are now less predictable because the multitude of elements that comprise organizations' information systems makes it difficult to predict how the attacks will come (Devine & Bastian, 2021). The richness that DT brings in terms of architectures and technological capabilities (e.g., AI cloud infrastructure, IoT devices, and software as a service) allows hackers to discover new ways to carry out more sophisticated attacks in organizations' vast technological ecosystems (Hai et al., 2021). Hackers are constantly improving their strategies (Kaloudi & Li, 2020) by attempting to understand the implementation and internal state of the systems (Devine & Bastian, 2021).

Several technological solutions are mentioned in the literature as more efficient security approaches evolve in response to emerging security challenges (Mendhurwar & Mishra, 2021). They are used to secure communication between authorized users, monitor a network or systems for malicious activity, validate a computer system user's identity, examine and analyze material found in digital devices, and ensure data is secure, private, accurate, available, and usable (Sarker et al., 2021). Nonetheless, these approaches are classified as "standard" and have limitations. For starters, many of them are rule-based, which means that not all possibilities can be anticipated using an organization's information system (Raisch & Krakowski, 2021). Moreover, the complexity of specific technologies, such as the IoT, renders sequence analysis-based security approaches insufficient because thousands of connected systems interact, resulting in an exponential increase in the number of connections to be analyzed (Zeadally et al., 2020).

It should be noted that technological limitations are not the only source of cybersecurity challenges in a DT context. DT implies increased employee responsibility for cybersecurity and, as a result, a behavior change. This is particularly true given that experts and literature have identified the human factor as the weakest link in an organization's information security (D'Arcy & Basoglu, 2022).

The Human Factor in Cybersecurity Challenges

According to a Verizon company survey, 81 percent of organizational data breaches were facilitated by employees' weak or stolen passwords due to a lack of compliance with strong password creation policies (Vance et al., 2022). Kweon et al. (2021) argue that employees are typically a firm's weakest link in terms of information security. They state that "Firms' core information assets leak out due to employees' careless behavior, for instance, downloading e-mails sent by the unidentified sender, checking linked pages incautiously, or setting passwords by their birthdays" (p. 361). Employees may endanger not only the assets of the organizations for which they work but also those of the organizations to which they provide services, such as cloud services. Cloud services models foster interconnection with external entities, which raises security concerns (Al Nafea & Almaiah, 2021). While security experts have numerous technical solutions, human behavior remains their focal point of concern, determining whether security efforts succeed or fail (Cram et al., 2019). Employees' misunderstanding, carelessness, or deliberate disregard for cybersecurity policies and measures frequently render security solutions ineffective (Chen et al., 2021). This situation worsens when managers fail to foster a cybersecurity culture within an organization or when cybersecurity issues are not prioritized at the top of the organization's priorities (Uchendu et al., 2021). Organizations attempting to reduce policy noncompliance frequently employ reward and punishment strategies toward employees, but these strategies are rarely effective due to employees' anxiety and frustration (Cram et al., 2020).

Organizations also provide cybersecurity learning programs to employees, but employees are uninterested in these programs because they see them as more of a burden than a benefit (Cram et al., 2021). As a result, organizations have to rekindle their employees' interest in cybersecurity and, eventually, make cybersecurity activities a more natural part of their daily operations. The level of cyber threats has become more complex and greater than what traditional human-centric cybersecurity approaches can handle. Organizations are constantly under attack, with hackers exploiting vulnerabilities and taking advantage of human mistakes. Therefore, businesses require a reliable partner who can provide a comprehensive strategy to strengthen their cybersecurity and overcome vulnerabilities caused by human errors. One solution could be a technology that can swiftly analyze massive amounts of data, effectively addressing the issues of scale and speed in the realm of cybersecurity. An advanced system that can constantly monitor networks, endpoints, and systems, tirelessly scanning for anomalies and potential breaches that could be undetected by humans. It can also identify intricate and evolving attack patterns that may be difficult for human operators to recognize. AI is an ideal candidate for these different tasks, as it possesses a wide range of algorithms that meet many of the needs that organizations require to minimize the likelihood of human errors that often lead to breaches. Furthermore, it can suggest an adaptable defense mechanism that allows systems to evolve according to real-time threat intelligence, thereby staying ahead of emerging attack vectors.

AI for a cybersecurity management framework

Organizations are encountering difficulties in managing huge amounts of data, verifying user identities, detecting illegal intrusions, and complying with policies. To address these issues, they are turning to automated and dynamic systems that rely on AI (Abbas et al., 2019). AI has significantly impacted human life and is one of the fourth industrial revolution's critical technologies used to protect internet-connected systems from cyber threats, attacks, damage, or unauthorized access (Raisch & Krakowski, 2021). AI's computing power and capabilities improved organizational cybersecurity capabilities, responsiveness, and effectiveness against cyberattacks (Siroya & Mandot, 2021). For instance, AI can also help identify new threats that are not yet well known in the industry or have resulted in so few victims that no one is talking about them. Organizations can use AI to explore and analyze hacker discussion platforms to identify new threats and criminal trends (Ebrahimi et al., 2022). AI has the computational power to simultaneously test and simulate multiple hacking scenarios in a real-world testing environment to discover and patch vulnerabilities (Berente et al., 2021). AI can probe software by sending bogus instructions to determine which components have security flaws with high accuracy (Obaidat et al., 2022). Finally, organizations can use AI to identify, assess, and control risks in their cybersecurity risk management plan (Bitton et al., 2021).

While AI has certain strengths, such as the ability to process massive amounts of heterogeneous data in a short period (Sarker et al., 2021), to automate simple decisions that require a large amount of information (Loebbecke et al., 2020), the potential of AI in cybersecurity management is either underestimated or overestimated, leading to frustrations or disasters (Westenberger et al., 2022). To discover the untapped potential of AI in cybersecurity management, guidelines and frameworks are required (Sarker et al., 2021). As a result, scholars and practitioners must concentrate on how organizations can use AI to manage cybersecurity (Fügener et al., 2022; Jain et al., 2021).

This section delves into the frontier of AI-driven cybersecurity management, where machine intelligence is harnessed to fortify digital defenses, enhance policy adherence, and empower the collective cybersecurity consciousness. Figure 10.1 depicts the framework we propose for using AI for cybersecurity management. First, the data sources and the scope of the organizations differ. Human resources data about employees, IT and security team reports (network, database, application, and user activities), and management reports are examples of internal reports. Data can also be obtained from the government, a trade association, the internet, or various experts. Each data source is critical, and organizations must use the ones that best suit the task at hand. Organizations can use natural language processing (NLP) to increase the amount of data considered in internal and external document searches and process this data automatically and more quickly to produce cybersecurity policies. Organizations are implementing learning programs to update users on cybersecurity policies. They can use recommendation systems based on user attributes (role, position, department, system accessed, and so on) to deliver content best suited to their status to maintain or increase their awareness of cybersecurity behavior. Organizations can assist their employees in adhering to cybersecurity policies by deploying an intelligent agent based on reinforcement learning (RL). This agent will educate itself on policy compliance states and analyze user activity data to identify noncompliant activities and notify users so that they can improve their behavior.

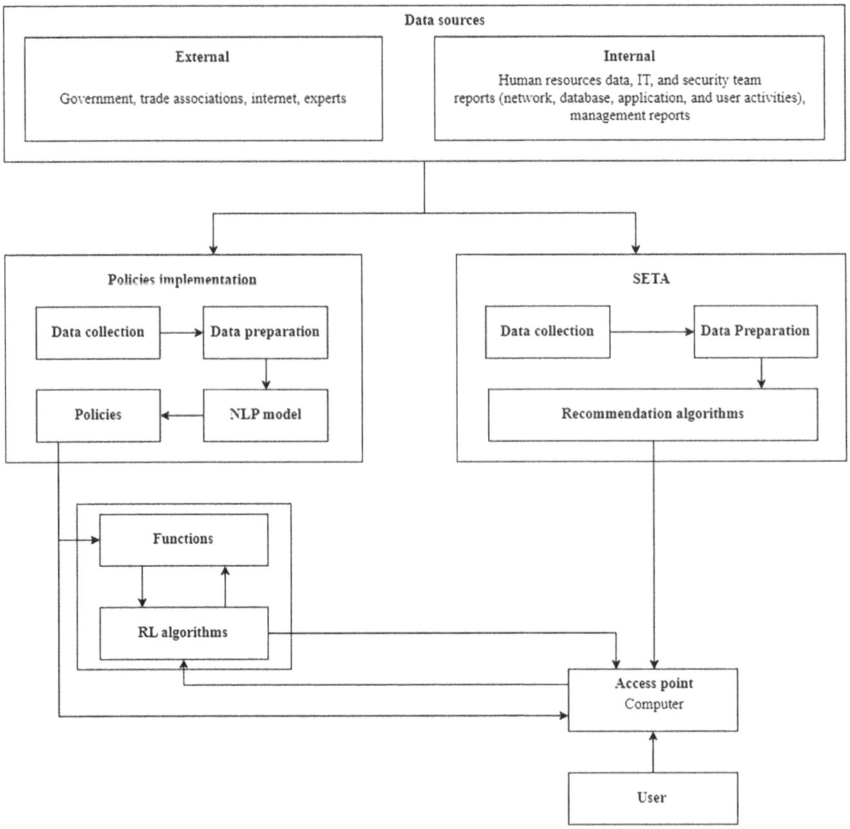

Source: Authors.

Figure 10.1 AI for a cybersecurity framework

The approaches proposed in this chapter have implications for research and practice. For research, they emphasize first a human–machine approach that permits the human to use the machine as a tool rather than as a separate entity that will make decisions for him. This chapter contributes to the concept of augmentation and automation by highlighting the improved cybersecurity management capabilities of managers and employees using AI. It suggests a specific application of AI systems that are widely used in business and services, but less so in helping managers make strategic decisions about human resource management.

Our proposed approaches also have implications for practice. First, organizations can communicate real-time cybersecurity policies to users. They will communicate the appropriate learning program at the appropriate time to meet user expectations, reduce resistance, and increase employee enthusiasm for learning about cybersecurity policies. Second, managers will save time and effort. Managers will save on the resources required to create, communicate, and maintain their cybersecurity policies. Although implementing an AI model could be costly, hiring consultants for its creation could be costly both monetarily and in terms of accessibility. Because they leave with their knowledge, they are present for a well-defined task and knowledge objectives. In addition, using AI will allow optimizing the costs, the efforts of the organizations, and the time employees spend on awareness campaigns, allowing managers to focus on strategic issues. Thirdly, businesses will have greater control over their cybersecurity. They will be able to receive rapid feedback so they can adapt to any challenges that arise. This will enable managers make upstream decisions, such as expanding awareness campaigns on a specific topic. Over time, they can regulate, modify, and audit the knowledge underlying their models.

In the following sections, we explain how AI can improve cybersecurity managerial efficiency within organizations through time management, complex decision-making, and communication, by using NLP, RL, and recommendation systems.

Involving AI in cybersecurity policies specifications

Cybersecurity management refers to comprehensive, safe, and secure information security operation management structures and practices (Li et al., 2019; Soomro et al., 2016). According to the National Institute of Standards and Technology (NIST) framework, effective cybersecurity management should include five phases: identification, protection, detection, response, and recovery (Whitman & Mattord, 2016). These stages are supported by policies and standards for mitigating organizational cybersecurity risks (Jaeger & Eckhardt, 2021). Organizations are constantly developing new procedures to raise employee awareness of cybersecurity practices' importance and encourage security-oriented behavior (Tsohou et al., 2015). Organizations ensure that their cybersecurity strategy applicable to human and technological resources is specified in policies, as stated by the UK National Cybersecurity Centre (HM Government, 2016).

Cybersecurity policies are a collection of statements management makes to protect the organization from internal or external security threats (Whitman & Mattord, 2016). Solid policies are the foundation of effective security programs (Whitman & Mattord, 2016). Security policies seek to create a productive and effective work environment by removing unnecessary distractions and inappropriate employee behavior.

Types of Policies

In cybersecurity, there are three types of security policies that an organization must define to establish the general strategic cybersecurity direction, provide specific and detailed instructions to solve cybersecurity issues, and provide procedures for configuring or maintaining systems. These are: enterprise information security policy (EISP), issue-specific security policy (ISSP), and system-specific security policy (SysSP). Swanson and Guttman (1996) from the NIST argue that organizations need to define these three types of policies to create a complete information security policy.

EISP is a high-level information security policy that sets the strategic direction, scope, and tone for all security efforts within an organization (Whitman & Mattord, 2016). It is a plan for the entire organization's security program, so it sets the security goals and implementation strategies. For example, in an EISP, a data security policy that describes the entire organization's data management, ownership, and encryption will remain relevant even as technical and organizational changes occur (Grimmick, 2022). The EISP document includes a statement of purpose, elements, needs, roles, responsibilities, and references (Whitman & Mattord, 2016). ISSP is an administrative policy that provides specific, detailed instructions to all organization members on using a resource (Whitman & Mattord, 2016). It describes a specific problem and provides security instructions to the appropriate employees to resolve it. For example, a remote access policy is an ISSP describing how and when employees can access company resources remotely (Grimmick, 2022). The ISSP document includes a statement of purpose, authorized and prohibited uses, system management, violation policy, policy review and modification, limitations, and liability (Whitman & Mattord, 2016). SysSP is an organizational policy that often functions as standards or procedures for configuring or maintaining systems (Whitman & Mattord, 2016). It is concerned with the security of a specific computer system, which means it is concerned with hardware, software, and technical infrastructure. For example, a security system policy describes which traffic an organization's firewall should allow or deny (Grimmick, 2022).

Although the components of EISP, ISSP, and SysSP differ, they all follow the same development and implementation guidelines in response to the increasing need for robust security measures in information systems. A framework and approach called Security System Development Life Cycle (SecSDLC) has been developed to tackle the issue of insufficient security practices and vulnerabilities (Whitman & Mattord, 2016). It is recommended that organizations use the SecSDLC to complete a successful policy development project, to ensure robustness in their security processes, to create a trustworthy information system that meets regulations, minimizes security risks, and earns the confidence of our customers. SecSDLC is a formal approach to designing information security programs that adheres to traditional information system development life cycle methodology (Whitman & Mattord, 2016).

Policy Specification Challenges

Investigation, analysis, design, implementation, and maintenance are different phases of the SecSDLC. The two first phases outline senior management involvement, clear articulation of goals, employee communities, essential reference materials to gather, and risk assessment. All the specifications and restrictions gathered during the investigation and analysis phases are presented in a detailed draft of the policy document during the design stage. This phase can be challenging for two main reasons: information availability and time and resource constraints (Whitman & Mattord, 2016). Organizations use external resources to gather information because they require assistance in developing a policy document from scratch. These resources include the web, government, professional literature, peer network, and reports to get ideas (Whitman & Mattord, 2016). This type of data collection can yield structured and unstructured data that is difficult to analyze due to the length of the documents, text complexity, language barrier, and complex structure (Ebrahimi et al., 2022). Consequently, this task can be accomplished effectively by using NLP.

Natural Language Processing

NLP refers to a computer's ability to read, listen to, and emit human language unambiguously and efficiently (Goodfellow et al., 2016). It is essentially a branch of AI concerned with making computers capable of understanding text and spoken words like humans do. NLP has many applications, including marketing, human resources, grammar checking, and cybersecurity (Kang et al., 2020). For example, in email spam filtering, NLP is an efficient alternative to decision tree models because it saves time and money in the long run due to self-learning, it reduces human intervention in maintenance and training, resulting in efficient resources, and it is efficient in sentiment analysis (Srinivasan et al., 2021). Furthermore, NLP can categorize text and construct hierarchies of categories from text data by identifying the corresponding type using semantically relevant text elements, allowing organizations to determine hierarchy in text data (Goodfellow et al., 2016). In addition, the ability of NLP to translate from foreign languages enables organizations to collect more data by generating multilingual text representations using generative adversarial networks to automatically extract transferable text representations and facilitate the analysis of multilingual content (Ebrahimi et al., 2022). Lastly, NLP enables the discovery of relationships between diverse information sources, allowing organizations to discover connections between texts by grouping them according to shared meaning and identifying the most prominent semantic drivers of those meanings (Bachura et al., 2022).

NLP-based Policy Specification Model

NLP has several advantages over other methods for developing cybersecurity policies. First, NLP is concerned with how computers interact with human language and how they precisely analyze and process vast amounts of natural language data (Goodfellow et al., 2016). As mentioned previously, cybersecurity policies are presented in written documents, and organizations' resources also consist of written text (Whitman & Mattord, 2016). In addition, NLP aims to make computers comprehend text in the same manner as humans (Kang et al., 2020). Therefore, NLP is better suited than other AI techniques for exploring and analyzing this type of data. Second, NLP employs semantic analysis focusing on analyzing text data to extract insightful information, such as context, and syntactic analysis, which checks the relationship between words and their global meaning and understanding (Goodfellow et al., 2016). Thus, NLP is best suited to comprehend the meaning of the data in the examined documents and their relevance to the task of implementing a cybersecurity policy.

Our proposed NLP-based policy development framework is illustrated in Figure 10.2. Phase 1 is the collection of data. Organizations must gather policy documents from the internet, government, professional literature, peer networks, and reports. These official documents can be obtained from official sources predefined for each country, organization, and professional. Thus, organizations can scrape and download policy documents from official websites. Additionally, organizations should add their internal management policy requirements documents to the collected documents. The second phase is preprocessing. Due to the variety of native formats including PDF, HTML, and Word, the document must be in plain text file format for computational processing. Thus, this preprocessing phase aims to convert all documents into simple text files, split each document into sentences since policies are written as sentences, and remove unnecessary tags using tools such as the National Language Toolkit (NLTK) library in Python (Hardeniya et al., 2016). The third phase is dynamic translation. Organizations must translate non-English documents in order to capitalize on them. For accurate translation, they can use AI deep adversarial representation learning to create a picture of the context in which the words are written (Ebrahimi et al., 2022). Phase 4 involves classification. Organizations should classify or categorize documents into the types of policy (EISP, ISSP, and SysSP). They could first use deep learning convolutional neural networks (CNNs) or recurrent neural networks (RNNs) to analyze and classify the document based on attributes such as document length and language model, and then use named entity recognition (NER) to identify and organize named entities (person, organization, location, date, and location) (Nadeau & Sekine, 2007). The fifth phase is search and extraction. Organizations would have a corpus of each type of policy from which they could search and extract relevant information using latent Dirichlet allocation (LDA), a technique for discovering and extracting hidden topics from text documents (Blei et al., 2003). The specificity and type of information contained by each type of policy (EISP, ISSP, and SysSP) will determine search and extraction.

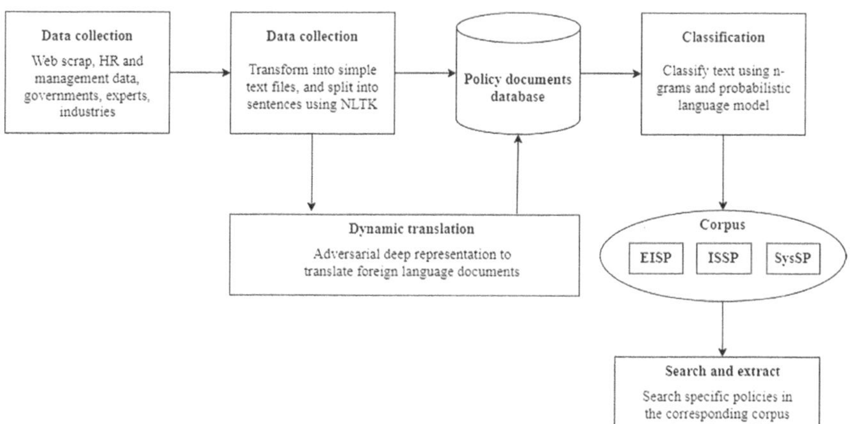

Source: Authors.

Figure 10.2 NLP-based policy development framework

NLP is a viable option for policy development because it can reduce policy analysis time from weeks to minutes (Planas et al., 2022) and automatically extract relevant text properties and characteristics (Goodfellow et al., 2016). For example, if cyberattacks originate in countries where organizations have already implemented appropriate policies, organizations would save time by using NLP for translating and analyzing these foreign policies (Ebrahimi et al., 2022). Second, because it can process massive text data, NLP ensures organizations full coverage of all policy documents that are electronically available in the various data sources identified, regardless of the number of documents (Goodfellow et al., 2016). Whitman and Mattord (2016) argue that for policies to be effective and legally defensible, they must meet the following criteria: (1) developed using industry-accepted practices; (2) distributed using all appropriate methods; (3) read by all employees; (4) comprehended by all employees; (5) formally agreed to by act or affirmation; (6) uniformly applied and enforced. NLP for policy development is a means of enhancing analytical capabilities. To effectively integrate it into their strategy, organizations must have a clear business plan for utilizing NLP, the required technical, data science, and management skills for NLP, the required technology platforms and computation power for data collection and NLP model-building, and an NLP pipeline that is integrated upstream into their continuity strategy.

Managerial Implications

NLP for policy development has several managerial implications. First, using NLP for dynamic and contextual translation of policies would remove language barriers and increase document completeness, making external resources more accessible. If organizations were limited to their geographic area in the document collection, they could now collect industry data worldwide. Second, NLP would maintain the textual data's structure, making it easier for managers to consult documents and update policies. Thus, managers could use policy mapping based on NLP analysis to find information without going through all the documents. These reports help allocate cybersecurity mitigation and investment funds. Finally, managers could save on cybersecurity policy consultants. Implementing an NLP-based system may be costly, but hiring consultants to create it may be costly financially, in terms of availability because they are present for a well-defined mandate, and in terms of knowledge because they leave with their knowledge.

AI-based system to improve policy compliance

Humans are identified in the literature as the weakest link in an organization's cybersecurity (Kweon et al., 2021). Employee noncompliance reduces cybersecurity regardless of policy effectiveness (Fügener et al., 2022). According to Forbes Expert Panel (2021), top employees' policy violations include never turning the equipment off, personal use of company equipment, carelessness with emails, bad passwords, using unapproved software, not updating systems, and using insecure internet. Policies underpin cybersecurity programs (Whitman & Mattord, 2016). Thus, if a policy includes behaviors no one is expected to follow, compliance with other parts will be weakened (Coventry et al., 2014).

Cram et al. (2020) recommend that organizations hire employees with a positive and ethical attitude toward cybersecurity, establish a commitment to cybersecurity initiatives, provide cybersecurity training, assist employees with their compliance intentions, and highlight the benefits of compliance to maximize employee compliance with cybersecurity policies.

These recommendations, however, have significant limitations. First, employees can prepare themselves for job interviews on cybersecurity topics even if they are not interested in or believe that basic cybersecurity knowledge is sufficient. Second, an organization's commitment to cybersecurity may be less effective because users' awareness is dependent on their willingness to follow policies (McCormac et al., 2017). Third, while training is beneficial, employees can become tired of it and see it as a burden rather than a solution (Cram et al., 2021). Finally, policies may be perceived differently by different employees in other roles, departments, and locations (Cram et al., 2020).

Cram et al. (2020) recommend providing employees with the resources necessary to comply with the cybersecurity policy. These resources may be technological, such as RL. RL is a subfield of machine learning concerned with how intelligent agents should behave in an environment to maximize cumulative rewards (El-Alfy & Mohammed, 2020).[1] RL is characterized by an agent interacting directly with its environment and generating learning experiences. The core concepts of RL are state, action, and reward (El-Alfy & Mohammed, 2020). The agent employs a trial-and-error strategy in which it takes actions that alter the current state of the environment and receives a reward or penalty from the environment, where the reward is a function that indicates how good or bad an action is (Russell & Norvig, 2010).

RL can be an effective approach to cybersecurity for three reasons. First, in both supervised and unsupervised learning, each observation in the data is independent (i.e., each line represents a unique, unrelated case) (Sarker et al., 2021). However, the actions employees take during their work constitute a series of interdependent events. In addition, the data is represented by a dynamic environment that would be challenging to represent in a table with rows and columns. Due to its suitability for a dynamic environment and sequence of actions as input data, RL is a superior solution for this type of problem. Second, both supervised and unsupervised learning make decisions based on the initial data they are given after training and cannot self-correct for poor decisions (Sarker et al., 2021). RL can adapt the agent's state and subsequent decisions based on the agent's previous state (Russell & Norvig, 2010). In a cybersecurity context, for instance, RL could use the user's action sequence to determine if s/he is permitted to access a resource. Thirdly, the objective of RL is to maximize a score based on the positive and negative rewards it receives for these real-time actions (Russell & Norvig, 2010). Consequently, RL is better aligned than other learning techniques with regard to compliance or violation of cybersecurity policies, which also results from employees' real-time actions.

Reinforcement Learning to Help Employees with Compliance

In cybersecurity, RL can be used locally, on employees' devices, or on the company's network (Nguyen & Reddi, 2021). Because there are various types of policies (EISP, ISSP, and SysSP), RL should be tailored to each to ensure they are all adequately covered. When standards, guidelines, and procedures are developed, EISP is supposed to be followed (Whitman & Mattord, 2016). ISSP and SysSP, on the other hand, are specific, allowing RL to learn the state promoted by the policy and determine whether or not it is respected. A policy, for example, can specify restricted access to resources such as data. If an employee attempts to access them, the agent can notify them of the impending policy violation and block access to this resource. Furthermore, if a policy requires employees to turn off their computers every day after work, and some employees forget, the agent can notify the employee's inactivity and turn off the devices. Another example is a policy requiring employees to use a secure or virtual private network when working abroad. The agent can learn a secure network's signature, detect a nonsecure network, and avoid connection. There are three approaches to implementing RL in cybersecurity: value-based, policy-gradient, and actor-critic. Value-based approaches are best suited to problems with discrete action spaces, whereas policy-gradient and actor-critic approaches are better suited to problems with continuous action spaces (Nguyen & Reddi, 2021). The environment in which the agents will evolve and learn is the network logs of the organizations (Nguyen & Reddi,

2021). RL can solve complex, dynamic, and particularly high-dimensional cyber-defense problems.

Organizations frequently face ethical issues when collecting data. Because of data collection legislation, organizations are not permitted to collect employee data. RL does not collect data; instead, the agent develops a behavior based on actions classified as good or bad. Organizations should define clear objectives for RL implementation in information systems to align with their business requirements. Because it does not require massive and labeled datasets, RL is a good solution for policy compliance. Furthermore, it can be used for sequences of actions, whereas supervised learning is predominantly used in an input–output manner. Finally, RL does not require retraining because it adapts to new environments automatically.

Managerial Implications

RL for cybersecurity has several managerial implications. First, using RL to help employees better comply with cybersecurity policies can aid managers' efforts to automatically assign, sense, and respond to their teams' individual needs in real time with appropriate responses. Thus, managers would communicate cybersecurity concepts to users in real time via the RL channel. Second, RL could optimize expenses, organization efforts, and employee time spent on awareness campaigns so managers could focus on employees with an approach based on user–machine interaction. Thus, various managerial teams of the organizations could better collaborate on how the RL agent should respond to the various actions. Third, using RL will save organizations money because it allows them to run tests in simulation environments to determine where their teams fall short of cybersecurity policy compliance. Organizations can train their various agents by simulating their existing systems in a simulation environment. Managers would be able to make decisions upstream, such as increasing awareness campaigns on a specific topic. As a result, they would avoid making decisions in the aftermath of a security breach that could cost them money and reputation.

SETA recommendation system

Employees' compliance with policies is central to studies examining the role of employees' behavior in cybersecurity (Yazdanmehr & Wang, 2021). Compliance with cybersecurity policies refers to accepting organizational standards and regulatory requirements to secure information assets (Cram et al., 2020). Thus, organizations invest in learning programs to raise employee awareness of cybersecurity policy compliance and boost self-efficacy. Self-efficacy is an individual's perception of their capability to perform specific actions (Xue et al., 2021). To accomplish this, organizations run SETA programs. All the knowledge and skills necessary to become an IT security specialist or professional are integrated into security education, including formal coursework (Kweon et al., 2021). Security training involves providing organization members with detailed information and hands-on cybersecurity instruction skills to prepare them to perform tasks securely (Kweon et al., 2021). The awareness training aims to improve a person's capacity to identify and address cybersecurity issues. It is intended to keep users' minds focused on information security (Kweon et al., 2021). Despite increasing efforts invested in SETA programs, employees misunderstand, disregard, and even purposefully violate policies (Chen et al., 2021). Employees do in fact view SETA programs more as a burden than a solution (Cram et al., 2021; Kweon et al., 2021). Employees have a limited capacity for memory retention, so they can only retain some of what they learn (Kweon et al., 2021). Employees may also be less willing to follow policies if they need assistance remembering and fulfilling their obligations (Whitman & Mattord, 2016). Employees continue to act carelessly and unsafely as a result, leaving vulnerable organizations open to security breaches. By spending money on learning programs that are not effectively delivered to the employee, organizations also lose money (Chen et al., 2021).

An organization's cybersecurity program relies on SETA (Kweon et al., 2021). A robust and relevant information security awareness and training program encourages employees to learn and use the information and tools needed to protect an organization's critical information (Caballero, 2017; Xue et al., 2021). Organizations that train employees in cybersecurity policies and role-based security responsibilities can better protect data (Bowen et al., 2007). The Federal Information Security Management Act (FISMA) suggests that cybersecurity education must receive more and better attention (Bowen et al., 2007).

Cybersecurity is a human issue for SETA (Burns et al., 2017). Thus, depending on the targeted employee groups within the organization, it aims to raise awareness, train, and educate all members of the organization on responsible cybersecurity behavior (Kweon et al., 2021). Awareness answers the question "what?" It's about educating employees about good and bad cybersecurity practices (Caballero, 2017). It employs teaching methods such as videos, newsletters, and posters, with a short-term impact (Caballero, 2017). The answer to the question "how?" is training. It is about providing knowledge to organization members in order for them to gain practical skills in order to solve cybersecurity problems (Caballero, 2017). For an intermediate impact timeframe, its teaching methods include lectures, case study workshops, and hands-on practice (Caballero, 2017). The question "Why?" is answered by education. It helps members of the organization understand and interpret cybersecurity concepts (Caballero, 2017). For a long-term impact timeframe, its teaching methods are discussion seminars and background reading (Caballero, 2017).

Instead of overloading employees with numerous courses, some of which are out of context, organizations should use machine learning recommender systems to recommend learning programs based on the needs of their employees. The recommender systems aim to predict a user's rating or preference for an item (Han et al., 2022). They are essential in several industries because they optimize income and provide organizations with a significant competitive advantage. For example, Netflix held a challenge (Netflix Prize) in 2009 to develop a better recommender system that would allow them to offer their customers content better suited to their needs and thus take the lead among video-on-demand companies (Rocca, 2019). There are two broad types of recommendation systems, collaborative filtering and content-based. Collaborative filtering recommendation systems use inputs from sources other than the user receiving the recommendation (Sarwar et al., 2001). It is appropriate when there is no information about the user and works on the similarity or association of the items. Content-based recommendation systems recommend based on the user's previous actions and improve over time (Pazzani & Billsus, 2007).

Implementing a SETA recommendation system in organizations is similar to a video-on-demand recommendation system, except that organizations own users' and course data.

The SETA learning programs recommendation system we suggest is shown in Figure 10.3. Business understanding is the first phase. Organizations should have a clear idea of their goals and parameters of the project by discussing with employees and different directions. They should explain that implementing a recommendation system will give employees the appropriate training program. Phase 2 is data collection. Organizations should seek data. Human resources departments typically have data on employees' ages, genders, roles, locations, system accreditation, and other personal information. Employee electronic actions, such as resource usage and emails, are recorded in logs by the information systems department. Moreover, SETA learning programs teams will have data about courses such as length, department, roles, specific issues, and systems. These are not exhaustive lists, and much more information could be included. The third stage is data preprocessing. Organizations should use NLP and statistical approaches to explore, clean, and prepare the data, eliminating nonrelevant business variables and transforming the remaining data in the correct format. Phase 4 is a recommendation. Because organizations have a limited number of employees and learning programs, they could use a machine learning probabilistic association rule and frequent itemset methods to consider a recommendation as an interaction between employee roles and course features.

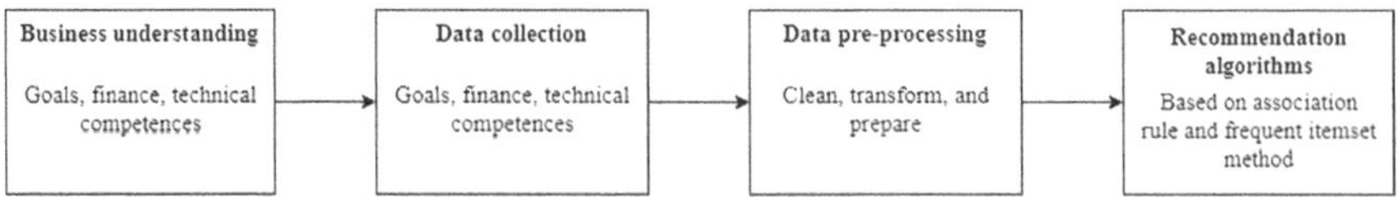

Source: Authors.

Figure 10.3 SETA learning programs recommendation system

Managerial Implications

Using a recommender system in the context of cybersecurity has several managerial implications. First, the recommender system seeks to segment elements important to the user (Han et al., 2022). Aside from systematically gathering and analyzing information about users' profiles, it also allows users to provide information that helps the system continuously adapt its recommendations. It enables managers to make the right decision at the right time to complete the mission quickly and efficiently, with minimal errors, and in accordance with the users' expectations. As a result, managers can ensure that employees spend as little time as possible on learning programs irrelevant to their jobs. Second, a recommender system could improve its user experience and engagement with cybersecurity learning programs by providing employees with the needed and desired content. As a result, managers would receive less resistance and more interest from employees in learning about cybersecurity policies. Third, a recommender system would reduce managers' workload by providing them with a strategic tool that would allow them to focus their efforts on increasing employee awareness. Managers would also save time allocating cybersecurity learning programs because they would have a dynamic and adaptive tool. Assume an employee is temporarily assigned to another department or has access to new resources. In this case, managers would not have to look for learning resources that match the employee's new responsibilities but could instead rely on the recommendation system. Managers could then devote their time to other organizational challenges.

Conclusion

In light of the current global DT, this chapter emphasizes the potential of using AI for cybersecurity management. We started by defining the various security difficulties brought on by DT. We have proposed three strategies to assist managers in enhancing their organizations' cybersecurity management. These include the use of NLP for the creation of cybersecurity policies, the use of recommendation algorithms to better suggest cybersecurity learning materials to employees, and the use of an intelligent agent based on RL to provide feedback to workers who exhibit risky behaviors. The AI methods outlined in this chapter are extensively used for profit in other fields. However, they can also be effectively used to manage cybersecurity. Effective implementation of these proposals will enable the practical implications recommended for each strategy to be realized.

Note

1. Machine learning, which is a subfield of AI that enables computers to learn without being explicitly programmed to solve a problem, is divided into four learning families: supervised, semi-supervised, unsupervised, and reinforcement learning.

References

Abbas, N. N., Ahmed, T., Shah, S. H. U., Omar, M., & Park, H. W. (2019). Investigating the applications of artificial intelligence in cyber security. *Scientometrics*, *121*(2), 1189–1211.

Al Nafea, R., & Almaiah, M. A. (2021). Cyber security threats in cloud: Literature review. *2021 International Conference on Information Technology (ICIT)*, 779–786.

Bachura, E., Valecha, R., Chen, R., & Rao, H. R. (2022). The OPM data breach: An investigation of shared emotional reactions on Twitter. *MIS Quarterly*, *46*(2), 881–910.

Berente, N., Gu, B., Recker, J., & Santhanam, R. (2021). Managing artificial intelligence. *MIS Quarterly*, *45*(3), 1433–1450.

Bitton, R., Maman, N., Elovici, Y., Shabtai, A., Singh, I., & Momiyama, S. (2021). Evaluating the cybersecurity risk of real-world, machine learning production systems. *ACM Computing Surveys (CSUR)*. https:// doi .org/ 10 .48550/ arXiv .2107 .01806.

Blei, D. M., Ng, A. Y., & Jordan, M. I. (2003). Latent Dirichlet allocation. *Journal of Machine Learning Research*, *3*, 993–1022.

Bowen, P., Hash, J., & Wilson, M. (2007). NIST special publication 800–100. Information security handbook: A guide for managers. https://nvlpubs.nist.gov/nistpubs/Legacy/SP/nistspecialpublication800-100.pdf.

Burns, A., Posey, C., Courtney, J. F., Roberts, T. L., & Nanayakkara, P. (2017). Organizational information security as a complex adaptive system: Insights from three agent-based models. *Information Systems Frontiers, 19*(3), 509–524.

Caballero, A. (2017). Information security essentials for IT managers: Protecting mission-critical systems. In J. R. Vacca (Ed.), *Computer and Information Security Handbook* (pp. 242–253). Morgan Kaufmann.

Chen, Y., Galletta, D. F., Lowry, P. B., Luo, X., Moody, G. D., & Willison, R. (2021). Understanding inconsistent employee compliance with information security policies through the lens of the extended parallel process model. *Information Systems Research, 32*(3), 1043–1065.

Coventry, L., Briggs, P., Blythe, J., & Tran, M. (2014). Using behavioural insights to improve the public's use of cyber security best practices. Government Office for Science. https:// discovery .ucl .ac .uk/ id/ eprint/ 1508276/ 1/ using _behavioural _insights_cybersecurity.pdf.

Cram, W. A., D'Arcy, J., & Proudfoot, J. G. (2019). Seeing the forest and the trees: A meta-analysis of the antecedents to information security policy compliance. *MIS Quarterly, 43*(2), 525–554.

Cram, W. A., Proudfoot, J. G., & D'Arcy, J. (2020). Maximizing employee compliance with cybersecurity policies. *MIS Quarterly Executive, 19*(3). https://doi.org/10.17705/2msqe.00032.

Cram, W. A., Proudfoot, J. G., & D'Arcy, J. (2021). When enough is enough: Investigating the antecedents and consequences of information security fatigue. *Information Systems Journal, 31*(4), 521–549.

D'Arcy, J., & Basoglu, A. (2022). The influences of public and institutional pressure on firms' cybersecurity disclosures. *Journal of the Association for Information Systems, 23*(3), 779–805.

Devine, S., & Bastian, N. (2021). An adversarial training-based machine learning approach to malware classification under adversarial conditions. *Proceedings of the 54th Hawaii International Conference on System Sciences*, 1–10.

Dremel, C., Wulf, J., Herterich, M. M., Waizmann, J.-C., & Brenner, W. (2017). How AUDI AG established big data analytics in its digital transformation. *MIS Quarterly Executive, 16*(2), 81–100.

Ebrahimi, M., Chai, Y., Samtani, S., & Chen, H. (2022). Cross-lingual cybersecurity analytics in the international dark web with adversarial deep representation learning. *MIS Quarterly, 46*(2), 1209–1226.

El-Alfy, E.-S. M., & Mohammed, S. A. (2020). A review of machine learning for big data analytics: Bibliometric approach. *Technology Analysis & Strategic Management, 32*(8), 984–1005.

FBI (2021). Internet crime report 2021. Federal Bureau of Investigation. https://www.ic3.gov/Media/PDF/AnnualReport/2021_IC3Report.pdf.

Forbes Expert Panel (2021). 13 bad habits that can compromise company tech devices and cybersecurity. Forbes. https://www.forbes.com/sites/forbestechcouncil/2021/10/12/13-bad-habits-that-can-compromise-company-tech-devices-and-cybersecurity/?sh=bd0490458874.

Fügener, A., Grahl, J., Gupta, A., & Ketter, W. (2022). Cognitive challenges in human–artificial intelligence collaboration: Investigating the path toward productive delegation. *Information Systems Research, 33*(2), 678–696.

Goodfellow, I., Bengio, Y., & Courville, A. (2016). Applications. In I. Goodfellow, Y. Bengio & A. Courville, *Deep Learning* (pp. 443–478). MIT Press.

Grimmick, R. (2022). What is a security policy? Definition, elements, and examples. *Inside Out Security*. https://www.varonis.com/blog/what-is-a-security-policy.

Gurbaxani, V., & Dunkle, D. (2019). Gearing up for successful digital transformation. *MIS Quarterly Executive, 18*(3), 6.

Hai, T. N., Van, Q. N., & Thi Tuyet, M. (2021). Digital transformation: Opportunities and challenges for leaders in the emerging countries in response to COVID-19 pandemic. *Emerging Science Journal, 5*, 21–36.

Han, J., Pei, J., & Tong, H. (2022). *Data Mining: Concepts and Techniques*. Morgan Kaufmann.

Hardeniya, N., Perkins, J., Chopra, D., Joshi, N., & Mathur, I. (2016). *Natural Language Processing: Python and NLTK*. Packt Publishing.

Hartmann, P. M., Zaki, M., Feldmann, N., & Neely, A. (2016). Capturing value from big data: A taxonomy of data-driven business models used by start-up firms. *International Journal of Operations & Production Management, 36*(10), 1382–1406.

Hess, T., Matt, C., Benlian, A., & Wiesböck, F. (2016). Options for formulating a digital transformation strategy. *MIS Quarterly Executive, 15*(2), 123–139.

HM Government (2016). National cyber security strategy 2016–2021. https://assets.publishing.service.gov.uk/government/uploads/system/uploads/attachment_data/file/567242/national_cyber_security_strategy_2016.pdf.

Jaeger, L., & Eckhardt, A. (2021). Eyes wide open: The role of situational information security awareness for security-related behaviour. *Information Systems Journal, 31*(3), 429–472.

Jain, H., Padmanabhan, B., Pavlou, P. A., & Raghu, T. S. (2021). Editorial for the special section on humans, algorithms, and augmented intelligence: The future of work, organizations, and society. *Information Systems Research, 32*(3), 675–687.

Kabanov, I., & Madnick, S. (2021). Applying the lessons from the equifax cybersecurity incident to build a better defense. *MIS Quarterly Executive, 20*(2), 4.

Kaloudi, N., & Li, J. (2020). The AI-based cyber threat landscape: A survey. *ACM Computing Surveys, 53*(1), 1–31.

Kang, Y., Cai, Z., Tan, C.-W., Huang, Q., & Liu, H. (2020). Natural language processing (NLP) in management research: A literature review. *Journal of Management Analytics, 7*(2), 139–172.

Kumar, A., Glisson, W., & Benton, R. (2020). Network attack detection using an unsupervised machine learning algorithm. *Proceedings of the 53rd Hawaii International Conference on System Sciences*, 6496–6505. https://doi.org/10.24251/HICSS.2020.795.

Kweon, E., Lee, H., Chai, S., & Yoo, K. (2021). The utility of information security training and education on cybersecurity incidents: An empirical evidence. *Information Systems Frontiers, 23*(2), 361–373.

Li, L., He, W., Xu, L., Ash, I., Anwar, M., & Yuan, X. (2019). Investigating the impact of cybersecurity policy awareness on employees' cybersecurity behavior. *International Journal of Information Management, 45*(7), 13–24.

Loebbecke, C., El Sawy, O. A., Kankanhalli, A., Markus, M. L., Te'Eni, D., Wrobel, S., Rydén, P., & Obeng-Antwi, A. (2020). Artificial intelligence meets is researchers: Can it replace us? *Communications of the Association for Information Systems, 47*(1), 48.

McCormac, A., Zwaans, T., Parsons, K., Calic, D., Butavicius, M., & Pattinson, M. (2017). Individual differences and information security awareness. *Computers in Human Behavior, 69*, 151–156.

Mendhurwar, S., & Mishra, R. (2021). Integration of social and IoT technologies: Architectural framework for digital transformation and cyber security challenges. *Enterprise Information Systems, 15*(4), 565–584.

Mou, J., Cohen, J. F., Bhattacherjee, A., & Kim, J. (2022). A test of protection motivation theory in the information security literature: A meta-analytic structural equation modeling approach. *Journal of the Association for Information Systems, 23*(1), 196–236.

Nadeau, D., & Sekine, S. (2007). A survey of named entity recognition and classification. *Lingvisticae Investigationes, 30*(1), 3–26.

Naseer, A., Naseer, H., Ahmad, A., Maynard, S. B., & Siddiqui, A. M. (2021). Real-time analytics, incident response process agility and enterprise cybersecurity performance: A contingent resource-based analysis. *International Journal of Information Management, 59*(8), 102334.

Naseer, H., Ahmad, A., Maynard, S. B., & Shanks, G. (2018). Cybersecurity risk management using analytics: A dynamic capabilities approach. *39th International Conference on Information Systems, San Francisco.* https:// web .archive .org/ web/ 20210812092158id _/ https:// aisel .aisnet .org/ cgi/ viewcontent .cgi ?article = 1063 & context=icis2018.

Nguyen, T. T., & Reddi, V. J. (2021). Deep reinforcement learning for cyber security. *IEEE Transactions on Neural Networks and Learning Systems, 34*(8), 3779–3795.

Obaidat, I., Sridhar, M., Pham, K. M., & Phung, P. H. (2022). Jadeite: A novel image-behavior-based approach for Java malware detection using deep learning. *Computers & Security, 113*, 102547.

Pan, J., & Yang, Z. (2018). Cybersecurity challenges and opportunities in the new "edge computing + IoT" world. *Proceedings of the 2018 ACM International Workshop on Security in Software Defined Networks & Network Function Virtualization*, 29–32.

Pang, M.-S., & Tanriverdi, H. (2022). Strategic roles of IT modernization and cloud migration in reducing cybersecurity risks of organizations: The case of US federal government. *The Journal of Strategic Information Systems, 31*(1), 101707.

Pazzani, M. J., & Billsus, D. (2007). Content-based recommendation systems. In P. Brusilovsky, A. Kobsa, & W. Nejdl (Eds.), *The Adaptive Web: Methods and Strategies of Web Personalization* (pp. 325–341). Springer.

Planas, J., Firebanks-Quevedo, D., Naydenova, G., Sharma, R., Taylor, C., Buckingham, K., & Fang, R. (2022). Beyond modeling: NLP pipeline for efficient environmental policy analysis. https://arxiv.org/abs/2201.07105.

Rai, A., Constantinides, P., & Sarker, S. (2019). Next generation digital platforms: Toward human-AI hybrids. *MIS Quarterly, 43*(1), iii–ix.

Raisch, S., & Krakowski, S. (2021). Artificial intelligence and management: The automation–augmentation paradox. *Academy of Management Review, 46*(1), 192–210.

Rocca, B. (2019). Introduction to recommender systems: Overview of some major recommendation algorithms. Towards Data Science. https:// towardsdatascience.com/ introduction-to-recommender-systems-6c66cf15ada.

Russell, S., & Norvig, P. (2010). Reinforcement learning. In S. Russell & P. Norvig, *Artificial Intelligence: A Modern Approach* (pp. 789–821). Pearson.

Samtani, S., Chai, Y., & Chen, H. (2022). Linking exploits from the dark web to known vulnerabilities for proactive cyber threat intelligence: An attention-based deep structured semantic model. *MIS Quarterly*, *46*(2), 911–946.

Sarker, I. H., Furhad, M. H., & Nowrozy, R. (2021). AI-driven cybersecurity: An overview, security intelligence modeling and research directions. *SN Computer Science*, *2*(3), 1–18.

Sarwar, B., Karypis, G., Konstan, J., & Riedl, J. (2001). Item-based collaborative filtering: Recommendation algorithms. *Proceedings of the 10th International Conference on World Wide Web*, 285–295.

Sipior, J. (2021). Monitoring remote employees at FinPro. *Communications of the Association for Information Systems*, *49*(1), 14.

Siroya, N., & Mandot, M. (2021). Role of AI in cyber security. In N. Bhargava, R. Bhargava, P. Singh Rathore, & R. Agrawal (Eds.), *Artificial Intelligence and Data Mining Approaches in Security Frameworks* (pp. 1–9). Scrivener.

Soomro, Z. A., Shah, M. H., & Ahmed, J. (2016). Information security management needs more holistic approach: A literature review. *International Journal of Information Management*, *36*(2), 215.

Srinivasan, S., Ravi, V., Alazab, M., Ketha, S., Al-Zoubi, A. M., & Kotti Padannayil, S. (2021). Spam emails detection based on distributed word embedding with deep learning. In Y. Maleh, M. Shojafar, M. Alazab, & Y. Baddi (Eds.), *Machine Intelligence and Big Data Analytics for Cybersecurity Applications* (pp. 161–189). Springer.

Swanson, M., & Guttman, B. (1996). *Generally Accepted Principles and Practices for Securing Information Technology Systems*. National Institute of Standards and Technology, Technology Administration, US Department of Commerce.

Tan, F. T. C., Ondrus, J., Tan, B., & Oh, J. (2020). Digital transformation of business ecosystems: Evidence from the Korean pop industry. *Information Systems Journal*, *30*(5), 866–898.

Taylor, A., & Associated Press. (2017). IRS: Computer breach bigger than first thought, with 700K victims. NewsHour Productions. https://www.pbs.org/newshour/politics/irs-computer-breach-bigger-than-first-thought-with-700k-victims.

Tsohou, A., Karyda, M., Kokolakis, S., & Kiountouzis, E. (2015). Managing the introduction of information security awareness programmes in organisations. *European Journal of Information Systems*, *24*(1), 38–58.

Turton, W. (2021). Hackers breach thousands of security cameras, exposing Tesla, jails, hospitals. https://www.bloomberg.com/news/articles/2021-03-09/hackers-expose-tesla-jails-in-breach-of-150-000-security-cams.

Uchendu, B., Nurse, J. R. C., Bada, M., & Furnell, S. (2021). Developing a cyber security culture: Current practices and future needs. *Computers & Security*, *109*, 1.

Vance, A., Eargle, D., Eggett, D., Straub, D. W., & Ouimet, K. (2022). Do security fear appeals work when they interrupt tasks? A multi-method examination of password strength. *MIS Quarterly*, *46*(3). https://doi.org/10.25300/MISQ/2022/15511.

Vial, G. (2019). Understanding digital transformation: A review and a research agenda. *The Journal of Strategic Information Systems*, *28*(2), 118–144.

Weill, P., & Woerner, S. L. (2018). Is your company ready for a digital future? *MIT Sloan Management Review*, *59*(2), 21–25.

Wessel, L., Baiyere, A., Ologeanu-Taddei, R., Cha, J., & Blegind Jensen, T. (2020). Unpacking the difference between digital transformation and IT-enabled organizational transformation. *Journal of the Association for Information Systems*, *22*(1), 102–129.

Westenberger, J., Schuler, K., & Schlegel, D. (2022). Failure of AI projects: Understanding the critical factors. *Procedia Computer Science*, *196*(2), 69–76.
Whitman, M. E., & Mattord, H. J. (2016). Information security policy. In M. E. Whitman & H. J. Mattord, *Management of Information Security* (pp. 169–209). Cengage Learning.
Xue, B., Warkentin, M., Mutchler, L. A., & Balozian, P. (2021). Self-efficacy in information security: A replication study. *Journal of Computer Information Systems*, *63*(11), 1–10.
Yazdanmehr, A., & Wang, J. (2021). Can peers help reduce violations of information security policies? The role of peer monitoring. *European Journal of Information Systems*, *32*(3), 1–21.
Zeadally, S., Adi, E., Baig, Z., & Khan, I. A. (2020). Harnessing artificial intelligence capabilities to improve cybersecurity. *IEEE Access*, *8*, 23817–23837.
Zeadally, S., & Tsikerdekis, M. (2020). Securing internet of things (IoT) with machine learning. *International Journal of Communication Systems*, *33*(1), e4169.

11 Data analysis for digital transformation: the example of willingness to share personal information

Christopher Schumacher, Felix Eggers, Peter C. Verhoef and Peter Maas

Digital transformation refers to firms integrating digital technologies into their business operations to fundamentally change the way they do business. As such, digital transformation can be regarded as a change catalyst. In an increasingly global and digital world, in which consumer data are relatively accessible and information-technology capabilities are continually expanding, firms have unparalleled opportunities to collect, analyze, and exploit consumer data to create value (Beke et al., 2018). The amount of data that consumers provide—willingly or unwillingly—is skyrocketing (Wedel & Kannan, 2016). However, as data become more readily available, customer databases become considerably larger and noisier; firms must handle, select, analyze, and interpret customer data to create valuable insights and provide consumer-specific solutions. Addressing consumers' heterogeneous needs and preferences within and across countries constitutes a considerable challenge for firms (Steenkamp & Ter Hofstede, 2002). Therefore, international market segmentation poses a significant challenge (Douglas & Craig, 2006).

On some factors, such as sharing personal information with firms, consumers from different countries may have more in common than consumers from the same country. Notably, none of the many rigorous segmentation studies (e.g., De Keyser et al., 2015; Herhausen et al., 2019; Konuş et al., 2008) consider information-sharing tendencies. Therefore, we propose that consumers' willingness to share (WTS) personal information with firms offers a viable segmentation basis. WTS has attracted considerable attention in marketing (Bleier et al., 2020; Eggers et al., 2023; John et al., 2011), information systems (Dinev & Hart, 2006; Malhotra et al., 2004; Smith et al., 1996), and organizational studies (Culnan & Armstrong, 1999). Additionally, we consider the privacy calculus (Beke et al., 2022; Culnan & Bies, 2003; Laufer & Wolfe, 1977) and consumers' relationships with firms (White, 2004) as potentially relevant segmentation criteria that may offer valuable insight into consumer decision-making processes in information-sharing contexts. The privacy calculus has been neglected in prior segmentation studies despite being viewed as essential in the information-sharing literature; it reflects both the costs (e.g., privacy concerns) and benefits (e.g., personalization) of sharing information (Culnan & Bies, 2003). Furthermore, we argue that consumers' relationships with firms are related to and help to predict WTS (White, 2004). We assess the relationship quality with various indicators, including trust (Kehr et al., 2015), satisfaction (Verhoef, 2003), word of mouth (WOM) (Zeithaml et al., 1996), and behavioral intention/loyalty (Cronin et al., 2000). To account for sociodemographic differences within and across countries, we control for gender, age, and income (Reynolds et al., 2003). Furthermore, existing research has shown that WTS is influenced by the sensitivity of information being requested (Eggers et al., 2023; Malhotra et al., 2004). Considering different types of information allows firms to better segment their customers. Thus, we consider information type in our international market segmentation, enabling us to draw more nuanced conclusions about consumers' data-sharing behaviors. Thus, overall, we consider perspectives from both the supply side (i.e., the firm) and the demand side (i.e., the consumer).

In light of the aforementioned research gaps, the purpose of this chapter is to perform a global market segmentation based on WTS that identifies consumer segments and country classes. In turn, we emphasize the importance and relevance of international market segmentation in the international marketing literature. Using multilevel latent class analysis (LCA), we segment 15,068 consumers across 24 countries based on WTS. We find three managerially meaningful consumer segments and two country classes that predict WTS. We label the consumer segments as follows: privacy-concerned consumers (segment size: 20.41 percent), privacy pragmatists (segment size: 51.40 percent), and relationship-seekers (segment size: 20.62 percent). Privacy-concerned consumers are characterized by their privacy concerns. Privacy pragmatists share personal information when they feel that doing so is worthwhile. Relationship-seekers tend to willingly share information, recognizing and appreciating the benefits they gain from such exchanges. The two country classes represent data-prone countries (50.6 percent) and data-reluctant countries (49.4 percent). Consumers in data-prone countries are more likely than those in data-reluctant countries to share their personal information with firms.

Our empirical findings illustrate significant differences both within and across countries, thereby contributing to the literature on information sharing, international market segmentation, and international marketing in three main ways. First—to the best of our knowledge—this is the first global segmentation study to investigate WTS while considering the privacy calculus and consumers' relationships with firms. We highlight the need to explore WTS more deeply—especially in the increasingly global world with skyrocketing amounts of consumer data—to enable firms to more precisely profile consumers and aim solutions at individual needs and preferences (Wedel & Kannan, 2016). In addition to establishing consumer segments and country classes, we suggest some critical variables to include in future segmentation efforts.

Second, our multilevel LCA simultaneously includes individual- and country-level influences, addressing calls for rigorous global research into international consumer segments (Burgess & Steenkamp, 2006; Steenkamp & Ter Hofstede, 2002). Our empirical findings show significant differences at both the individual and country levels, contributing to the debate on standardization versus adaptation in international market segmentation (Agarwal et al., 2010; Kraus et al., 2016). In contrast to prior segmentation studies, which have largely grouped consumers by country (Steenkamp & Ter Hofstede, 2002), we show that consumers from different countries have more in common than consumers from the same country and that regional proximity (on a country level) does not imply similar country class membership. Thus, we recommend mixed international market segmentation strategies with as much standardization as possible at the global level but as much customization as possible on the country and individual levels. This approach combines the benefits of standardization and adaptation by considering both cross-national and cross-cultural market segments (Agarwal et al., 2010).

Third, we advance discussions on the economic value of personal information (John et al., 2011) by providing insights into consumer decision-making processes through the consideration of information sensitivity (Eggers et al., 2023; Malhotra et al., 2004). Our findings show to what extent highly sensitive information is associated with a low likelihood of sharing (i.e., a low WTS). Among all identified segments, demographic information is shared most eagerly, followed by behavioral information. More sensitive information, such as health and financial information, is considerably less likely to be shared. Thus, consumers are protective of more sensitive information. Accordingly, we show the positive relationship between the economic value and sensitivity of personal information.

This chapter proceeds as follows. First, we develop our conceptual model and introduce the segmentation variables and covariates. Second, we detail our processes of data collection, measurement operationalization, and controlling for data equivalence and common method variance (CMV). Third, we present our empirical findings and discuss the various consumer segments and country classes. Finally, we elaborate on the managerial implications of our findings, the limitations of this study, and future research opportunities.

Theoretical background

Prior Segmentation Studies

Westin (1967) was the first to segment consumers based on privacy considerations. He proposed three essential categories: (1) "privacy fundamentalists," who are strongly concerned about their privacy and less willing to share personal information, (2) "privacy pragmatists," who are concerned about privacy but to a lesser extent, and (3) "privacy unconcerned," who have low privacy concerns and are largely willing to share personal information.

In a study of U.S. internet users' privacy preferences, Ackerman et al. (1999) confirmed the segments identified by Westin (1967) using a multivariate clustering technique. They argued that it is hardly possible to complete transactions online without revealing at least some personal information (e.g., billing information, shipping address). One of their key findings is that consumers are less likely to share personal information if the required information is personally identifiable. Strikingly, while consumers' comfort levels vary across clusters depending on information type, some consumers in different clusters share similar views about which information is the least and most sensitive (Ackerman et al., 1999). However, as Ackerman et al. (1999) acknowledged, their sample of 381 U.S. internet users was neither statistically nor globally representative.

With their longitudinal study of U.S. consumers' preferences, knowledge, and attitudes regarding data practices in online and mobile markets, Hoofnagle and Urban (2014) questioned Westin's (1967) long-standing assumptions and provided new insights into topical privacy knowledge and preferences. For example, with regard to the description of pragmatic consumer decisions, they asserted that Westin (1967) did not explain whether privacy pragmatists actually engage in deliberations or actions that reflect pragmatism. Furthermore, they showed that pragmatists and fundamentalists reject information-intensive service options—in contrast to Westin's (1967) depiction. Moreover, they outlined that many individuals are misinformed about legal protection and business practices and that Westin's (1967) privacy pragmatists are less knowledgeable than privacy unconcerned or privacy fundamentalists. Ultimately, Hoofnagle and Urban (2014) suggested revisiting Westin's (1967) work to reflect on more modern privacy-related challenges.

Another study suggested a segmentation approach for responsible direct marketing based on consumer privacy concerns and privacy-related behaviors (Dolnicar & Jordaan, 2007). The identified consumer segments differ significantly on these factors, revealing patterns that enable firms to address segment-specific consumer needs and preferences. Consumers want to know why firms collect their data, how they protect them, and which data are shared with other parties (Dolnicar & Jordaan, 2007). Thus, firms benefit from offering stronger privacy-protection options, as such offerings lay the foundation for a trusting relationship. In addition to using consumers' perceptions of information sensitivity to improve their targeting efforts, firms can target the right consumers with more appropriate offerings and an appealing marketing approach (Dolnicar & Jordaan, 2007). While Dolnicar and Jordaan (2007) acknowledged that privacy concerns extend beyond local businesses, their research did not address privacy concerns from a global perspective.

Consumers' Willingness to Share Personal Information

Consumers' willingness to share (WTS) personal information with firms represents the extent to which individuals are open to providing their personal information to firms. Existing research has identified several factors that can influence WTS, including personalization (Xu et al., 2009), financial rewards (Xu et al., 2011), and information sensitivity (Malhotra et al., 2004). It has also been established that the type of information requested by a firm can affect consumers' privacy concerns (Eggers et al., 2023; Phelps et al., 2000), referred to by Malhotra et al. (2004) as *information sensitivity*. Accordingly, we define information sensitivity as the level of discomfort that consumers perceive when sharing personal information with a firm (Malhotra et al., 2004). Existing research indicates that most users are selective when sharing personal information online (Acquisti & Gross, 2006). For instance, Phelps et al. (2000) found that demographic and lifestyle information tend to be shared readily, followed by purchase-related data; however, consumers are far less likely to share financial and personally identifiable information. Consumers are less willing to share more sensitive information, as it evokes greater risk beliefs (Malhotra et al., 2004). In other words, consumers generally perceive there to be less risk when sharing less sensitive information and greater risk when sharing more sensitive information with a firm (Dinev et al., 2013). Hence, there is a negative relationship between information sensitivity and WTS. Furthermore, while most social media users refuse to publish their address, class schedules, and phone numbers, they gladly share their political views, date of birth, and sexual orientation (Acquisti & Gross, 2006). Importantly, WTS increases when consumers receive something valuable in exchange for their information, such as shopping benefits (Phelps et al., 2000). As Dinev and Hart (2006) proposed, idiosyncratic preferences may determine consumers' privacy concerns (Anderson & Agarwal, 2011) and influence WTS.

Segmentation Variables and Covariates: The Privacy Calculus and Consumers' Relationships with Firms

The concept of a calculus that represents an antecedent to sharing information has garnered considerable attention from researchers in various disciplines (Beke et al., 2022; Dinev & Hart, 2006). The *privacy calculus* can be viewed as a cognitive computation that considers the costs, benefits, and situational constraints (e.g., institutional norms of appropriate behavior, anticipated benefits, unpredictable consequences) of sharing personal information (Laufer & Wolfe, 1977). Following this logic, consumers share personal information if the benefits exceed the costs of disclosure—if they achieve a positive net outcome (Culnan & Bies, 2003). This cost–benefit trade-off influences consumers in various privacy-related contexts, such as online personalization (Chellappa & Sin, 2005), profiling by online vendors (Awad & Krishnan, 2006), disclosing personal information to marketers (Malhotra et al., 2004), sharing personal health data (Anderson & Agarwal, 2011), participating in social media (Krasnova et al., 2010) or online financial portals (Hann et al., 2007), conducting e-commerce transactions (Dinev & Hart, 2006), and engaging in location-based services (Xu et al., 2009). Lastly, consumers raise concerns over privacy when sharing information with firms on account of the increasing economic value of their personal information (Culnan & Armstrong, 1999; Smith et al., 1996). As a result, consumers assess the risks and benefits of sharing their personal information before actually disclosing any data (Kehr et al., 2015). Although some studies (e.g., Dinev & Hart, 2006; Xu et al., 2009) consider risks and benefits to be independent of each other, we follow the notion of more recent research, suggesting that the risks and benefits of sharing personal information are interdependent (Dinev et al., 2013).

Privacy concerns

Warren and Brandeis (1890) were the first to conceptualize privacy as the right to be left alone. Even though this definition may seem straightforward, modern information privacy is affected by many factors, such as industry sectors, state regulation, and culture (Culnan & Bies, 2003; Malhotra et al., 2004). We define information privacy concerns as consumers' apprehension about firms collecting, storing, and using their personal information (Beke et al., 2018; Malhotra et al., 2004; Smith et al., 1996). Regardless of their complexity, privacy concerns are vital to the privacy calculus (Culnan & Bies, 2003; Dinev & Hart, 2006; Malhotra et al., 2004). Prior literature has established a relationship between privacy concerns and WTS (Phelps et al., 2000), explored how data privacy affects customer and firm performance (Martin et al., 2017), and suggested that consumers can be segmented according to their privacy types to tailor products and services to their distinct needs (John et al., 2011). As firms collect ever-increasing amounts of consumer data, privacy concerns have surged (Beke et al., 2018). Given that individuals from similar geographical regions may vary significantly in their online activities, privacy concerns (Bellman et al., 2004), and perceptions of fairness (with regard to how firms collect and use information) due to their individual characteristics and past experiences (Malhotra et al., 2004), privacy remains challenging to grasp, and estimating its psychological value is even more challenging than quantifying its material value (John et al., 2011).

Perceived benefits

In line with the privacy calculus, consumers are willing to take risks associated with sharing personal information as long as the benefits they receive in exchange for their information exceed the costs (Beke et al., 2022; Dinev et al., 2013). In other words, privacy can be seen as an economic good that can be freely exchanged for some benefits (Eggers et al., 2023; Smith et al., 2011). One major benefit of sharing personal information with firms is personalization; firms can use consumer data to tailor their offerings to meet individual consumer needs and preferences (Wedel & Kannan, 2016). With consumer data and digitization, firms can define an entire marketing mix for individual consumers with personalized products, services, prices, and promotions (Rust & Huang, 2014). Furthermore, firms may incentivize consumers to share their information by compensating them with monetary benefits (Culnan & Bies, 2003). In a study, Kehr et al. (2015) explored the effects of perceived benefits in an information-sharing context. They found perceived benefits to be positively associated with perceived privacy and trust. At the same time, they found a negative relationship between perceived benefits and perceived risk of sharing personal information, suggesting that perceived benefits increase WTS.

Relationships with Firms

Existing research has demonstrated that consumers with a stronger relationship with a firm are more likely to share personal information with said firm (White, 2004). We operationalize consumers' relationships with firms using four variables: trust, satisfaction, WOM, and behavioral intention/loyalty.

Trust

Trust refers to the "willingness to be vulnerable to the actions of another party based on the expectation that the other will perform a particular action important to the trustor, irrespective of the ability to monitor or control that other party" (Mayer et al., 1995, p. 712); it is essential for mitigating risk beliefs. Prior experience with a firm may help to build trust (Chellappa & Sin, 2005), as consumers are more likely to share their information with a firm they trust and when they believe that fair procedures are in place (Culnan & Armstrong, 1999).

Satisfaction

Satisfaction refers to an overall evaluation of a firm based on the entire customer experience over time (Garbarino & Johnson, 1999). Satisfied customers appreciate a firm's attention, willingness to explain procedures, service quality, claims responsiveness, employee expertise, customer relationship, and alertness (Verhoef, 2003). We define satisfaction as "the emotional state that occurs as a result of a customer's interactions with the firm over time" (Verhoef, 2003, p. 33). While unsatisfied customers may complain about a firm, leading to negative WOM (Singh, 1990), satisfied customers are more likely to share their personal information with firms.

Word of Mouth (WOM)

The literature has shown that WOM is among the most influential communication channels in the marketplace (Allsop et al., 2007). WOM is perceived as a more credible means of persuasion than communication initiated by a firm, as it reflects people's blunt evaluations (Allsop et al., 2007). WOM can be measured with the net promoter score (NPS), which reflects the ratio of promoters to detractors of a firm (Reichheld, 2003). It is a forward-looking customer feedback metric, as it considers consumers' willingness to recommend a particular firm in the future, indicating their relationship with the firm (de Haan et al., 2015). For instance, loyal customers spend more over their customer life cycles as their wallets grow over time (Reichheld, 2003).

Furthermore, the literature affirms that the NPS effectively predicts customer retention (de Haan et al., 2015) and, therefore, is an important indicator of consumers' relationship with a firm.

Behavioral intention/loyalty

Behavioral intention/loyalty indicates whether a customer is likely to remain with or defect from a firm (Zeithaml et al., 1996). In terms of relationship quality, customers with favorable behavioral intentions are more likely to form a stronger relationship with the firm (Zeithaml et al., 1996). Consumers become more loyal by developing a preferred firm, continuing to purchase from it, and increasing future business (Zeithaml et al., 1996).

Demographic variables

We control for gender, age, and income in our analyses to account for demographic factors (Reynolds et al., 2003). However, based on prior studies (Konuş et al., 2008), we do not expect there to be a strong impact of demographics on WTS segmentation. Figure 11.1 illustrates the conceptual framework.

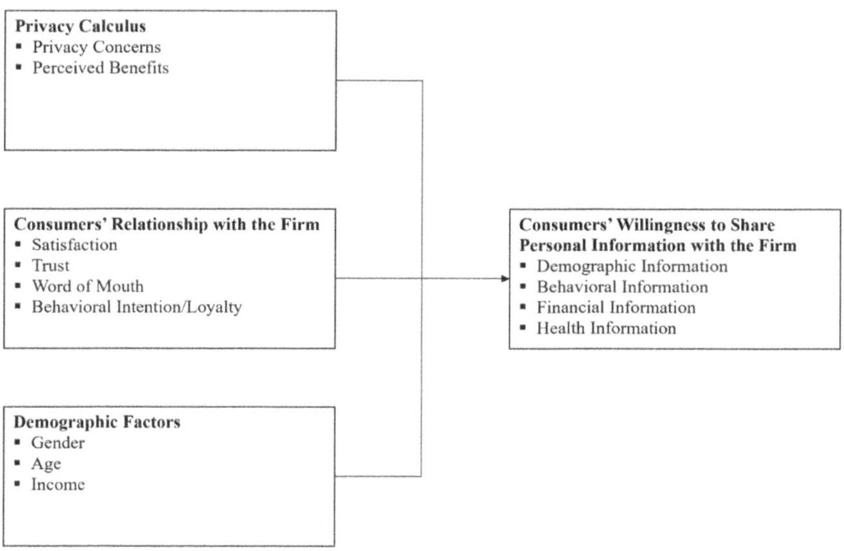

Source: Authors.

Figure 11.1 Conceptual framework

Methodology

Data Collection

We collected data on WTS using a large-scale global online survey that gathered data in 24 countries,[1] which collectively account for 54.95 percent of the global population (United Nations Department of Economic and Social Affairs, 2020) and 77.68 percent of the global gross domestic product (GDP) (World Bank, 2020). We developed a preliminary questionnaire in English and pretested it with a student sample. To ensure translation equivalence, we verified the questionnaire with bilingual country representatives. Following revision, the questionnaire was translated into all relevant languages by a professional translation agency.[2] The survey was done in 2017, with respondents being randomly sampled via an international market research agency. We only received completed questionnaires. If respondents could not finish the questionnaire immediately, they were permitted to pause and finish it later. As a result, we have no missing values. We received online questionnaires completed by 15,838 consumers. We excluded 131 respondents with a uniform response style[3] (Baumgartner & Steenkamp, 2001) and 639 respondents who appeared to have rushed through the questionnaire.[4] The final data set comprises 15,068 consumers with a mean age of 42.81 years (standard deviation = 13.88 years) and is well balanced in terms of gender (50.03 percent men and 49.97 percent women). The data set is also well balanced in terms of nationality (see Appendix A). We received information on six income brackets. Respondents provided their absolute income in their national currency, which we converted into U.S. dollars for our analyses.[5] Appendix A illustrates the sample characteristics.

Measures

We operationalized WTS inspired by the scale provided by Gupta et al. (2009). More specifically, we measured WTS by considering information sensitivity according to four data clusters: demographic, behavioral, financial, and health. Demographic information (α = 0.896, CR = 0.913, AVE = 0.570) refers to name, email address, date of birth, home address, work address, home phone number, work phone number, and gender. Behavioral information (α = 0.878, CR = 0.908, AVE = 0.624) refers to media habits, driving behavior, shopping behavior, consumption behavior, location data, and social media profiles. Financial information (α = 0.824, CR = 0.895, AVE = 0.741) refers to income, credit card details, and further financial information. Health information (α = 0.897, CR = 0.951, AVE = 0.907) refers to health data and medical history. While Malhotra et al. (2004) investigated collection, control, and awareness of privacy practices in the context of online privacy, we were more interested in the nuanced dimensions of different types of information. Furthermore, we operationalized the privacy calculus by considering both the costs and benefits of sharing personal information with a firm (Culnan & Bies, 2003; Laufer & Wolfe, 1977). We used the privacy concerns construct developed by Malhotra et al. (2004) to operationalize the equation's cost side ($\alpha = 0.848$, CR = 0.888, AVE = 0.667) and Dinev at al.'s (2013) perceived benefits scale ($\alpha = 0.874$, CR = 0.923, AVE = 0.799) to operationalize its benefit side. To operationalize relationships with firms (White, 2004), we used satisfaction (Verhoef, 2003), trust (Kehr et al., 2015), WOM (Zeithaml et al., 1996), and behavioral intention/loyalty (Cronin et al., 2000). Lastly, we considered gender, age, and income to control for sociodemographic factors. Table 11.1 presents descriptive statistics and correlations. Appendix B contains detailed information about construct measurement and operationalizations. All measures are reflective and were measured using multi-item 5-point Likert scales.

Data Equivalence and Common Method Variance

Data equivalence is "the extent to which the elements of a research design have the same meaning, and can be applied in the same way, in different cultural contexts" (Hult et al., 2008, p. 1027). In Appendix C, we outline how we established construct, measurement, and data collection equivalence to ensure that differences among countries and cultures stem from data that are equivalent across countries and cultures rather than distinct measurement scales or construct operationalizations (Hult et al., 2008).

Furthermore, given that we derived predictor and outcome variables from the same survey respondents, we control for *common method variance* (CMV)—the "variance that is attributable to the measurement method rather than to the constructs the measures represent" (Podsakoff et al., 2003, p. 879)—which may generate type I and type II errors (Chang et al., 2010). We outline the procedural and statistical remedies we applied to control for CMV in Appendix D.

Model

Our data vary on three levels. First, we obtain multiple observations for each individual regarding their WTS depending on information type and category (demographic, behavioral, financial, and health). Second, we account for individual-level data with covariates (privacy concerns, perceived benefits, trust, satisfaction, WOM, behavioral intention/loyalty, gender, age, and income). Third, we consider that individuals are nested within countries. Thus, we employ multilevel latent class analysis (LCA) to identify consumer

Table 11.1 Descriptive statistics and correlation matrix

	Correlation Matrix										
Variable	1	2	3	4	5	6	7	8	9	10	11
1. WTS - Demographic Information	1.000										
2. WTS - Behavioral Information	0.540**	1.000									
3. WTS - Financial Information	0.521**	0.678**	1.000								
4. WTS - Health Information	0.521**	0.624**	0.627**	1.000							
5. Privacy Concerns	0.013	-0.025**	-0.059**	0.000	1.000						
6. Perceived Benefits	0.346**	0.469**	0.400**	0.380**	0.067**	1.000					
7. Satisfaction	0.287**	0.297**	0.247**	0.210**	0.223**	0.402**	1.000				

	Correlation Matrix										
Variable	1	2	3	4	5	6	7	8	9	10	11
8. Trust	0.347**	0.327**	0.257**	0.249**	0.193**	0.432**	0.754**	1.000			
9. Word of Mouth	0.388**	0.419**	0.327**	0.271**	0.112**	0.459**	0.518**	0.547**	1.000		
10. Behav-ioral Intention/ Loyalty	0.391**	0.365**	0.269**	0.214**	0.102**	0.415**	0.532**	0.564**	0.791**	1.000	
11. Age	0.039**	-0.124**	-0.152**	-0.119**	0.087**	-0.100**	-0.023**	-0.005	-0.060**	-0.012	1.000
Mean	3.425	2.786	2.293	2.561	4.121	3.296	3.741	3.789	3.499	3.650	42.81
Standard Deviation	1.013	1.080	1.135	1.135	0.797	0.943	0.800	0.823	0.965	0.927	13.88

Notes: ** = correlations significant at the 0.01 level (two-tailed). N = 15,068 consumers from 24 countries. Variables, means, and standard deviations appear in their original values.

segments that share a similar sensitivity in terms of WTS and its categories (demographic, behavioral, financial, and health) as predictors. As the segments (or classes) are latent, individuals can only be assigned to a class with a certain probability. In order to accurately differentiate these segments and classes and reduce the classification error, we assume that the segments and classes can be separated further via the covariates (privacy concerns, perceived benefits, trust, satisfaction, WOM, behavioral intention/loyalty, gender, age, and income).

Using these covariates, we model the segment/class membership probability with a multinomial logit model. Moreover, we employ multilevel modeling to account for the country-level data by specifying group-level latent classes for the countries and including them as group-level covariates (Vermunt & Magidson, 2005). With LCA, the number of classes is not determined a priori; rather, it can be selected based on information criteria, such as the Bayesian information criterion (BIC) and the Akaike information criterion (AIC). Initially, we estimate the fit of a 1-segment 1-country class model to the data, making theoretical and empirical considerations as recommended by Nylund et al. (2007). We fit the model using a robust maximum likelihood estimation (Asparouhov & Muthén, 2014). Next, we specify additional segments and country classes before estimating the model for solutions with one to six segments and one to six country classes. We use BIC and CAIC (consistent Akaike's information criterion) criteria to identify the final number of segments and country classes. When differences in information criteria are ambiguous, we employ segment and country class interpretability as supplementary selection criteria. Moreover, we aim for a solution that minimizes classification error. Ultimately, we obtained a minimum BIC and CAIC for the 6-segment 2-country class solution. This model minimized the classification error (0.037) while maximizing R^2 (0.443). Thus, we chose this solution as our final model. Table 11.2 displays the model selection.

Findings

The 6-segment 2-country class solution is illustrated in Table 11.3. It presents the model parameters that indicate the average WTS score (intercept) and how the data-sharing behavior differs across WTS category types. We identify six consumer segments, of which segments 1–3 are most relevant. Segment 1 is the largest with 51.4 percent. Segments 2 (20.6 percent) and 3 (20.4 percent) are nearly equal in size. Segments 4–6 (with a combined size of just 7.6 percent) only represent differences in response styles that correspond to midpoint responding (segment 4), nay-saying (segment 5), or yea-saying (segment

Table 11.2 Model selection

	LL	BIC(LL)	AIC(LL)	AIC3(LL)	CAIC(LL)	Npar	Class. Err.	R^2
Segment Solution								
6-Segment 1-Country Class	-329,851	660,665.183	659,903.151	660,003.151	660,765.183	100	0.037	0.443
6-Segment 2-Country Class	-329,682	660,382.978	659,575.223	659,681.223	660,488.978	106	0.037	0.443
6-Segment 3-Country Class	-329,658	660,393.384	659,539.908	659,651.908	660,505.384	112	0.037	0.443
6-Segment 4-Country Class	-329,682	660,499.392	659,600.193	659,718.193	660,617.392	118	0.037	0.443
6-Segment 5-Country Class	-329,632	660,456.056	659,511.135	659,635.135	660,580.056	124	0.037	0.443
6-Segment 6-Country Class	-329,604	660,458.284	659,467.641	659,597.641	660,588.284	130	0.037	0.443
Country Class Solution								
1-Segment 2-Country Class	-500,288	1,000,634.602	1,000,588.880	1,000,594.880	1,000,640.602	6	0.000	0.089

	LL	BIC(LL)	AIC(LL)	AIC3(LL)	CAIC(LL)	Npar	Class. Err.	R^2
2-Segment 2-Country Class	-461,031	922,312.210	922,114.081	922,140.081	922,338.210	26	0.022	0.342
3-Segment 2-Country Class	-442,413	885,269.919	884,919.384	884,965.384	885,315.919	46	0.026	0.413
4-Segment 2-Country Class	-413,872	828,380.621	827,877.680	827,943.680	828,446.621	66	0.028	0.422
5-Segment 2-Country Class	-360,262	721,352.179	720,696.831	720,782.831	721,438.179	86	0.028	0.428
6-Segment 2-Country Class	-329,682	660,382.978	659,575.223	659,681.223	660,488.978	106	0.037	0.443

Notes: LL = Log-likelihood, BIC = Bayesian information criterion, AIC = Akaike information criterion, AIC3 = adapted Akaike information criterion, CAIC = consistent Akaike's information criterion, Npar = number of parameters, Class. Err. = classification error.

6) without further variation (Baumgartner & Steenkamp, 2001). As these segments were not meaningful from a managerial perspective, we excluded them from further analyses. Segments 1–3 are consistent regarding the order in which consumers share information types: Demographic data (e.g., name, email address, date of birth, home address, work address, work phone number, home phone number, gender) are the most likely to be shared, followed by behavioral data (e.g., media habits, driving, shopping, consumption behavior, location data, social media profiles), health information (e.g., medical history, health data), and financial data (e.g., income, credit card details, further financial information). However, the segments differ substantially in their overall level of WTS and regarding relative differences between the categories. In particular, segment 1 shows a moderate level of WTS (intercept = 2.678); it is open to sharing demographic data but is more reluctant to provide other types of information. Segment 2 shows a high level of WTS (intercept = 3.960); it is the most likely to share any type of information, though it is reluctant to share financial data. Segment 3 shows a low level of WTS (intercept = 1.673); it is the most hesitant to provide personal information, especially health and financial data. In turn, based on average WTS scores, one can identify medium (segment 1), strong (segment 2), and weak sharers (segment 3).

Table 11.3 Predictors of WTS

WTS	Segment 1 Medium Sharers	Segment 2 Strong Sharers	Segment 3 Weak Sharers	Segment 4	Segment 5	Segment 6
Intercept	2.678 (0.006)	3.960 (0.006)	1.673 (0.007)	3.000 (0.000)	1.000 (0.000)	5.000 (0.000)
Segment Size	51.4%	20.6%	20.4%	3.6%	2.1%	1.9%
Predictors: Type of Information						
Demographic	0.955 (0.006)	0.310 (0.006)	0.527 (0.008)	-0.000 (0.000)	0.000 (0.000)	0.000 (0.000)
Behavioral	-0.017 (0.006)	0.044 (0.007)	0.096 (0.007)	0.000 (0.000)	-0.000 (0.000)	-0.000 (0.000)
Financial	-0.635 (0.008)	-0.379 (0.008)	-0.346 (0.009)	0.000 (0.000)	-0.000 (0.000)	-0.000 (0.000)
Health	-0.303 (0.009)	0.025 (0.009)	-0.277 (0.010)	-0.000 (0.000)	0.000 (0.000)	0.000 (0.000)

Notes: Segments 4–6 were omitted from further analyses. Standard errors in parentheses.

Table 11.4 Predictors of segment membership

Covariates	Relationship-Seekers (Segment 2)	Privacy-Concerned Consumers (Segment 3)
Privacy Concerns	-0.416 (0.032)	0.195 (0.033)
Perceived Benefits	0.209 (0.036)	-0.886 (0.034)
Trust	0.180 (0.055)	-0.350 (0.053)
Satisfaction	-0.385 (0.053)	-0.325 (0.053)
WOM	0.221 (0.051)	-0.455 (0.046)
Behavioral Intention/ Loyalty	0.446 (0.051)	0.263 (0.047)
Gender		
Female	-0.025 (0.024)	-0.007 (0.024)
Male	0.025 (0.024)	-0.007 (0.024)
Age	0.006 (0.002)	0.013 (0.002)
Income		
Less than $16,000	-0.442 (0.074)	-0.223 (0.066)
Between $16,001 and $31,000	-0.001 (0.057)	-0.117 (0.053)
Between $31,001 and $48,000	0.334 (0.053)	0.060 (0.050)
Between $48,001 and $72,000	0.588 (0.053)	0.157 (0.052)
More than $72,000	0.348 (0.052)	-0.051 (0.050)
Prefer not to say	-0.827 (0.121)	0.174 (0.086)

Notes: Privacy pragmatists (segment 1) are used as the reference segment. Segments 2 and 3 are compared to this reference segment. Standard errors in parentheses.

Table 11.4 contains the multinomial logit model parameters that indicate how the covariates affect segment membership (Konuş et al., 2008) relative to the medium sharer segment (segment 1). We use the medium sharer segment (segment 1) as the reference category, as it is by far the largest of all segments. We label the medium sharers *privacy pragmatists*, as they appear to share personal information when they feel that doing so is worthwhile.

A negative coefficient indicates that consumers in the strong (segment 2) and weak sharer segments (segment 3) are lower on the variable than the privacy pragmatists while a positive coefficient indicates that they are higher on that variable. According to the Wald tests, the parameters differ significantly across clusters ($p < 0.05$). *Strong sharers* (segment 2) have relatively minor privacy concerns; they favor the benefits they receive in exchange for their information. Accordingly, firms should emphasize and enhance the benefits that they provide to increase WTS. The relationship with the firm is crucial for strong sharers. Compared to medium sharers, they trust the firm with whom they share information; they tend to be more loyal and engage in positive WOM. Interestingly, strong sharers do so despite being less satisfied with the firm than medium sharers. This may stem from the fact that the positive overall relationship with the firm is more critical to strong sharers than a single dimension (e.g., satisfaction). Furthermore, strong sharers have relatively high incomes, especially in the income brackets above $31,000. At the same time, strong sharers do not seem to hesitate to disclose their income. Compared to medium sharers, fewer strong sharers opted to avoid disclosing their income. Consequently, we label strong sharers as *relationship-seekers*.

Weak sharers (segment 3) are characterized by their privacy concerns. Privacy is more important to them than it is to medium sharers. At the same time, weak sharers value benefits to a lesser degree than medium sharers. Thus, to target weak sharers, firms must protect their privacy. Furthermore, weak sharers do not value strong relationships with firms that aim to collect their data. Our empirical evidence indicates that weak sharers do not trust these firms, that their satisfaction scores are fairly low, and that they would not recommend these firms. However, once convinced, they may become loyal and stick with the firm. Weak sharers tend to be in income brackets between $31,000 and $72,000, though the number of these consumers unwilling to disclose their income is high compared to medium sharers. Consequently, we label weak sharers as *privacy-concerned consumers*. Furthermore, the Wald test shows that the parameters for gender do not differ significantly (Wald = 4.640, $p = 0.46$), indicating that gender does not influence segment membership or, in turn, WTS. The parameters for age are quite similar across all segments and do not provide insightful findings. Lastly, we must highlight that merely considering differences in income would yield a biased picture due to the heterogeneity within and across segments and country classes.

Segmentation on the Country Level

Our 6-segment 2-country class solution identifies two country classes. Table 11.5 illustrates how the three consumer segments are distributed across the two country classes. Given their mean scores, we label country class 1 as data-prone countries (mean = 3.051) and country class 2 as data-reluctant countries (mean = 2.843). Consumers in *data-prone countries* are more likely to share their personal information with firms while those from *data-reluctant countries* are less likely to do so. In our sample, the number of consumers from data-prone countries (50.6 percent of consumers) is roughly equal to the number of consumers from data-reluctant countries (49.4 percent of consumers). The data-prone countries are Brazil, Canada, China, India, Malaysia, Mexico, Singapore, South Africa, Spain, Sweden, Turkey, and the United States. The data-reluctant countries are Australia, Austria, Belgium, the Czech Republic, France, Germany, Japan, the Netherlands, Poland, South Korea, Switzerland, and the United Kingdom. Data-prone countries contain more relationship-seekers (26.19 percent) than privacy-concerned consumers (17.24 percent). The opposite is true for data-reluctant countries, where privacy-concerned consumers account for 23.65 percent of the population while relationship-seekers account for just 14.91 percent. Privacy pragmatists account for the largest proportion in both country classes—48.68 percent in data-prone countries and 54.20 percent in data-reluctant countries.

Table 11.5 Country classes

	Data-Prone Countries (Country Class 1)	Data-Reluctant Countries (Country Class 2)
Country Class Size	50.60%	49.40%
Segments		
Privacy Pragmatists (Segment 1)	48.68%	54.20%
Relationship-Seekers (Segment 2)	26.19%	14.91%
Privacy-Concerned Consumers (Segment 3)	17.24%	23.65%
Mean WTS	3.051	2.843

Table 11.6 Segments per country

	Privacy Pragmatists (Segment 1)	Relationship-Seekers (Segment 2)	Privacy-Concerned Consumers (Segment 3)
Data-Prone Countries (Country Class 1)			
Brazil	44.8%	33.2%	9.9%
Canada	53.4%	21.1%	19.0%
China	38.6%	42.5%	15.0%
India	40.0%	47.3%	5.7%
Malaysia	44.0%	30.3%	19.1%
Mexico	50.7%	26.6%	16.6%
Singapore	51.9%	21.4%	22.4%
South Africa	55.0%	27.7%	11.1%
Spain	49.8%	23.1%	18.5%
Sweden	50.7%	16.4%	21.8%
Turkey	47.6%	27.9%	13.4%
USA	42.5%	32.2%	16.3%
Data-Reluctant Countries (Country Class 2)			
Australia	55.5%	13.7%	24.1%
Austria	60.5%	8.5%	25.2%
Belgium	53.9%	12.7%	25.1%
Czech Republic	57.2%	12.9%	22.6%
France	51.1%	17.9%	22.1%
Germany	61.0%	9.9%	23.7%
Japan	44.3%	13.0%	34.9%
Netherlands	55.6%	9.3%	26.6%
Poland	49.8%	11.2%	29.1%
South Korea	54.9%	16.7%	25.5%

	Privacy Pragmatists (Segment 1)	Relationship-Seekers (Segment 2)	Privacy-Concerned Consumers (Segment 3)
Switzerland	58.3%	12.0%	24.5%
United Kingdom	54.0%	16.5%	20.4%

Table 11.6 summarizes the segments per country, revealing considerable differences. In data-prone countries, privacy pragmatists are the largest segment by far, followed by relationship-seekers and privacy-concerned consumers. For privacy pragmatists, segment membership ranges from 38.6 percent (China) to 55.0 percent (South Africa) with an average of 47.4 percent. Segment membership for relationship-seekers ranges from 16.4 percent (Sweden) to 47.3 percent (India) with an average of 29.1 percent. In China and India, relationship-seekers constitute the biggest segment, accounting for 42.5 percent and 47.3 percent, respectively. In other words, there are more relationship-seekers than privacy pragmatists. Privacy-concerned consumers range from 5.7 percent (India) to 22.4 percent (Singapore) with an average of 15.7 percent. More consumers are in the privacy-concerned segment in Singapore (22.4 percent) and Sweden (21.8 percent) than in the relationship-seeker segment. Notably, less than 10 percent of all consumers in Brazil (9.9 percent) and India (5.7 percent) are privacy-concerned consumers.

In data-reluctant countries, privacy pragmatists constitute the biggest segment, followed by privacy-concerned consumers and relationship-seekers. Segment membership for privacy pragmatists ranges from 44.3 percent (Japan) to 61.0 percent (Germany) with an average of 54.7 percent. Segment membership for relationship-seekers ranges from 8.5 percent (Austria) to 17.9 percent (France) with an average of just 12.9 percent. The relationship-seeker segment is the smallest in all of the data-reluctant countries. In fact, it falls below 10 percent in Austria (8.5 percent), Germany (9.9 percent), and the Netherlands (9.3 percent). Lastly, segment membership for privacy-concerned consumers ranges from 20.4 percent (United Kingdom) to 34.9 percent (Japan) with an average of 25.3 percent. Figure 11.2 depicts the country-level classification.

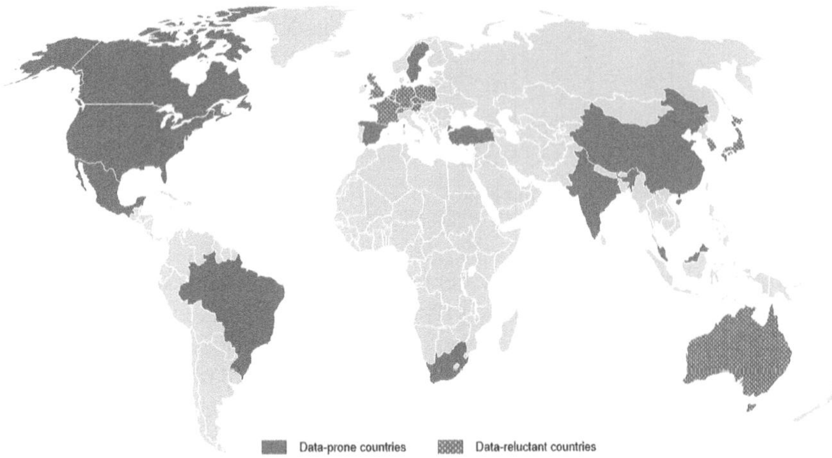

Figure 11.2 Country-level classification

Discussion

Prior literature has highlighted the fact that effectively identifying market segments has a considerable impact on a firm's financial performance (Agarwal et al., 2010). However, international market segmentation remains a significant challenge (Douglas & Craig, 2006). Segments do not occur naturally as a group of homogeneous consumers; rather, they are defined by the marketer's strategic view of the market (Wedel & Kamakura, 2002). The purpose of this chapter was to perform a global market segmentation that identifies consumer segments and country classes based on consumers' WTS. We segmented consumers based on WTS, investigated the privacy calculus and consumers' relationships with firms as segmentation criteria, and explored WTS. Drawing on multilevel LCA and data from 15,068 consumers across 24 countries, we identified three consumer segments—privacy-concerned consumers, privacy pragmatists, and relationship-seekers—and two country classes—data-prone and data-reluctant countries—that help to predict WTS. Our empirical findings demonstrate that the identified segments differ considerably from one another, enabling multinational firms to adapt their marketing strategies and segmentation efforts to appeal to each distinct consumer segment within and across countries.

Theoretical Implications

Our findings contribute to the literatures on information sharing, international market segmentation, and international marketing in several ways. First—to the best of our knowledge—this is the first global segmentation study to investigate WTS while considering the privacy calculus and consumers' relationships with firms. Our findings reaffirm the need to deeply explore WTS given the increasingly global and data-driven nature of the modern world. Amid the ever-increasing accessibility of consumer data, firms can more precisely profile consumers and target solutions to individual needs and preferences (Wedel & Kannan, 2016). Effectively identifying consumer segments enables firms to more effectively target customers, which can have a positive effect on firm performance.

We address the shortcomings of prior segmentation studies by revisiting WTS in the context of modern privacy-related challenges (Hoofnagle & Urban, 2014) from a global perspective (Ackerman et al., 1999; Dolnicar & Jordaan, 2007). Extending the work of Ackerman et al. (1999), who drew conclusions based on the responses of just 381 internet users, we employed a far broader sample that represents consumers from all over the world. Consequently, our findings should be more generalizable. Dolnicar and Jordaan (2007), for example, explored consumers from just two countries in their study: Australia and South Africa. This narrow focus likely limited their findings. In contrast, our vast data set allows us to address privacy concerns from a global perspective. Lastly, our investigation considers up-to-date privacy-related challenges, addressing the call of Hoofnagle and Urban (2014) to revisit Westin's (1967) privacy segmentation in light of modern privacy considerations.

Conducting an international market segmentation in the information-sharing realm is particularly relevant given the fact that prior segmentation studies (e.g., De Keyser et al., 2015; Herhausen et al., 2019; Konuş et al., 2008) have not yet considered information sharing. Moreover, existing research has neglected the privacy calculus and consumers' relationships with firms as segmentation criteria. This study demonstrated that the privacy calculus is essential in the information-sharing literature, as it helps to explain consumer differences in information disclosure. Consequently, we drew on the privacy calculus because it considers the opposing dimensions of information disclosure (i.e., privacy concerns and benefits) and, thus, more aptly resonates with the complex nature of sharing personal information.

Furthermore, research on how firms' privacy practices affect the customer–firm relationship is fragmented (Beke et al., 2018). We argue that consumers with a stronger relationship with a firm are more likely to share their personal information with said firm (White, 2004). We used four variables to operationalize consumers' relationships with firms: trust (Kehr et al., 2015), satisfaction (Verhoef, 2003), WOM (Zeithaml et al., 1996), and behavioral intention/loyalty (Cronin et al., 2000). We shed light on both the supply side (i.e., the firm) and the demand side (i.e., the consumer). Based on the notion that consumers are increasingly willing to actively protect their information privacy, firms can create a competitive advantage (Bleier et al., 2020) by improving their relationships with customers.

Our second contribution answers calls for rigorous research into international consumer segments on a global level (Burgess & Steenkamp, 2006; Steenkamp & Ter Hofstede, 2002). Global trends may have increased commonalities across countries while also increasing heterogeneity within countries (Agarwal et al., 2010). Our multilevel LCA enabled us to simultaneously explore individual- and country-level influences, revealing significant differences in both the individual and country level, which highlights the need to consider both types of information in international segmentation. We identified the 6-segment 2-country class solution to minimize information criteria (e.g., BIC or CAIC). While this solution identified six consumer segments, only three of them are managerially relevant. We labeled consumers in these segments as privacy-concerned consumers, privacy pragmatists, and relationship-seekers. Privacy pragmatists represent the largest segment (51.4 percent), followed by relationship-seekers (20.6 percent) and privacy-concerned consumers (20.4 percent). Additionally, we considered demographic variables, such as gender, age, and income, to assess their impact on segment and country class membership. The remaining three segments correspond to consumers with a uniform response style (i.e., yea-saying, nay-saying, or midpoint responding) for the variables that we were interested in (Baumgartner & Steenkamp, 2001). We excluded these segments from our analyses, as they only collectively account for 7.6 percent of all consumers.

We gathered new insights by comparing relationship-seekers and privacy-concerned consumers with privacy pragmatists. We found that privacy concerns are less relevant and perceived benefits are more relevant to relationship-seekers than to privacy pragmatists. This finding suggests that relationship-seekers have a considerably favorable cost–benefit trade-off (i.e., privacy calculus), resulting in a higher WTS (Dinev & Hart, 2006). In contrast, privacy-concerned consumers have higher privacy concerns and value benefits to a far lesser degree than privacy pragmatists. Consequently, their cost-benefit trade-off yields a lower WTS. As their label suggests, privacy-concerned consumers are less likely to share their personal information with firms due to their concerns over privacy. Thus, it is more challenging for firms to convince these consumers to disclose data. To confront this challenge, they could address either end of the privacy calculus: increase consumers' perception of benefits or address consumers' privacy concerns (e.g., better protect consumers' privacy). The latter approach could be particularly beneficial for firms and, if implemented appropriately, could lead to a competitive advantage (Bleier et al., 2020).

As their label suggests, relationship-seekers value good relationships with firms. They score highest on trust, WOM, and behavioral intention/loyalty. In other words, a good relationship with the firm is key to relationship-seekers. Firms that succeed in building such relationships (e.g., through building trust) can expect these consumers to engage in positive WOM and become more loyal. Only satisfaction is lower compared to privacy pragmatists. This is somewhat counterintuitive given that satisfaction is among the key drivers of a good customer–firm relationship (Verhoef, 2003). However, there may actually be more unsatisfied consumers in the relationship-seeker segment than in the privacy pragmatist segments, resulting in their desire to build strong relationships, which could be seen as a precursor to sharing information (Chellappa & Sin, 2005). Lastly, more relationship-seekers earn above $31,000 than do privacy pragmatists, suggesting that relationship-seekers generally have higher incomes.

In contrast, privacy-concerned consumers score lower on trust, satisfaction, and WOM than privacy pragmatists. Overall, their relationships with firms are worse than those of privacy pragmatists. Interestingly, however, privacy-concerned consumers exhibit a higher value on behavioral intention/loyalty than privacy pragmatists. It is possible that privacy-concerned consumers, once loyal to a firm, become more willing to readily share their information. Of course, firms must first be able to turn these privacy-concerned consumers into loyal consumers. Lastly, there are more privacy-concerned consumers than privacy pragmatists in the income brackets from $31,001 to $72,000 and fewer privacy-concerned consumers in the income brackets below $31,000. Accordingly, most privacy pragmatists are in the lower-income brackets (e.g., up to $31,000).

As expected, differences in gender and age were insignificant, as shown in prior segmentation studies (Konuş et al., 2008). The Wald tests demonstrated that the parameters for gender and age did not differ significantly, suggesting that they do not influence segment membership or, in turn, WTS. Accordingly, we can confirm that neither gender nor age has a strong impact on WTS segmentation.

Country classes. Our 6-segment 2-country class solution identified two relevant country classes: data-prone (50.6 percent) and data-reluctant countries (49.4 percent). Consumers in data-prone countries (i.e., Brazil, Canada, China, India, Malaysia, Mexico, Singapore, South Africa, Spain, Sweden, Turkey, and the United States) are more likely to share their personal information (mean = 3.051) than those in data-reluctant countries (i.e., Australia, Austria, Belgium, the Czech Republic, France, Germany, Japan, the Netherlands, Poland, South Korea, Switzerland, and the United Kingdom; mean = 2.843). Privacy pragmatists are the largest segment in both classes, with 48.68 percent in data-prone countries and 54.20 percent in data-reluctant countries. However, there are more relationship-seekers in data-prone countries (26.19 percent) than in data-reluctant countries (14.91 percent) and fewer privacy-concerned consumers in data-prone countries (17.24 percent) than in data-reluctant countries (23.65 percent).

Exploring the segments per country, we identified that the largest segment across all countries is privacy pragmatists, except for China and India, where most consumers are relationship-seekers. At the same time, the proportion of privacy-concerned consumers in these two countries is considerably small (China: 15.0 percent, India: 5.7 percent). However, these findings must be treated with caution, as these values may be influenced by regulation and local laws (Cockcroft & Rekker, 2016). Relationship-seekers constitute the second-largest segment in data-prone countries while privacy-concerned constitute the smallest. In contrast, privacy-concerned consumers follow privacy pragmatists in data-reluctant countries, where relationship-seekers constitute the minority. Strikingly, the proportion of relationship-seekers is less than 10 percent in Austria, Germany, and the Netherlands. Overall, good relationships with firms are far more relevant to consumers in data-prone countries than to those in data-reluctant countries.

For instance, Spain is a data-prone country while France is a data-reluctant country. Likewise, South Korea and Japan are data-reluctant countries while China is data-prone. Multinational firms may find it easier to target data-prone countries, as their consumers tend to more readily share information. Nevertheless, there are still relationship-seekers (i.e., strong sharers) in data-reluctant countries and privacy-concerned consumers (i.e., weak sharers) in data-prone countries. We have illustrated that consumer behavior regarding WTS varies significantly, even among neighboring countries. In other words, consumers from different countries can have more in common than consumers from the same country; regional proximity on the country level does not imply identical country class membership. This finding extends previous segmentation approaches that have grouped consumers by country

(Steenkamp & Ter Hofstede, 2002). Thus, multinational firms should be careful when addressing consumers from different countries. Our evidence indicates that approaches that target regional clusters (i.e., groups of geographically proximate countries) are not appropriate, as the countries may differ in terms of WTS. Instead, firms should adopt a highly differentiated view. Thus, it may be best for multinational firms to deploy mixed international market segmentation strategies with as much standardization as possible at the global level but as much customization as possible at the country and individual levels. For instance, firms that operate in data-prone countries may want to address relationship-seekers and enable further data collection. This could be facilitated through increasing levels of customer satisfaction and developing trust. Firms operating in data-reluctant countries may want to tackle privacy-concerned consumers by protecting their privacy more effectively. They could achieve this by maintaining a strong privacy policy on their website (Awad & Krishnan, 2006; Milne & Culnan, 2004) and implementing privacy-protection seals (Hui et al., 2007).

Our third contribution pertains to the ongoing discourse surrounding the economic value of personal information (John et al., 2011). We provided further insight into consumer decision-making processes through the consideration of information sensitivity (Malhotra et al., 2004). Prior literature highlighted that information sensitivity increases alongside the potential for loss associated with sharing information (Mothersbaugh et al., 2012). More sensitive information should be more valuable to consumers and, thus, be better protected. Accordingly, more sensitive information is less likely to be shared due to its greater economic value (Brandimarte et al., 2013; John et al., 2011).

Across all three consumer segments, demographic information (i.e., name, email address, date of birth, home address, work address, home phone number, work phone number, and gender) is shared most eagerly, followed by behavioral information (i.e., media habits, driving behavior, shopping behavior, consumption behavior, location data, and social media profiles). Demographic information is readily accessible and generic (i.e., less sensitive), suggesting that consumers are willing to share it with a lower degree of sensitivity. The findings regarding behavioral information and health information (i.e., health data and medical history) are mixed. While relationship-seekers and privacy-concerned consumers are largely willing to share behavioral information, privacy pragmatists are hesitant. Privacy pragmatists are also reserved in sharing their health data, which is also the case for privacy-concerned consumers. In contrast, relationship-seekers are willing to share their health information. More sensitive information about consumers' finances (i.e., income, credit card details, and further financial information) is shared to a considerably lesser degree.

Our findings show that consumers are less likely to share more sensitive information with firms, confirming existing research (e.g., John et al., 2011; Malhotra et al., 2004; Phelps et al., 2000). Instead, consumers aim to protect their sensitive information. These findings align with those of previous studies showing that consumers are more likely to disclose purchasing or lifestyle information than medical or financial information (Lwin et al., 2007; Mothersbaugh et al., 2012). Overall, there is a positive relationship between the economic value of personal information and information sensitivity. Nevertheless, the probability of sharing information differs across segments; firms that critically depend on more sensitive information can target segments that are generally more open to sharing information. Hence, firms need a distinctive strategy for requesting different types of consumer information, as there is no one-size-fits-all approach.

Managerial Implications

As consumer data becomes more readily accessible, firms should deploy data analytics to segment their customer base (Wedel & Kannan, 2016). Firms that identify consumer and country segments should also develop specific strategies to target these segments and differentiate their offerings (Konuş et al., 2008). In other words, multinational firms must adapt their marketing strategies and segmentation efforts based on the existence of distinct consumer segments within and across countries. Firms need to develop distinct strategies to target relationship-seekers, privacy pragmatists, and privacy-concerned consumers. As demonstrated by Bleier et al. (2020) and Eggers et al. (2023), there are promising approaches to making information privacy a strength that can lead to a competitive edge. These approaches help consumers to trust firms, increasing their propensity to disclose personal information. Furthermore, multinational firms should distinguish between data-prone and data-reluctant countries and acknowledge cultural differences across countries. To develop effective global marketing strategies, multinational firms must adopt a market segmentation approach that is both cross-national and cross-cultural.

Limitations and Further Research

This study is characterized by some limitations that offer avenues for further research. First, we recognize that the segmentation approach we chose is, at best, an approximation of reality (Wedel & Kamakura, 2002). We cannot assert that the consumer segments and country classes really exist, and we cannot claim to know exactly how heterogeneity is distributed. However, the segments we identified may serve as a sound basis for managers and marketers to better address consumer needs in information-sharing contexts. Second, we relied on the privacy calculus (Culnan & Bies, 2003; Laufer & Wolfe, 1977) and consumers' relationships with firms (White, 2004) to segment consumers. We encourage scholars to consider further segmentation variables that reflect the nature of data, such as data use transparency and customer control (Martin et al., 2017). It may be of interest to explore how more granular dimensions of privacy concerns—such as those pertaining to data collection, unauthorized secondary use, improper access, and errors (Smith et al., 1996)—shape WTS. Third, we used a multilevel LCA model to determine consumer segments and country classes. We individually assessed each of the 24 countries. Further research may consider a more fine-grained geographical segmentation (e.g., regions, states) to better account for within-country heterogeneity (Burgess & Steenkamp, 2006). Lastly, context specificity (John et al., 2011) and information sensitivity (Malhotra et al., 2004; Phelps et al., 2000) were crucial determinants of this study, but the segmentation variables we used may not be entirely appropriate for segmenting consumers in non-information-sharing contexts. Noting that information sensitivity significantly affects WTS, we highlight the need to include other types of information pertaining to additional aspects of consumers' lives that may influence segment membership. Despite its limitations, our research approach offers a key insight: International marketing scholars and multinational firms must consider WTS in a highly differentiated manner by considering consumers' segment and country class membership in international market segmentation efforts.

Notes

1. The countries are Australia, Austria, Belgium, Brazil, Canada, China, the Czech Republic, France, Germany, India, Japan, Malaysia, Mexico, the Netherlands, Poland, Singapore, South Africa, South Korea, Spain, Sweden, Switzerland, Turkey, the United Kingdom, and the United States.
2. The languages are Chinese, Czech, Dutch, French, Japanese, Korean, Malay, Polish, Portuguese, Spanish, Swedish, and Turkish.
3. A uniform response style characterizes consumers that answer all questions identically. In other words, there is no variation across their questionnaire responses.
4. We excluded consumers who finished the questionnaire in less than one-third of the median time.
5. There can be substantial differences in average incomes across countries. This is particularly relevant given that our sample comprises both higher-income

countries (e.g., Belgium) and lower-income countries (e.g., Turkey). To account for differences in average incomes per country, we relied on the help of an economist from the IBM Institute for Business Value. The economist developed a sophisticated estimation model to equalize and harmonize cross-country differences in national currencies. For each country, he developed income ranges that match the five income brackets we display in our chapter. These are: (1) < \$16,000, (2) \$16,001–\$31,000, (3) \$31,001–\$48,000, (4) \$48,001–\$72,000, (5) > \$72,000. In other words, this estimation method ensured that the five income brackets per country (in a country's national currency) were identical across countries. For instance, the second income bracket in Belgium (i.e., higher-income country) ranges from approximately 12,000 to 22,800 Euros, while the same income bracket in Turkey (i.e., lower-income country) ranges from approximately 150,000 to 300,000 Turkish Lira. Through this adjusting estimation approach, country differences were equalized and income in a country's national income was converted to U.S. dollars.

6. This is a qualitative assessment that requires no statistical testing.

References

Ackerman, M. S., Cranor, L. F., & Reagle, J. (1999). Privacy in E-Commerce: Examining User Scenarios and Privacy Preferences. *Proceedings of the 1st ACM Conference on Electronic Commerce*, 1–8. https://doi.org/10.1145/336992.336995.

Acquisti, A., & Gross, R. (2006). Imagined Communities: Awareness, Information Sharing, and Privacy on the Facebook. *Proceedings of the 6th Privacy Enhancing Technologies Symposium*, 36–58. https://doi.org/10.1007/11957454_3.

Agarwal, J., Malhotra, N. K., & Bolton, R. N. (2010). A Cross-National and Cross-Cultural Approach to Global Market Segmentation: An Application Using Consumers' Perceived Service Quality. *Journal of International Marketing, 18*(3), 18–40.

Allsop, D. T., Bassett, B. R., & Hoskins, J. A. (2007). Word-of-Mouth Research: Principles and Applications. *Journal of Advertising Research, 47*(4), 398–411.

Anderson, C. L., & Agarwal, R. (2011). The Digitization of Healthcare: Boundary Risks, Emotion, and Consumer Willingness to Disclose Personal Health Information. *Information Systems Research, 22*(3), 469–490.

Asparouhov, T., & Muthén, B. (2014). Auxiliary Variables in Mixture Modeling: Three-Step Approaches Using Mplus. *Structural Equation Modeling: A Multidisciplinary Journal, 21*(3), 329–341.

Awad, N. F., & Krishnan, M. S. (2006). The Personalization Privacy Paradox: An Empirical Evaluation of Information Transparency and the Willingness to be Profiled Online for Personalization. *MIS Quarterly, 30*(1), 13–28.

Baumgartner, H., & Steenkamp, J.-B. E. M. (2001). Response Styles in Marketing Research: A Cross-National Investigation. *Journal of Marketing Research, 38*(2), 143–156.

Beke, F. T., Eggers, F., & Verhoef, P. C. (2018). Consumer Informational Privacy: Current Knowledge and Research Directions. *Foundations and Trends in Marketing, 11*(1), 1–71.

Beke, F. T., Eggers, F., Verhoef, P. C., & Wieringa, J. E. (2022). Consumers' Privacy Calculus: The PRICAL Index Development and Validation. *International Journal of Research in Marketing, 39*(1), 20–41.

Bellman, S., Johnson, E. J., Kobrin, S. J., & Lohse, G. L. (2004). International Differences in Information Privacy Concerns: A Global Survey of Consumers. *The Information Society, 20*(5), 313–324.

Bleier, A., Goldfarb, A., & Tucker, C. (2020). Consumer Privacy and the Future of Data-Based Innovation and Marketing. *International Journal of Research in Marketing, 37*(3), 466–480.

Brandimarte, L., Acquisti, A., & Loewenstein, G. (2013). Misplaced Confidences: Privacy and the Control Paradox. *Social Psychological and Personality Science, 4*(3), 340–347.

Burgess, S. M., & Steenkamp, J.-B. E. M. (2006). Marketing renaissance: How research in emerging markets advances marketing science and practice. *International Journal of Research in Marketing, 23*(4), 337–356.

Chang, S. J., van Witteloostuijn, A., & Eden, L. (2010). From the Editors: Common Method Variance in International Business Research. *Journal of International Business Studies, 41*(2), 178–184.

Chellappa, R. K., & Sin, R. G. (2005). Personalization versus Privacy: An Empirical Examination of the Online Consumer's Dilemma. *Information Technology and Management, 6*(2–3), 181–202.

Cockcroft, S., & Rekker, S. (2016). The Relationship between Culture and Information Privacy Policy. *Electronic Markets, 26*(1), 55–72.

Craig, C. S., & Douglas, S. P. (2000). *International Market Research* (2nd edn.). Wiley.

Cronin, J. J., Brady, M. K., & Hult, G. T. M. (2000). Assessing the Effects of Quality, Value, and Customer Satisfaction on Consumer Behavioral Intentions in Service Environments. *Journal of Retailing, 76*(2), 193–218.

Culnan, M. J., & Armstrong, P. K. (1999). Information Privacy Concerns, Procedural Fairness, and Impersonal Trust: An Empirical Investigation. *Organization Science, 10*(1), 104–115.

Culnan, M. J., & Bies, R. J. (2003). Consumer Privacy: Balancing Economic and Justice Considerations. *Journal of Social Issues, 59*(2), 323–342.

de Haan, E., Verhoef, P. C., & Wiesel, T. (2015). The Predictive Ability of Different Customer Feedback Metrics for Retention. *International Journal of Research in Marketing, 32*(2), 195–206.

De Keyser, A., Schepers, J., & Konuş, U. (2015). Multichannel Customer Segmentation: Does the After-Sales Channel Matter? A Replication and Extension. *International Journal of Research in Marketing, 32*(4), 453–456.

Dinev, T., & Hart, P. (2006). An Extended Privacy Calculus Model for E-Commerce Transactions. *Information Systems Research, 17*(1), 61–80.

Dinev, T., Xu, H., Smith, H. J., & Hart, P. (2013). Information Privacy and Correlates: An Empirical Attempt to Bridge and Distinguish Privacy-Related Concepts. *European Journal of Information Systems, 22*(3), 295–316.

Dolnicar, S., & Jordaan, Y. (2007). A Market-Oriented Approach to Responsibly Managing Information Privacy Concerns in Direct Marketing. *Journal of Advertising, 36*(2), 123–149.

Douglas, S. P., & Craig, C. S. (2006). On Improving the Conceptual Foundations of International Marketing Research. *Journal of International Marketing*, *14*(1), 1–22.
Eggers, F., Beke, F. T., Verhoef, P. C., & Wieringa, J. E. (2023). The Market for Privacy: Understanding How Consumers Trade Off Privacy Practices. *Journal of Interactive Marketing*. https://doi.org/10.949968221140061.
Fornell, C., & Larcker, D. F. (1981). Evaluating Structural Equation Models with Unobservable Variables and Measurement Error. *Journal of Marketing Research*, *18*(1), 39–50.
Garbarino, E., & Johnson, M. S. (1999). The Different Roles of Satisfaction, Trust, and Commitment in Customer Relationships. *Journal of Marketing*, *63*(2), 70–87.
Gold, A. H., Malhotra, A., & Segars, A. H. (2001). Knowledge Management: An Organizational Capabilities Perspective. *Journal of Management Information Systems*, *18*(1), 185–214.
Gupta, B., Iyer, L. S., & Weisskirch, R. S. (2009). Willingness to Disclose Personal Information Online and Its Effect on Ensuring and Protecting Privacy: A Two Country Study. *AMCIS 2009 Proceedings*, 172. https://aisel.aisnet.org/amcis2009/172.
Hann, I.-H., Hui, K.-L., Lee, S.-Y., & Png, I. (2007). Overcoming Online Information Privacy Concerns: An Information-Processing Theory Approach. *Journal of Management Information Systems*, *24*(2), 13–42.
Henseler, J., Ringle, C. M., & Sarstedt, M. (2015). A New Criterion for Assessing Discriminant Validity in Variance-Based Structural Equation Modeling. *Journal of the Academy of Marketing Science*, *43*(1), 115–135.
Henseler, J., Ringle, C. M., & Sarstedt, M. (2016). Testing Measurement Invariance of Composites Using Partial Least Squares. *International Marketing Review*, *33*(3), 405–431.
Herhausen, D., Kleinlercher, K., Verhoef, P. C., Emrich, O., & Rudolph, T. (2019). Loyalty Formation for Different Customer Journey Segments. *Journal of Retailing*, *95*(3), 9–29.
Hoofnagle, C. J., & Urban, J. M. (2014). Alan Westin's Privacy Homo Economicus. *Wake Forest Law Review*, *49*, 261–317.
Hui, K.-L., Teo, H. H., & Lee, S.-Y. (2007). The Value of Privacy Assurance: An Exploratory Field Experiment. *MIS Quarterly*, *31*(1), 19–33.
Hult, G. T. M., Ketchen, D. J., Griffith, D. A., Finnegan, C. A., Gonzalez-Padron, T., Harmancioglu, N., Huang, Y., Talay, M. B., & Cavusgil, S. T. (2008). Data Equivalence in Cross-Cultural International Business Research: Assessment and Guidelines. *Journal of International Business Studies*, *39*(6), 1027–1044.
John, L. K., Acquisti, A., & Loewenstein, G. (2011). Strangers on a Plane: Context-Dependent Willingness to Divulge Sensitive Information. *Journal of Consumer Research*, *37*(5), 858–873.
Kehr, F., Kowatsch, T., Wentzel, D., & Fleisch, E. (2015). Blissfully Ignorant: The Effects of General Privacy Concerns, General Institutional Trust, and Affect in the Privacy Calculus. *Information Systems Journal*, *25*(6), 607–635.
Kock, N. (2015). Common Method Bias in PLS-SEM: A Full Collinearity Assessment Approach. *International Journal of E-Collaboration*, *11*(4), 1–10.
Konuş, U., Verhoef, P. C., & Neslin, S. A. (2008). Multichannel Shopper Segments and their Covariates. *Journal of Retailing*, *84*(4), 398–413.
Krasnova, H., Spiekermann, S., Koroleva, K., & Hildebrand, T. (2010). Online Social Networks: Why We Disclose. *Journal of Information Technology*, *25*(2), 109–125.

Kraus, S., Meier, F., Eggers, F., Bouncken, R. B., & Schuessler, F. (2016). Standardisation vs. Adaption: A Conjoint Experiment on the Influence of Psychic, Cultural and Geographical Distance on International Marketing Mix Decisions. *European Journal of International Management*, *10*(2), 127–156.
Laufer, R. S., & Wolfe, M. (1977). Privacy as a Concept and a Social Issue: A Multidimensional Developmental Theory. *Journal of Social Issues*, *59*(2), 243–261.
Lindell, M. K., & Whitney, D. J. (2001). Accounting for common method variance in cross-sectional research designs. *Journal of Applied Psychology*, *86*(1), 114.
Lwin, M., Wirtz, J., & Williams, J. D. (2007). Consumer Online Privacy Concerns and Responses: A Power–Responsibility Equilibrium Perspective. *Journal of the Academy of Marketing Science*, *35*(4), 572–585.
Malhotra, N. K., Kim, S. S., & Agarwal, J. (2004). Internet Users' Information Privacy Concerns (IUIPC): The Construct, the Scale, and a Causal Model. *Information Systems Research*, *15*(4), 336–355.
Martin, K. D., Borah, A., & Palmatier, R. W. (2017). Data Privacy: Effects on Customer and Firm Performance. *Journal of Marketing*, *81*(1), 36–58.
Mayer, R. C., Davis, J. H., & Schoorman, F. D. (1995). An Integrative Model of Organizational Trust. *Academy of Management Review*, *20*(3), 709–734.
Milne, G. R., & Culnan, M. J. (2004). Strategies for Reducing Online Privacy Risks: Why Consumers Read (or Don't Read) Online Privacy Notices. *Journal of Interactive Marketing*, *18*(3), 15–29.
Mothersbaugh, D. L., Foxx, W. K., Beatty, S. E., & Wang, S. (2012). Disclosure Antecedents in an Online Service Context: The Role of Sensitivity of Information. *Journal of Service Research*, *15*(1), 76–98.
Mullen, M. R. (1995). Diagnosing Measurement Equivalence in Cross-National Research. *Journal of International Business Studies*, *26*(3), 573–596.
Nylund, K. L., Asparouhov, T., & Muthén, B. (2007). Deciding on the Number of Classes in Latent Class Analysis and Growth Mixture Modeling: A Monte Carlo Simulation Study. *Structural Equation Modeling: A Multidisciplinary Journal*, *14*(4), 535–569.
Phelps, J. E., Nowak, G., & Ferrell, E. (2000). Privacy Concerns and Consumer Willingness to Provide Personal Information. *Journal of Public Policy & Marketing*, *19*(1), 27–41.
Podsakoff, P. M., MacKenzie, S. B., Lee, J. Y., & Podsakoff, N. P. (2003). Common Method Biases in Behavioral Research: A Critical Review of the Literature and Recommended Remedies. *Journal of Applied Psychology*, *88*(5), 879–903.
Reichheld, F. F. (2003). The One Number You Need to Grow. *Harvard Business Review*, *81*(12), 46–57.
Reynolds, N. L., Simintiras, A. C., & Diamantopoulos, A. (2003). Theoretical Justification of Sampling Choices in International Marketing Research: Key Issues and Guidelines for Researchers. *Journal of International Business Studies*, *34*(1), 80–89.
Rust, R. T., & Huang, M. H. (2014). The Service Revolution and the Transformation of Marketing Science. *Marketing Science*, *33*(2), 206–221.
Singh, J. (1990). Voice, Exit, and Negative Word-of-Mouth Behaviors: An Investigation across Three Service Categories. *Journal of the Academy of Marketing Science*, *18*(1), 1–15.
Smith, H. J., Dinev, T., & Xu, H. (2011). Information Privacy Research: An Interdisciplinary Review. *MIS Quarterly*, *35*(4), 989–1016.

Smith, H. J., Milberg, S. J., & Burke, S. J. (1996). Information Privacy: Measuring Individuals' Concerns about Organizational Practices. *MIS Quarterly*, *20*(2), 167–196.
Steenkamp, J.-B. E. M., & Maydeu-Olivares, A. (2021). An Updated Paradigm for Evaluating Measurement Invariance Incorporating Common Method Variance and Its Assessment. *Journal of the Academy of Marketing Science*, *49*(1), 5–29.
Steenkamp, J.-B. E. M., & Ter Hofstede, F. (2002). International Market Segmentation: Issues and Perspectives. *International Journal of Research in Marketing*, *19*(3), 185–213.
United Nations Department of Economic and Social Affairs (2020). World Population Prospects. https://population.un.org/wpp/Download/Standard/Population/.
Verhoef, P. C. (2003). Understanding the Effect of Customer Relationship Management Efforts on Customer Retention and Customer Share Development. *Journal of Marketing*, *67*(4), 30–45.
Vermunt, J. K., & Magidson, J. (2005). *Latent Gold 4.0 User's Guide*. Statistical Innovations Inc.
Warren, S. D., & Brandeis, L. D. (1890). The Right to Privacy. *Harvard Law Review*, *4*(5), 193–220.
Wedel, M., & Kamakura, W. (2002). Introduction to the Special Issue on Market Segmentation. *International Journal of Research in Marketing*, *19*(3), 181–183.
Wedel, M., & Kannan, P. K. (2016). Marketing Analytics for Data-Rich Environments. *Journal of Marketing*, *80*(6), 97–121.
Westin, A. F. (1967). *Privacy and Freedom*. Atheneum.
White, T. B. (2004). Consumer Disclosure and Disclosure Avoidance: A Motivational Framework. *Journal of Consumer Psychology*, *14*(1–2), 41–51.
World Bank (2020). World Development Indicators: GDP. https://data.worldbank.org/indicator/NY.GDP.MKTP.CD?view=map.
Xu, H., Luo, X., Carroll, J. M., & Rosson, M. B. (2011). The Personalization Privacy Paradox: An Exploratory Study of Decision Making Process for Location-Aware Marketing. *Decision Support Systems*, *51*(1), 42–52.
Xu, H., Teo, H.-H., Tan, B. C. Y., & Agarwal, R. (2009). The Role of Push-Pull Technology in Privacy Calculus: The Case of Location-Based Services. *Journal of Management Information Systems*, *26*(3), 135–174.
Zeithaml, V. A., Berry, L. L., & Parasuraman, A. (1996). The Behavioral Consequences of Service Quality. *Journal of Marketing*, *60*(2), 31–46.

APPENDIX A

Table 11A.1 Sample characteristics

Criterion	Sample Size
Gender	
Female	7,530 (49.97%)
Male	7,538 (50.03%)
Age (years)	
Mean	42.81
Standard Deviation	13.88
Income	
Less than $16,000	1,282 (8.51%)
Between $16,001 and $31,000	2,621 (17.39%)
Between $31,001 and $48,000	3,414 (22.66%)
Between $48,001 and $72,000	3,391 (22.50%)
More than $72,000	3,429 (22.76%)
Prefer not to say	931 (6.18%)
Sample size per country	
Australia	628
Austria	638
Belgium	622
Brazil	649
Canada	623
China	622
Czech Republic	643
France	596

Criterion	Sample Size
Germany	628
India	620
Japan	607
Malaysia	634
Mexico	655
Netherlands	593
Poland	625
Singapore	617
South Africa	656
South Korea	639
Spain	623
Sweden	615
Switzerland	633
Turkey	615
United Kingdom	588
USA	699

Note: N = 15,068.

APPENDIX B

Table 11A.2 Measurement and operationalizations

Measure	Loading	α	CR	AVE
WTS - Demographic Information (Gupta et al., 2009)		0.896	0.913	0.570
Name	0.752			
Email address	0.738			
Date of birth	0.758			
Home address	0.805			
Work address	0.768			
Home phone number	0.753			
Work phone number	0.810			
Gender	0.641			
WTS - Behavioral Information (Gupta et al., 2009)		0.878	0.908	0.624
Media habits	0.836			
Driving behavior	0.768			
Shopping behavior	0.832			
Consumption behavior	0.830			

Measure	Loading	α	CR	AVE
Location data	0.658			
Social media profiles	0.801			
WTS - Financial Information (Gupta et al., 2009)		0.824	0.895	0.741
Income	0.882			
Credit card details	0.786			
Financial information	0.909			
WTS - Health Information (Gupta et al., 2009)		0.897	0.951	0.907
Health data	0.951			
Medical history	0.954			
Privacy Concerns (Malhotra et al., 2004)		0.848	0.888	0.667
I am sensitive to the way companies handle my personal information	0.834			
It is important to keep my privacy intact from online companies	0.890			
Personal privacy is very important, compared to other subjects	0.851			
I am concerned about threats to my personal privacy	0.676			
Perceived Benefits (Dinev et al., 2013)		0.874	0.923	0.799
Providing my personal information to this company will entail benefits	0.897			

Measure	Loading	α	CR	AVE
Revealing my personal information to this company will help me obtain the services I want	0.893			
I believe that as a result of my personal information disclosure to this company, I will benefit from a better, more customized service	0.891			
Satisfaction (Verhoef, 2003)		0.943	0.953	0.745
How satisfied are you with the company regarding its ...				
... attention to you personally?	0.874			
... willingness to explain procedures?	0.869			
... service quality?	0.853			
... claims responsiveness?	0.845			
... employees' expertise?	0.862			
... relationship with you?	0.874			
... alertness?	0.862			
Trust (Kehr et al., 2015)		0.907	0.941	0.843
This company is trustworthy in handling client data	0.911			
This company would tell the truth and fulfill promises related to the information provided by me	0.919			
This company is always honest with customers when it comes to using the information that I would provide	0.923			

Measure	Loading	α	CR	AVE
Word of Mouth (Zeithaml et al., 1996)		0.929	0.955	0.876
How likely are you to …				
… say positive things about this company to other people?	0.936			
… recommend this company to someone who seeks your advice?	0.938			
… encourage friends and others to do business with this company?	0.933			
Behavioral Intention/Loyalty (Cronin et al., 2000)		0.913	0.945	0.852
The probability that I will use this company's products and services again	0.926			
The probability that I will recommend this company's products and services to a friend	0.926			
If I had to do it over again, I would make the same choice	0.917			
Gender				
What is your gender?				
Age				
What is your age?				
Income				

Measure	Loading	α	CR	AVE
What is your current net income of your household per year?				
Less than $16,000				
Between $16,001 and $31,000				
Between $31,001 and $48,000				
Between $48,001 and $72,000				
More than $72,000				
Prefer not to say				

Notes: All measures are reflective and were measured using multi-item 5-point Likert scales. Loading = factor loadings, α = Cronbach's alpha, CR = composite reliability, AVE = average variance extracted.

APPENDIX C: Data equivalence

Based on a thorough literature review, we used validated survey instruments to establish functional, conceptual, and category equivalence (Craig & Douglas, 2000). Furthermore, we assessed construct reliability and validity—including both convergent and discriminant validity (Hult et al., 2008). Convergent validity was confirmed as all items loaded substantively with factor loadings above 0.5 (Fornell & Larcker, 1981). Further, the square root of the AVE must be greater than the correlation of the construct with all other constructs. Values for AVE are in line with recommended thresholds (Fornell & Larcker, 1981). Noting recent critiques of the Fornell-Larcker criterion for reliably identifying discriminant validity, we also used the heterotrait–monotrait (HTMT) ratio (Henseler et al., 2015), which describes average heterotrait–heteromethod correlations (i.e., correlations of the indicators measuring the same construct) relative to average monotrait–heteromethod correlations (i.e., correlations of the indicators across constructs measuring different phenomena) (Henseler et al., 2015). The conservative threshold for the HTMT ratio is 0.9 (Gold et al., 2001), with HTMT ratios closer to 1 indicating a lack of discriminant validity, which we did not exceed (Henseler et al., 2015).

Measurement equivalence pertains to whether constructs (e.g., operationalization, scaling, and scoring) can be compared across different populations (Mullen, 1995). We addressed measurement invariance by following the three-step approach suggested by Henseler et al. (2016). First, we assessed configural invariance by ensuring equality across groups in terms of having the same indicators to determine the measurement models, data treatment (e.g., coding), and optimization criteria (or algorithm settings).[6] Second, we tested for compositional invariance using a permutation test over the correlation between the composite scores. Estimating the model with 5,000 permutation runs demonstrates that the value of the correlation is not significantly different from 1; in other words, it exceeded the 5 percent quantile, suggesting that compositional invariance was achieved. Third, we established full measurement invariance by demonstrating equal composite mean values and variances; in other words, the differences between mean values across groups (and between variance values across groups) needed to be insignificant (or zero). As in the second step, we did a test with 5,000 permutation runs to demonstrate that differences between means and variances across groups did not differ significantly given that the p-values exceeded 0.05. Overall, we established full measurement invariance (Henseler et al., 2016).

Data collection equivalence describes the equivalence of techniques and sampling frames used to collect data across countries and cultures (Reynolds et al., 2003). We ensured that the country samples were roughly equal in size and demographically representative. We minimized the time needed to collect data by standardizing the data collection process; both the survey and sampling methods were uniform across all countries. We included several sociodemographic variables—gender, age, and income—in our model to confirm comparability across all considered countries (Reynolds et al., 2003).

APPENDIX D: Common method variance

Procedural remedies help to control for CMV by eliminating or minimizing commonalities of the independent and dependent variables through the study design (Podsakoff et al., 2003). For instance, we protected respondents' anonymity and limited ambiguity by keeping questions simple, concise, and specific. To reduce respondents' evaluation apprehension, we ensured that their answers were anonymous and encouraged them to answer honestly. Moreover, we used different formats and scale endpoints to measure independent and dependent variables. However, not even the strictest procedural remedies can confirm the absence of CMV (Steenkamp & Maydeu-Olivares, 2021).

Therefore, we also used *statistical remedies* to control for CMV. First, we performed a Harman single-factor test to determine the maximum variance explained by a single factor in exploratory factor analysis (Chang et al., 2010). The first unrotated factor accounted for 33.04 percent of the variance in the data, indicating that the study does not suffer from CMV, as it was under 50 percent (Podsakoff et al., 2003). We ran this analysis separately for each country and found no concerns regarding CMV. Additionally, we performed a collinearity diagnostic in which we explored variance inflation factors (VIFs). If VIFs exceed 3.3, they indicate collinearity and CMV in models with formative scales (Kock, 2015). In order to be thorough and conservative, we also connected all of the variables to the dependent variable—one at a time—and tested for any other latent variables. All VIFs were below 3.3, so CMV does not appear to be a concern in this study. Finally, we also used a marker variable as a variable that is theoretically unrelated to at least one of the other variables of the study (Lindell & Whitney, 2001). We used "emotion violation" as a marker variable and obtained consistent correlations below 0.3, suggesting that CMV is not a large concern (Lindell & Whitney, 2001).

12 Business ethics for digital transformation

Daniel Malan

Over the last few centuries, the introduction of new and innovative technology has resulted in several societal transformations. The most common way to describe our current understanding of these transformations is to refer to the different industrial revolutions. The first industrial revolution (mid eighteenth to mid nineteenth centuries) involved the introduction of new energy sources such as the steam engine to mechanise production processes and to enable mass production. This resulted in the creation of factories, as well as new ways of transport and communication. The second industrial revolution (late nineteenth to early twentieth centuries) involved rapid scientific discovery and industrialisation, largely driven by the invention of electricity. The third industrial revolution, also referred to as the digital revolution, started in the middle of the twentieth century and is associated with the advent of the Information Age. The symbols of the third industrial revolution are computers, cellular phones and the Internet. The fourth industrial revolution is a term that describes the very rapid advances enabled by the digital revolution, and refers specifically to so-called frontier technologies such as artificial intelligence (AI), big data and advanced robotics. The fourth industrial revolution was popularised by Klaus Schwab, the executive director of the World Economic Forum, who described it as the "fusion of technologies that is blurring the lines between the physical, digital, and biological spheres" (World Economic Forum, 2016). In this chapter, digital transformation is defined specifically with reference to the profound changes that were introduced by the fourth industrial revolution.

All these revolutions have had profound impacts on society and humanity. It is therefore not surprising that they could be subjected to moral scrutiny, because we want to answer one of the most fundamental, but also complex, questions: Were they good or bad? This chapter focuses on the moral and ethical dimensions of digital transformation, specifically as it applies to the more recent developments associated with the fourth industrial revolution. In the words of Klaus Schwab, "[the fourth industrial revolution] does not only change the way we do things, it changes us" (World Economic Forum, 2016).

The structure of this chapter is as follows. Firstly, digital transformation is discussed in more detail, with specific reference to the concepts of frontier technology and the fourth industrial revolution. Secondly, a brief overview of ethics is provided, with a focus on the main theoretical traditions in Western philosophy. Thirdly, ethical issues associated with digital transformation are examined with reference to a systematic review of recent academic literature in the field. This review involved a process of both open and thematic coding, resulting in the identification of three main themes: firstly design principles and considerations, secondly the impact of digital transformation and thirdly the governance and regulation of digital transformation. Fourthly, recommendations are made about practical ways to manage and govern these issues. Finally, recommendations are made about a future research agenda.

Digital transformation and frontier technology

Digital transformation describes the process of profound and fundamental change that has taken place as the result of digital technology. It is an ongoing process and therefore should be discussed in terms of change that has already taken place (the historical perspective), change that is currently happening (an assessment of the status quo) as well as change that will likely take place in future (this involves making recommendations and predictions based on our current understanding).

Kingsnorth (2016: 175) describes digital transformation as a mindset, and describes its most important traits: a relentless focus on the end consumer and their needs, agility and adaptable ways of working and a focus on value creation and breakthroughs rather than incrementalism. Within this context, Kingsnorth (2016: 176) argues, "[t]echnology is a smart enabler ... rather than the adoption of technology being an end in itself".

Verhoef et al. (2021: 889) define digital transformation as "a change in how a firm employs digital technologies [in order] to develop a new digital business model that helps to create and appropriate more value for the firm". They identify three phases of digital transformation (Verhoef et al., 2021: 891): digitisation (changing analogue information into digital format), digitalisation (the application of digital technology to change existing business processes, for example improving the communication between customers and firms) and digital transformation (a more fundamental change to the business logic or value creation processes).

The process of transformation can be assessed from different perspectives, for example in terms of the impact on organisational performance or the way in which the process is governed and managed. Within the context of the industrial revolutions, digital transformation has been a feature for a relatively short period (the third and fourth revolutions). During this period of about 75 years we can identify clearly defined phases based on historical perspectives on what was viewed as relevant. To mention a few, there were different moments where the cutting-edge technology of the time was either having a personal computer, having a website, having an app or having a social media presence (Kingsnorth, 2016: 175).

At the moment, our focus is on so-called frontier technology, defined by the Organisation for Economic Co-operation and Development (OECD) as technology that will "reshape industry and communications and provide urgently needed solutions to global challenges like climate change and have the potential to displace existing processes". The most prevalent example of frontier technology is AI, and it includes the related examples of big data, blockchain, the Internet of Things (IoT) and virtual reality (VR). At this stage it forms the frontier, but we are conscious of the fact that websites or apps were also once at the forefront and we therefore have to acknowledge that different technologies will claim this space in future.

As noted above, one of the hallmarks of digital transformation is the relentless focus on the end consumer. Big data has enabled innovations that have been embraced by consumers, but also raised ethical concerns. Consumers are not always conscious of the sacrifices they need to make – for example in terms of privacy – to enable the innovations they appreciate.

Within a business-to-consumer (B2C) environment, individual consumers experience frontier technology in the form of chatbots, virtual assistants like Alexa and Siri, smart devices in their homes (e.g. smart fridges) and cryptocurrencies. Within a business-to-business (B2B) environment, companies employ frontier technology to increase sales by tracking and predicting consumer behaviour, to improve productivity through the employment of technology such as robotics and to streamline human resource processes through the use of AI screening processes to automate recruitment. AI is also increasingly utilised in the corporate e-learning environment.

Vial (2019: 118) defines digital transformation as "a process that aims to improve an entity by triggering significant changes to its properties through combinations of information, computing, communication, and connectivity technologies". Vial specifically calls for research to study the strategic importance of ethics in the context of digital transformation.

In 2022, the *Journal of Business Ethics* published a special edition with a focus on "Business Ethics in the Era of Artificial Intelligence". In their guest editorial, Haenlein et al. (2022: 868) acknowledge that research in the area is "emerging, scattered across many domains, thus lacking a coherent theoretical perspective". They highlight the importance of regulation, but also argue that ethical leadership could mitigate against the need for excessive regulation and therefore enhance competitiveness. The next section provides a very rudimentary overview of the ethical perspective.

The ethical perspective

According to the *Encyclopaedia Britannica*, ethics is the "discipline concerned with what is morally good and bad and morally right and wrong".[1] Even though most human beings are not familiar with ethical theory, we all seem to have that general sense of right and wrong – this is sometimes referred to as common morality.[2] According to Blackburn:

> Human beings are ethical animals. I do not mean that we naturally behave particularly well, nor that we are endlessly telling each other what to do. But we grade and evaluate, and compare and admire, and claim and justify. We do not just 'prefer' this or that, in isolation. We prefer that our preferences are shared; we turn them into demands on each other. (2001: 4)

Ethics is defined by Norman (1998: 1) as "the attempt to arrive at an understanding of the nature of human values, of how we ought to live, and of what constitutes right conduct". With reference to Norman's use of "right conduct", one of the familiar ways we describe ethical behaviour is the ability to distinguish between right and wrong, and then to commit to do what is right. Right and wrong in this context needs the moral imperative of making things better or doing what we ought to do – it is not the same as giving a right or wrong answer to a factual question (Parfit, 2011: 150).

Another important distinction that has to be made is between descriptive ethics and prescriptive ethics. Descriptive ethics – as the name suggests – simply describes the way things are. For example: *x* per cent of employees believe that AI technology cannot be trusted. Prescriptive ethics suggests ways in which we can make a contribution to improve things towards how they should be. For example: in order to improve trustworthiness, bias should be avoided when algorithms are developed. When the two are confused, the naturalistic fallacy occurs. That is when people argue that things should be the way they are simply because things are the way they are. For example: the majority of software engineers in industry *X* believe that it is acceptable to hide certain design elements from consumers, therefore it is acceptable.

It is also useful to be reminded that almost everything can be subjected to moral scrutiny. The philosopher G. E. Moore developed the "open question argument" in the early twentieth century. According to this approach, any state of affairs in the world can be subjected to the open question: "Is it good?"

Consequentialism, deontology and virtue ethics are three of the most popular ethical theories that are part of the Western philosophical tradition. According to consequentialism, ethical decisions are made based on an assessment of the consequences of an action. Whatever will result in the best outcome is the right thing to do. On the other hand, deontology requires decisions to be made based on rights and duties. Social contract theory (the idea that members of society should agree amongst themselves the terms upon which society functions) forms part of this tradition. Virtue ethics relates back to the work of the Greek philosophers, in particular Aristotle. According to virtue ethics, the right decision is one made by a virtuous person, and cannot be determined by external factors such as consequences, rights or duties.

The trolley problem is a classical hypothetical case that is used to illustrate different ethical theories, and has also found a new lease of life by being applied to the field of autonomous vehicles. There are many different versions of the trolley problem, but in essence it comes down to the following: a runaway trolley is speeding down a track where many people are working, and an individual has the ability to flick a switch that would divert the trolley to another track where only one person is working. A slightly different, but similar, example is the shipwreck situation, where eleven people jump into a lifeboat designed for ten occupants. The lifeboat starts to sink, and the ethical dilemma is whether one person should be thrown overboard to save ten lives.

Consequentialism provides the easy solution, because in both cases it is a simple cost–benefit analysis that has to be performed. When more lives can be saved, you have the right answer, even if it involves killing. Deontology provides the opposite advice: the duty of the decision maker is *not* to kill, therefore they should not interfere in the trolley situation and cannot authorise the killing of one person in the shipwreck situation, even if more lives will be saved. Virtue ethics cannot be applied as a tool to solve these dilemmas, because the focus is on being virtuous, not giving practical advice.

Today, most people are familiar with the way in which the trolley problem has been transposed into the world of AI and autonomous vehicles. How should algorithms be developed that would deal with decisions that would have an impact on the safety of the driver, passengers, innocent bystanders (e.g. pedestrians on a pavement) and offending bystanders (e.g. jaywalkers). The same applications of the different ethical theories would apply. Although consequentialism provides the easiest way to deal with the dilemma, complexity increases when decisions need to be made about which lives to sacrifice.

From a business ethics point of view, the work of Tom Donaldson has been hugely influential. In the late 1990s, Donaldson and the late Tom Dunfee published a book on Integrative Social Contracts Theory (Donaldson and Dunfee, 1999). Their ambitious aim was to propose a theory that could be applied by multinational corporations when developing and implementing organisational integrity programmes across different countries and cultures. The most basic summary of their theory – which does not do justice at all to the theoretical sophistication – is that there are certain universal ethical norms that apply everywhere (they call them hypernorms), but that context must always be taken into account when making ethical decisions. They therefore allow communities or industries to develop local rules or conventions (they call them micro contracts) that would be valid in those communities only, on condition that these micro contracts cannot contravene any hypernorms. Donaldson and Dunfee believed that this approach would avoid the pitfalls of both relativism and absolutism. For example, companies can have different gifs policies in different parts of the world that would align with local customs. Another example is that companies can subscribe to the hypernorm of non-discrimination, yet allow for affirmative action in jurisdictions where there are ethical or legal requirements to support marginalised or previously disadvantaged communities.

In 2015, a further development of this theory was published by Donaldson, this time in association with Jim Walsh. In this important contribution the authors enquired about the purpose of business, and proposed a theory of business as an alternative to the dominant theory of the firm (Donaldson and Walsh, 2015). It is beyond the scope of this chapter to discuss their work in detail, but in a nutshell they suggested that there is an important distinction between value creation for individual firms and value creation for business in general. They proposed that the purpose of business (in general) is to create optimised collective value, a concept that could be compared with prosperity.

To summarise, ethics is a theoretical discipline that has been in existence for a few thousand years. Different theoretical approaches will yield different solutions to the same ethical problem, and this will also be the case when we talk about ethics and digital transformation.

In addition to different theoretical approaches, context is always important. In many cases the ethical answer will be prefaced with "it depends", not as a consequence of relativism, but because the answer will be determined by who is using the technology and to what purpose. Often, the ethical lens will therefore be on the *application* of the technology, not the technology itself.

Ethics and digital transformation

The ethical implications of digital transformation can be categorised into three broad categories: concerns about the technology itself, concerns based on the perceptions of those who engage with digital technology, and concerns about the actual outcomes of technological changes. Each of these categories presents challenges.

The ethical issues that relate to the technology itself include concerns about fairness, accountability and transparency, with specific reference to concerns about bias, security and nudging. One of the major challenges in this area is a mismatch of expertise. In general, ethicists do not have a sophisticated understanding of technology, and similarly scientists often have a superficial understanding of ethical issues. Constructive dialogue therefore becomes difficult. For example, ethicists might have sophisticated views about bias in recruitment processes, while computer programmers often lack those insights when they develop selection algorithms.

The ethical issues that concern individual perceptions relate to trust, privacy, autonomy, alienation and job security. Again, there is a potential mismatch because consumers who use technology might have the double disadvantage of not understanding either the ethical or the technological issues. Concerns about issues such as trust or autonomy could potentially fall through conceptual cracks because they are not well articulated. For example, consumers might enjoy the perceived accuracy with which online retailers recommend purchases, without understanding how these recommendations take away their freedom of choice.

Concerns about the outcomes related to possible unemployment, quality of life, workplace safety and product safety. The challenges here relate to regulation and policy issues that are based on incomplete information or conflicting interpretations. For example, factory workers might appreciate the employment of robotic technology that eases the burden of manual labour, but the same technology can make their jobs obsolete.

With these anecdotal issues in mind, a basic literature review was conducted by identifying articles published in three- and four-star journals, as categorised in the Ethics, CSR and Management field of the Chartered Association of Business Schools (ABS) Academic Journal Guide. It was decided to focus specifically on AI as the most topical current representative of frontier technology. The following search string was applied: (Artificial Intelligence OR "AI") (trust OR integrity OR ethics OR control OR fairness OR prejudice OR bias OR discrimination OR privacy OR security OR unemployment OR moral*).[3] An initial search returned more than 500 results, and a refined search that only looked at title, abstract and keywords returned 58 results, which were used in the subsequent analysis. These articles were published in the journals listed in Table 12.1.

Table 12.1 Frequency of articles in selected journals

Journal	ABS category	Number of articles
MIT Sloan Management Review	3	17
Journal of Business Research	3	16
Journal of Business Ethics	3	12
Harvard Business Review	3	3
Business Ethics Quarterly	4	2
Academy of Management Review	4*	2
California Management Review	3	2
Business & Society	3	1
Academy of Management Annals	4*	1
Journal of Management Studies	4	1
Academy of Management Perspectives	4	1

Note: The category 4* indicates a "Journal of Distinction" according to the ratings - this is reserved for a small number of journals recognized as world leading.

Using Atlas TI software, an initial round of inductive open coding was performed that revealed almost 30 codes that were identified with the frequencies (Figure 12.1).

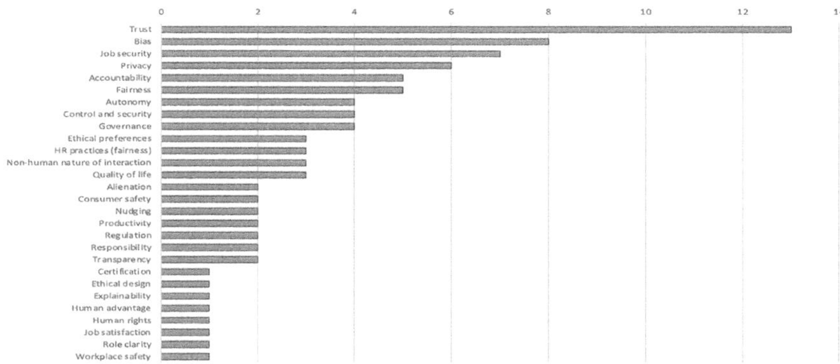

Source: Author.

Figure 12.1 Open codes and their frequency

The codes are briefly summarised in Table 12.2.

Table 12.2 Open codes and descriptions

Code	Description
Accountability	Similar to broader discussions about ethics and governance, accountability evokes the idea of responsibility, mostly in the context of potential harm. Howard (2019) suggests that the time is long gone where companies can simply ask the world to trust AI-powered products. In order to ensure accountability, Howard discusses the need for regulation. Accountability is also directly related to the question of fairness (Prasanna et al., 2019; Tambe et al., 2019). Tóth et al. (2022) propose a new framework of AI Robot accountability, with reference to the examples such as driverless cars and lethal autonomous weapon systems. They propose the concept of "accountability clusters" to take into account the variety of actors and institutions, e.g. designers, users and regulators.
Alienation	Alienation refers to the idea that artificial intelligence dehumanises individuals, and reduces their feelings of belonging in the world. Braganza et al. (2021) examine the effects of AI on levels of engagement and trust in organisations - they refer to this as the psychological contract. With reference to the 8th Sustainable Development Goal (the promotion of productive employment and decent work) they find that the adoption of AI detracts from these goals, an effect that they describe as alienational.
Autonomy	This is reflected to some extent in the fear of "machines taking over", but at a more realistic level simply questions where decision-making authority resides. As a result, the concept of autonomy is closely related to accountability. Concerns about autonomy can change behaviour. Carmon et al. (2020) discuss how consumers actually violate their own preferences to re-establish their sense of autonomy by not choosing predictably.
Bias	This refers to "algorithmic institutionalization of income, gender, racial and geographic prejudices" (Candelon et al., 2021b) leading to reduced inclusiveness (De Keyser et al., 2021). Bias can be explained by the lack of diversity in the human teams that build algorithms, which then results in questionable assumptions made by the alogrithms themselves (Silverman, 2020). Van Giffen et al. (2022) identify eight distinct machine learning biases.

Code	Description
Certification	Certification has been raised as a possible remedy to increase trust in algorithms and their underlying models (Davenport, 2019). Research by Gartner suggests that frontier technology is at the peak of a "hype cycle" and is headed towards a "trough of disillusionment" (Davenport, 2019).
Consumer safety	There is an argument that consumer behaviour can be enhanced by artificial intelligence: "Because the bots will have deep knowledge about individuals' habits and preferences, they'll be able to anticipate a consumer's needs even better than the consumer herself can" (Dawar and Bendle, 2018). This argument is put forward with specific reference to virtual assistants and as a way to increase trust. The more consumers perceive the predictions and suggestions of assistants like Alexa and Siri to be reliable and accurate, the more they will trust them. This opens up a new marketing battlefield, potentially with its own ethical pitfalls, where companies will focus on getting the attention of these assistants.
Control and security	This is related to the concern that "criminal innovation often outpaces defensive efforts" (Huang et al., 2019). It is the constant push/pull between forces for good and forces for evil. Companies need to employ the most advanced technology to ramp up security, but they know that criminals will use the very same technology in an attempt to undermine their efforts. For example, the AV-Test Institute identified more than 350,000 new malware samples per day in 2019. Concerns about privacy, security, storage and safety will all have an impact on trust.
Ethical design	Ethical design is linked to the concept of design thinking, and proposes that ethical principles need to be embedded into algorithms from the very beginning. This is to ensure fairness and accountability and ultimately required to increase trust.
Ethical preferences	Similar to the broader field of ethics, there is no consensus and ongoing debates about preferred theoretical approaches. This results, for example, in the inability to create a universally acceptable definition of "fairness" (Howard, 2019). To explore ethical preferences, a more detailed discussion of different ethical theories is required.

Code	Description
Explainability	Explainability refers to the right that individuals have to understand products and processes that will have an influence on their lives. Although AI and other frontier technologies are extremely complex, an attempt should be made to explain it to users in terms they can understand. Candelon et al. (2021a) suggest that, even if regulators require firms to explain how software makes decisions, it might not be that easy to understand.
Fairness	Fairness is one of the core concepts in moral philosophy, with particular emphasis on the work of John Rawls, who explored fairness through his famous "veil of ignorance" thought experiment. Rawls argued that - if we do not know whether we will be in power or without power when we make the rules (something only possible as a thought experiment) - we will agree to rules that are fair. In the context of digital transformation, the argument is that design flaws based on bias will lead to unfair decisions (Van Giffen et al., 2022). Fairness should inform product design and regulation. However, as Howard (2019) pointed out, fairness is very difficult to define and therefore depends on different ethical theories.
Governance	Governance is a system of direction and control, mostly associated with boards or governing bodies. The term is used more loosely, and sometimes confusingly, to describe ways in which processes are managed. The concept of "data governance" is of particular importance. Kelley (2022) describes eleven components that could impact the adoption of AI principles - these could be loosely defined as a combination of governance and management principles. They are: communication, management support, training, an ethics office or ethics officer, a reporting mechanism, enforcement, measurement, technical processes, technical infrastructure, organisational structure and an interdisciplinary approach.
HR practices (fairness)	Fairness with regard to HR practices stands out as a specific issue because of concerns about the influence of AI on recruitment practices. Tambe et al. (2019) identify four challenges in using data science for HR purposes: complexity of phenomena, constraints imposed by small data sets, accountability questions associated with ethical constraints, and possible adverse employee reactions in response to data-driven management decisions.

Code	Description
Human advantage	The emphasis on human advantage is a way to counter concerns that calculations and decisions based on big data will always be superior. Felin and Zenger (2018) use the example of Steve Jobs (Apple), Howard Schultz (Starbucks) and Sam Walton (Walmart) to argue that humans remain better at "asking novel questions that prompt fresh insight".
Human rights	A focus on human rights is aimed at ensuring that the benefits brought about by digital technology do not infringe on human rights. Stahl et al. (2021) use the concept of human flourishing to make some recommendations on the responsible use of technology with specific reference to AI.
Job satisfaction	The use of digital technology is linked to job satisfaction. If individuals can employ technology in a way to save time and/or enhance productivity it is clear that there will be a positive correlation. Marikyan et al. (2022) studied the impact of digital assistants like Amazon's Alexa, and found that "performance expectancy, perceived enjoyment, intelligence, social presence and trust were positively related to satisfaction with digital assistants", which in turn correlated with productivity and engagement.
Job security	Job security has been an issue for a longer time than many of the others listed here, because the impact of robotics (e.g. in the automotive industry) has been a concern for some time. On the one hand, the use of robots makes work easier for employees on assembly lines but, on the other hand, they have the potential to make human labour obsolete in some instances, leading to job losses. Concerns have also been expressed about AI and job security in the accounting industry. Bughin (2018) argues that job losses will occur, but that these can also sometimes be explained by companies that are unable or unwilling to use AI for innovative purposes. Carmon et al. (2020) argue that even with major disruption of labour markets, humanity will be - on balance - better off.
Non-human nature of interaction	Giroux et al. (2022) argue that increased interaction with automated technology will result in what they call "declined guilt". For example, if people use self-checkout machines at a supermarket and an error is made, individuals are less likely to report the error because they do not feel the same moral obligation towards the machine that they would feel towards another human being. Glikson and Wolley (2020) discuss the role of AI's anthropomorphism in terms of the development of emotional trust.

Code	Description
Privacy	The invasion of privacy is one of the major concerns with digital technology, and this issue is often framed as a human rights issue. This is related to the developing field of people analytics, where technology is used to assess potential or predict talents (Chamorro-Premuzic, 2020). More generally, the collection and storage of biometric data raise various concerns in terms of privacy and security (De Keyser et al., 2021). Another important dimension is consumer privacy, related to the vast amounts of data that consumers share with companies on a daily basis, often without understanding how that data will be used (Du and Xie, 2021). To address privacy in a comprehensive way, a combination of regulation and consumer education is required. Like most of the other dimensions of frontier technology, the way in which privacy is addressed often depends on the ethical intention behind it. For example, while some might argue that emotion-sensing technology constitutes an invasion of privacy, Philips and ABN AMRO Bank have collaborated to develop technology that can reduce the risk of trading in financial markets. They have done this by identifying traders in heightened emotional states that are likely to overpay for assets and downplay risk (Whelan et al., 2018).
Productivity	One of the biggest arguments in favour of more advanced digital technology is the increase in productivity; for example, the ability to perform remote surgery and training (Morvan et al., 2020). In addition, it is argued that emotion-sensing technologies can improve productivity through alleviating stress and improving concentration. This is done through the assessment of eye movements, facial expressions and skin conductance (Whelan et al., 2018).
Quality of life	Perhaps seen as the negative flipside of concerns about job security, it is argued that digital technology can improve quality of life. This is achieved by reducing the time humans have to spend on tedious activities such as driving and shopping (Carmon et al., 2020). While some argue that advanced technologies like AI can improve quality of life by saving us from time-consuming activities that could be described as annoyances, Friedland (2019) argues that these annoyances play a key adaptive role because they help us to adjust to others and the world around us.

Code	Description
Regulation	The issue of regulation is critical to deal with both ethical and operational issues in terms of frontier technology. Candelon et al. (2021a) discuss three main challenges with regards to regulation: fairness, transparency and preventing dangerous or discriminatory evolvement of algorithms.
Responsibility	Although the concept of responsibility is often used as the catch-all phrase to describe the need for responsible (i.e. ethical) technology, it is also used in a more specific way to describe the responsibility gap: the fear that machines will become autonomous and that humans can therefore not be held responsible for their actions (Johnson, 2015). New models of responsibility are therefore required to take these changes into account (John-Mathews, 2022). This also involves the development of role clarity in a collaborative environment involving humans and technology (Chowdhury et al., 2022).
Transparency	Transparency is one of the key concerns in terms of digital technology. It is linked to the concepts of understandability and explainability. It is one of the issues raised in relation to regulation as well (Candelon et al., 2021a), and is particularly important in terms of explaining how software makes decisions.
Trust	Trust is the issue raised most frequently in terms of digital technology. When people do not understand something, they don't trust it. When people feel threatened by something, they don't trust it. Howard (2019) argues that "the time when companies could simply ask the world to trust artificial intelligence and AI-powered products is long gone". According to Howard (2019), trust requires fairness, transparency and accountability. Trust is associated with concepts such as reliance, dependability and predictability. In a survey of US consumers, only 4% of respondents indicated that they trust AI in the employee hiring process (Davenport, 2019). Trust is usually also viewed as the end result of a process – it has to be earned. For example, it is only if virtual assistants demonstrate over a period of time that their answers and recommendations are useful that they will be trusted by consumers (Dawar and Bendle, 2018). Concerns about deep fakes and the more fundamental concept of truth are also relevant here.
Workplace safety	In the same way as consumer safety is addressed, digital technology can make the workplace safe. Chamorro-Premuzic (2020) discusses various ways in which AI can make the workplace safe.

Thematic coding

The next step was to analyse the open codes and to cluster them into thematic codes. Three main thematic codes emerged. These are presented in Table 12.3, with reference to the open codes that support them.

Table 12.3 Thematic codes

Thematic codes	Open codes
Design principles and considerations for digital transformation	Accountability, Autonomy, Bias, Consumer safety, Ethical design, Ethical preferences, Explainability, Fairness, HR practices, Human advantage, Human rights, Privacy, Responsibility, Transparency, Trust
Impact of digital transformation	Alienation, Job satisfaction, Job security, Non-human nature of interaction, Productivity, Quality of life, Workplace safety
Governance and regulation of digital transformation	Certification, Control, Human rights, Regulation, Security

There seems to be an iterative, but sequential, relationship between these three thematic codes: governance and regulation will impact and inform the design principles and considerations, which will then be reflected in technological products, and the subsequent use of these products will determine impact. Impact will be assessed and will result in new regulation and governance activities, and so the process will continue.

It is interesting to compare these codes to the three specific ethical areas identified in one of the most cited literature reviews on digital transformation (Vial, 2019): the role of ethics as a means to account for multilevel implications of digital transformation, the need to balance the tension between organisational performance and ethics, and the need to address concurrent but often conflicting needs of value co-creators.

The Multilevel Nature of Digital Transformation

Vial (2019: 135) quotes the familiar "don't be evil" motto of Google and "do the right thing" from Alphabet as examples of companies that try to align their business models with espoused values. It then becomes very easy to ask fundamental ethical questions when the very same companies impose self-censorship in order to access the Chinese market: it presents a clear clash between the business model and the ethical values. Vial (2019: 136) suggests that the ethical implications of digital transformation lie beyond the strategy of the firm and can impact society itself. Although different terms are used here, this articulation is basically the same as the familiar distinction between different levels of business ethics that has been in use for decades: systemic (the crudest example here is capitalism versus socialism), industry (initially focused on the usual suspects like tobacco, alcohol and gambling, then extended to fast food, and today also focusing on previously uncontroversial industries like financial services and technology), company (focusing on the corporate level, e.g. corporate governance and corporate responsibility) and finally the individual level (even in a company with a good reputation for integrity which operates in an uncontroversial industry, employees can (and do) engage in unethical and sometimes criminal behaviour, e.g. bribery or insider trading).

The Role of Ethical Performance

Vial (2019: 136) argues that companies should incorporate ethical issues related to digital transformation into their overall discussions about ethical performance. This is necessary because of undesirable consequences, for example the scandal that involved Facebook and Cambridge Analytica related to the United States presidential election in 2016: "the undesirable outcomes of such tactics do not occur because they are illegal. Rather, it is because they are deemed morally reprehensible by some of the stakeholders who are co-creators of value for the firm."

Accounting for Conflicting Demands of Value Co-creators

Vial (2019: 137) points out that technology is very often no longer only the by-product of a firm's operations, but integral to the value proposition itself: "the business model of a firm may depend on the collection, the sharing and the selling of data." This points to the theme – introduced later – of the tension between privacy and transparency: as a consumer, I want *my* data to be private, but I often argue that the data of *others* should be in the public domain to increase transparency. This is where the concept of optimised collective value, introduced by Donaldson and Walsh (2015) and discussed earlier, could be particularly helpful.

Ethical design tensions

Upon further investigation, three ethical design tensions can be identified (Figure 12.2).[4] The success with which they can be negotiated will determine whether the impact will be positive or negative, and sophisticated regulation could also take them into account, hence they can potentially be superimposed on all three thematic codes.

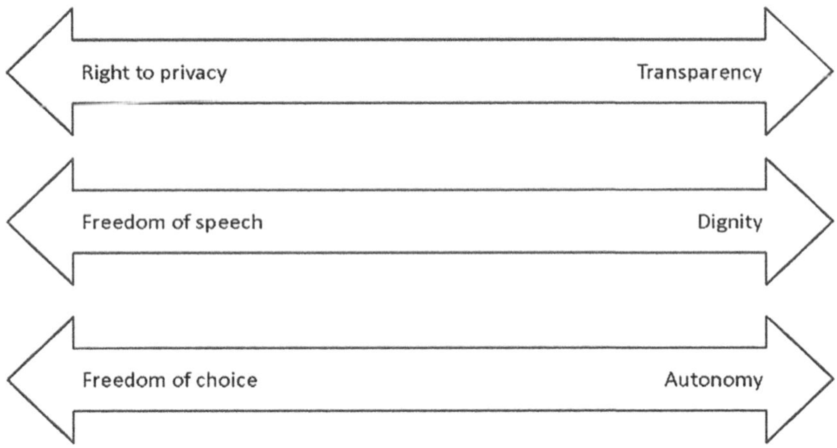

Source: Author.

Figure 12.2 Ethical design tensions

Privacy and Transparency

The basic argument is that privacy has been sacrificed as a result of digital transformation. Examples include targeted online marketing, digital health technology (wearable tech) that captures private data and recommender systems such as the one employed by Netflix. This tension can also be experienced between the privacy afforded by blockchain, juxtaposed against the need for transparency, for example in the call for beneficial ownership registers.

Freedom of Speech and Dignity

This tension is often played out in the area of social media, and more specifically the debates around the regulation of Twitter. Extreme proponents of absolute freedom of speech will argue that anybody should be allowed to say whatever they want on any platform available to them, while most people would argue that the dignity of individuals should be protected. This is the type of threshold that is aligned with the work of Tom Donaldson. Respect for human dignity is one of the hypernorms identified in his work, and suggested as a threshold that should govern human activity, including freedom of speech. Yes, there might be scope for micro contracts – what is allowed on Twitter will be different from what is allowed on other platforms such as the printed media or election campaigns, but the idea of a threshold is a very useful one.

Freedom of Choice and Autonomy

The tension between freedom of choice and autonomy is particularly relevant for the world of AI. Recommender systems might guide decision-making up to the point of manipulation, while human autonomy might be questioned because decision-making and human behaviour in general are always mediated by a specific context.

These tensions are also interrelated. Invasion of privacy impedes freedom of choice. Freedom of speech could enhance transparency. And a responsible application of the right to privacy can enhance human autonomy.

Management and governance recommendations

Specific recommendations for organisations (including those in the non-profit sector) in terms of management and governance can be broadly articulated as the need to strike a balance between the tensions identified above. This is also the requirement for regulators, and will most likely play out in the sphere of soft law. Elsewhere, I have argued that regulation is critical in this space, but that it cannot rely on traditional box-tick compliance.[5]

The most important recommendations for organisations are:

- Ensure that governing bodies (usually boards of directors) have sufficient awareness and understanding of the issues to make informed decisions. This might require the establishment of a technology-oriented board committee, but all board members should have a basic understanding of the core issues.
- Specific focus is required on the issue of data governance. The ways in which organisations gather, use and dispose of data are regulated, but given the immense risks and opportunities involved, most organisations would

be well advised to move beyond compliance and think strategically about these issues.

- Finally, there is a general trend to move away from compliance towards a more comprehensive concept of integrity (Malan et al., 2022). In line with the views expressed by Vial (2019), organisations should view digital transformation and the ethical issues associated with it as a strategic issue and deal with it accordingly.

Future research agenda

As mentioned by Vial (2019: 135), the ethical implications of digital transformation are currently understudied. Three areas for future research are recommended.

Firstly, at a conceptual level, the intersection between ethics and technology deserves more attention. Vial (2019: 136) argues that consequentialist and deontological theories can both be helpful: "Together these theoretical foundations can help us to gain a deeper understanding of the rationale behind firms' strategic decisions and the impacts of those decisions." It is acknowledged that these approaches can collide, and according to Vial (2019: 136), "our knowledge on these important questions [...] is limited". To put it bluntly, the trolley problem remains unresolved when transposed to an autonomous vehicle. More work is required. This will increasingly require multidisciplinary research and possible extensive preparatory work, simply for researchers from different paradigms to understand each other's worlds. We can only hope that researchers on both sides will have the patience to spend time to ensure that this is done properly.

Secondly, there is a need to position these discussions within the broader context of discussions about the purpose of business. We live in a world that is dominated by discussions about environmental, social and governance (ESG) issues. Debates about old-style corporate social responsibility (CSR) and the more traditional "ethics and compliance" function in corporations are fading fast. Integration and integrity are going to become the new buzzwords, and discussions about digital transformation should feature strongly in this dialogue.

Finally, there is a need for specific research that investigates ethics and the law within the context of digital transformation, and more specifically frontier technology. Soft law and "comply or explain" regimes can be of particular relevance here. Regulation is critical, but this cannot be a separate and technical legal discussion. We have to find ways to integrate all of these research areas in a way that can advance the research agenda and at the same time address the very real risks and opportunities that exist.

Conclusion

The second and third industrial revolutions have placed digital transformation at the forefront of discussion about business and its impact on society. While there is no denial that this transformation has made a huge contribution to human progress, the ethical challenges associated with the transformation are also real. Technological progress will not slow down, and it is difficult to keep up with new challenges as they arise, yet many of the ethical issues associated with digital transformation could perhaps be described as new wine in old casks. The ethical challenges associated with the trolley problem and the algorithms informing autonomous vehicles are exactly the same. Issues of design, impact and regulation need to be addressed in order to ensure a future that is characterised by prosperity, fairness and trust.[6]

Notes

1. See https://www.britannica.com/topic/ethics-philosophy.
2. It should be noted that there is a conceptual distinction between morality and ethics. Morality is usually associated with a more personal approach (e.g. the moral convictions of an individual), while ethics is associated with standards agreed upon by specific communities (e.g. the code of ethics of an organisation). However, they both have to do with the distinctions between good and bad or right and wrong and can often be used interchangeably.
3. The generous assistance of David Macnaughton, subject librarian at Trinity College Dublin, is acknowledged. The use of the asterisk indicates a truncated search for the word moral, including morals, morality, etc.
4. For an initial discussion of these tensions based on the literature review, see https://www.weforum.org/agenda/2023/03/frontier-technologies-against-corruption/.
5. See https://www.weforum.org/agenda/2018/06/law-too-slow-for-new-tech-how-keep-up/.
6. This chapter is based on a presentation that was given at the World Congress of the International Society of Business, Economics, and Ethics (Barcelona, July 2022).

References

Blackburn, S. (2001). *Ethics: A Very Short Introduction*. Oxford University Press.

Braganza, A., Chen, W., Canhoto, A., & Sap, S. (2021). Productive employment and decent work: The impact of AI adoption on psychological contracts, job engagement and employee trust. *Journal of Business Research, 131*, 485–494. https://doi.org/10.1016/j.jbusres.2020.08.018.

Bughin, J. (2018). Why AI isn't the death of jobs. *MIT Sloan Management Review, 59*(4), 42–46. https://www.mckinsey.com/mgi/overview/in-the-news/why-ai-isnt-the-death-of-jobs.

Candelon, F., Di Carlo, R. C., De Bondt, M., & Evgeniou, T. (2021a). AI regulation is coming. *Harvard Business Review, 99*(5), 102–111. https://hbr.org/2021/09/ai-regulation-is-coming.

Candelon, F., Di Carlo, R. C., & Mills, S. D. (2021b). AI-at-scale hinges on gaining a 'social license'. *MIT Sloan Management Review, 63*(1), 1–4. https://sloanreview.mit.edu/article/ai-at-scale-hinges-on-gaining-a-social-license/.

Carmon, Z., Schrift, R., Wertenbroch, K., & Yang, H. (2020). Designing AI systems that customers won't hate. *MIT Sloan Management Review, 61*(2), 1–6. https://sloanreview.mit.edu/article/designing-ai-systems-that-customers-wont-hate/.

Chamorro-Premuzic, T. (2020). Can surveillance AI make the workplace safe? *MIT Sloan Management Review, 62*(1), 13–15. https://sloanreview.mit.edu/article/can-surveillance-ai-make-the-workplace-safe/.

Chowdhury, S., Budhwar, P., Dey, P. K., Joel-Edgar, S., & Abadie, A. (2022). AI-employee collaboration and business performance: Integrating knowledge-based view, socio-technical systems and organisational socialisation framework. *Journal of Business Research, 144*(3), 31–49. https://doi.org/10.1016/j.jbusres.2022.01.069.

Davenport, T. H. (2019). Can we solve AI's 'trust problem'? *MIT Sloan Management Review, 60*(2), 1. https://hbsp.harvard.edu/product/SMR730-PDF-ENG.

Dawar, N., & Bendle, N. (2018). Marketing in the age of Alexa. *Harvard Business Review, 96*(3), 80–86. https://hbr.org/2018/05/marketing-in-the-age-of-alexa.

De Keyser, A., Bart, Y., Gu, X., Liu, S. Q., Robinson, S. G., & Kannan, P. K. (2021). Opportunities and challenges of using biometrics for business: Developing a research agenda. *Journal of Business Research, 136*, 52–62. https://doi.org/10.1016/j.jbusres.2021.07.028.

Donaldson, T., & Dunfee, T. (1999). *Ties that Bind: A Social Contracts Approach to Business Ethics*. Harvard University Press.

Donaldson, T., & Walsh, J. (2015). Toward a theory of business. *Research in Organizational Behavior, 35*, 181–207. https://doi.org/10.1016/j.riob.2015.10.002.

Du, S., & Xie, C. (2021). Paradoxes of artificial intelligence in consumer markets: Ethical challenges and opportunities. *Journal of Business Research, 129*, 961–974. https://doi.org/10.1016/j.jbusres.2020.08.024.

Felin, T., & Zenger, T. (2018). What sets breakthrough strategies apart? *MIT Sloan Management Review, 59*(2), 86–88. https://sloanreview.mit.edu/article/what-sets-breakthrough-strategies-apart/#:~:text=Innovative%20strategies%20depend%20more%20on,than%20on%20well%2Dcrunched%20numbers.

Friedland, J. (2019). AI can help us live more deliberately. *MIT Sloan Management Review, 60*(4), 45–51. https://sloanreview.mit.edu/article/ai-can-help-us-live-more-deliberately/.

Giroux, M., Kim, J., Lee, J. C., & Park, J. (2022). Artificial intelligence and declined guilt: Retailing morality comparison between human and AI. *Journal of Business Ethics, 178*, 1027–1041. https://doi.org/10.1007/s10551-022-05056-7.

Glikson, E., & Woolley, A. W. (2020). Human trust in artificial intelligence: Review of empirical research. *Academy of Management Annals, 14*(2), 627–660. https://www.researchgate.net/publication/340605601_Human_trust_in_artificial_intelligence_Review_of_empirical_research_Academy_of_Management_Annals_in_press.

Haenlein, M., Huang, M.-H., & Kaplan, A. (2022). Guest editorial: Business ethics in the era of artificial intelligence. *Journal of Business Ethics, 178*(2), 867–869. https://doi.org/10.1007/s10551-022-05060-x.

Howard, A. (2019). The regulation of AI: Should organizations be worried? *MIT Sloan Management Review, 60*(4), 1–3. https://sloanreview.mit.edu/article/the-regulation-of-ai-should-organizations-be-worried/#:~:text=So%20should%20organizations%20be%20worried,also%20safe%20for%20consumer%20use.

Huang, K., Siegel, M., Pearlson, K., & Madnick, S. (2019). Casting the dark web in a new light. *MIT Sloan Management Review, 60*(4), 1–9. https://sloanreview.mit.edu/article/casting-the-dark-web-in-a-new-light/.

John-Mathews, J.-M., Cardon, D., & Balagué, C. (2022). From reality to world: A critical perspective on AI fairness. *Journal of Business Ethics, 178*(2), 945–959. https://doi.org/10.1007/s10551-022-05055-8.

Johnson, D. (2015). Technology with no human responsibility? *Journal of Business Ethics, 127*(4), 707–715. https://doi.org/10.1007/s10551-014-2180-1.

Kelley, S. (2022). Employee perceptions of the effective adoption of AI principles. *Journal of Business Ethics, 178*(4), 871–893. https://doi.org/10.1007/s10551-022-05051-y.

Kingsnorth, S. (2016). *Digital Marketing Strategy: An Integrated Approach to Online Marketing*. Kogan Page.

Malan, D., Taylor, A., Tunkel, A., & Kurtz, B. (2022). Why business integrity can be a strategic response to ethical challenges. *MIT Sloan Management Review*. https://sloanreview.mit.edu/article/why-business-integrity-can-be-a-strategic-response-to-ethical-challenges/.

Marikyan, D., Papagiannidis, S., Rana, O. F., Ranjan, R., & Morgan, G. (2022). 'Alexa, let's talk about my productivity': The impact of digital assistants on work productivity. *Journal of Business Research, 142*, 572–584. https://doi.org/10.1016/j.jbusres.2022.01.015.

Morvan, L., Hintermann, F., & Ovanessoff, A. (2020). Preparing for the risky world of extended reality. *MIT Sloan Management Review, 61*(2), 1–4. https://sloanreview.mit.edu/article/preparing-for-the-risky-world-of-extended-reality/.

Norman, R. (1998). *The Moral Philosophers*. Oxford University Press.

Parfit, D. (2011). *On What Matters: Volume 1*. Oxford University Press.

Prasanna, T., Cappelli, P., & Yakubovich, V. (2019). Artificial intelligence in human resources management: Challenges and a path forward. *California Management Review, 61*(4). https://doi.org/10.1177/0008125619867910.

Silverman, K. (2020). Why your board needs a plan for AI oversight. *MIT Sloan Management Review, 62*(1), 1–6. https://sloanreview.mit.edu/article/why-your-board-needs-a-plan-for-ai-oversight/.

Stahl, B. C., Andreou, A., Brey, P., Hatzakis, T., Kirichenko, A., Macnish, K., Laulhé Shaelou, S., Patel, A., Ryan, M., & Wright, D. (2021). Artificial intelligence for human flourishing: Beyond principles for machine learning. *Journal of Business Research, 124*, 374–388. https://doi.org/10.1016/j.jbusres.2020.11.030.

Tambe, P., Cappelli, P., & Yakubovich, V. (2019). Artificial intelligence in human resources management: Challenges and a path forward. *California Management Review, 61*(4), 15–42. https://doi.org/10.1177/00081256198679.

Tóth, Z., Caruana, R., Gruber, T., & Loebbecke, C. (2022). The dawn of the AI robots: Towards a new framework of AI robot accountability. *Journal of Business Ethics, 178*, 895–916. https://doi.org/10.1007/s10551-022-05050-z.

Van Giffen, B., Herhausen, D., & Fahse, T. (2022). Overcoming the pitfalls and perils of algorithms: A classification of machine learning biases and mitigation methods. *Journal of Business Research, 144*(6), 93–106. https://doi.org/10.1016/j.jbusres.2022.01.076.

Verhoef, P., Broekhuizen, T., Bart, Y., Bhattacharya, A., Qi Dong, J., Fabian, N., & Haenlein, M. (2021). Digital transformation: A multidisciplinary reflection and research agenda. *Journal of Business Research, 122*, 889 – 901. https://doi.org/10.1016/j.jbusres.2019.09.022.

Vial, G. (2019). Understanding digital transformation: A review and a research agenda. *Journal of Strategic Information Systems, 28*(2), 118–144. https://doi.org/10.1016/j.jsis.2019.01.003.

Whelan, E., McDuff, D., Gleasure, R., & Vom Brocke, J. (2018). How emotion-sensing technology can reshape the workplace. *MIT Sloan Management Review, 59*(3), 7–10. https://sloanreview.mit.edu/article/how-emotion-sensing-technology-can-reshape-the-workplace/#:~:text=New%20emotion%2Dsensing%20technologies%20can,must%20address%20important%20privacy%20issues.

World Economic Forum (2016). *Values and the Fourth Industrial Revolution: Connecting the Dots between Value, Values, Profit and Purpose.* https://www.weforum.org/whitepapers/values-and-the-fourth-industrial-revolution-connecting-the-dots-between-value-values-profit-and-purpose.

Index